CW01240026

**The Roma and Their Struggle for Identity
in Contemporary Europe**

ROMANI STUDIES
Edited by Sam Beck, Cornell University

In the course of the twenty-first century, Europe has become aware that the Roma are its largest minority, with an estimated population of eleven million people. As a result, Romani Studies has emerged as an interdisciplinary field that offers perspectives derived from the humanities and social sciences in the context of state and transnational institutions. One of its aims is to remove the stigma surrounding Roma scholarship, to engage with the controversies regarding Roma identity and, in this way, to counter anti-Roma racism.

Volume 3
THE ROMA AND THEIR STRUGGLE FOR IDENTITY IN CONTEMPORARY EUROPE
Edited by Huub van Baar and Angéla Kóczé

Volume 2
INWARD LOOKING: THE IMPACT OF MIGRATION ON ROMANIPE FROM THE ROMANI PERSPECTIVE
Aleksandar G. Marinov

Volume 1
ROMA ACTIVISM: REIMAGINING POWER AND KNOWLEDGE
Edited by Sam Beck and Ana Ivasiuc

THE ROMA AND THEIR STRUGGLE FOR IDENTITY IN CONTEMPORARY EUROPE

❋ ❋ ❋

Edited by
Huub van Baar and Angéla Kóczé

berghahn
NEW YORK • OXFORD
www.berghahnbooks.com

First published in 2020 by
Berghahn Books
www.berghahnbooks.com

© 2020 Huub van Baar and Angéla Kóczé

All rights reserved. Except for the quotation of short passages
for the purposes of criticism and review, no part of this book
may be reproduced in any form or by any means, electronic or
mechanical, including photocopying, recording, or any information
storage and retrieval system now known or to be invented,
without written permission of the publisher.

Library of Congress Cataloging-in-Publication Data
Names: Baar, Huub van, 1970- editor. | Kóczé, Angéla, 1970- editor.
Title: The Roma and their struggle for identity in contemporary Europe /
 edited by Huub van Baar and Angéla Kóczé.
Description: New York : Berghahn, 2020. | Series: Romani studies; vol. 3 |
 Includes bibliographical references and index.
Identifiers: LCCN 2019045999 (print) | LCCN 2019046000 (ebook) | ISBN
 9781789206425 (hardback) | ISBN 9781789206432 (ebook)
Subjects: LCSH: Romanies--Europe--Ethnic identity. | Romanies--Cultural
 assimilation--Europe.
Classification: LCC DX145 .R595 2020 (print) | LCC DX145 (ebook) | DDC
 305.8914/9704--dc23
LC record available at https://lccn.loc.gov/2019045999
LC ebook record available at https://lccn.loc.gov/2019046000

British Library Cataloguing in Publication Data
A catalogue record for this book is available from the British Library

ISBN 978-1-78920-642-5 hardback
ISBN 978-1-78920-643-2 ebook

We dedicate this volume to Damian John Le Bas (Sheffield, 30 January 1963–Worthing, 9 December 2017) and acknowledge the vital role he and his artworks played and continue to play in the Romani movement, and in critically and spiritedly redirecting the ways in which Roma, Gypsies and Travellers have been portrayed in culture and society.

Damian Le Bas in front of his artwork 'Deutschland Roma Armee Fraktion', outside the Maxim Gorki Theatre in Berlin, 20 October 2017. Courtesy of Delaine Le Bas.

Contents

✳ ✳ ✳

List of Illustrations   ix

Foreword. Roma, Jews and European History   xi
   Malachi H. Hacohen

Acknowledgements   xv

List of Abbreviations   xviii

PART I. INTRODUCTIONS

Introduction. The Roma in Contemporary Europe: Struggling for Identity at a Time of Proliferating Identity Politics   3
   Huub van Baar with Angéla Kóczé

Chapter 1. Decolonizing Canonical Roma Representations: The Cartographer with an Army   46
   Huub van Baar

PART II. SOCIETY, HISTORY AND CITIZENSHIP

Chapter 2. The Impact of Multifaceted Segregation on the Formation of Roma Collective Identity and Citizenship Rights   69
   Júlia Szalai

Chapter 3. Reflections on Socialist-Era Archives in Hungary and Shifting Romani Identity   94
   Nidhi Trehan

Chapter 4. Gendered and Racialized Social Insecurity of Roma in East Central Europe   124
   Angéla Kóczé

PART III. EUROPE AND THE CHALLENGE OF 'ETHNIC MINORITY GOVERNANCE'

Chapter 5. Governing the Roma, Bordering Europe: Europeanization, Securitization and Differential Inclusion 153
  Huub van Baar

Chapter 6. Ethnic Identity and Policymaking: A Critical Analysis of the EU Framework for National Roma Integration Strategies 179
  Iulius Rostas

PART IV. GENDER AND SOCIAL MOVEMENTS

Chapter 7. Intersectional Intricacies: Romani Women's Activists at the Crossroads of Race and Gender 205
  Debra L. Schultz

Chapter 8. Can the Tables Be Turned with a New Strategic Alliance? The Struggles of the Romani Women's Movement in Central and Eastern Europe 230
  Violetta Zentai

PART V. ART AND CULTURE

Chapter 9. Ethnicity Unbound: Conundrums of Culture in Representations of Roma 257
  Carol Silverman

Chapter 10. Identity as a Weapon of the Weak? Understanding the European Roma Institute for Arts and Culture – An Interview with Tímea Junghaus and Anna Mirga-Kruszelnicka 281
  Tina Magazzini

Chapter 11. A *Gypsy Revolution*: The Ongoing Legacy of Delaine and Damian Le Bas 305
  Annabel Tremlett and Delaine Le Bas

Epilogue. The Challenge of Recognition, Redistribution and Representation of Roma in Contemporary Europe 328
  Angéla Kóczé and Huub van Baar

Index 335

Illustrations

※ ※ ※

Figures

Figure 1.1 'Roma Armee Fraktion Berlin', Damian Le Bas, 2017.	47
Figure 1.2 'Gypsyland. The Atlantic Side of the Pyrenees', Damian Le Bas, 2007.	48
Figure 1.3 'Frontier De Luxe Vienna', Damian Le Bas, 2016.	49
Figure 1.4 'The World of Gypsy Romance?' (detail), Delaine and Damian Le Bas, 2012.	55
Figure 1.5 'Table for a Romani Embassy', Rotor, Graz. Damian Le Bas, 2017.	56
Figure 1.6 'Back to the Future! Safe European Home 1938', Damian Le Bas, 2013.	60
Figure 1.7 'They Don't Want Us in the EU' (*Italia Antiqua*), Damian Le Bas, 2015.	61
Figure 3.1 'Gypsies on the Road to Socialist Development', *Székesfehérvár Újsag*, July 1951.	105
Figure 3.2 'Outside the Gate', *Magyar Hírlap*, 9 January 1972.	107
Figure 3.3 'The Problems of Gypsies and the Society', *Népszava*, 5 August 1979.	109
Figure 3.4 'Brothers, Gypsies!', *Élő Szó* (Living Word), 20 March 1990.	111
Figure 11.1 'Bin Bag Dolls', Delaine Le Bas, 2005. Image taken from ROOM catalogue.	309

Figure 11.2 'The World of Gypsy Romance?' (Carmen painting, detail), Delaine and Damian Le Bas. From the exhibition *The Buccaneers*, 2012.   310

Figure 11.3 'Don't Tell Us Who We Are' and 'Gypsy Anarchy' print, Delaine and Damian Le Bas. Original artwork produced in 2011 for HIAP Residency, Finland.   311

Figure 11.4 'The Fighting Irish', Damian Le Bas, 2008.   313

Figure 11.5 'Roma Pavilion Got Lost', Delaine and Damian Le Bas, 2009. Intervention postcard: 'Roma Europe', Damian Le Bas, 2007.   319

Figure 11.6 'CHAVI', Delaine and Damian Le Bas, 2007. Invitation for *Chavi Exhibition: Daniel Baker, Damian Le Bas, Delaine Le Bas*, Novas Contemporary Urban Centre, London, 2007.   320

Table

Table 4.1 Poverty rates among the Roma population in three countries, 1992 (age range 20–57).   136

FOREWORD

✸ ✸ ✸

ROMA, JEWS AND EUROPEAN HISTORY

Malachi H. Hacohen

With the destruction of the European Jewish and German diasporas – the former in the Holocaust and the latter in post-Second World War ethnic cleansings – the Roma became Europe's largest diaspora. The European Union (EU) has viewed Roma integration as a major challenge, and has launched several grand projects to advance it. A Romani intelligentsia has emerged, seeking to combat traditional anti-Roma prejudice and negotiate Europeanization. They have entered the academy and the arts, and have deployed advanced feminist, postcolonial and postnationalist approaches to explore possibilities for Romani politics and culture. 'The Roma/Gypsy Question' has become, in a sense, postwar Europe's 'Jewish Question' – the standard by which Europe's ability to make good on its promise of universal citizenship may be judged.

Yet, the Roma have not played centre stage in either European politics or the academy. The growth of European Muslim communities and, more recently, new migration waves have created greater political anxieties, and the dilemmas of European Muslim identity have attracted much more academic attention. Indeed in 2014, when the Council for European Studies at Duke University launched, under my direction, a Mellon-funded project on 'Reasonable Accommodations? Minorities in the Globalized Nation State', we did not have the Roma foremost in our minds. 'Reasonable Accommodation' is a rubric encapsulating national policies that seek to accommodate minorities whose culture diverges from the national norms. Pushed to an extreme, militant democracy ends up in coercive enforcement (i.e. in illiberalism and conflict), whereas reasonable accommodation of 'illiberal' communities enhances pluralist coexistence, which far outweighs the cost of liberal concessions in its benefits. Traditional religious communities are the prime example of beneficiaries of such accommodation. Precisely because the Roma are 'old Europeans', diverse and indefinite in their religious affinities, their communal culture does not present a similar challenge to liberal national cultures. At Duke, as in Europe, they were offstage.

As a Jewish European historian, writing a history seeking to incorporate traditional Jews into the European narrative, I noticed, however, that the Roma represented an opportunity for exploring the dilemmas of European integration. Among the minorities who had inhabited multi-ethnic Central and Eastern Europe prior to the murderous ethno-nationalization before, during and after the Second World War, Jews and Roma were the major diasporas lacking a European homeland, hence, they were the great losers of nationalization. Imperial and federalist arrangements could prove life-sustaining to diasporas representing divergent acculturation and hybrid identities, and postwar Europeanization held a promise for both Jews and Roma. The first two decades of the EU represented a highpoint of Jewish acceptance and cultural pre-eminence. As Part II of this book shows, this was also the time when the EU launched projects to advance Roma Europeanization. The results were mixed but, as Huub van Baar suggests in Chapter 5, if Europeans negotiated the Roma difference, they could purge Europeanization of its hubris.

The Roma thus represented an opportunity for the Council for European Studies at Duke to address issues that were at the centre of European politics and reflected our special concern with the accommodation of minorities in national cultures. In April 2015, more than twenty scholars and artists from four continents met at Duke University and Wake Forest University for two days of meetings on 'Reasonable Accommodations and Roma in Contemporary Europe'. The participants came from the global academic community of Romani Studies and the Romani intelligentsia, and they were supported by funds from both universities.

The Roma and Their Struggle for Identity in Contemporary Europe has emerged from these meetings. Romani identity is the focus of this volume. The authors are well aware of the pitfalls associated with 'identity', and intersectionality is their common rubric. They begin by exploring segregation and dire poverty, the economic and social conditions that defy the best efforts of Roma to advance. Gender commands their attention, and the Roma women's movement, the difficulties it encounters in the Roma community and its European ramifications are the focus of several chapters. The authors display theoretical virtuosity in deploying postcolonial theory to discuss strategic essentialism, and have a refined understanding of artistic and cultural representation. If they appear preoccupied with Romani identity, it is not because they wish to rescue a vestige of ethnic identity – they decidedly refuse it – but because the label 'Roma' continues to carry heavy liability in European culture and politics. Our authors are haunted by the arbitrary way in which the label is applied, and the diminution of life chances it entails. The thrust of the discussion was to deconstruct Romani identities as constructed by Europeans. To an extent surprising for a Jewish historian, and even more so for any historian of nationalism, the Romani intelligentsia has difficulty positing the 'We'. Chastened by postcolonial theory, they are aware of the gap separating the intelligentsia and the people. But it is also true that Romani diversity presents a special challenge for scholars and activists wishing to think of the Roma diaspora as a collective.

What is to be done? History is not our authors' preferred mode for arbitrating identity, but it offers opportunities for working around the problem of Romani diversity. By telling Romani narratives, history creates, almost *malgré lui*, a collective. The diversity of communities, which recognized themselves as Romani or were pegged as Gypsies by hostile Europeans, become the subjects of a history that allows all to take part without demanding that they first arbitrate their identity. Such a history could also become Romani European, mitigating public discourse that 'others' the Roma, and expanding Europeanization without requiring that they be other than that which they wish.

Jewish European history, an emergent historiographical genre, may be instructive for Romani European history. Focusing on the cosmopolitan Jewish intelligentsia, Jewish European history has told pluralist and international stories that Europeans, in search of a unifying cultural legacy, love to hear. In *Jacob & Esau: Jewish European History Between Nation and Empire*, I expanded the genre to include traditional rabbinic Jews. I used the trope of Jacob and Esau, the competing biblical brothers, to tell the story of Christian-Jewish relations over two millennia. I focused on modern European Jewish integration, and highlighted the European nation-state's dilemmas and the opportunities opened to Jewish identity in pluralist continental empires. The Jews and Roma share diasporic features, and Romani historians may find they can proceed in constructing history along similar lines to Jewish ones. From the grouping of Roma, vagabonds and criminals as 'Gypsies' in sixteenth-century England to the conscious hybridity of Romani European art in the twenty-first century, displayed in this book, Romani history tells European stories. It may represent the next frontier in advancing cultural and political prospects for the Roma.

Will Europe still have, in the foreseeable future, a space for such a history? The viability of reasonable accommodation, Romani studies and Romani European history depends on European attentiveness to minority needs. The meetings at Duke and Wake Forest took place at a unique juncture when the progressive US academy, the global Romani intelligentsia and the EU all saw a mission in Roma advance. The volume highlights the paradoxes of EU policies and their shortcomings, but it does not question the goodwill. Meanwhile, however, political and cultural realities have changed radically. The rise of populist nationalism and authoritarian politics on both sides of the Atlantic have undermined support for minority rights, and made the crisis of constitutionalism and liberal democracy more urgent. Scholars from the Central European University (CEU) in Budapest were prominent during the discussions and are among this volume's authors. As this Foreword is written, the CEU is leaving Budapest for Vienna, forced out by Hungarian government harassment. Resistance to Europeanization is waxing and ever fewer people view it as desirable, let alone as tenable. This book already sounds as if coming from a golden past, when dreaming of a Romani European future was possible. Let it be a testimony that such times and hopes existed. When a future age reopens possibilities for Roma advance, it may derive some guidance and inspiration from the present book.

Duke University, Durham NC
25 December 2018

Malachi H. Hacohen (PhD, Columbia University) is Bass Fellow and Professor of History, Political Science and Religion, as well as of Eurasian, German and Jewish Studies at Duke University, Durham NC, USA. He directs the Religions and Public Life Initiative at the Kenan Institute for Ethics. His *Karl Popper – The Formative Years, 1902–1945: Politics and Philosophy in Interwar Vienna* (Cambridge University Press, 2000) won the Herbert Baxter Adams Prize of the AHA and the Victor Adler State Prize. He has published essays on the Central European Jewish intelligentsia, Cold War liberalism and cosmopolitanism, and Jewish identity in *The Journal of Modern History, The Journal of the History of Ideas, History and Theory, History of Political Economy, Jewish Social Studies,* and other journals and collections. His *Jacob & Esau: Jewish European History Between Nation and Empire* has just been published by Cambridge University Press. It provides a new account of two millennia of Jewish European history, and integrates the cosmopolitan narrative of the Jewish diaspora with that of traditional Jews and Jewish culture.

Acknowledgements

✺ ✺ ✺

We would like to extend our warmest thanks to the people and institutions without whose help this project and book would not have been possible. First and foremost, our special thanks to all of the contributors for supporting this project from the outset and for following through with timely, insightful and inspiring chapters. We feel privileged to have been able to exchange ideas with each of them, and thank them for their intellectual labour, commitment and enthusiasm while working on this project. Their knowledge of specific aspects and dimensions of the situation of Roma, and their eagerness to share their insights, have been key to realizing this book.

We thank the Council for European Studies at Duke University, Durham, NC, as well as the Department of Women's, Gender and Sexuality Studies at Wake Forest University (WFU) in Winston Salem, NC, for hosting discussions about 'Reasonable Accommodations and Roma Issues in Contemporary Europe: A Symposium on Global Governance, Democracy and Social Justice' (7–8 April 2015), as part of the CES series 'Reasonable Accommodations: Minorities in Globalized Nation States', funded by the 'Partnership in a Global Age' grant of the Andrew W. Mellon Foundation. We thank the Council for European Studies at Duke University, The Provost's Fund for Academic Excellence at WFU, IPLACe and the Humanities Institute at WFU for sponsoring this event, which laid the grounds for this volume. For their attendance, chairing, presentation and energizing participation in the discussions, we are grateful to, among many others, Glenda Bailey-Mershon, Cristina Bejan, David Crowe, Petra Gelbart, Jelena Jovanović, Tímea Junghaus, Lynn Hooker, Barbara Rose Lange, Márton Rövid and José Villalba. At Duke University, we thank Giovanni Zanalda, Director of the Duke University Center for International and Global Studies and Associate Research Professor in the Department of Economics, the Department of History and the Social Science Research Institute. We also would like to thank Amy Vargas-Tonsi, the former associate director of the Council for

European Studies at Duke University. We are especially grateful for the support of WFU faculty members Wanda Balzano and David Coates. We grieve for David, who died on 7 August 2018 and unfortunately cannot enjoy the deliberation of this volume.

We also thank the Duke University Center for International and Global Studies and the Council for European Studies at Duke University for financially supporting the realization of this publication. We are specifically grateful to Malachi H. Hacohen, Bass Fellow and Professor of History, Political Science and Religion, and Director of the Religions and Public Life Initiative at the Kenan Institute for Ethics at Duke University for his encouragement and generosity in supporting this project from the very beginning. We also thank him very much for writing the foreword to this book.

Angéla Kóczé, who initiated this book project, would like to thank Wake Forest University, and the Department of Women's, Gender, and Sexuality Studies in particular, for offering an excellent academic environment for organizing the 2015 international symposium. She also expresses her gratitude to the Romani Studies Program at Central European University, Budapest, for the supportive environment while working on this edited volume.

Huub van Baar thanks his colleagues from the collaborative research centre 'Dynamics of Security: Forms of Securitization in Historical Perspective' at the Justus Liebig University in Giessen, the Philipps University in Marburg and the Herder Institute for Historical Research on East Central Europe in Marburg. Especially, he would like to thank Regina Kreide, Ana Ivasiuc, Laura Soréna Tittel, Horst Carl and Angela Marciniak. He thanks the German Research Foundation (DFG), which has, through grant SFB/TRR 138 (2014–21), financed the inspiring research, and which includes his and his colleagues' research project 'Between Minority Protection and Securitization: Roma Minority Formation in Modern European History'. He also thanks very much Yolande Jansen and Sammy and Benjamin van Baar for their loving support and patience during the course of co-editing this volume.

We particularly wish to thank very much Delaine Le Bas for allowing us to include images of several of her artworks and those of her late husband, Damian le Bas. It was with great sorrow that we learned that, on 9 December 2017, Damian had suddenly died, at the age of 54. We have dedicated this volume to Damian Le Bas to underscore the role that he and his artworks played and continue to play in the international Romani art movement, as well as in and beyond the Roma movement more generally.

Damian John Le Bas was born in Sheffield, UK, in 1963. He studied at the Royal College of Art London (1985–87). He was one of the sixteen artists who were part of *Paradise Lost*, the first Roma pavilion at Venice Biennale

2007. Together with Delaine Le Bas, he created *Safe European Home?*, a series of public art installations that have been seen across Europe since 2011. *Gypsy Revolution* and *Gypsy DaDa* were two other artistic creations initiated by Damian Le Bas. He worked extensively with cartographies and maps. His works have been exhibited internationally since the late 1980s, including at Prague Biennale 2005 and 2007, Venice Biennale 2007, The Third Edition of The Project Biennale Art D-O Ark Underground Bosnia & Herzegovina 2015 and Goteborg International Biennale For Contemporary Art Extended 2015. Damian Le Bas produced the artwork and paintings for the theatre production *Roma Armee* (2017) at the Maxim Gorki Theatre in Berlin and was the initiator of *Come Out Now! First Roma Biennale*, organized at the same place in April 2018.

We wish to thank Marion Berghahn as well as Sam Beck, the editor of the Romani Studies series, for providing us with the opportunity for this cooperation. At Berghahn Books, we would also like to thank Tom Bonnington and Harry Eagles for their guidance and support in the editorial and production processes that have enabled the publication of this book. We are grateful to Thomas Acton, Sam Beck and the anonymous reviewers for their valuable commentaries on the proposal for and draft version of this volume. We also thank Gwen Jones, Nigel Smith and Caroline Kuhtz for their careful and thorough reading and copy-editing of the entire manuscript.

Last but not least, we, the editors, thank each other for being dedicated and supportive colleagues and friends during the long course of undertaking this book project together.

Abbreviations

❀ ❀ ❀

AWID	Association for Women's Rights in Development
CEE	Central and Eastern Europe
CEU	Central European University
CRT	Critical Race Theory
DCIS	Department of Control and Inspection Service (Slovakia)
EANRS	European Academic Network of Romani Studies
ENAR	European Network against Racism
ERIAC	European Roma Institute for Art and Culture
ERRC	European Roma Rights Centre
ERTF	European Roma and Travellers Forum
EU	European Union
FRA	European Union Agency for Fundamental Rights
EWL	European Women's Lobby
LGBTQI+	Lesbian, Gay, Bisexual, Transgender, Queer (Questioning), Intersex
MSzMP	Magyar Szocialista Munkáspárt (Hungarian Socialist Workers' Party)
MSzP	Magyar Szocialista Párt (Hungarian Socialist Party)
NGO	Non-governmental Organization
NRCP	National Roma Contact Points
NRIS	National Roma Integration Strategies
NWP	Network Women's Program
OSCE	Organization for Security and Co-operation in Europe
OSA	Open Society Archives (Budapest)
OSF	Open Society Foundation
OSI	Open Society Institute
RWI	Roma Women's Initiative
SzDsZ	Szabad Demokraták Szövetsége (Alliance of Free Democrats [Hungary])

UN	United Nations
CEDAW	Convention on the Elimination of All Forms of Discrimination against Women
UNDP	United Nations Development Programme
UNESCO	United Nations Educational, Scientific and Cultural Organization

PART I

❀ ❀ ❀

INTRODUCTIONS

INTRODUCTION

✻ ✻ ✻

THE ROMA IN CONTEMPORARY EUROPE
Struggling for Identity at a Time of Proliferating Identity Politics

Huub van Baar with Angéla Kóczé

Thirty Years On

> Under communism we were denied any identity; now we have to have one.
> —Female Slovak Romani journalist, August 2005

In 1992, the non-governmental human rights organization Helsinki Watch published a report under the title 'Struggling for Ethnic Identity: Czechoslovakia's Endangered Gypsies'. It was the successor to two earlier reports published in 1991 under the title 'Destroying Ethnic Identity' on the position of Roma in the aftermath of the fall of communism in Bulgaria and Romania respectively (Helsinki Watch 1991a, 1991b, 1992). These reports were among the first international non-governmental documents that, directly after the changes of 1989, discussed the position of Roma and called for national and international political, legal and institutional action to improve their societal position. Nearly thirty years on, a discussion of what these relatively unknown and largely forgotten reports assessed in terms of a 'struggle for identity' would be helpful in order to introduce several of the thematic dimensions of identity that the contributors to this study will analyse and revisit.

One of the prominent issues discussed throughout the three Helsinki Watch reports is the lack of recognition of the Roma's status as victims of racially motivated violence against them. The reports highlight the rapid emergence of mob and institutional violence against Roma throughout Central and Eastern Europe in the immediate aftermath of 1989. The report on Romania, for instance, states:

> The single, most dramatic change for Gypsies since ... 1989 ... has been the escalation of ethnic hatred and violence directed against them by the non-Gypsy population. Prior to 1990, anti-Gypsy sentiments took more subtle forms of expression. Now, rarely a month goes by ... without another Gypsy village being attacked. Many of those interviewed ... expressed their growing sense of insecurity and fear for their families and homes. (Helsinki Watch 1991b: 33)

These early reports and several later ones – such as the many reports published by the Budapest-based European Roma Rights Centre (ERRC) since its establishment in 1996 – clarify that the eruption of violence against Roma was directly related to the lack of adequate responses from public authorities, or to the denial of or even support for this violence from their side. Since 1989, numerous cases have been documented in which the racially motivated character of attacks was denied, in which the police or health authorities refused to investigate or report assaults, in which independent investigations or court cases were frustrated, in which police officers passively or actively supported violence against Roma – sometimes in collaboration with extremist factions – and in which the police themselves violated the rights of Roma or even reversed charges against the police in their own favour.

A second key identity-related theme discussed in the reports is the racial dimension of several persistent and severe practices of segregation, such as those related to education (special schools or classes), residence and housing (in separate shantytowns, ghettoes or so-called 'settlements' that are occasionally the targets of police raids or removals by authorities), health care (separate rooms in hospitals, practices of sterilization, denied access to emergency services) and other public services and facilities (separate or denied seats on public transport; lacking or substandard infrastructure; denied access to restaurants, pubs, discos and cultural or sport clubs; no refuse collection). The reports also put these diverse aspects of segregation in the context of the often devastating impact of assimilation policies during (and before) state socialism, and of the neglect or active denial of Romani culture and ethnic identity, such as in Bulgarian socialist policies that forbade Roma from speaking the Romani language, and in socialist policies that limited or denied Romani forms of cultural association more generally.

A final major element that these reports relate to the then 'struggle for identity' is the ways in which authorities, politicians, citizens and media negatively or one-sidedly identified Roma, through various overlapping and intersecting processes of stigmatization, criminalization, pathologization and dehumanization. The reports also pay attention to how these processes of stereotyping and interrelated practices of marginalization had led to a culture of fear in which many Roma tried to hide their identity in order to avoid as much as possible the negative attitudes and behaviours towards them. At the same time, the reports discuss the emergence of new forms of political and cultural association, organized by Roma themselves and for various reasons, including activism to improve their situation, their self-articulation and their self-representation.

Thirty years on, an assessment of these three complex dimensions of identity related to the denial of racially motivated violence against Roma, radical practices of marginalization and exclusion, and the interconnection between outside identification and self-representation is still highly relevant to understand adequately the contemporary Romani struggle for identity. Therefore, in the next two sections, we begin with this threefold assessment. Then, in the following two sections, we discuss in greater detail how we will approach the issue of identity in this volume. First, we will consider identity in the context of the contemporary proliferation of identity politics, and then in terms of debates of essentialism versus constructivism, and how to move beyond this binary. In the final section, we will present the structure of the book and introduce the individual chapters.

While significant developments have been achieved with regard to each of the three identity-related domains that we have briefly discussed above, the challenges that relate to these dimensions are astonishingly similar to those of the early 1990s, as the contributions to this volume will demonstrate. Although it is beyond the scope of this study to indicate all the significant changes that have taken place since the 1990s, it is helpful to delineate a few of the more important ones, beginning with those in the context of the relationship between outside identification and multiple practices of self-identification.

Significant Changes: Romani Presence, Voice and Participation

The post-1989 widening and deepening of various formal and more informal Romani social movements have had a profound impact on making Roma publicly visible and audible on political, policy, cultural and public debates about their societal position within and beyond the contested borders of Europe.

Throughout the 1990s and since the beginning of the new millennium, what has become known as 'the Romani movement' (Puxon 2000; Vermeersch 2006) has increasingly become more diverse, intersectional and transnational (Vermeersch 2006; Nicolae and Slavik 2007; Sigona and Trehan 2009; McGarry 2010; van Baar 2011a; Bunescu 2014; Bhabha, Mirga and Matache 2017; Beck and Ivasiuc 2018; Law and Kovats 2018; Kóczé et al. 2019). By developing their own heterogeneous social movements, those Roma who have associated themselves with these movements and their various more or less institutionalized practices have increasingly entered the sociopolitical and cultural scene as active agents of representation, not merely as passive 'victims' of representations and disputable identifications by others. As part of these developments, discussions about self-representation – for instance, about the contested use of 'Gypsies', 'Roma', 'Travellers' or other terms as homogeneous or homogenizing labels – have become an almost permanent ingredient in debates at diverse institutional levels, ranging from everyday encounters at the local level to institutionalized European and international fora dealing with politics, policy and culture. Today, it has become odd and even controversial to implement a social, political, cultural or academic programme without some form of Roma participation – notwithstanding the fact that this still continues to take place.

Consequently, Roma have now become more than simply the subject of discourses, programmes and tools of inclusion, antidiscrimination, development, empowerment, participation and cultural and media production and consumption. They are also critical voices in debates about their status, identity, history, memory and more general representation as minorities; as such, they have tried to influence the policy fabric around their position and the debates about how they could or should be represented in society, culture, media and history at various levels. The momentum of '1989' and the dynamic interactions between formal and informal Romani activisms, advocacy networks, non-governmental organizations and international governmental structures have led, for instance, to a wide and diversified landscape of Romani and 'pro-Roma' activism and engagement in and beyond Europe. These debates have increasingly emphasized the vital role of intersectional dimensions (Kóczé 2009; Schultz, this volume; Szalai, this volume; Zentai, this volume). Those who have raised their voices in public and academic debates have increasingly articulated the importance of paying attention both to the connections between different societal sectors (economy, culture, society, politics, religion, media, environment, science, etc.) and the intersections of – in particular – ethnicity, race, gender, class, age and nationality.

These social, political, civil and cultural movements have had diverse impacts throughout European cultures and societies, some of which will be explicitly and more extensively discussed in the contributions to this volume. In the domain of history and memory, for instance, we have been able to observe a hard-won, but nevertheless increased sense of ownership over Romani histories and memories, and over the sites, archives, institutions and narratives key to historical awareness and collective, cultural memories. This is particularly true for the histories and memories related to the Romani Holocaust (see, for instance, Rose 1987; Hancock 1996; Bársony and Daróczi 2008; Mirga-Kruszelnicka, Acuña and Trojański 2015). In this field, we have seen the continuation of struggles for the recognition of the occurrence and huge human and societal consequences of genocide and violent persecution. Although these struggles began soon after the Second World War and, for decades, primarily took place in Germany,[1] since the 1990s they have increasingly taken place all over Europe and become more impactful. Romani claims for the recognition of their histories have become public and more robust and, moreover, have found significant inroads into institutional, cultural and political infrastructures, to allow for narrating and imagining Romani histories and memories as integral rather than marginal parts of national and European narratives. This development has not remained limited to the Romani Holocaust; for instance, regarding the position and situation of Roma during processes of modern European nation- and state-building, as well as during communism (Majtényi and Majtényi 2016; Donert 2017; Trehan, this volume), we have been able to observe the trend of increasing attention being paid to Roma, and also on their own terms, even while this trend is still preliminary. In this context, both access to archives and Roma mobilization for the production of new archives – such as the ones included in the *RomArchive* project[2] – have been vital not only in terms of reconsidering the position of Roma in European histories. They have also been fundamental in the creation and performance of new narratives and memories regarding Romani identities, implicitly or explicitly critical of how canonical discourses about Europe have historically and until now often managed to exclude and marginalize them (Picker 2017; Tremlett and Le Bas, this volume; van Baar 2011a, and Chapter 1, this volume).

In this respect, the establishment of the European Roma Institute for Arts and Culture (ERIAC) in June 2017 in the centre of Berlin can be considered one of the key moments in this development in which Roma actors themselves create, perform and institutionalize new narratives regarding their identities, histories and memories – notwithstanding the complex history and disputes in the course of the 2010s, out of which ERIAC emerged (Ryder 2018; Magazzini, this volume). These processes have not been homogeneous, just as the emergence and development of the Roma social and civil movement have, throughout history, been a highly heterogeneous societal process (Mayall 2004; Klímova-Alexander 2005; Vermeersch 2006;

van Baar 2015a). In the more recent development of and within the Roma social movement, we have been able to observe the emergence of various new movements, overlapping but at times also conflicting with other, more mainstream factions of the movement. Here, we particularly want to mention the Romani women's movement (Kóczé et al. 2019; Schultz, this volume; Zentai, this volume) and various intersecting movements that could be qualified as the Romani LGBTQI+ movement (Kurtić 2014; Fremlová 2017; Fremlová and McGarry 2019). In all these instances of Roma involvements and movements, the possibilities to claim their own history and gain ownership over its dominant discourses, imageries, sources and representations, as we will see in this volume, have been key to organizing critical debates about important and often delicate issues such as citizenship, political voice and representation, cultural ownership, poverty, sustainable development, racism, displacement, gender, domestic violence, public visibility, and equality and justice more generally.

In the other two identity-related contexts of the denial of racially motivated violence against Roma and the challenging of radical practices of Roma marginalization, the situation has been more ambiguous. In the broader context of the 'Europeanization of the representation of the Roma' (van Baar 2011a, Chapter 5, this volume) and the interrelated emergence of 'the Roma political phenomenon' (Law and Kovats 2018) in Europe, substantially more attention has been paid, at various institutional levels and scales, to the causes and impact of practices of physical and symbolic violence against Roma. During the 1990s, international non-governmental organizations such as Helsinki Watch and the ERRC, and local and transnational networks of Romani and pro-Roma activists, played a crucial role in representing the situation of Roma as a 'human emergency' and in bringing them onto Europe's political and institutional agendas (Ram 2010; van Baar 2011b). Several scholars have also shown how, since the second half of the 1990s, mechanisms that should guarantee the protection of Roma have steadily been developed at both national and international levels (Rooker 2002; Klímova-Alexander 2005; O'Nions 2007; Agarin and Cordell 2016; Bhabha, Mirga and Matache 2017). Over the years, in an increasing number of national and European court cases that have dealt with violence and marginalization affecting Roma, the role of racism has been acknowledged (ERRC 2010), as has the profound impact of institutional racism and racial discrimination on the daily, personal and professional lives of Roma, as well as on 'interethnic' relations and the formations and transformations of their identities.

More generally, from a programmatic point of view, it is probably reasonable to say that issues related to various forms and practices of segregation – and their impact on life quality, health, education, human security, social mobility, family planning, gender, future prospects, self-esteem, societal participation and trust in authorities, as well as other intersecting issues of identity and identity formation – have come to the fore and been acknowledged much more prominently in political, socioeconomic and cultural contexts than they were in the early 1990s. This development could not have taken place without another significant change that we have been able to observe and which we have also highlighted at the beginning of this section: in various contexts and at many different levels throughout Europe, Roma have become involved much more prominently and constructively in affairs that directly or indirectly concern them – even while phenomena such as tokenism and at best consultative inclusion, rather than full and equal participation, are still omnipresent in processes of decision making that affect or pertain to Roma in contemporary societies and cultures.

Similar Challenges: Displacement and Racial Reversibility

As diverse evaluations of the situation of the European Roma over the last thirty years have concluded, there is not much ground for optimism if we consider the impact of the various societal changes and developments on the quality of life of many Roma, and particularly the poorest and most marginalized among them. For them, daily realities are still bleak and often characterized by miserable future prospects. Academic and public discussions about identity struggles and transformations will probably not hold great appeal for them, if at all. Nevertheless, this study hopes to clarify why these debates do matter – and are meaningful.

The Relation between Outside Identification and Self-Representation

We have been able to observe, for instance, important advantages of migration, ranging from the escape from social malaise and increased socioeconomic mobility to support for relatives through remittances, less (direct) discrimination and improvement of future prospects. And yet, many Roma who have experienced new lifeworlds through migration have chosen to hide their identity abroad in order to be able to navigate these worlds. Nonetheless, they have been confronted with exploitation in the labour and housing markets as well as high degrees of precariousness and, in the UK, with additional uncertainties caused by the debate about and possibility of Brexit. At the same time, those who, for various reasons, have not been able to hide their identities have often been faced with 'spectacular' displacement and violent removal through eviction or deportation.

Various influential media spectacles have turned Roma into some of Europe's most visibly politicized subjects. Here, we can think of spectacles such as the 'nomad emergency', the 'security pacts' and the policy of fingerprinting of Roma in Italy (Clough Marinaro and Sigona 2011); the expulsion of mostly Romanian Roma from France and also Spain (van Baar 2011b; Parker 2012; Vrăbiescu 2019); the hype about 'poverty migration' of Roma in the UK, Austria, Germany, the Benelux countries and Scandinavia (Benedik 2010; Fox 2012, Fox, Morosanu and Szilassy 2012; Djuve et al. 2015; Hemelsoet and Van Pelt 2015; Lausberg 2015; Olesen and Karlsson 2018); the hysteria about supposed 'child stealing' Roma in Greece, Italy and Ireland (van Baar 2014; Kóczé and Rövid 2017); and the 'repatriation' of Kosovo Roma from Germany followed by the alleged 'asylum shopping' of Roma from Albania and ex-Yugoslavia in Germany (Castañeda 2014; van Baar 2017b). At the same time, in Central and Eastern Europe, similar practices of the hypervisibilization of Roma have repeatedly been articulated through events and practices such as anti-Roma demonstrations (Albert 2012; Balogh 2012; Efremova 2012), anti-Roma neighbourhood watch initiatives (Balogh 2012; Mireanu 2013), mandatory public works (van Baar 2012; Grill 2018; Kóczé, this volume; Szalai, this volume) and zero tolerance measures, evictions and police raids throughout the region (Vincze 2013; Trlifajová et al. 2015; Picker 2017; van Baar forthcoming).

Yet, as the diversity of these examples already indicates, it would be misleading to relate the irregularization of the sociopolitical identity and status of Romani migrants, refugees and citizens primarily to the dramatization generated by political rhetoric, crisis talk and media coverage, or even to the persistent present-day manifestations of extremism, nationalism and populism in and beyond Europe. More is involved. These processes of irregularization and the correlated, unorthodox measures affecting Roma have been and are becoming an integral and normalized part of 'unspectacular' everyday bureaucratic practices that are often presented as 'reasonable' and 'justifiable' ways to deal with Roma. In this respect, something highly peculiar and influential has taken place in the diverse institutional commitments towards Roma that have emerged throughout Europe. Huub van Baar and Peter Vermeersch (2017) have argued that those Roma representations that have been operationalized in decision- and policymaking bodies often exclusively fall within the categories of either 'risky people' or 'people at risk', and thus invoke the disputable assumption that there is a close or even inherent link between 'Roma' and 'risk'. Consequently, these institutionalized representations of Roma along the lines of risk contribute significantly to rendering Roma hypervisible. They make them visible, legible and governable, but only in very specific ways, and operate in a regime of visuality that strongly affects Romani agency and identity negatively (see also Tremlett and Le Bas, this volume). On the ground, the impact of these operational Roma representations has frequently resulted in a situation in which 'positive' 'anti-policies' – programmes that focus on the socially desirable aims such as antidiscrimination, antiracism, antipoverty and desegregation – have ambiguously merged with their 'negative' counterparts – 'anti-policies' that focus on socially undesirable phenomena such as antisocial behaviour, crime, trafficking, mobile banditry, illegal migration, zero tolerance and the like (van Baar 2019).

Practices of Marginalization and Exclusion

At the complex juncture of citizenship, security and development, the clear and ongoing trend to hypervisibilize and securitize Roma thus limits how others identify them – mainly negatively, with suspicion or as vulnerable victims with limited agency – and also limits the ways in which Roma can negotiate their own identities in everyday intersubjective, bureaucratic, cultural, economic or sociopolitical encounters. And even though desegregation programmes have been developed and court decisions against the segregation of Roma are numerous, their implementation on the ground has been incomplete at best, for a variety of reasons – corruption, a lack of political will, institutional racism, inadequate policies and their problematic top-down implementation, and hampered or inadequate decentralization (ERRC 2010; Rostas 2012; Hornberg and Brüggemann 2013; Miskovic 2013; Szalai and Zentai 2014). In particular, at the nexus of security and development, where attempts to combat exclusion and marginalization have tended to contribute more to the maintenance of a fragile and delicate status quo, and thus supported governing rather than solving poverty among Roma, we have been able to notice a radical but mostly negative impact on how Roma can exercise their citizenship rights. Within contexts of durable or even deepening segregation – often organized along a historically structural and well-established (though not necessarily steady) colour line between Roma and their fellow citizens – constructive or recuperative processes of identity formation and transformation of Roma have remained incredibly difficult, as both Júlia Szalai and Angéla Kóczé show in their contributions to this volume.

While this delicate relation between segregation and identity formation is highly tangible in Europe's rural and urban peripheries, it is equally tangible, though at a more symbolic level, in political, policy and academic debates on the multiple borders in and of Europe. Media spectacles such as those related to the still ongoing deportation of Romanian Roma from France have illuminated the highly ambiguous character of the Europeanization of the representation of the Roma. Indeed, if these spectacles have clarified one thing, it is that they function as a political technology of separation in which citizenship has been dealt with differentially and in which Roma have often ended up on the 'wrong' side of the border (van Baar 2017a, forthcoming; see also van Baar, Chapter 5, this volume). Despite the political rhetoric of Roma inclusion in Europe and the fact that many of the Romani migrants targeted for eviction or deportation are EU citizens who exercise and practise their EU right to free movement, these Roma have nevertheless been relegated to the domain of 'non-' and 'not-yet Europeans', and thus to the 'imaginary waiting room of history' (Chakrabarty 2000: 8) in which they do not yet 'belong' to Europe, and nor are they yet considered as its full citizens.

Therefore, in debates on the relationship between Romani identity formation and their symbolic or physical separation, we have to challenge the open or hidden manifestations of both political and methodological Eurocentrism that are present in any suggestion that the 'Roma problem' is only an internal or 'intra-European' affair, just as we still have to revisit how the 'Gypsy Question' was once considered an integral part of the 'National Question' in the decades of state socialism (Stewart 2001: 77–82; Trehan, this volume). The consideration of Roma in terms of a 'problem' has not only turned things radically upside down and rendered the underlying societal problematic significantly invisible, but the European domestication of how this alleged 'Roma problem' should be solved has also resulted in a positivist kind of European Studies that does not question how Europe itself has historically been complicit in these narrow Roma problematizations. Indeed, it is perhaps not despite, but precisely *because of* the Europeanization of Roma representation that Roma could be qualified and approached as Europe's racialized, second-rank citizens (van Baar 2011a, 2017a, 2018, and Chapter 5, this volume; Yıldız and De Genova 2018; De Genova 2019).

The incomplete shift in the Europeanization of Roma representation, from considering them a 'European minority' to perceiving them primarily as a 'European problem' (van Baar 2011b), has shown how their Europeanization has gone hand in hand with a highly disputable biopolitical bordering of Europe that, at the same time, has more clearly opened up the opportunities to discuss critically the position and identities of Roma from a postcolonial and critical race point of view as well (Imre 2005; Trehan and Kóczé 2009; New Keywords Collective 2016; Picker 2017; van Baar 2017a, 2018, 2019; Baker 2018). From such a perspective, it becomes clear that contemporary mechanisms of excluding and segregating minoritized groups are deeply rooted in Europe's notorious colonial, imperial and otherwise racial pasts, as Giovanni Picker (2017), Catherine Baker (2018) and Geraldine Heng (2018) have eloquently shown for the case of the Roma in their recent monographs. Such a point of view also reveals how these mechanisms are related to problematic racial and biopolitical processes in which, both historically and currently, minoritized lives and bodies – 'migrants', 'refugees', 'minorities' and 'their' practices – are radically called into question, such as in the notorious and recurring articulations of the 'Jewish Question', the 'Gypsy/Roma Question', the 'Muslim Question' and, most recently, the 'Migrant/Refugee Question' (De Genova 2016; New Keywords Collective 2016).

At the same time, this double process – both revealing the links with Europe's 'present pasts' and interrelating the fate of various racialized and minoritized groups in Europe's global histories – has also enabled the kinds of 'travelling activism' (van Baar 2013) that have created productive spaces for dialogue between different global social movements, such as Romani, women's, Black, feminist, indigenous and LGBTQI+ movements (Szalai and Schiff 2014; Bhabha, Mirga and Matache 2017; McGarry 2017; Beck and Ivasiuc 2018; Corradi 2018; Kóczé et al. 2019; Magazzini, this volume; Schultz, this volume; Silverman, this volume; Tremlett and Le Bas, this volume; Zentai, this volume). Moreover – and this is crucial for any critical understanding of contemporary policies and the development of better future ones – the ambiguity of the Europeanization of Roma representation has turned into a *positive* ambiguity, in which travelling activism and the creation of productive spaces for dialogue have generated opportunities for critical interchanges and negotiations about the ways in which Roma have implicitly or explicitly been addressed in policy, political, cultural, social and media discourses. Furthermore, the peculiarities regarding the hypervisibilization of Roma in several European contexts have attracted the interest of scholars in fields as diverse as citizenship studies, migration and border studies, critical race studies, gender studies, queer studies, critical legal studies, critical security studies, social movement studies, visual studies and political geography, and, thus, in turn have indirectly contributed to a desirable interdisciplinary diversification of Roma-related scholarship – even though we are still at the beginning of this process (see also van Baar, Chapter 5, this volume).

We have been able to observe similarly ambiguous challenges in the context of the so-called 'refugee/migration crisis'.[3] In particular, some East Central European populist and nationalist politicians have rendered this crisis 'successfully' productive by managing to gain political capital through connecting the recent arrival of migrants to the long-term presence of Roma in their countries and, thus, by suggesting that both the international 'Refugee/Migration Question' and the domestic 'Roma Question' are 'untameable' and, most importantly, 'irreconcilable' with the 'National Question'. A notorious case in point is the way in which Viktor Orbán, Hungary's prime minister, has connected his anti-migrant rhetoric and measures with the suggestion that Hungarian Roma are an 'unruly' population, with whom 'the Hungarians' have been 'burdened' 'at some point' in their history (Kóczé and Rövid 2017). Similarly, when, after the 'hot summer' of 2015, Angela Merkel's *Willkommenskultur* (welcoming culture) was increasingly disputed in Germany, a bifurcation of its asylum system took place in which those migrants arriving from South Eastern Europe – among them a significantly high number of Roma – were relegated to newly established reception centres dealing with 'chanceless' asylum claimants. Similar to those who are advantaged in airport queues because they are 'speedy boarders' making use of specific priority lanes, these South East European migrants are *disadvantaged* because they have to be 'deported with priority' through these new and separate *Transitzentren* (transit centres) that some media and politicians have called *Sonderlager* (special camps). As Romani Rose, the chair of the Central Council of German Sinti and Roma, emphasizes – and particularly in the context of Germany's dark past – it is cynical, dangerous and unacceptable to discuss and install such 'special camps', which was the term used for many Nazi camps in order to disguise their real function (Staffen-Quandt 2015). Thus, in the context of the recent 'tests' to the EU's border regime, the proliferation of co-constituted and interrelated crises and crisis formations has coincided with the renewal and reinforcement of differential and racial treatment, not only of those who come from 'outside', but also of those who live within Europe's contested borders (van Baar 2015b, 2017a, and Chapter 5, this volume).

At the same time, however, and as in the case of the 'refugee/migration crisis', we have been able to notice the emergence of a productive synergy of Roma-related scholarship with diverse strands in, for instance, migration and border studies, citizenship studies, critical race studies, critical security studies and social movement studies (see, for instance, Bigo, Carrera and Guild 2013; Jansen, Celikates and de Bloois 2015; New Keywords Collective 2016; Yıldız and De Genova 2018). Even though we have to be critically aware of what crisis narratives do for scholarship about (not only) Roma and their problematization in all sorts of political and cultural communication (De Genova, Garelli and Tazzioli 2018; Pulay 2018), these synergies have helped to reveal and interrogate the ambiguous links between, on the one hand, the ongoing and renewed racialization of the European Roma and, on the other, Europe's commitment to them in programmes officially dedicated to its 'largest ethnic minority' (Yıldız and De Genova 2018; see also Rostas, this volume; van Baar 2018, and Chapter 5, this volume). In other words, silencing or neglecting the presence of Europe's diverse racial legacies in the very tissue of what is supposedly '*ethnic* minority governance' in Europe equals a denial of the impact of racialization on Romani identities and their position in Europe more generally, and the articulation of an oft-overlooked colour line that traverses Europe. Thus, our emphasis on race and racialization is not necessarily meant as a general critique of the notions of ethnicity or ethnic identity as 'essentializing concepts' (Pulay 2018: 185), but is a specific critique of those uses of ethnicity that overlook the racializing impact of institutionalized practices of 'ethnic' minority governance in Europe regarding Roma. This topic directly relates to racially motivated violence against Roma, and leads us to revisit what it looks like and how it is dealt with in contemporary Europe.

The Denial of Racially Motivated Violence against Roma

In the domain of racial violence against Roma, many battles are still to be won. For instance, attacks on Roma have recently taken place in Bulgaria, Romania and Ukraine, while police brutality against Roma continues to be endemic in several European countries beyond the East–West divide. One outstanding case in point is the way in which Slovak authorities have dealt with the police raid that took place in the town of Moldava nad Bodvou on 19 June 2013. In the early morning of that day, sixty-three heavily equipped and masked police officers from special riot units entered the local, entirely segregated Romani shantytown, where they physically and verbally attacked thirty-one Roma, who offered them no resistance. In addition to committing physical and psychological violence against these people, including their children, the police damaged their property. They also detained fifteen Roma, who were again abused during detention. Medical reports have confirmed the serious injuries of those who were targeted.

At the moment of writing (June 2019) and, thus, about six years after the raid, no adequate or thorough investigation of the case has taken place. Only seven months after the police actions, in early 2014, the Department of Control and Inspection Service (DCIS) of the Slovak Ministry of Interior began examining the events. The DCIS did not find any police misconduct, did not refer the case for criminal proceedings, and ultimately closed it in August 2017, after the Slovak Constitutional Court – the highest court in the country – had investigated the case and reached similar findings, largely based on the testimonies of police personnel. As the body responsible for investigating police misconduct of police officers, the DCIS was widely criticized both domestically and internationally for not fulfilling the essential requirements of independence and impartiality; moreover, the Slovak Ombudsperson was repeatedly critical in her reports on the case (Public Defender of Rights 2013; Zalešák 2015).

Local and international human rights organizations, including the ERRC and Amnesty International, have condemned the ways in which the Slovak authorities have thus far dealt with the raid, and therefore brought the case to the European Court of Human Rights in Strasbourg in 2018, where it is still pending.[4] Over the years, those who had to examine the raid took the testimonies of intervening police officers as the accurate truth, while those of the Roma were repeatedly disputed. Already in the first year of inquiries, an investigating police officer ordered 'psychological' examinations of many of the Romani victims and witnesses. As Michal Zalešák (2015) has suggested, 'this unusual step [gave] the impression that instead of concentrating on finding the perpetrators, the investigation [was] now focused on undermining the credibility of those giving evidence against the police officers'. He considered it as 'harassment and re-victimisation of the victims', and this is exactly what has happened. In the spring of 2017, it turned out that the irregularities in the testimonies of the Romani victims were attributed to their 'Roma mentality' (*mentalita romica*) which, according to psychologists and police officers involved in the investigations, was characterized by features such as 'a lack of self-discipline, neglect of commitments towards others, aggression, being asocial and an inability to adapt to social standards' (Zalešák 2018; see also Bán 2017). From there it was only a small step to what happened later in 2017, when the relevant Slovak police authorities stated that four of the Romani victims who were official witnesses in the case had fabricated their stories of being assaulted by officers during the raid. Even more disturbingly, the police brought charges against these four victims on 18 May and 30 August 2017 and have officially indicted them of perjury (Romea 2017). This development brings us literally back to the 1990s when, in the ERRC's third country report, Claude Cahn and Nidhi Trehan wrote that one tried and tested method of 'denying Roma due process when they are subject to an attack by a law enforcement official is to bring charges against them' (ERRC 1997: 27).

We have outlined this case in detail because it illustrates a deep and structural pattern of anti-Roma racism in Europe that has enormously impacted Romani struggles for identity. Spectacles such as those related to police raids, zero tolerance practices and evictions strongly interrelate to the securitization of Roma – that is, their problematization in terms of security threats to, for instance, public order or even national security (van Baar, Ivasiuc and Kreide 2019). In these and similar contexts, we are able to observe a form of racial dismissal that can be characterized by a persistent reversal:

> Racial dismissal trades on the dual logic of reversal. It charges the historically dispossessed as the now principal perpetrators of racism, while dismissing as inconsequential and trivial the racisms experienced by the historical targets of racism. In doing so, racial dismissal renders opaque the structures making possible and silently perpetuating racially ordered power and privilege. (Goldberg 2015: 30)

The logic of reversal outlined by David Theo Goldberg – even though this logic is historically not new when discussing the position of Roma, and certainly not always fully reversed to the extent that it charges the Roma 'as the now principal perpetrators of racism' – has become increasingly manifest throughout Europe. For sure, the kinds of media spectacles discussed above have significantly contributed to what Goldberg calls rendering 'opaque the structures making possible and silently perpetuating racially ordered power and privilege'. Thus, the discourses and practices of ostensibly 'reasonable' antigypsyism that have emerged with this diabolic logic of reversal have significantly contributed to both the invisibilization and legitimization of contemporary anti-Roma racisms (Powell and van Baar 2019).[5] This finding does not imply that everything is reducible to racism or racialization – or, for that matter, to other '-izations' such as securitization, stigmatization, neoliberalization, globalization or Europeanization – as if we were dealing here with a kind of master signifier or category of analysis. As the contributors to this volume clarify however, various intersectionalities – in which 'race' has also been assiduously present – have played a profound role in both the marginalization of Roma and possible ways out of this troublesome present-day condition.

At the same time, the racial reversal characteristic of currently ubiquitous 'reasonable antigypsyist' practices is directly related to the emergence of what Arjun Appadurai, in *Fear of Small Numbers: An Essay on the Geography of Anger*, calls 'predatory identities':

> Predatory identities emerge ... out of pairs of identities, sometimes sets that are larger than two, which have long histories of close contact, mixture and some degree of mutual stereotyping ... [V]iolence may or may not be parts of these histories, but some degree of contrastive identification is always involved. One of these pairs or sets of identities often turns predatory by mobilizing an understanding of itself as a *threatened majority*. (Appadurai 2006: 51, emphasis added)

Predatory identities, Appadurai maintains, are almost always majoritarian identities that fear that they themselves could be turned into minorities, thus losing the power and privilege that Goldberg connects with racial dismissal and attempts to maintain its logics of reversal. Here, with the relationship between racial reversal and predatory identities, we enter one of the central themes that will be taken up in several of the contributions to this volume, namely the theme of identity politics at a time when this is seen as one of the most common terms of abuse in popular political but also academic arenas. For a long time now, 'identity politics' has been considered a 'dirty word' and a kind of politics that one should, particularly when one is in a minority position, rather avoid if one wants to escape becoming the target of harsh criticism. And when one starts discussing identity politics, one should also discuss what is actually meant by 'identity' and whether this is approached along the lines of, for instance, essentialism, strategic essentialism, anti-essentialism, constructivism or poststructuralism. In the following two sections, we will discuss how both 'identity' and 'identity politics' are relevant to this volume's general topic of Romani struggles for identity in contemporary Europe. To be sure, the authors in this volume explore different dimensions and understandings of identity and identity politics, as well as critiques of these notions and practices relating to them. Thus, we refrain from the suggestion that what we discuss in this volume represents one specific approach to these themes. Instead, the authors will present various approaches to these topics, including the ways in which identity and identity politics have been or become relevant to Roma in diverse contexts and settings, ranging from segregation, labour, social mobility, sociopolitical participation and decision- and policymaking, to discrimination, racism, social movement formation, everyday encounters, artistic and cultural practice and trans-local or transnational solidarity.[6]

A final caveat is in order. The contributions to this study primarily deal with issues of *collective* identity formation and transformation, even while personal and collective identities are always dialectically intertwined and the boundaries between the personal/individual and public/collective have historically been incorporated in governmentalities that tend to render delicate and important political and socioeconomic issues 'private', 'technical' or 'natural'. Indeed, crucial public and political Romani identity-related topics have often been rendered private (as in neoliberal, 'responsibilizing' programmes which suggest that Roma should solve 'their own' matters), technical (as in quasi-neutral policy interventions that suggest technical solutions to political problems), or natural (as in suggestions that it is Romani 'culture' or 'behaviour' that causes the problems with which they and their neighbours are faced) (van Baar 2011a, 2018). In this respect, we share the provocatively *repoliticizing* way in which Angela Davis has addressed the nexus of the personal and the collective, and consider the analyses in this volume as radically feminist:

> [O]ur analysis [has] to be feminist – not simply in the sense of attending to gender, but also in the sense of attending to the circuits that lead from the intimate to the institutional, from the public to the private and from the personal to the political. (Davis 2017: 263)

This perspective also allows a different and critical take on identity and identity politics, as we will show below.

Articulating Identity within and beyond Identity Politics

Francis Fukuyama, in *Identity: The Demand for Dignity and the Politics of Resentment* (2018), claims that in the present liberal democratic struggle for the recognition of all kinds of identities, we are willing to fritter away vital achievements such as justice, privacy and even democracy. According to him, it is identity politics and the interrelated demand for dignity and recognition that have now radically taken over a politics, focusing on redistribution, the strengthening of democratic institutions, and other major themes such as combating poverty and striving for equality. With reference to two concepts in Friedrich Nietzsche's philosophy, Fukuyama suggests that 'megalothymia' – a desire not just for respect and recognition, but a need to dominate others in excessive and spectacular ways – has begun to be at odds with the more reasonable 'isothymia', which stands for the human desire to be seen and treated by others as equals. Fukuyama connects the struggle for identity of groups such as LGBTQI+ and Romani communities to isothymia. At the same time, he suggests that some of these struggles – such as the Black Power movement in the United States – have gone further, if not too far, by asking not only for equal treatment, but also for recognition as a *separate* group. This is something that Fukuyama also criticizes in what he considers to be the cultural particularisms inherent in multiculturalism.

Critical debates about Fukuyama's latest reflection on modern liberal democracies should clarify to what extent this analysis of identity politics represents a continuation of, or a welcome break from, the much criticized liberal-conservative position he took in his seminal 1992 book *The End of History and the Last Man*. While his suggestion that Western multiculturalism has unsettled and weakened national identities, and his defence of the state's right to control its own borders suggest a continuation of his conservatism, he nevertheless brings up some key issues of concern. One of them is that, according to him, '[r]esentment over lost dignity or invisibility [of particular groups] often has economic roots, but fights over identity often distract us from focusing on policies that could concretely remedy those issues' (Fukuyama 2018: 179). Another of his main concerns is that politicians such as Donald Trump have played a 'critical role in moving the focus of identity politics from the left, where it was born, to the right, where it is now taking root', and that, consequently, 'white nationalism has moved from a fringe movement to something much more mainstream' (ibid.: 119, 120). He clarifies that one of the key problems of present-day identity politics is strongly linked to what he calls 'white nationalism', or to what others call 'white identity politics' (Jardina 2019) or 'white innocence' (Wekker 2016). As the African-American writer Ta-Nahisi Coates has argued so powerfully in *We Were Eight Years in Power* (2017), leaders such as Trump are not just openly sexist and racist, but have plainly turned 'whiteness' into a political strategy for governing; this is the reason why – although it is perhaps not entirely accurate historically – Coates has ingeniously called Trump the first *white* president of the United States.

We have been able to notice similar developments in Europe. Indeed, in different ways and to different degrees, influential populist or extremist politicians across Europe have used anti-migrant and anti-minority rhetoric or measures, as well as ideas about white supremacy to re-articulate a complex but tangible colour line throughout Europe. These uses and abuses have also significantly influenced the agendas and discourses of other, more conventional political parties and thus – most importantly – contributed to 'mainstreaming racism' in key institutions of Europe's democracies. Therefore, the question is perhaps not so much to what extent identity politics itself is problematic, regardless of who is politicizing identities here. Rather, the question is to what extent a politics of identity regarding historically disadvantaged minorities could still be legitimately articulated at a time when all kinds of 'white' identity politics are proliferating, in which the logic of reversal has pushed majoritarian identities towards the brink of becoming predatory – thereby often rehabilitating some of the darkest moments and legacies of national, colonial and imperial histories.

Recently, questions of whiteness, white supremacy and majoritarian identity politics have also been discussed in the context of the position of Roma, scholarship regarding them and the role of Romani actors in academic, political, feminist, artist, activist and other kinds of social networks and movements (Imre 2005; van Baar 2014; Bogdán 2015; Vajda 2015; Matache 2016a, 2016b; Stewart 2017; Corradi 2018; Kóczé 2018). Violeta Vajda, for instance, makes the successful development of collective Romani emancipation considerably dependent on how it deals with issues of whiteness:

> [T]he project of Romani emancipation will have difficulty moving forward until the concept of critical whiteness is incorporated into it, both theoretically and practically. I contend that until such time that non-Romani people are willing and able to examine their own racialized identity, even those non-Roma who are committed to dismantling the discrimination experienced by Romani communities will be unable to play a powerful role in this process; whereas those non-Roma who are indifferent, resentful of or actively hostile to Roma could be persuaded to budge from their positions through a deeper understanding of the history of their own identities and how these are formed and performed in the present. (Vajda 2015: 48)

In order to incorporate the concept of critical whiteness adequately, Vajda calls for a hermeneutic learning process in which 'non-Romani people and communities ... reach back into history to gain an understanding of their own *prejudices*, engage in a process of *Bildung* designed to open them up to the possibility of new insights into their own and Romani identity and be ready to seek out and genuinely accept the *provocation* (or learning experience) held up by Romani people and communities that they encounter' (ibid.: 54, emphasis in the original). Margareta Matache has similarly appealed for a shift away from the currently dominant, excessive focus on the Roma and their 'vulnerabilities' to a concentration on the impact of racism and whiteness:

> We should be able to start exploring critically the social power and privilege of dominant majority populations and their impact on the education and other social and economic rights of Romani people. We need to start exploring the language and the mechanisms of racism and whiteness in law, policy and practice. (Matache 2016b)

In the specific context of scholarship, Matache contends that, for too long, '[a]cademics have neglected to pay attention to the historic and present-day dynamics of power between Roma and non-Roma, including academia, leading to reaffirming and constructing unequal power dynamics' (ibid.). This persistent neglect by scholars and the lack of a 'serious effort to employ critical and self-reflexive analysis of their position in the social hierarchy' has led, Matache maintains, to the problematic and still ongoing reproduction of whiteness and white supremacy. In order to contest the 'long history of cultural domination of white Europeans and subalternization of Roma in Europe', she proposes to rigorously shift 'the frameworks of thought and Romani scholarly production' to, most notably, 'white privileges', 'perpetual institutionalized racism' and 'the means of liberating non-Roma from long-held racist *doxa* or commonly held beliefs' (ibid.).

These recent contributions to the debate are welcome interventions that focus on the analysis and historicization of power structures and relations, including the ways in which canonical institutions and discourses of knowledge production tend to continue sidelining Roma from society, culture and their centres of power, policymaking and knowledge formation. To some extent, these interventions continue the debate that Wim Willems (1997) initiated in the 1990s, when he emphasized the importance of postcolonial studies – mostly Said's *Orientalism* (1978) – for analysing Roma-related scholarship and its close relation to the persistence of the marginalization of the Roma in European cultures, societies and academies.[7] What scholars such as Matache and Vajda add to this debate is, among other key issues, the crucial importance of reflecting on positionality, privilege and the conditions under which they are maintained or challenged in and beyond scholarship. At the same time, however, if we want to maintain the *criticality* of postcolonial studies – or, for that matter, of critical race studies, whiteness studies, citizenship studies, migration studies, gender studies and, last but certainly not least, critical Romani studies – scholarship should avoid falling into the trap of tribalizing 'white people' (or 'white scholars'), which can all too easily coincide with a shift of focus to white privileges, institutional racism and calls for the self-reflexivity of, in particular, 'non-Romani' people (and scholars).[8] Indeed, without suggesting that Vajda's or Matache's interventions do or imply so, such a tribalization and the interrelated reductionist understanding of racialization and racism would bring with them exactly the kinds of problems that Fukuyama and his like have addressed regarding the proliferation of identity politics.

'Unlike fights over economic resources, identity claims are usually unnegotiable' (Fukuyama 2018: 122) and, therefore, an all-too-narrow focus on racism and racialization could easily lead to fights over identity that distract us from the larger socioeconomic and sociopolitical contexts that should be addressed simultaneously. Therefore, in order to avoid the anger and fear that Appadurai (2006) connects to the emergence of predatory identities, and to circumvent the politics of resentment that Fukuyama (2018) relates to current identity politics, the contributors to this volume underscore the indispensability of a focus on intersectionality. Here, we mean the 'classic' intersections of race, ethnicity, class, gender, age, nationality and the like (Kóczé 2009, 2011), but also how these intersecting categories are relevant for analyses of traversing sectors such as housing, education and labour (Rostas 2012; Szalai, this volume) and for examinations of the security–development, security–citizenship or security–mobility nexuses (Clough Marinaro and Daniele 2011; van Baar 2011b, 2017a, 2018; Nagy 2018; van Baar, Ivasiuc and Kreide 2019).

At a fundamental level, the extent to which a politics of identity for disadvantaged minorities such as Roma can still be legitimately articulated depends considerably on how it manages to deal with various identity-related dilemmas and traps (see also McGarry and Jasper 2015). Almost fifteen years ago, in his eloquent notes on the ambiguities of Romani activism and identity politics, Peter Vermeersch suggested that Romani activists 'must make sure that the emancipatory potential of [their] act of group construction is not overshadowed by a discourse of oppressive essentialism' (2005: 468). Here, Vermeersch was referring in particular to an oppressive essentialism in their own (Romani) identity formation. Based on what we have discussed above in terms of the risk of tribalizing 'white people' and of discussing the impact of racism too much in isolation, we should add that the 'counter-movement' towards a narrative of reified 'oppressors' should be equally carefully avoided.[9] This extension can also be connected with some of the other valuable remarks from Vermeersch on identity politics:

> [I]dentity politics should always fight a twofold battle. Defending the interests of an oppressed identity group always needs to be accompanied by an interrogation of the categorization schemes that have constructed the very identity group one is defending ... [R]ecuperative identity politics and the politics of deconstruction need not be mutually exclusive. The politics of recuperation may *avoid the tacit reproduction of essential identities* on the *condition* that the advocacy of specific identities is *accompanied by targeted acts of contestation*. (Vermeersch 2005: 468, emphasis added)

Vermeersch concluded these observations with an appeal for making a conceptual difference between identity- and interest-based advocacy, suggesting that 'activism is not simply about the demand for recognition of group identities, but rather about the demand for the elimination of unequal access to opportunities and resources' (ibid.: 469). Several of the contributions to this volume prove that a shift to the latter kinds of demand has indeed taken place, including 'targeted acts of contestation'; yet *without* losing a critical focus on the role and impact of discussions regarding identity.

Therefore, we make a subtle though important distinction between 'recuperative identity politics' and a 'critical politics of identity'. While the former usually tends to start from a relatively reified notion of identity – whether it is based on strategized essentialism or not – the latter does not necessarily reify collective identity but leaves its materialization considerably open. A 'critical politics of identity' – with greater emphasis on critical politics than on identity – questions those kinds of 'politics' and enactments of 'political communities', as well as those structural mechanisms of governing and policing that, through various irregularization processes, differentiate and hierarchize identities, thus demarcating them in ways that lead or have already led to exclusion. The openness towards identity could also be approached from Stuart Hall's suggested change of perspective:

> [The question is not] how do we effectively mobilize those identities which are already formed, so that we could put them on the train and get them onto the stage at the right moment, [but rather] how can we organize ... human subjects into positions where they can recognize one another *long enough to act together*, and thus to take up a position that one of these days might *live out and act through as an identity*? Identity is at the end, not the beginning of the paradigm. (Hall 1997: 291, emphasis added)

Hall's suggestion that identity is not at the beginning, but 'at the end of the paradigm' also helps to make a critical politics of identity resistant to the easy suggestions that thinking along the lines of ethnic identity, or ethnicity more generally, is automatically equal to thinking in terms of more or less reified, unified groups. In the early 2000s, in articles with telling titles such as 'Ethnicity without Groups' and 'Beyond "Identity"', Rogers Brubaker called for a rethinking of ethnicity 'without groups' and rejected the use of identity-based groups because of the implied 'groupism'. Here, groupism is 'the tendency to take discrete, sharply differentiated, internally homogeneous and externally bounded groups as basic constituents of social life, chief protagonists of social conflicts and fundamental units of social analysis' (Brubaker 2002: 164; see also 2004: 8).

Brubaker's critique of groupism is relevant to challenge any kind of 'thick' identity politics based on strong forms of compartmentalization, but less so regarding what we consider a critical politics of identity. As some of Brubaker's critics have convincingly argued, he tends to 'set a very high standard for recognizing identity', suggesting that 'only perfectly bounded, fixed, and internally homogenous categories share identity' (Calhoun 2003b: 565) and, therefore, that these forms of 'groupism' should be critically examined, if not abandoned, at least as categories of analysis. However, as Craig Calhoun maintains, '[t]he problems lie not in the terms "group", or even "identity", but in certain tendencies of usage' (ibid.: 562). Alternatively, '[g]roups should not be presumed to be sharply bounded or internally homogeneous; they should be seen *as variably solidary, salient and stable*' (ibid., emphasis added). Therefore, Calhoun argues – and, we think, rightly so – that Brubaker underestimates the role of collectivities, particularly in the context of the cultural and the social, and how they are always constitutive of the personal (see also Silverman, this volume). Accordingly, Calhoun claims, ethnic identity or ethnicity is 'not merely an attribute of individuals, nor is it any specific attribute shared by all members of one set of people and no others' (ibid.: 560). It is, rather:

> a commonality of understanding, access to the world, and mode of action that facilitates the construction of social relationships and provides a common rhetoric even to competition and quarrels. In one sense it is helpful to say something like people participate to varying degrees in ethnicity, rather than that they simply are or are not members of ethnic groups. *It is indeed a relational phenomenon not simply a substance.* But it is also reproduced in ways that bind people into certain relationships and not others. (Ibid., emphasis added)

What is at stake for Calhoun, as well as for Hall, is an understanding of ethnicity and identity in the context of social solidarities. This is also how we interpret Hall's question: 'How can we organize ... human subjects into positions where they can recognize one another long enough to act together?' (Hall 1997: 291) Put differently, in Calhoun's words, identities and solidarities are 'neither simply fixed nor simply fluid, but may be more fixed or more fluid under different circumstances' (Calhoun 2003a: 537). In line with critical readings of identity politics such as those of Appadurai or Fukuyama, Calhoun admits that solidarities have been produced partly to engage in new conflicts. However, it would be a mistake 'to think that this is the only work that ethnicity or community do for people. They provide networks of mutual support, capacities for communication, frameworks of meaning' (ibid.). This approach to ethnic identity in terms of social solidarities that may (or may not, as in Hall's formulation) exist 'long enough to act together' is at the heart of how we understand a critical politics of identity. Such an understanding of identity acknowledges that 'a rigorously anti-essentialist attitude, with respect to things like identity, culture, tradition, gender ... is not really a position one can sustain in a consistent way' (Clifford 2003: 62). With this acknowledgement, we are in the middle of the discussion about how we could approach identity beyond the opposition between essentialism and constructivism – the topic of our penultimate section.

Identity beyond Essentialism versus Constructivism

> I saw myself as being mixed – this, that and the other – but people, they'd like to be able to put you in a perfect little box
> —Damian John Le Bas, June 2012 (quoted from Tremlett and Le Bas, this volume)

Once in a while, the debate over essentialism versus constructivism pops up again in discussions about Romani identity. Furthermore, Roma-related scholarship that mentions identity issues often refers to this dualistic debate as if it reflected the current state of affairs. An intense discussion over essentialism versus constructivism had taken place in the late 1990s and early 2000s, most notably in academic debates between Judith Okely, Wim Willems, Leo Lucassen, Yaron Matras, Ian Hancock, Thomas Acton and, to a lesser extent, Annamarie Cottaar, Will Guy, David Mayall and Michael Stewart. Largely, this debate began in reply to a few key publications by Judith Okely (1983) and the Dutch historians Lucassen, Willems and Cottaar (Willems 1997; Lucassen, Willems and Cottaar 1998).

From an anti-essentialist, constructivist point of view, the latter three scholars have argued that Gypsy identity formation – they use 'Gypsy' rather than 'Roma' for reasons that become clear below – is the result of historically fluctuating, yet nevertheless intense and fundamentally influential processes of labelling and stigmatization. In particular, Willems has argued that the use of the term 'ethnicity' in debates about Romani/Gypsy identity has to be considered as a 'death trap' (Lucassen, Willems and Cottaar 1998: 17–34). Any use of the term 'ethnic identity' – even when mobilized strategically – would lead to a re-articulation of the problematic essentialization of Gypsy identities that has dominated the long, unceasing European history of stigmatizing and marginalizing them. Based on a rather monolithic assessment of Enlightenment legacies and an inadequate analysis of the role of the Romani language,[10] Willems and Lucassen were highly sceptical towards the growing use of ethnic categories in articulations of Romani identity formation and politics in the 1990s. Lucassen, for instance, has suggested that 'this habit' of 'using the ethnic term *Sinti und Roma* instead of Gypsies' does not spring 'from historical considerations, but it is the fruit of the actual political (and politically correct) struggle of interest groups from among and for Gypsies' (ibid.: 92–93). He continues that, 'from a scholarly point of view, the disadvantage of the *Sinti und Roma* approach is that all kinds of contemporary racist as well as present-day ethnic categories are ... used' (ibid.: 93). He concludes that 'assuming that there ever was a clearly ethnically defined *Sinti und Roma* group in the past means that we in fact accept the point of departure ... that it was possible to define who was a "real" Gypsy' (ibid.). The latter refers to the historically highly ambiguous 'search for the "true" Gypsy' and her origins, which was the central focus of Willems's (1997) critical study of Gypsy-related orientalism in Europe. There, he concluded:

> It remains questionable ... whether corrections [regarding the required re-evaluation of extant historical knowledge] are to be anticipated from this corner [of Gypsy groups involved in the process of emancipation] since the intelligentsia in Gypsy circles are not likely to profit very much by challenging the core concepts of Gypsy Studies. For political and pragmatic reasons, they will sooner close ranks in support of the idea of a *collective* Gypsy identity, including a language which belongs to them. Recognition as an ethnic minority culminates, to be sure, in more agreements pertaining to specific rights. (Willems 1997: 307; Lucassen, Willems and Cottaar 1998: 34, emphasis in original)

This debate over the political reasons behind Romani identity struggles and the politicization of Romani identity more generally has recently returned once more, along surprisingly similar lines of essentialism versus constructivism (Surdu and Kovats 2015; Surdu 2016; Law and Kovats 2018; Mirga 2018). Most notably, Mihai Surdu and, to a lesser extent, Ian Law and Martin Kovats, have been critical about the involvement of Romani activists and scholarship in debates about Romani identity, as well as about the ways in which various kinds of policy and academic experts have been highly influential in politicizing, classifying and stigmatizing Roma. Surdu goes the furthest by suggesting that 'Roma activists and scholars have their role in reproducing and reinforcing a stereotyped and negative Roma identity'

(Surdu 2016: 32). He claims that 'Roma activists in fact *mirror* a negative generalized Roma group image', and that, because of the 'perniciousness of ethnic policies and politics to sooner or later *trigger ethnic conflict*', the 'scholarly community and policymakers should *de-ethnicize* (in the sense of *de-essentialize*) *Roma identity*' (ibid.: 32–33, emphasis added). This leads him to conclude that 'I do not affirm that Roma people do not exist, but I assert that [the] Roma population exists *as a negative and oppositional construction made by dominant groups* and *self-internalized by many of those labelled as Roma*' (ibid.: 39, emphasis added). This position brings Surdu's view remarkably close to the constructivist one of Willems, Lucassen and their like.

Yet one of the dominant alternative positions that criticizes the constructivist position through a positivist reaffirmation of Romani identity (Matras 2004) is equally problematic (for an extensive critique, see van Baar 2011a: 75–149). Whereas Willems had lumped divergent eighteenth-century legacies within Romani Studies together as being equally involved in stigmatizing Roma, Yaron Matras (1999, 2004) has, appropriately, differentiated between them, and fervently and repetitively criticized the debatable views of, most notably, Okely (1983) and Willems (1997) regarding the Romani language. However, in turn, Matras has politically neutralized what he calls the 'objective' eighteenth-century 'sensational discovery' (2002: 2) of the Indian origins of the Romani language by considering it the rational, well-explained 'foundation for Romani linguistics' (1999: 89). This argument in favour of an argued 'objectivity' (1999: 94) – one that would articulate Romani identity through linguistic communality – positivistically brings essentialism in again through the backdoor.

Not only have the sources underpinning the two main positions in the essentialism versus constructivism debate largely run dry, at a second order of analysis, they have also remained problematically preoccupied with 'origins' (van Baar 2011a: 92–105). According to Willems, Lucassen, Surdu and their like – even though their positions should certainly not be conflated – the influential legacy of the persistent, relentless labelling, classification and stigmatization of Roma has its incontestable origins in the emergence of modern scientific mechanisms of quantification and qualification that, as political technologies, are deeply rooted in the modern, mostly Enlightenment history of Europe. On the other hand, in the case of Matras, the legacy of the Enlightenment is mobilized differently, namely to (try to) rigorously sift pseudo-scientific or mystifying, and thus 'politicized' approaches to Roma from objective, scientific, demystifying, and thus 'politically neutral' ones. This search for origins represents a scientistic pursuit of neutral, objective scientific methods – one that arguably detaches the emergence of scientific methods of comparison in the eighteenth century from the simultaneous emergence of new minority-related governmentalities and the interrelated problematization of Roma (among other minoritized groups) in terms of their cultural, linguistic and diasporic origins (van Baar 2011a: 99–149; see also Ivasiuc 2018).[11]

Poststructuralist approaches to the essentialism versus constructivism debate have seriously challenged the 'either-orism' central to this debate. In several strands of critical scholarship – for instance, in cultural studies (e.g. Clifford, Gilroy, Hall, Pratt), gender studies (e.g. Butler, Haraway, hooks, Fraser) and post/decolonial and subaltern studies (e.g. Bhabha, Chakrabarty, Chatterjee, Mignolo, Spivak) – the identity-related binary opposition of essentialism and constructivism has been thoroughly challenged for a relatively long time now, and mostly through mobilizing poststructuralist and deconstructivist strands of philosophy (e.g. Derrida, Foucault). However, in Roma-related scholarship, the deconstruction of this binary seems curiously difficult to achieve – despite several serious attempts to do so (for instance, Imre 2005, 2009; Trehan and Kóczé 2009; Tremlett 2009; van Baar 2011a; Silverman 2012; Corradi 2018; Szeman 2018). Although we could observe a serious delay of the influence of Said's *Orientalism* (1978) in Roma-related scholarship – Willems's study appeared almost two decades later – Romani Studies is also confronted with the delayed influence of those pioneering scholars in postcolonial, decolonial and cultural studies who have critiqued, for example, the remnants of essentialism and constructivism in earlier postcolonial studies.

Homi Bhabha's (1994) seminal critique of Said's reified juxtaposition of 'colonizer' and 'colonized', for instance, and the former's introduction of the concepts of 'hybridity' and 'mimicry' to challenge such binaries, are also highly relevant to the debate about the Romani struggle for identity, as several scholars have emphasized (Tremlett 2009; Okely 2010; Silverman 2012; Toninato 2014; French 2015). However, as Carol Silverman (2012: 39–56) has persuasively argued with reference to poststructuralist thinkers such as Rey Chow, Arif Dirlik and Paul Gilroy, the use of such new-fangled concepts should result neither in a kind of easy celebration of difference or multicultural diversity, nor in the embrace of how notions such as hybridity have been globally marketized. Instead, she has called for both critically translating them to Roma-related scholarship and grounding them in material realities, rather than just projecting them abstractly onto Roma-related contexts and suggesting that they 'apply' there (for the latter critical view, see also Bogdal 2018).

In a similar fashion, Huub van Baar (2011a) has mobilized poststructuralist and postcolonial frameworks of analysis to historicize not only Roma stigmatization – as the constructivists in the debate have done, and extensively so – but also, and *co-constitutively*, Roma agency. His attempt at renewing more canonical Roma-related historiographies could also be read through the lens of Bhabha's notion of mimicry, which offers a welcome critique of an all-too-rigid and binary reading of the relationship between what Willems and Lucassen call the 'stigmatizer' and the 'stigmatized', or between what Surdu, Kovats and Law call the 'classifier' and the 'classified'. Notwithstanding highly influential Roma-related histories of stigmatization and classification, readings such as Surdu's – which claim that Roma can merely 'mirror' a 'negative generalized Roma group image' (Surdu 2016: 32) and thus only 'self-internalize' a 'negative and oppositional construction made by dominant groups' (ibid.: 39) – leave little if any room for Roma agency, subversion, and their histories and memories. An understanding of Roma agency through the lens of mimicry, however, helps to explain why the ways in which those who are classified as 'Roma' always do more than just mirror the power relationships (of being classified, stigmatized, and so on) in which they are implicated. Indeed, mimicry implies not just the imitation, copying or mirroring of such relations, but the ambiguous reworking of them to the extent that it could disrupt the classifying or stigmatizing authority (see Bhabha 1994: 121–31).

Particularly here, in the context of the complex relationship between agency and continued and renewed mechanisms and processes of stigmatization, several of the contributions to this volume try to intervene and contribute to debates beyond reproductions of the essentialism versus constructivism debate. For sure, finding the right balance between recuperative identity politics and a critical politics of identity is not easy, and will also lead to developments where, once in a while, the balance will be unstable – as in every trial and error process. Yet the contributors show that beyond the horizon of the trite debate of essentialism versus constructivism, new discussions have become vital to rethinking Romani struggles for identities in contemporary Europe.

Structure of the Book and Chapter Overview

This book is composed of five closely interconnected parts in the form of a circle that will bring us back to Part I. In Part II, entitled *Society, History and Citizenship*, topics will be discussed that are primarily related to the impact of historical and societal mechanisms of marginalization and exclusion on present-day processes of Romani identity formation, and particularly on the opportunities and constraints for Roma to articulate adequately their agency and exercise their citizenship (rights, ownership over their own affairs, access to public debate, etc.). In Chapter 2, *Júlia Szalai* explains why segregation, as a ubiquitous and influential force of separating and subordinating

Roma in Central and East European societies, has to be considered as one of the most dominant characteristics of contemporary interethnic relations in the region. By looking at key domains of everyday life, such as education, labour and housing, Szalai explores those majoritarian interests that have made significant contributions to the prevailing arrangements for Roma through mechanisms of reproduction and intersectionality. She shows how segregation has become an increasingly powerful social mechanism of splitting universal social and political rights, and of erecting, for the Roma, a second-class order in which their citizenship rights are seriously threatened. By explaining how segregative forces strongly and negatively impact practices of Romani recuperative identity formation, including opportunities for upward social mobility, Szalai illuminates the radical ways in which contemporary mechanisms of segregation have reduced Roma agency.

In Chapter 3, *Nidhi Trehan* follows close in the footsteps of scholars such as Celia Donert (2017), who have challenged the prevailing image of the socialist past as a period in which Romani and pro-Roma citizens were denied any opportunity to critically discuss and influence debates regarding issues that were highly relevant to the societal position of Roma. Trehan examines socialist-era ethnographic materials in Hungary with a view to revisit and elucidate the complexities of Romani collective identity formation in the region. To a significant extent, Romani identity has been influenced by various forces such as, most notably, state policy interventions as well as ambivalent displays of both social prejudice and social solidarity by the majority. What is striking about the record – based on an interrogation of the archives from the 1950s to the 1980s as sites of the epistemological enterprise (Stoler 2002) – are the continuities and discontinuities, at times ruptures, with post-socialist regimes. Trehan offers an analysis of how, from the 1970s onwards, scholars, journalists and policymakers – including Hungarian Roma – dealt with what was then considered as the 'Gypsy Question'. She argues that a subtler, historicized approach to the socialist-era experience of Romani communities – including the question of Romani identity – is empirically, methodologically and conceptually necessary to arrive at a richer understanding of socialist-era and post-socialist experiences for Roma.

In Chapter 4, *Angéla Kóczé* focuses on the relationship between the restructured welfare state in post-1989 East Central Europe, the growth of poverty, and their impact on Roma at the intersection of class, race and gender. Kóczé intervenes in debates about long-term poverty among Roma and the ways in which it has become manifest both in materialized social structures and in gendered, racialized and class-based discourses about the welfare state, during its transition from a 'state socialist' one to the current 'embedded neoliberal' welfare state. She explains how the restructuring of welfare in the region has intensified poverty in terms of both width and depth, and how it has also produced material and discursive devastation, particularly in the lives of gendered and racialized groups such as Roma. Kóczé brings together the findings of two groups of scholars who are often presented in relative isolation. She shows how scholars working on Roma-related issues and those working on gender inequality have both, often independently, come to the conclusion that Roma and women are among the most serious 'losers' of the processes of welfare reform, particularly as a result of restricting social rights and political guarantees. Kóczé cross-fertilizes these two strands of scholarships to highlight and interrogate the vulnerable position of Romani women in particular, who lie at the intersection of gender, race and class.

In Part III, entitled *Europe and the Challenge of 'Ethnic Minority Governance'*, the focus shifts to the Europeanization of the representation of the Roma, and its relevance for the ways in which Romani identity has been problematized in and beyond the sphere of transnational European policymaking. The two chapters in this part continue to concentrate on the relevance of citizenship and societal participation, but now relate this debate to the transnational dimension of EU citizenship and how its arrangement in and through European policies has often led to a continuation of mechanisms of marginalization affecting Roma, rather than a decisive break with them. In Chapter 5, *Huub van Baar* revisits the discussion over the Europeanization of Roma representation that he initiated about a decade ago to clarify how it differs from what others have called the Europeanization of the Roma issue, identity or policy. The focus on the Europeanization of Roma representation, seen as a specific and contestable practice of transnational governmentality, helps to challenge the remnants of Eurocentrism that are still present in discussions of the Europeanization of Roma identity or policy. This Eurocentrism, for instance, leaves the question of the normativity of European programmes meant for Roma considerably untouched, and therefore problematically undisputed and analytically underexposed. Van Baar goes on to discuss how his perspective on Europeanization is relevant for a critical analysis of the current position of Roma at the nexuses of security and citizenship, and security and development. By means of a brief exploration of these nexuses, he first demonstrates how, despite their European citizenship, Roma have often ended up as the 'internalized outsiders' in the current European Union, whose exercise of citizenship has been seriously hampered. Second, he shows how, despite the launch of Europe-wide development programmes, Roma have been faced with practices of development that have contributed less to the alleviation of their poverty, and more to their governance and to the maintenance of the ambiguous societal status quo. Finally, van Baar proposes a research agenda beyond the existing preponderance of Eurocentric and Roma-centric approaches that helps to diversify Roma-related research and to 'de-exceptionalize' practices of displacement that affect Roma.

In Chapter 6, *Iulius Rostas* reflects on three decades of Roma-related European policies, and argues that, despite all institutional and transnational efforts, we have not been able to observe serious improvements in the position of Roma or in their opportunities for societal participation. Even more delicately, he points to the paradox that the more policy attention the situation of the European Roma receives and the more measures targeting them are adopted and implemented, the worse their situation seems to become. In his analysis of how we could understand this grim impasse, Rostas interrogates the role that ethnicity has played in the design, process, implementation and outcome of European policies dedicated to Roma, thereby using insights from policy design, policy analysis and critical race theory. In particular, he analyses the policy framework for Roma launched by the EU in 2011, and to which all its members have committed themselves in terms of devising, implementing and evaluating so-called 'national Roma integration strategies'. By focusing on questions such as: how do policymakers define 'the Roma'?; who exactly is part of the group that these policies target?; and how are their 'problems' defined?, Rostas shows that the kinds of defining parameters involved have greatly influenced the design, process and outcome of policies dedicated to Roma. Rostas demonstrates not only that the various actors involved in policy design and implementation have used different definitions and problematizations of their 'Roma' target groups, but also that these policies have failed to take their ethnic relevance and, thus, Romani ethnic identity adequately into consideration.

In Part IV, called *Gender and Social Movements*, the focus remains on the transnational dimension, but now zooms in on the specific context of the Romani women's movement, and how it has interconnected with the broader Romani social movement and various other social movements, and with international women's movements in particular. The two chapters in this part show how the Romani women's movement has developed considerably over the years, moving through various difficult phases in which their main actors were confronted with the difficulty of gaining recognition both within the Romani social movement and the broader European and global women's movements. The chapters illustrate how actors within the Romani women's movement have nevertheless been able to set their agendas and develop, both domestically and internationally, ongoing dialogues with key stakeholders about the main issues to be addressed. This process has resulted in a situation in which the actors in the Romani women's movement have increasingly managed to claim their rightful place in key debates about the situation of the Roma in and beyond Europe. In Chapter 7, *Debra Schultz* revisits two decades of Romani women's activism in Central and Eastern Europe, specifically the feminist-inspired claims Romani women have made on the Romani movement, the women's movement, nation-states, multilateral institutions, donors, partners, and on themselves and each other. She shows how Romani women's activism and their claims have impacted individual and collective Romani identity quests and social change discourse. On the basis of Schultz's research with leading Romani women activists and a reconsideration of the seminal 'Roma Women's Initiative' (1999–2007), she demonstrates that Romani women's unique intersectional location challenged them to examine the combined effects of ethnic, racial, class, national and gender identities while developing influential intellectual and activist agendas. In her reflection on the role that she herself has played vis-à-vis the Romani women's movement, she also offers a good example of the critical whiteness inquiries that scholars such as Matache and Vajda have called for. Moreover, in her discussion of several mini-biographies of Romani women activists, she eloquently demonstrates feminist epistemological interventions that articulate the dialectical relationships between personal and collective activist practices of identity formation.

In Chapter 8, *Violetta Zentai* investigates recent trends in the formations of the Romani women's movement in Europe, with a particular focus on Central and Eastern Europe. Her research is conceived within the larger puzzle of what explains this movement's standing and voice, shaped in a multi-scalar European political space in the 2010s. She examines the acts of and within the Romani women's movement in relation both to wider gender equality struggles and the broader Romani movement for equal citizenship, by acknowledging a recent trend that repositions Romani women's claims and alliances in a wider political and social landscape. One of the important developments that Zentai brings to our attention is how Romani women, who have acted in accordance with relational identity configurations and social justice agendas, have addressed, developed and encouraged strategies of what she calls 'transformative anti-essentialism'. These new strategies, Zentai argues, have increasingly (but not entirely) replaced the intersectional reasoning and punctuated strategic essentialism that inspired these women and their allies in the recent past.

In Part V, entitled *Art and Culture*, the focus shifts to culture and Romani art movements, and their relevance for discussions about Romani identity formation and transformation. In different ways, the three chapters in this part adopt a critical stance towards narrow interpretations of culture, both in the broader societal sense and more specifically in terms of cultural and artistic artefacts and expressions. In Chapter 9, *Carol Silverman* interrogates current debates about ethnicity and culture regarding the representation of Roma. She explains that the label 'Roma' may be used, on the one hand, to essentialize a diverse group, or, on the other, to serve as an umbrella term for political mobilization. Using three examples, Silverman discusses the 'essentialism' conundrum to unmask the tension between the danger of reifying Romani culture and the need to define it. She suggests that culture and tradition are not static givens, but rather tools in representational projects. Silverman views Romani claims to identity and culture as performative works in progress, situated on a hierarchical political playing field. In dialogue with several key authors in cultural studies, she argues in favour of understanding culture and ethnicity in the context of shared commonalities, thereby taking a critical stance towards those scholars such as Rogers Brubaker (2004) who have called for a departure from using the concepts of 'identity' and 'groups' in discussions about ethnicity. Finally, Silverman suggests that in the discussion about Romani ethnicity and identity, one of the main challenges is to reject both a pro- and anti-essentialist position, and to embrace what James Clifford has called an 'anti-anti-essentialist' position. This does not simply imply, through the double negation, a return to essentialism, but is an attempt to move beyond the binary opposition between essentialism and constructivism.

In Chapter 10, *Tina Magazzini* interviews Tímea Junghaus and Anna Mirga-Kruszelnicka, who co-direct the Europe Roma Institute of Arts and Culture (ERIAC), established in 2017 in central Berlin. In her conversation with them, Magazzini discusses three broader themes that relate to ERIAC, its development prior to its launch and its institutional position in the field of European politics and knowledge formation. First, she focuses on 'the making of ERIAC' and some of the challenges and controversies that coincided with the trajectory towards the opening of the institute. Junghaus and Mirga-Kruszelnicka emphasize that the emergence of ERIAC should be placed in the context of a long struggle to establish an institute that would deal with Romani art and culture, which began in the 1970s. The second part of the interview concentrates on the position of ERIAC vis-à-vis the Council of Europe and the European Roma and Travellers Forum (ERTF), and on the more general question of what ERIAC has to offer as an institution that explicitly focuses on Romani arts and culture. Finally, Magazzini encourages Junghaus and Mirga-Kruszelnicka to reflect on the role that ERIAC has played and wants to play in the context of social responsibility, identity formation and knowledge production. In her critical interview with the directors of ERIAC, Magazzini aims to understand its activity and the broader institutional context of its emergence. She triggers a constructive debate about Romani art and culture in the context of identity formation and identity politics in contemporary Europe.

Last but not least, in Chapter 11, *Annabel Tremlett and Delaine Le Bas* focus on the contemporary Romani art movement and what it can offer to our understanding of processes of Romani identity formation and transformation, and their relationship to issues of social justice in contemporary Europe. The chapter is based on interviews with the artists Delaine and Damian Le Bas who have, for more than a decade now, been two of the leading figures in the contemporary European Romani art movement. The interviews are about their histories, beliefs and desires, and were conducted mostly in June 2012, five years before Damian Le Bas's unexpected death at the age of 54 on 9 December 2017, causing shock to and beyond the European Romani art world. The chapter is primarily dedicated to the larger question of the relevance and impact of the Romani art movement – or better, *movements* in the plural – but is also meant as a special tribute to the life and work of Damian, to what he created on his own and also to what he created and developed over the years together with Delaine, his wife and ultimate partner in artistic production. The chapter is in three parts. First, it looks at art as emancipatory and a way to connect with others about the lived experiences of inclusion and exclusion. For Delaine and Damian Le Bas, throughout their lives as artists, 'identity politics' first and foremost meant something emancipatory, based on learning about oneself and one's position in and beyond one's own community, in order to better understand others and relationships with them and, thus, to transform the personal into the political. Gayatri Spivak (2012) has suggested that their work shows the 'fragile staging of Roma life and history' in which theory and art practice merge in the act of making visible and staging, and thus where theory could be considered as a kind of theatre. The second part of the chapter looks at how the exhibitions of works by Damian and Delaine Le Bas have created space for relationships and social change. It discusses how their very presence at their exhibitions and their direct engagement with their audiences has been instrumental to their art as activism, and how the kinds of artwork they have produced are often interactively situated, as public art, in dialogue with mainstream Roma and Gypsy representations as well as with their audiences, by inviting them explicitly 'to Gypsyland' as an imagined space of interpersonal exchange. Finally, the chapter looks at the constraints of the art and social world, and how structural barriers and the politics of labelling can obstruct the work Romani artists strive to create.

We, the editors of this volume, have dedicated this book to Damian Le Bas and his legacy. The chapter by Annabel Tremlett and Delaine Le Bas ends with Damian's wish to initiate an alternative to the Roma pavilion of the 2007 Venice Biennale: what he imagined to be a Roma Biennale. In collaboration with several artists, and curated by Delaine le Bas and Hamze Bytyçi, this first Roma Biennale, entitled 'Come Out Now!', was finally realized in April 2018, after Damian's death and thus in his memory. During the Biennale, the theatre play *Roma Armee* (Roma Army) was also performed again, following its premiere on 14 September 2017 in the presence of Damian. For this play, directed by Yael Ronen & Ensemble after an idea of the Romani actors Sandra and Simonida Selimović, Delaine and Damian Le Bas produced the theatrical sceneries and costumes.

To complete the circle, we will start this volume with our first chapter in which *Huub van Baar* reflects on some of the key themes in Damian's oeuvre, including those that are clearly present in the sceneries he made for *Roma Armee*.

Huub van Baar is an Assistant Professor of Political Theory at the Institute of Political Science at the Justus-Liebig University of Giessen in Germany. He is also a Senior Research Fellow at the Amsterdam Centre for Globalisation Studies (ACGS) at the Faculty of Humanities of the University of Amsterdam, and an affiliated researcher at the Amsterdam Centre for European Studies (ACES). He coordinates a research project on the formation and transformation of Romani minorities in modern European history, which is part of the research programme Dynamics of Security: Forms of Securitization in Historical Perspective (2014–2021), funded by the German Research Foundation (DFG). He has published widely on the position and political and cultural representation of Europe's Romani minorities, predominantly from the angle of how their situation has changed at the nexus of citizenship, security and development. He has published peer-reviewed articles in, for instance, *Social Identities, Antipode, Journal of Ethnic and Migration Studies, City, Third Text, Citizenship Studies, International Journal of Cultural Policy* and *Society and Space*. He is the author of *The European Roma: Minority Representation, Memory and the Limits of Transnational Governmentality* (F&N, 2011) and the main co-editor of *Museutopia: A Photographic Research Project by Ilya Rabinovich* (Alauda, 2012, with Ingrid Commandeur) and *The Securitization of the Roma in Europe* (Palgrave Macmillan, 2019, with Ana Ivasiuc and Regina Kreide). He is currently finalizing a monograph entitled *The Ambiguity of Protection: Spectacular Security and the European Roma*.

Angéla Kóczé is an Assistant Professor of Romani Studies and Academic Director of the Roma Graduate Preparation Program at Central European University in Budapest, Hungary. In 2013–2017, she was a Visiting Assistant Professor in the Department of Sociology and Women's, Gender and Sexuality Studies Program at Wake Forest University in Winston Salem, NC, USA. She has published several peer-reviewed articles and book chapters with various international presses, including Palgrave Macmillan, Ashgate, Routledge and CEU Press, as well as several thematic policy papers related to social inclusion, gender equality, social justice and civil society. In 2013, the Woodrow Wilson International Center for Scholars in Washington, DC, honoured Kóczé with the Ion Ratiu Democracy Award for her interdisciplinary research approach, which combines community engagement and policymaking with in-depth participatory research on the situation of the Roma. She is a co-editor of *The Romani Women's Movement: Struggles and Debates in Central and Eastern Europe* (Routledge, 2019, with Violetta Zentai, Jelena Jovanović and Enikő Vincze).

Notes

Huub van Baar wrote this introductory chapter and, afterwards, Angéla Kóczé commented on the text. We would like to thank Thomas Acton, Sam Beck, Debra Schultz, Júlia Szalai, Nidhi Trehan and Violetta Zentai for their valuable comments on draft versions of this chapter.

1. This struggle for the recognition of the Romani Holocaust was a difficult and long-lasting one against the denial of racially motivated and genocidal violence against Roma (see, for instance, Rose 1987; Margalit 2002; for the ambiguities of this struggle, see von dem Knesebeck 2011; van Baar 2011a, 2015a).
2. *RomArchive* is a large digital archive for Roma arts and cultures. It archives works from all genres, and augments them with contemporary documents and scholarly appraisals. More information about the archive is available at https://www.romarchive.eu/en/.
3. The framing of the situation of Roma in terms of the 'refugee/migration crisis' should not be analysed in isolation from the much broader proliferation of crisis narratives ('economic crisis', 'financial crisis', 'debt crisis', 'crisis of the Euro-zone' or 'banking crisis') that, at least since 2007, have been mobilized to manage societal problems and processes in and beyond Europe (New Keywords Collective 2016: 8–15). In many countries across Europe – and Central and Eastern Europe in particular – the European and domestic 'financial crisis' has been mobilized to legitimate various drastic measures that have affected Roma negatively, ranging from evictions to harsh, racializing labour market policies (van Baar 2012, 2017a, this volume; Grill 2018; Kóczé, this volume; Szalai, this volume).
4. The case is known as 'M.H. and Others against Slovakia', and was lodged on 19 March 2018 under application number 14099/18 of the European Court of Human Rights. The applicants are eight Slovak nationals, who live in Moldava nad Bodvou, and are represented by the European Roma Rights Centre in Budapest.
5. 'Reasonable antigypsyism' (van Baar 2014) is the kind of anti-Roma racism in which racial reversibility has become prominent, and which follows a logic whereby one would rightfully be entitled to act against Roma and treat them differently, based on the idea that not 'we', but 'they' violate rights and fail in their duties (ibid. 30).
6. Of course, the ways in which just one volume can deal with complex issues of identity and identity formation are limited; therefore, we do not want to suggest

that we cover the field comprehensively. Some key dimensions of present-day Roma-related identity formation and struggles for identity – such as, most notably, those connected with religion and the emergence of new religious affiliations and movements – are underrepresented in our analysis.

7. In Michael Stewart's (2017: 127) recent attempt both 'to retrace the history of Romani Studies' and to assess what postcolonial studies, feminist critique, intersectionality and critical race theory have contributed to Roma-related scholarship, remarkably enough he does not include the contributions of Willems or others who have discussed the societal position and imagery of Roma through the lens of manifestations of orientalism. However, this exclusion seems to be based on Stewart's narrow understanding of postcolonial studies and theorizations of intersectionality as primarily preoccupied with 'questions of identity' and of the 'authority to speak' (ibid.: 127, 128). Although we should be wary of manifestations of the tribalization of either 'white' or 'black' people (or for that matter, group reifications based on class, gender or other categories), any suggestion that the theorizations in postcolonial studies, feminist critique, intersectionality or critical race theory tend to reify identity and, therefore, contribute to questionable forms of identity politics or troublesome mixtures of activism and scholarship, misses the point of what 'reigning deities, such as Spivak and Chakraborty [sic]' (Stewart 2017: 128), as well as later postcolonial authors, have tried to argue. Moreover, Stewart's identification of recent scholars (who have used one or more of the mentioned theoretical lenses to analyse the position of Roma) with those who are predominantly preoccupied with issues of identity and activism, creates artificial boundaries between academic and activist work (ibid.: 127, 137–44), between different generations of scholars (127), between Romani and non-Romani scholars, and also between more established and newly developed conceptual or methodological scholarly paradigms.

8. In his review of Coates's *We Were Eight Years in Power*, Cornel West has accused him of such tribalization: 'Coates rightly highlights the vicious legacy of white supremacy – past and present. He sees it everywhere and ever reminds us of its plundering effects. Unfortunately, he hardly keeps track of our fightback, and never connects this ugly legacy to the predatory capitalist practices, imperial policies (of war, occupation, detention, assassination) or the black elite's refusal to confront poverty, patriarchy or transphobia. In short, Coates fetishizes white supremacy. He makes it almighty, magical and unremovable . . . Note that his perception of white people is tribal and his conception of freedom is neoliberal. Racial groups are homogeneous and freedom is individualistic in his world . . . It is clear that his narrow racial tribalism and myopic political neoliberalism has no place for keeping track of Wall Street greed, U.S. imperial crimes or black elite indifference to poverty' (West 2017).

9. Similarly, this dialectic was also missing in Willems's analyses. To remain with Said's terms, while Willems (1997) was primarily focusing on the role of orientalism and orientalist Gypsy identity formations, he largely overlooked the simultaneous formation of occidentalist European identities through (for Said, fundamental) occidentalism. We return to an even more substantial critique of Willems's work below.

10. Willems (1997: 82–83) suggested that we could assess various historical and contemporary uses of Romani vocabularies primarily in terms of something like argot and, thus, not as the dialects of an existing, practised language. For a valuable critique, see Matras (2004: 63–68), who, in turn, overemphasizes the importance of

Willems' view on language to invalidate several of the latter's important insights on other key issues (see van Baar 2011a: 75–149).
11. For similar reasons, Thomas Acton has suggested that Matras's 'common-sense positivistic search for a magic epistemological bullet to kill off sloppy scholarship is fundamentally a mistaken approach' (Acton 2008: 33). In the first volume to Berghahn's book series Romani Studies, and in the context of activism, Ana Ivasiuc (2018: 6) has likewise problematized views that all too strictly distinguish between 'neutral', 'objective' knowledge claims and forms of knowledge production that would be 'contaminated' by 'political' or 'activist' preoccupations, and which, therefore, are less reliable.

References

Acton, T. 2008. 'Has Rishi Gone out of Style? Academic and Policy Paradigms in Romani Studies', *Roma* 56/57: 31–38.
Agarin, T., and K. Cordell (eds). 2016. *Minority Rights and Minority Protection in Europe*. Lanham, MD: Rowman & Littlefield.
Albert, G. 2012. 'Anti-Gypsyism and the Extreme Right in the Czech Republic', in M. Stewart (ed.), *The Gypsy 'Menace': Populism and the New Anti-Gypsy Politics*. London: Hurst & Company, pp. 137–65.
Appadurai, A. 2006. *Fear of Small Numbers*. Durham, NC: Duke University Press.
Baker, C. 2018. *Race and the Yugoslav Region: Postsocialist, Post-Conflict, Postcolonial?* Manchester: Manchester University Press.
Balogh, L. 2012. 'Possible Responses to the Sweep of Right-Wing Forces and Anti-Gypsyism in Hungary', in M. Stewart (ed.), *The Gypsy 'Menace': Populism and the New Anti-Gypsy Politics*. London: Hurst & Company, pp. 241–63.
Bán, A. 2017. 'Prípad Moldava: Razia a "mentalita romica"', *Týždeň*, 18 June. Retrieved 29 September 2018 from https://www.tyzden.sk/reportaze/40301/razia-a-mentalita-romica/.
Bársony, J., and Á. Daróczi (eds). 2008. *Pharrajimos: The Fate of the Roma during the Holocaust*. New York: Idebate Press.
Beck, S., and A. Ivasiuc (eds). 2018. *Roma Activism: Reimagining Power and Knowledge*. Oxford: Berghahn Books.
Benedik, S. 2010. 'Harming "Cultural Feelings"', in M. Stewart and M. Rövid (eds), *Multi-Disciplinary Approaches to Romani Studies*. Budapest: CEU Press, pp. 71–88.
Bhabha, H. 1994. *The Location of Culture*. London: Routledge.
Bhabha, J., A. Mirga and M. Matache (eds). 2017. *Realizing Roma Rights*. Philadelphia: University of Pennsylvania Press.
Bigo, D., S. Carrera and E. Guild (eds). 2013. *Foreigners, Refugees or Minorities?* Farnham: Ashgate.
Bogdal, K.-M. 2018. 'Review of *Roma Voices in the German-Speaking World* by Lorely French', *Monatshefte* 110(3): 480–84.
Bogdán, M. 2015. 'Challenging Perspectives: The Role of Media Representation in Knowledge Production about Roma', *Roma Rights* 2: 71–74.
Brubaker, R. 2002. 'Ethnicity without Groups', *Archives européennes de sociologie* 43(2): 163–89.

———. 2004. *Ethnicity without Groups*. Cambridge, MA: Harvard University Press.
Bunescu, I. 2014. *Roma in Europe: The Politics of Collective Identity Formation*. London: Routledge.
Calhoun, C. 2003a. '"Belonging" in the Cosmopolitan Imaginary', *Ethnicities* 3(4): 531–53.
———. 2003b. 'The Variability of Belonging: A Reply to Rogers Brubaker', *Ethnicities* 3(4): 558–68.
Castañeda, H. 2014. 'European Mobilities or Poverty Migration? Discourses on Roma in Germany', *International Migration* 53(3): 87–99.
Chakrabarty, D. 2000. *Provincializing Europe*. Princeton, NJ: Princeton University Press.
Clifford, J. 2003. *On the Edges of Anthropology*. Chicago, IL: Prickly Paradigm Press.
Clough Marinaro, I., and U. Daniele. 2011. 'Roma and Humanitarianism in the Eternal City', *Journal of Modern Italy Studies* 16(5): 621–36.
Clough Marinaro, I., and N. Sigona (eds). 2011. 'Anti-Gypsyism and the Politics of Exclusion: Roma and Sinti in Contemporary Italy', special issue, *Journal of Modern Italy Studies* 16(5): 583–666.
Coates, T.-N. 2017. *We Were Eight Years in Power: An American Tragedy*. New York: One World Publishing.
Corradi, L. 2018. *Gypsy Feminism: Intersectional Politics, Alliances, Gender and Queer Activism*. London: Routledge.
Davis, A.Y. 2017. 'Policing the Crisis Today', in J. Henriques, D. Morley and V. Goblot (eds), *Stuart Hall: Conversations, Projects and Legacies*. London: Goldsmiths Press, pp. 257–65.
De Genova, N. 2016. 'The European Question: Migration, Race and Postcoloniality in Europe', *Social Text* 128: 75–102.
———. 2019. 'The Securitization of Roma Mobilities and the Re-bordering of Europe', in H. van Baar, A. Ivasiuc and R. Kreide (eds), *The Securitization of the Roma in Europe*. New York: Palgrave Macmillan, pp. 29–44.
De Genova, N., G. Garelli and M. Tazzioli. 2018. 'Autonomy of Asylum? The Autonomy of Migration: Undoing the Refugee Script', *The South Atlantic Quarterly* 117(2): 239–65.
Djuve, A.B., et al. 2015. *When Poverty Meets Affluence: Migrants from Romania on the Streets of the Scandinavian Capitals*. Copenhagen: Fafo and Rockwool Foundation.
Donert, C. 2017. *The Rights of the Roma: The Struggle for Citizenship in Postwar Czechoslovakia*. Cambridge: Cambridge University Press.
Efremova, G. 2012. 'Integralist Narratives and Redemptive Anti-Gypsy Politics in Bulgaria', in M. Stewart (ed.), *The Gypsy 'Menace': Populism and the New Anti-Gypsy Politics*. London: Hurst & Company, pp. 43–66.
ERRC (European Roma Rights Centre). 1997. 'Time of the Skinheads: Denial and Exclusion in Slovakia'. Budapest.
———. 2010. 'Implementation of Judgments', special issue, *Roma Rights* 1. Budapest.
Fox, J. 2012. 'The Uses of Racism: Whitewashing New Europeans in the UK', *Ethnic and Racial Studies* 36(11): 1871–89.
Fox, J., L. Morosanu and E. Szilassy. 2012. 'The Racialization of the New European Migration to the UK', *Sociology* 46(4): 680–95.
Fremlová, L. 2017. 'The Experiences of LGBTIQ Romani People: Queer(y)ing Roma'. PhD dissertation. Brighton: University of Brighton.

Fremlová, L., and A. McGarry. 2019. 'Negotiating the Identity Dilemma: Crosscurrents across the Romani, Romani Women's and Romani LGBTIQ Movements', in A. Kóczé et al. (eds), *The Romani Women's Movement*. London: Routledge, pp. 51–68.
French, L. 2015. *Roma Voices in the German-Speaking World*. New York: Bloomsbury.
Fukuyama, F. 2018. *Identity: The Demand for Dignity and the Politics of Resentment*. London: Profile Books.
Goldberg, D.T. 2015. *Are We All Postracial Yet?* Cambridge: Polity.
Grill, J. 2018. 'Re-learning to Labour?', *Journal of the Royal Anthropological Institute* 24(1): 105–19.
Hall, S. 1997. 'Subjects in History: Making Diasporic Identities', in W. Lubiano (ed.), *The House That Race Built*. New York: Pantheon, pp. 289–300.
Hancock, I. 1996. 'Responses to the *Porrajmos*: The Romani Holocaust', in A. Rosenbaum (ed.), *Is the Holocaust Unique? Perspectives on Comparative Genocide*. Oxford: Westview Press, pp. 39–64.
Helsinki Watch. 1991a. 'Destroying Ethnic Identity: The Gypsies of Bulgaria'. New York.
———. 1991b. 'Destroying Ethnic Identity: The Persecution of the Gypsies in Romania'. New York.
———. 1992. 'Struggling for Ethnic Identity: Czechoslovakia's Endangered Gypsies'. New York.
Hemelsoet, E., and P. van Pelt. 2015. 'Questioning the Policy Framing of Roma in Ghent, Belgium', *Social Inclusion* 3(5): 148–60.
Heng, G. 2018. *The Invention of Race in the European Middle Ages*. Cambridge: Cambridge University Press.
Hornberg, S., and C. Brüggemann (eds). 2013. *Die Bildungssituation von Roma in Europa*. Münster: Waxmann.
Imre, A. 2005. 'Whiteness in Post-Socialist Eastern Europe: The Times of the Gypsies, the End of Race', in A.J. López (ed.), *Postcolonial Whiteness: A Critical Reader on Race and Empire*. Albany, NY: SUNY Press, pp. 79–102.
———. 2009. *Identity Games: Globalization and the Transformation of Media Cultures in the New Europe*. Cambrdige, MA: MIT Press.
Ivasiuc, A. 2018. 'Introduction: Renewing Research and Romani Activism', in S. Beck and A. Ivasiuc (eds), *Roma Activism: Reimagining Power and Knowledge*. Oxford: Berghahn Books, pp. 1–22.
Jansen, Y., R. Celikates and J. de Bloois (eds). 2015. *The Irregularization of Migration in Contemporary Europe: Deportation, Detention, Drowning*. Lanham, MD: Rowman & Littlefield.
Jardina, A. 2019. *White Identity Politics*. Cambridge: Cambridge University Press.
Klímova-Alexander, I. 2005. *The Romani Voice in World Politics*. Aldershot: Ashgate.
Kóczé, A. 2009. *Missing Intersectionality: Race/Ethnicity, Gender and Class in Current Research and Policies on Romani Women in Europe*. Budapest: Center for Policy Studies, Central European University.
———. 2011. 'Gender, Ethnicity and Class: Romani Women's Political Activism and Social Struggle in Post-Socialist Europe', PhD dissertation. Budapest: Central European University.
———. 2018. 'Race, Migration and Neoliberalism: Distorted Notions of Romani Migration in European Public Discourses', *Social Identities* 24(4): 459–73.
Kóczé, A., and M. Rövid. 2017. 'Roma and the Politics of Double Discourse in Contemporary Europe', *Identities* 24(6): 684–700.

Kóczé, A., et al. (eds). 2019. *The Romani Women's Movement: Struggles and Debates in Central and Eastern Europe*. London: Routledge.

Kurtić, V. 2014. *Džulvjarke: Roma Lesbian Existence*. Niš: Ženski proctor.

Lausberg, M. 2015. *Antiziganismus in Deutschland: Zuwanderung aus Bulgarien und Rumänien*. Marburg: Tectum Verlag.

Law, I., and M. Kovats. 2018. *Rethinking Roma: Identities, Politicisation and New Agendas*. New York: Palgrave Macmillan.

Lucassen, L., W. Willems and A. Cottaar. 1998. *Gypsies and Other Itinerant Groups: A Socio-historical Approach*. Basingstoke: Macmillan.

Majtényi, B., and G. Majtényi. 2016. *A Contemporary History of Exclusion: The Roma Issue in Hungary from 1945 to 2015*. Budapest: CEU Press.

Margalit, G. 2002. *Germany and its Gypsies*. Madison: University of Wisconsin Press.

Matache, M. 2016a. 'Word, Image and Thought: Creating the Romani Other', *The Huffington Post*, 10 March. Retrieved 16 October 2018 from https://www.huffingtonpost.com/entry/57f29d40e4b095bd896a156a?timestamp=1475519595732.

———. 2016b. 'The Legacy of Gypsy Studies in Modern Romani Scholarship', *The Huffington Post*, 10 November. Retrieved 16 October 2018 from https://www.huffingtonpost.com/entry/58253d92e4b02b1f52579f3a?timestamp=1479138689015.

Matras, Y. 1999. 'Johann Rüdiger and the Study of Romani in 18th Century Germany', *Journal of the Gypsy Lore Society* 9(1): 89–116.

———. 2002. *Romani: A Linguistic Introduction*. Cambridge: Cambridge University Press.

———. 2004. 'The Role of Language in Mystifying and Demystifying Gypsy Identity', in N. Saul and S. Tebbutt (eds), *The Role of the Romanies: Images and Counter-Images of 'Gypsies'/Romanies in European Cultures*. Liverpool: Liverpool University Press, pp. 53–78.

Mayall, D. 2004. *Gypsy Identities 1500–2000*. London: Routledge.

McGarry, A. 2010. *Who Speaks for Roma?* London: Continuum.

———. 2017. *Romaphobia*. London: Zed Books.

McGarry, A., and J. Jasper (eds). 2015. *The Identity Dilemma: Social Movements and Collective Identity*. Philadelphia, PA: Temple University Press.

Mireanu, M. 2013. 'The Spectacle of Security in the Case of Hungarian Far-Right Paramilitary Groups', *Fascism* 2: 1–26.

Mirga, A. 2018. 'Review of *Those Who Count* by Mihai Surdu', *Critical Romani Studies* 1(1): 114–26.

Mirga-Kruszelnicka, A., E. Acuña and P. Trojański (eds). 2015. *Education for Remembrance of the Roma Genocide*. Cracow: Libron.

Miskovic, M. (ed.). 2013. *Roma Education in Europe*. London: Routledge.

Nagy, V. 2018. 'The Janus Face of Precarity: Securitization of Roma Mobility in the UK', *Local Economy* 33(2): 127–46.

New Keywords Collective. 2016. 'Europe/Crisis: New Keywords of "the Crisis" in and of "Europe"', *Near Futures Online* 1. Retrieved 1 September 2016 from http://nearfuturesonline.org/europecrisis-new-keywords-of-crisis-in-and-of-europe/.

Nicolae, V., and H. Slavik (eds). 2007. *Roma Diplomacy*. New York: Idebate Press.

Okely, J. 1983. *The Traveller-Gypsies*. Cambridge: Cambridge University Press.

———. 2010. 'Constructing Culture through Shared Location, Bricolage and Exchange', in M. Stewart and M. Rövid (eds), *Multi-disciplinary Approaches to Romany Studies*. Budapest: CEU Press, pp. 35–54.

Olesen, C.L., and L.E. Karlsson. 2018. 'Roma Representations in Danish Roma Policy and Public Discourse', *Societies* 8(63): 1–11.
O'Nions, H. 2007. *Minority Rights Protection in International Law*. Farnham: Ashgate.
Parker, O. 2012. 'Roma and the Politics of EU Citizenship in France', *Journal of Common Market Studies* 50(3): 475–91.
Picker, G. 2017. *Racial Cities*. London: Routledge.
Powell, R., and H. van Baar. 2019. 'The Invisibilization of Anti-Roma Racisms', in H. van Baar, A. Ivasiuc and R. Kreide (eds), *The Securitization of the Roma in Europe*. New York: Palgrave Macmillan, pp. 91–113.
Public Defender of Rights. 2013. 'The Public Defender of Rights's Extraordinary Report Regarding Facts Indicating Serious Violation of Fundamental Rights and Freedoms by Actions Taken by some Bodies'. August. Bratislava.
Pulay, G. 2018. 'Crises, Securitizations and the Europeanization of Roma Representation', *Intersections* 4(3): 180–92.
Puxon, G. 2000. 'The Romani Movement', in T. Acton (ed.), *Scholarship and the Gypsy Struggle*. Hatfield: University of Hertfordshire Press, pp. 94–113.
Ram, M. 2010. 'Interests, Norms and Advocacy', *Ethnopolitics* 9(2): 197–217.
Romea. 2017. 'Amnesty International: We Demand Justice for the Victims of the Slovak Police Raid on the Roma Settlement of Moldava nad Bodvou', 19 September. Retrieved 19 September 2017 from http://www.romea.cz/en/news/world/amnesty-international-we-demand-justice-for-the-victims-of-the-slovak-police-raid-on-the-roma-settlement-of-moldava-nad.
Rooker, M. 2002. *The International Supervision of the Protection of Romany People in Europe*. Nijmegen: Nijmegen University Press.
Rose, R. 1987. *Bürgerrechte für Sinti und Roma: Das Buch zum Rassismus in Deutschland*. Heidelberg: Zentralrat Deutscher Sinti und Roma.
Rostas, I. (ed.). 2012. *Ten Years After: A History of Roma School Desegregation in Central and Eastern Europe*. Budapest: CEU Press.
Ryder, A. 2018. 'Paradigm Shifts and Romani Studies: Research "on" or "for" and "with" the Roma', in S. Beck and A. Ivasiuc (eds), *Roma Activism: Reimagining Power and Knowledge*. Oxford: Berghahn Books, pp. 91–110.
Said, E. 1978. *Orientalism*. London: Vintage.
Sigona, N., and N. Trehan (eds). 2009. *Romani Politics in Contemporary Europe*. New York: Palgrave Macmillan.
Silverman, C. 2012. *Romani Routes: Cultural Politics and Balkan Music in Diaspora*. Oxford: Oxford University Press.
Spivak, G.C. 2012. *Making Visible*. Retrieved 10 August 2018 from https://www.igkultur.at/artikel/making-visible.
Staffen-Quandt, D. 2015. '"Sonderlager sind inakzeptabel": Gespräch mit Romani Rose', *Migazin*, 28 July. Retrieved 20 September 2015 from http://www.migazin.de/amp/2015/07/28/sonderlager-sind-inakzeptabel/.
Stewart, M. 2001. 'Communist Roma Policy 1945–1989 as Seen through the Hungarian Case', in W. Guy (ed.), *Between Past and Future: The Roma of Central and Eastern Europe*. Hatfield: Universtity of Hertfordshire Press, pp. 71–92.
———. 2017. 'Nothing about Us without Us, or the Dangers of a Closed-Society Research Paradigm', *Romani Studies* 27(2): 125–46.
Stoler, A.L. 2002. 'Colonial Archives and the Arts of Governance', *Archival Science* 2: 87–109.

Surdu, M. 2016. *Those Who Count: Expert Practices of Roma Classification*. Budapest: CEU Press.
Surdu, M., and M. Kovats. 2015. 'Roma Identity as an Expert-Political Construction', *Social Inclusion* 3(5): 5–18.
Szalai, J., and C. Schiff (eds). 2014. *Migrant, Roma and Postcolonial Youth in Education across Europe*. New York: Palgrave Macmillan.
Szalai, J., and V. Zentai (eds). 2014. *Faces and Causes of Roma Marginalization in Local Contexts*. Budapest: Center for Policy Studies, Central European University.
Szeman, I. 2018. *Staging Citizenship: Roma, Performance and Belonging in EU Romania*. Oxford: Berghahn Books.
Toninato, P. 2014. *Romani Writing: Literacy, Literature and Identity Politics*. London: Routledge.
Trehan, N., and A. Kóczé. 2009. 'Postcolonial Racism and Social Justice: The Struggle for the Soul of the Romani Civil Rights Movement in the "New Europe"', in G. Huggan and I. Law (eds), *Racism, Post-colonialism, Europe*. Liverpool: Liverpool University Press, pp. 50–73.
Tremlett, A. 2009. 'Bringing Hybridity to Heterogeneity in Romani Studies', *Romani Studies* 19(2): 147–68.
Trlifajová, L., et al. 2015. *Analýza politik nulové tolerance v Litvínově a Duchcově* [An Analysis of the Politics of Zero Tolerance in Litvínov and Duchcov]. Prague: SPOT.
Vajda, V. 2015. 'Towards "Critical Whiteness" in Romani Studies', *Roma Rights* 2: 47–57.
van Baar, H. 2011a. *The European Roma: Minority Representation, Memory and the Limits of Transnational Governmentality*. Amsterdam: F&N.
———. 2011b. 'Europe's Romaphobia: Problematization, Securitization, Nomadization', *Environment and Planning D: Society and Space* 29(2): 203–12.
———. 2012. 'Socioeconomic Mobility and Neoliberal Governmentality in Postsocialist Europe', *Journal of Ethnic and Migration Studies* 38(8): 1289–304.
———. 2013. 'Travelling Activism and Knowledge Formation in the Romani Social and Civil Movement', in M. Miskovic (ed.), *Roma Education in Europe*. London: Routledge, pp. 192–203.
———. 2014. 'The Emergence of a Reasonable Anti-Gypsyism in Europe', in T. Agarin (ed.), *When Stereotype Meets Prejudice: Antiziganism in European Societies*. Stuttgart: Ibidem Verlag, pp. 27–44.
———. 2015a. 'Enacting Memory and the Hard Labour of Identity Formation', in A. McGarry and J. Jasper (eds). 2015. *The Identity Dilemma: Social Movements and Collective Identity*. Philadelphia, PA: Temple University Press, pp. 150–69.
———. 2015b. 'The Hidden Dimension of "The Refugee Crisis": Racializing Poverty and Bordering Europe Biopolitically'. Public Lecture held at the University of Freiburg, 11 October.
———. 2017a. 'Evictability and the Biopolitical Bordering of Europe', *Antipode* 49(1): 212–30.
———. 2017b. 'Boundary Practices of Citizenship: Europe's Roma at the Nexus of Securitization and Citizenship', in R. Gonzales and N. Sigona (eds), *Within and Beyond Citizenship*. London: Routledge, pp. 143–58.
———. 2018. 'Contained Mobility and the Racialization of Poverty in Europe: The Roma at the Development-Security Nexus', *Social Identities* 24(4): 442–58.
———. 2019. 'From "Lagging Behind" to "Being Beneath"? The De-developmentalization of Time and Social Order in Contemporary Europe', in H. van Baar, A. Ivasiuc

and R. Kreide (eds), *The Securitization of the Roma in Europe*. New York: Palgrave Macmillan, pp. 159–82.

———. Forthcoming. *The Ambiguity of Protection: Spectacular Security and the European Roma*. Book manuscript.

van Baar, H., A. Ivasiuc and R. Kreide (eds). 2019. *The Securitization of the Roma in Europe*. New York: Palgrave Macmillan.

van Baar, H., and P. Vermeersch. 2017. 'The Limits of Operational Representations: "Ways of Seeing Roma" beyond the Recognition–Distribution Paradigm', *Intersections* 3(4): 120–39.

Vermeersch, P. 2005. 'Marginality, Advocacy and the Ambiguities of Multiculturalism', *Identities* 12(4): 451–78.

———. 2006. *The Romani Movement*. Oxford: Berghahn Books.

Vincze, E. (ed.). 2013. 'Spatialization and Racialization of Social Exclusion', special issue, *Sociologia* 58(2): 1–288.

von dem Knesebeck, J. 2011. *The Roma Struggle for Compensation in Post-War Germany*. Hatfield: University of Hertfordshire Press.

Vrăbiescu, I. 2019. 'Voluntary Return as Forced Mobility', in H. van Baar, A. Ivasiuc and R. Kreide (eds), *The Securitization of the Roma in Europe*. New York: Palgrave Macmillan, pp. 207–29.

Wekker, G. 2016. *White Innocence: Paradoxes of Colonialism and Race*. Durham, NC: Duke University Press.

West, C. 2017. 'Ta-Nehisi Coates is the Neoliberal Face of the Black Freedom Struggle', *The Guardian*, 17 December.

Willems, W. 1997. *In Search of the True Gypsy: From Enlightenment to Final Solution*. London: Frank Cass.

Yıldız, C., and N. De Genova (eds). 2018. 'Un/Free Mobility: Roma Migrants in the European Union', special issue, *Social Identities* 24(4): 425–532.

Zalešák, M. 2015. 'Justice Denied: Victimising the Victims of Police Violence in Slovakia', European Roma Rights Centre blog. Retrieved 29 September 2018 from http://www.errc.org/news/justice-denied-victimising-the-victims-of-police-violence-in-slovakia.

———. 2018. 'Moldava nad Bodvou: Five Years On and Still No Justice for Roma Victims of Police Brutality', European Roma Rights Centre blog. Retrieved 29 June 2018 from http://www.errc.org/news/moldava-nad-bodvou-five-years-on-and-still-no-justice-for-roma-victims-of-police-brutality.

CHAPTER 1

❈ ❈ ❈

DECOLONIZING CANONICAL ROMA REPRESENTATIONS
The Cartographer with an Army
Huub van Baar

Setting up a Roma Army

One of Damian Le Bas's most ludic interventions in modern art history has undoubtedly been his materialized idea of the RAF, short for Roma Armee Fraktion or Roma Army Faction. Try to imagine colourful and confrontational images of soldier-like figures on maps of Berlin and Europe, accompanied by the letters 'RAF', all in the heart of Berlin, at the city's famous boulevard Unter den Linden, next to the Humboldt University, one of the city's main centres of knowledge production, and in front of the Maxim Gorki Theatre (Figure 1.1). Many people who saw these images in the public space between these buildings frowned when they read 'RAF'. RAF? The RAF?! The notorious Rote Armee Fraktion (Red Army Faction), once led by the terrorists Andreas Baader and Ulrike Meinhof, is back in the public space of Berlin, after all the violence, anger and fear that the RAF caused, particularly during the 1970s? What's up? Who's playing with this delicate legacy? Who's playing with fire here?

Damian Le Bas was and still is. His artworks have attained a kind of semi-permanent status in public space, just next to the Neue Wache, the Central Memorial of the Federal Republic of Germany for the Victims of War and Dictatorship. Le Bas created his artworks on the RAF as part of

Figure 1.1 'Roma Armee Fraktion Berlin', Damian Le Bas, 2017. Courtesy of The Le Bas Archive & Collection. Photographic credit: Huub van Baar.

the performance and sceneries he made for *Roma Armee*, a theatre play produced by Yael Ronen & Ensemble after an idea from the Serbian-Austrian Romani sisters Sandra and Simonida Selimović, and performed by mostly Romani actors from different European countries, including the Selimović sisters themselves. *Roma Armee* was performed for the first time on 14 September 2017 – and several times since – in Berlin's Gorki Theatre which, for many years now, has become a kind of headquarters – 'Gorki HQ' as Damian calls it on some of his paintings – of the European Romani art movement, together with Kai Dikhas, the Berlin-based Gallery for Contemporary Art of the Roma and Sinti.

Damian's RAF could be considered as a ludic, but also probing and thoughtful play with the idea of a Romani armed force – a militant force – that is not terrorizing other people, but combating the various ways in which, throughout European and global history, others have terrorized Roma, Gypsies, Travellers and their identities with highly impactful ideas and images of whom they would be. Damian's RAF is not about taking up guns to fight or plan terrorist attacks to threaten fellow citizens, but about using art, culture and their visual and discursive idioms to fight against a dreadful but often unnoticed history of terrorizing representations and imageries. This is what is in the job description of the virtual but effective Roma Army, and this is how Damian Le Bas, often together with his wife and partner in artistic crime Delaine Le Bas, has tempted and invited us 'to Gypsyland' (see Tremlett and Le Bas, this volume). Yet, 'Gypsyland' – a phrase often used in the couple's artworks – is never what it seems or is expected to be. It is not something marginal out there, a fringe phenomenon, but is fundamental to what our places of living, our Europe and our world constitute. 'Gypsyland' is where London changes into 'Romeville' and where the London Underground system changes into the Romany Underground system in Damian Le Bas's artwork *Romeville* (2007). 'Gypsyland' is where, in his paintings *Paris I* and *Paris II* (2009), Paris changes into an urban landscape in which, at each and every street corner, is a caravan. 'Gypsyland' is where entire cities or regions – Berlin, Freiburg, Fenland, Munich, Venice, Kirkby Stephen and Appleby, the Pyrenees, New Forest National Park, Scandinavia, Newfoundland, East Central Europe, the Balkans, the Alpine countries – turn into colourfully mapped landscapes where we meet, in Dada-like collages, all kinds of objects and figures, and most of all, faces and eyes that look and do not look at you at the same time (Figure 1.2). 'Gypsyland' is where, on the impressive opening scenery for *Roma Armee*, the map of Europe changes into 'Gypsyland *Europa*'; where, in one of Damian Le Bas's 1995 artworks, the 'New Commercial Map of the World' changes into a Magical

FIGURE 1.2 'Gypsyland. The Atlantic Side of the Pyrenees', Damian Le Bas, 2007. Courtesy of The Le Bas Archive & Collection. Photographic credit: Huub van Baar.

Figure 1.3 'Frontier De Luxe Vienna', Damian Le Bas, 2016. Courtesy of The Le Bas Archive & Collection. Photographic credit: Huub van Baar.

Gypsy World; and where, last but not least, on the various globes he used as the basis for some of his 2016 pieces, three-dimensional worlds change into multiple-planet earths with 'No Man's Lands', 'Motherlands of All of Us' and 'Frontier de Luxe' (see Figure 1.3). This imagining of 'Gypsyland' is not to suggest that Roma, Gypsies and Travellers are 'everywhere' – though they virtually are – but to unambiguously enact a regime of visuality that is clear about one thing: 'We are here'. As in the famous activist slogan related to contemporary struggles of migrants and refugees – 'We are here, because you were there' – Damian has created a visual regime that clearly states: 'We are here, although you have overlooked us'. The invitations 'to Gypsyland' are not a kind of pedagogical tour in which someone takes you by the hand to introduce you to Romani culture and traditions, or to teach you how stereotypes should be debunked or how the Roma 'really are'. Rather, they are invitations that encourage you to look at the world differently and to think about the powerful impact of representation, identification and identities more generally, and in dialogue with whom you would like to meet to seriously reconsider this impact.

An Epistemological Testing Ground for the European Imaginary

In her important 1992 essay 'The Time of the Gypsies: A "People without History" in the Narratives of the West', Katie Trumpener argues that in the past – in the ages of Enlightenment, Romanticism and literary modernism in particular – chroniclers, scholars and various kinds of artists primarily considered 'the Gypsies' as a people or group of wandering clans who were at odds with the modern structures of temporality, and with the paradigms of modernity more generally. They were often seen as a people that stood outside modern life, and the formation of the nation (state) in particular, and so they were consequently relegated to the domain of pre-modern, traditional, natural and 'history-less' societies. Particularly since the end of the eighteenth century, Trumpener argues, the 'Gypsies' also started to function as a trope for various kinds of escape routes, which led away from the modern socioeconomic, political and cultural order towards a mythical or mystical realm of freedom and dissipation. In the long history of Gypsy-related narratives and imageries, Gypsies were generally portrayed as representing either an escape from the order of modernity and its troubles, or a serious threat to its maintenance, stability and further development.

In Heinrich von Kleist's *Michael Kohlhaas*, for instance, a Gypsy fortune-teller appears as a figure that lives outside of history to introduce 'magical timelessness' (Trumpener 1992: 869) into the main narrative. And in Virginia Woolf's novel *Orlando*, Gypsy men and women appear as indistinguishable, 'genderless' people during Orlando's gender transition from man into woman and liberation from a patriarchal world (Bardi 2006). 'Gypsies' are required to make Orlando aware of her gender transition, and when she is fully conscious about her new status, she leaves them again as if she no longer needs them. In both these narratives, as well as in many others,

Trumpener argues, 'the Gypsies are ... reduced to a textual effect' (1992: 869). Everywhere they appear in these narratives, they seemingly 'begin to hold up ordinary life, inducing local amnesias or retrievals of cultural memory, and causing blackouts or flashbacks in textual, historical and genre memory as well' (ibid.). Trumpener contends that the Gypsies appear not only along a kind of timeless escape route from the order of modernity, but also as magical figures who ambivalently *disrupt* the structure of temporality of this modern order itself, as those whose main discursive job seems to be what she calls 'time-banditry' (ibid.).

The reduction of the 'Gypsies' to textual effects is not limited to pre-Second World War narratives. As various authors have analysed, in many ways the Gypsies have continued to play this role in various postwar and contemporary works, including film, exhibitions and popular culture. In postwar policy documents, the Gypsies and those who are usually associated with them also pop up as a people that has another sense of time and place, and that apparently belongs to another social order than that of the European majorities. A 1984 document of the European Parliament on 'education for children with parents who have no fixed abode', for instance, represents caravan dwellers as follows:

> [They] have a relatively casual attitude towards space and time. They live in the present and give little or no thought to the future. They do not live according to a fixed scheme of hours, days and weeks, etc. Work is integrated into the normal rhythm of the day so that there is no difference between work and leisure as such. (European Parliament 1984, cited Simhandl 2006: 106)

Back in 1984, the European Parliament suggested that the fact that the Gypsies live 'in the present and give little or no thought to the future' resulted in their suffering from 'educational backwardness' (cited Danbakli 2001: 30). Living in an eternal here and now and making no difference between work and leisure had apparently led to a situation in which their children were not 'integrated in normal education' (ibid.).

The 'historylessness' of the Gypsies has also been represented in academic writing, popularized or not. Some authors have claimed that Gypsy or Romani cultures could be characterized by an 'art of forgetting'. For instance, in a chapter on the Holocaust in her bestseller *Bury Me Standing: The Gypsies and their Journey*, Isabel Fonseca states that 'the Jews have responded to persecution and dispersal with a monumental industry of remembrance. The Gypsies – with their peculiar mixture of fatalism and the spirit, or wit, to seize the day – have made an art of forgetting' (1995: 276). Fonseca's theory of the Roma's 'art of forgetting' has been rephrased more authoritatively by Inge Clendinnen who, in *Reading the Holocaust*, claims that the European Roma are 'an example' of a people who have chosen 'not to bother with history at all' and who 'seek no meanings beyond those relevant to immediate survival' (1999: 8).

A similar, though perhaps somewhat more subtle point of view returns in the works of the anthropologists Michael Stewart and Paloma Gay y Blasco. The latter, for instance, claims that 'all Gypsies . . . elaborate on the contrast between themselves and the non-Gypsies and also share . . . a lack of an elaborate social memory' (Gay y Blasco 1999: 4). In her research on Spanish Gitanos, to which this lack of memory would apply, she suggests that, 'unlike many other minorities, the Gitanos do not look to a historical or mythical past for explanations of their way of life or of their difference from the dominant majority' (ibid.: 14). Both Stewart and Gay y Blasco relate this lack of an 'elaborate social memory' to a preoccupation with temporality that would be characteristic of the Roma. The former, for instance, concludes his much-read study *The Time of the Gypsies* with the remark that 'they live with *their gaze fixed on a permanent present* that is *always becoming*, a *timeless now* in which their continued existence as Rom is *all that counts*' (Stewart 1997: 246, emphasis added). Similarly, Gay y Blasco claims that the Gitanos 'lack an elaborate social memory and have no myths of origin in which their common identity could find its roots: they are intent on separating the past from the present, and on denying that the "before" . . . may hold the blueprint for the "now"' (1999: 174). The way in which the Gitanos allegedly deal with temporality leads Gay y Blasco to conclude that they 'seem to be permanently engaged in the "celebration of impermanence"' (ibid.: 173). This implies that 'the identity of the group is not objectified outside the group itself' (ibid.: 174).

Although most of the mentioned authors implicitly or explicitly suggest that the Roma's endurance as a people relates to how others have treated them throughout European history, they nevertheless strongly tend to reify Romani cultures and their external boundaries. Their cultures are represented as having 'timeless' characteristics, even though the Roma's relationships with others and among themselves may change over time. This reification manifests itself most clearly in the case of Stewart's and Gay y Blasco's representation of the Gypsies as those who would live in a 'permanent present' or 'timeless now'. Elsewhere, I have discussed how the political status of the Roma as citizens, refugees and migrants has often been 'irregularized' (van Baar 2015, 2017; see also van Baar with Kóczé, Introduction to this volume). On the basis of the examples I have discussed here, we could add that 'the time of the Roma' has also been irregularized and, since 'their gaze' would be 'fixed on a permanent present', considerably reified, if not racialized. These kinds of reifications tend to obscure how these Roma representations relate to the dynamic interrelationships between Roma and others, to internal variations across ethnic difference and space, and to how particular sociocultural mechanisms 'majoritize' some groups while at the same time 'minoritizing' or even inferiorizing others.

The ways in which timelessness has been repeatedly projected onto the figures of the Gypsies has led Trumpener to a general contemplation on the relationship between the continuous Western fascination with the Gypsies and the formative moments of cultural traditions themselves:

> If in the course of the nineteenth century the Gypsies became increasingly stylized, exoticized, 'generic' figures of mystery, adventure and romance, they also became intimately identified, on several different levels, with the formation of literary tradition itself, acting as figurative keys to an array of literary genres and to the relations between them . . . If at the end of the nineteenth century, apparently disparate branches of literary production are thus peculiarly connected by their common fascination with Gypsies' 'primitive magic', the longer list of authors and literary forms preoccupied with Gypsy life is . . . virtually synonymous with the modern European literary canon – and is synonymous as well, if the many thousands of popular novels, poems, songs, operettas, paintings and films featuring Gypsies are added to it, with European and American cultural literacy more generally. Over the last two hundred years, European literary and cultural mythology has repeatedly posed the Gypsy question as the key to the origin, the nature, the strength of cultural tradition itself. It could be argued, indeed, that as the Gypsies become bearers, par excellence, of the European memory problem in its many manifestations, they simultaneously become a *major epistemological testing ground for the European imaginary*, black box or limit case for successive literary styles, genres and intellectual movements. (Trumpener 1992: 873–74, emphasis added)

Trumpener argues that the very formation and celebration of successive Western artistic traditions and intellectual movements as innovative, progressive and radically and irreducibly 'other' have been made possible by the construction of the Gypsies as the ultimate and universal representatives of a premodern, traditional, natural and timeless order. Thus, the teleological time of modern, 'civilized' history could only have been set in motion by *immobilizing* and bringing to a stop 'the time of the Gypsies' – which is similar to suggesting that they live in a 'timeless now' – and by continually instrumentalizing related stereotypical representations. According to Trumpener, the cultural uses of such Gypsy or Roma representations can be considered as a crucial condition for the possibility of the temporal structures of modernity. This leads her to inherently relate the European memory problem to the silent erasure of Romani memory from Western canons, and the impossibility for the Roma to effectively claim a representative space for their own memories and histories.[1] Finally, this brings her to the conclusion that 'those peoples who do not claim a history, are relegated to nature, without a voice in any political process, represented only in the glass case of the diorama, the dehumanizing legend of the photograph, the tableaux of the open-air museum' (Trumpener 1992: 884).

Over the last decade, particularly but not exclusively in the German-speaking academic world, thorough and ground-breaking studies have been published on the various uses and abuses of Gypsy figures in European societies, cultures and artistic traditions (see, for instance, Solms 2008, 2018; Von Hagen 2009; Bogdal 2011; Brittnacher 2012; Patrut 2014; Reuter 2014). To some extent, these studies could be read as crucial elaborations and required refinements of Trumpener's analysis of the early 1990s, and of how 'Europe has invented the Gypsies' in a complex and variable 'history of contempt and fascination', as Klaus-Michael Bogdal (2011) put it in the title of his seminal study. Yet what is striking about this important recent historiography is that Roma self-representations and their histories have been largely if not entirely neglected, or only dealt with at the level of footnotes and epilogues. This is all the more remarkable since much has gone on at the level of self-representation over the decade in which these studies were undertaken, and in which Romani art movements developed with intensity (see, for instance, Junghaus and Székely 2007; Bahlmann and Reichelt 2011; Galerie Kai Dikhas 2011, 2012, 2013; Baker and Hlavajova 2013; Pankok 2019; Magazzini, this volume; Tremlett and Le Bas, this volume).

So, the question is what is happening now that, very clearly, the long and highly ambiguous history of Gypsy representations in 'the glass case of the diorama', in 'the dehumanizing legend of the photograph' and in 'the tableaux of the open-air museum' has been challenged by Romani artists themselves, and now that they have actually and unambiguously claimed a history – or, better, diverse histories.

Setting Time in Motion: When Carmen Starts Bleeding

In Delaine and Damian Le Bas's artwork 'The World of Gypsy Romance?' (2012, see Figure 1.4; see also Figure 11.2 in Tremlett and Le Bas, this volume) we see a classical stereotypical portrait of the beautiful Gypsy woman. It is the canonical figure that traverses European visual and discursive histories of Gypsy representations in which the Carmen-like character has both erotic and demonic power: she seduces men while simultaneously and ambiguously disrupting the spatiotemporal order in which these men and their likes are living. Yet the Carmen-like figure that Delaine portrayed bleeds heavily from her mouth. What is more, the painting bleeds as well, or is stained with blood, and is damaged with a sharp object close to the face of the no longer so beautiful Gypsy woman. The millions of Carmens who have catalysed virtual, and therefore not yet unreal escapes from bourgeois worlds do so

FIGURE 1.4 'The World of Gypsy Romance?' (detail), Delaine and Damian Le Bas, 2012. Courtesy of The Le Bas Archive & Collection. Photographic credit: Delaine Le Bas.

no more. Here, in this artwork, the tradition of the 'beautiful Gypsy girl' is bleeding to death. Full stop. However, the piece is not a mutilation or visual assassination of the 'beautiful Gypsy girl', but rather a critical artistic intervention in a still continuing tradition of violent, terrorizing Gypsy clichés

Figure 1.5 'Table for a Romani Embassy', Rotor, Graz. Damian Le Bas, 2017. Courtesy of The Le Bas Archive & Collection. Photographic credit: Huub van Baar.

and their impact on those associated with them. This artwork claims history by critically intervening in a long and often undisputed history of artistic and stereotypical representations (see also Tremlett and Le Bas, this volume).

Elsewhere, Delaine and Damian Le Bas have gone a step further. Imagine, for instance, the following design: a rectangular table of about 70 x 120 centimetres, with one chair on each side (Figure 1.5). The upper part of the table is decorated in the middle, with eyes, wheels, arrows and some inscriptions. The primarily white chairs are painted in different colours and with black letters. On the table is written 'Table for a Romani Embassy'; on one of the chairs we read 'Welcome to Romanistan'; on other chairs 'Lackademic fat cats hands off our Romani Embassy' and 'Time for a Romani Embassy'. Damian Le Bas created the table and the four chairs for an art exhibition in Graz, Austria, in 2017, in what would be the final year of his life. His table with chairs for a Romani Embassy is at one with various performances by Delaine on the same theme and at places as diverse as London (2015), Malmö (2015), Thessaloniki (2015), the University of Essex (2016), Bradford (2017), Czarna

Góra, Szczurowa, Poland (2017), Graz (2017) and, last but not least, Berlin (2017, 2018). On the website that is part of the embassy project, Delaine Le Bas explains it as follows:

> Romani Embassy is an information point, a living archive, an embodiment of reclaiming the stolen artefact that we have become. It can morph in size, change its appearance, appear and disappear. It is not contained within one building, it is a moving, flexible structure. It is a cardboard sign made on the move. It exists within real and virtual space and time. It can be one person, it can possibly be more. It can be a distribution point to question majority societies' opinion and ongoing mistreatment of us. It can be a silent act of resistance. Romani Embassy is an ongoing performance, artwork, activism.[2]

If philosophically informed studies, from Trumpener's to more recent texts, have primarily *interpreted* the history of Gypsy and Roma representations, then artists such as Damian and Delaine Le Bas want to *change* it by keenly intervening in it through their 'artivism'. In the Berlin version of the Romani Embassy performance, Delaine was in a long, completely white, Victorian dress, with black hair and sitting in a guard house-like construction made out of bare wood, its inside decorated with Damian's 'This is Gypsyland 2014' mirror and, on the outside, with images and texts that refer to, for instance, the Egyptian Act of 1530, an article about 'Counterfeit Egyptians' and the construction of criminal identity in early modern England, a book about the Winchester Confessions of 1615–1616, a historical image of a fortune-teller and an image of the girl Maria, who was found in a Greek Romani neighbourhood and taken away by the police for further investigation concerning 'the Gypsies' who had 'stolen' her in 2013.[3] During the performance, Delaine reads parts from the Egyptian Act of 1530, which was passed by the Parliament of England in 1531 to expel the 'outlandish people calling themselves Egyptians', meaning Gypsies, who 'using no craft nor feat of merchandise . . . have come into this realm and gone from shire to shire, and place to place, in great company; and used great subtlety and crafty means to deceive the people'. While she performs and brings in various episodes from more distant and more recent Roma-related histories – including the one of the Romani girl Maria – Delaine claws her dress to shreds, thereby symbolically getting rid of her Victorian armour. Theory has become theatre here, as Gayatri Spivak (2012) has said of Delaine and Damian Le Bas's art, and the various elements and artefacts from past and present – stories, laws, signs, images and the like – are turned into what Delaine calls 'a living archive' (see also Tremlett and Le Bas, this volume).

Consequently, the 'Romani Embassy' is neither the group of people who represent the Roma in a foreign place, nor the material structure – the building – in which these people work or live. It escapes these two canonical meanings of embassy, because it is the site and the activity in which a new (hi-)story emerges through the re-appropriation and reassembling of known and unknown elements from present pasts, and their strategic and active positioning within the politics of the present. Romani Embassy turns the imaginary yet highly tangible 'waiting room of history' to which the Roma have historically, and to this day, been so frequently relegated (Chakrabarty 2000: 8; see van Baar with Kóczé, Introduction to this volume) into the most important outpost of the Roma Army, which has no aim other than to both expose and challenge how canonical histories of Gypsy and Roma representations are fully complicit in violating lifeworlds and maintaining mechanisms of exclusion. 'Do not be an active participant' of these dominant histories, 'so history does not repeat itself', we read on one of the panels of Delaine and Damian Le Bas's public art installation *Safe European Home?* 'Don't tell us who we are', we read in red letters on the inside of one of its main art objects, 'We have a history'. This is meant as a disruption of the structure of temporality of the current European order, not to rearticulate it, but to radically question it. This is no 'time-banditry', but sabotaging the continued production, distribution and circulation of terrorizing Roma/Gypsy representations in European cultures and societies.

Maps as Mobile Engines: Moving and Reclaiming the World

> We are claiming this space for ourselves. We, the constrained, limited and defined by those who want to control, name and silence us. Here we are.
> —Damian Le Bas (*Romani History X*, November 2017)

Damian Le Bas is and will be remembered for how he mapped the world or, better, for how he mapped it *anew*. 'Maps are not mirrors of reality, but rather "mobile engines" that distort and co-constitute the outside world' (Loughan, Olsson and Schouten 2015: 23). In Damain's provocative distortion of the world, he has confronted his audience with the bothersome truth that the world is often not moved at all by the violence implied in the highly intimidating representations of whom Gypsies, Roma, Travellers or other 'outsiders' would be according to many mainstream views. Therefore, on his own and together with Delaine, he has turned the world upside down, not simply to replace images with counter-images, but to put representation and its impact at the eye of the storm – the eye that Damian has multiplied so frequently without reproducing it. His maps do not simply create alternative geographies of the spaces he mapped and the worlds he was critical of, since his way of doing art challenges both mapping in its classical mimetic understanding and familiar frameworks by which representational thinking tends to 'geo-graph' our worlds, fully populated with borders and other obstacles that actively produce insiders and outsiders, and hamper mutual understanding and respect.

However, Damian's maps are also not about projecting desirable spaces or utopias onto the world, as if he were just dealing with topography or, for that matter, with 'utopography'. If mapping 'domesticates the unknown and the invisible, making them known and visible, making them available for use', as John Pickles (2004: 7) states, then Damian Le Bas has tried to domesticate the invisibilization of Roma, Gypsies and Travellers, and the exclusion mechanisms that have affected them throughout history, in order to visibilize how these mechanisms could be countered. In his artworks, Damian Le Bas is a cartographer who is fully aware of the geopolitics of identity and representation, and who has turned maps into places of experimentation into how diverse tracings could be combined and set in motion to see things differently. The way in which Damian has worked as a ludic, inspiring, inventive and – not to forget – hardworking and highly productive cartographer 'leads the viewer of the "map" to realize how problematic it is to think in terms of outside/inside . . . but at the same time [how] our inclination to do so is permanently there' (Loughan, Olsson and Schouten 2015: 36).

This double confrontation – problematizing the common view and alienating the viewer from the familiar – is connected with what could perhaps be considered as the topological quality of his work. Topology is that discipline of mathematics that focuses on all kinds of possible deformations of objects through stretching or folding, but never through tearing and then gluing them together again. The topological quality of Damian Le Bas's work 'deconstructs our cartographic imagination based on clear borders and immutable positioning systems, while still allowing for a spatialized, albeit moving representation of social reality' (Loughan, Olsson and Schouten 2015: 36). Damian did not cut the original, geographic maps that he used as the starting points for many of his artworks; rather, he treated their original two-dimensional parameters with care, respecting their plain realities, but he stretched these parameters as much as possible to turn land into borderless oceans filled with faces and eyes that encourage the viewer to travel the world anew, and allowing, most importantly, the introduction of both perspective and introspection.

Particularly in the course of the last decade, Damian Le Bas mobilized his cartography to visibilize the politics of past mappings. In 2008, he used a map of *Österreich – Ungarn 1914* ('Austria – Hungary 1914') as the basis for one of his artworks, while, in 2013, he used a 1938 political map of Europe to create his 'Back to the Future! Safe European Home 1938' (Figure 1.6). Critically focusing on the ways in which Europe had been mapped on the eve of the

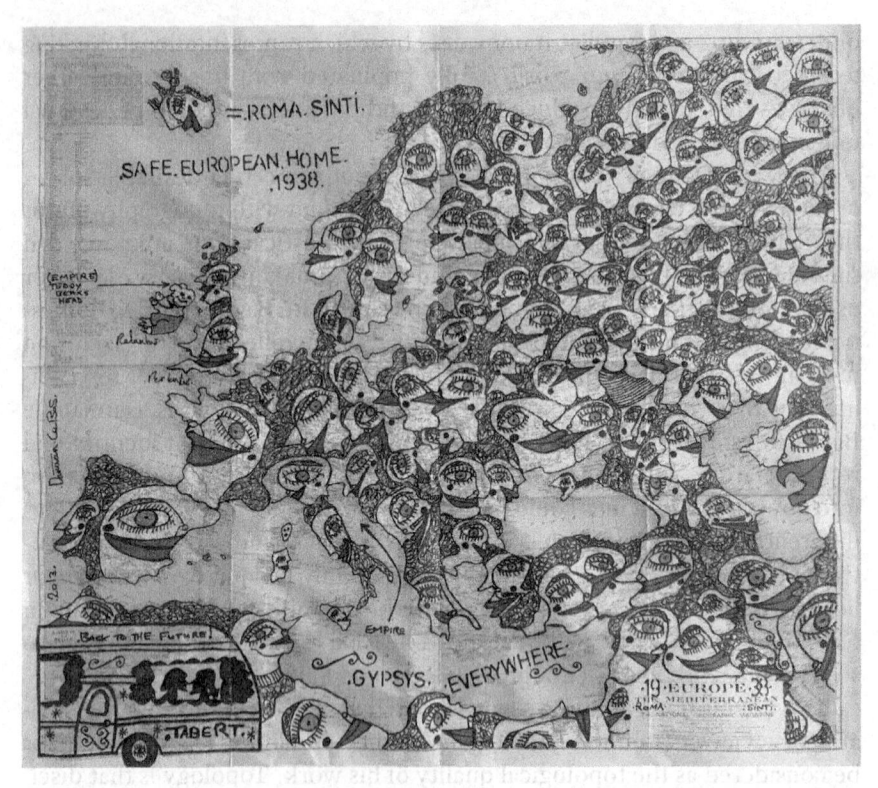

FIGURE 1.6 'Back to the Future! Safe European Home 1938', Damian Le Bas, 2013. Courtesy of The Le Bas Archive & Collection. Photographic credit: Huub van Baar.

two main catastrophes in its modern history, and linking past, present and future in the redirected *Safe European Home?* art project, Damian had given his work its fundamental signature. Then as now, Europe has been densely populated by his characteristic faces, eyes and lips, to give the continent and its cartographic history a new look, a novel taste, which, most of all, allows us to see Europe anew with and through other eyes. In the unforgettable scene in *The Great Dictator* (1940) in which a caricature of Hitler plays with the world as a huge balloon that finally and suddenly bursts in his own face, Charlie Chaplin had invented a new cinematic language to movingly and ironically cross-examine new manifestations of empire. Similarly, Damian Le Bas invented a novel visual language – that of his cartography – to reflect in a ludic yet critical way on past and present manifestations of empire, and most crucially on the dictatorship of canonical representation. For ages, maps have been weaponized visuals used by the powerful to manipulate how we look at the world, and to normalize its territorialization in geopoliticized entities. 'Conflict and War is all about borders', Damian once wrote,

FIGURE 1.7 'They Don't Want Us in the EU' (*Italia Antiqua*), Damian Le Bas, 2015. Courtesy of The Le Bas Archive & Collection. Photographic credit: Huub van Baar.

and 'conflicts are planned on maps'.⁴ In Damian Le Bas's new cartographic language, such territorializations of the world – creating borders and, thus, 'empires of privileged insiders' and 'realms of scapegoated outsiders' – have disappeared through the decolonization of cartographic imaginations that are based on separated, politicized identities.

Damian Le Bas went yet one step further. In the final years of his life, in 2015 and 2016, he totally reworked maps of *Italia Antiqua* (Ancient Italy, see Figure 1.7) and *Imperium Romanum* (the Roman Empire), changing the latter into 'the Romani Empire', thereby ironically dotting the 'i's in Europe's cartographic history since antiquity. Many cities in Europe are proudly exhibiting their ancient Roman origins. Often, old Roman excavations have been carefully preserved and turned into touristic attractions, such as in the old city centres of Vienna and Plovdiv. When you have Roman excavations, the archaeological argument seems to go, you are 'truly European'. Damian's final cartographic interventions in contemporary art history ridicule this kind of exhibitionism and the involved fetishism of origins, and the search for them. He could equally have ridiculed the Council of Europe's (1993) statement that 'the Gypsies', who are 'living scattered all over Europe, not having a country to call their own . . . are a true European minority'. The 'truth' is neither laid in vast territorialization nor in radical dispersion. Having neither Roman excavations nor a country to call their own does not imply that the true foundations are still somewhere else or somewhere underneath. 'There are no maps that show the infrastructure of the underground world of the Gypsy', Damian once stated,[5] thereby demythologizing the myth of whatever kind of the 'true origins' of the Roma. Damian Le Bas's conquests for the Romani Empire have taken place where the Roma Army has wholeheartedly started to exhaust the tyranny of established, stereotypical representation. Ultimately, this is how what Damian and Delaine Le Bas called 'the Gypsy revolution' has made a firm and impressive start.

Huub van Baar is an Assistant Professor of Political Theory at the Institute of Political Science at the Justus-Liebig University of Giessen in Germany. He is also a Senior Research Fellow at the Amsterdam Centre for Globalisation Studies (ACGS) at the Faculty of Humanities of the University of Amsterdam, and an affiliated researcher at the Amsterdam Centre for European Studies (ACES). He coordinates a research project on the formation and transformation of Romani minorities in modern European history, which is part of the research programme Dynamics of Security: Forms of Securitization in Historical Perspective (2014–2021), funded by the German Research Foundation (DFG). He has published widely on the position and political and cultural representation of Europe's Romani minorities, predominantly from the angle of how their situation has changed at the nexus of citizenship, security and development. He has published peer-reviewed articles in, for instance, *Social Identities, Antipode, Journal of Ethnic and Migration Studies, City, Third Text, Citizenship Studies, International Journal of Cultural Policy* and *Society and Space*. He is the author of *The European Roma: Minority Representation, Memory and the Limits of Transnational Governmentality* (F&N, 2011) and the main co-editor of *Museutopia: A Photographic Research*

Project by Ilya Rabinovich (Alauda, 2012, with Ingrid Commandeur) and *The Securitization of the Roma in Europe* (Palgrave Macmillan, 2019, with Ana Ivasiuc and Regina Kreide). He is currently finalizing a monograph entitled *The Ambiguity of Protection: Spectacular Security and the European Roma*.

Notes

I very much thank Delaine Le Bas and her son Damian James Le Bas for taking such great care over Damian's work and legacy, now that they have been confronted with the incredible loss of his enjoyable, friendly, lovely and humorous company. I thank Moritz Pankok of Gallery Kai Dikhas in Berlin for our discussions about Damian's work and for his hospitality during my visits to the gallery's archives and exhibitions.

1. Elsewhere, I have extensively discussed what Trumpener calls 'the European memory problem' in the context of Romani memorial cultures and the simultaneous, ambiguous trend to governmentalize Holocaust remembrance for pedagogical reasons of Roma inclusion (van Baar 2011: 271-313).
2. Retrieved 22 November 2018 from the site 'Romani.embassy.com', see http://romani-embassy.com/?page_id=45.
3. The 'blonde, blue-eyed angel Maria' – as she was portrayed in international media – is a Romani girl who lived in a Romani shantytown in Greece, when, in October 2013, she was taken away from her adoptive parents by the Greek police because they suspected that she was a non-Romani child 'stolen' by those who claimed – rightfully, it turned out – to be her adoptive parents. For more on this story and its wider context, see van Baar 2014.
4. Retrieved 22 November 2018 from http://damianlebasartbrut.com/category/shows-exhibitions/gypsyland/.
5. See the previous note.

References

Bahlmann, L., and M. Reichelt (eds). 2011. *Reconsidering Roma: Aspects of Roma and Sinti Life in Contemporary Art*. Göttingen: Wallstein.

Baker, D., and M. Hlavajova (eds). 2013. *We Roma: A Critical Reader in Contemporary Art*. Utrecht: BAK/Valiz.

Bardi, A. 2006. 'The Gypsy as Trope in Victorian and Modern British Literature', *Romani Studies* 16(1): 31-42.

Bogdal, K.-M. 2011. *Europa erfindet die Zigeuner*. Frankfurt am Main: Suhrkamp.

Brittnacher, H.R. 2012. *Leben auf der Grenze: Klischee und Faszination des Zigeunerbildes in Literatur und Kunst*. Göttingen: Wallstein.

Chakrabarty, D. 2000. *Provincializing Europe.* Princeton, NJ: Princeton University Press.
Clendinnen, I. 1999. *Reading the Holocaust.* Cambridge: Cambridge University Press.
Council of Europe. 1993. 'Gypsies in Europe', Recommendation 1203. Strasbourg.
Danbakli, M. (ed.). 2001. *Roma, Gypsies: Texts Issued by International Institutions.* Hatfield: University of Hertfordshire Press.
European Parliament. 1984. 'Education for Children of Parents who have No Fixed Abode', European Parliament Working Documents 1983–1984'. 12 March. Brussels.
Fonseca, I. 1995. *Bury Me Standing: The Gypsies and their Journey.* London: Vintage.
Galerie Kai Dikhas. 2011. *Ort des Sehens – Kai Dikhas – Place to See 1: Lita Cabellut, Delaine Le Bas, Alfred Ullrich.* Berlin: Braus.
———. 2012. *Ort des Sehens – Kai Dikhas – Place to See 2: Damian Le Bas, Gabi Jiménez, Imrich Tomáš, Ceija Stojka, Kiba Lumberg, Nihad Nino Pušija.* Berlin: Braus.
———. 2013. *Ort des Sehens – Kai Dikhas – Place to See 3: George Vasilescu, Manolo Gómez Romero, Tamara Moyzes, Kálmán Várady, András Kállai, Henrik Kállai.* Berlin: Braus.
Gay y Blasco, P. 1999. *Gypsies in Madrid: Sex, Gender and the Performance of Identity.* Oxford: Berg.
Junghaus, T., and K. Székely (eds). 2007. *Paradise Lost: The First Roma Pavilion.* Munich: Prestel.
Loughan, V., C. Olsson and P. Schouten. 2015. 'Mapping', in C. Aradau et al. (eds), *Critical Security Methods: New Frameworks for Analysis.* London: Routledge, pp. 23–56.
Pankok, M. (ed.). 2019. *Akathe Te Beshen: Die Sammlung Kai Dikhas.* Berlin: Braus.
Patrut, I.-K. 2014. *Phantasma Nation: 'Zigeuner' und Juden als Grenzfiguren des 'Deutschen' (1770–1920).* Würzburg: Königshausen & Neumann.
Pickles, J. 2004. *A History of Spaces: Cartographic Reason, Mapping and the Geo-coded World.* London: Routledge.
Reuter, F. 2014. *Der Bann des Fremden: Die fotografische Konstruktion des 'Zigeuners'.* Göttingen: Wallstein.
Simhandl, K. 2006. '"Western Gypsies and Travellers" – "Eastern Roma": The Creation of Political Objects by the Institutions of the European Union', *Nations and Nationalism* 12(1): 97–115.
Solms, W. 2008. *Zigeunerbilder: Ein dunkles Kapitel der deutschen Literaturgeschichte.* Würzburg: Königshausen & Neumann.
———. 2018. *'Zwei Zigeuner, schwarz und gräulich': Zigeunerbilder deutscher Dichter.* Frankfurt am Main: Klostermann.
Spivak, G. 2012. *Making Visible.* Retrieved 10 August 2018 from https://www.igkultur.at/artikel/making-visible.
Stewart, M. 1997. *The Time of the Gypsies.* Oxford: Westview.
Trumpener, K. 1992. 'The Time of the Gypsies: A "People without History" in the Narratives of the West', *Critical Inquiry* 18: 843–84.
van Baar, H. 2011. *The European Roma: Minority Representation, Memory and the Limits of Transnational Governmentality.* Amsterdam: F&N.
———. 2014. 'The Emergence of a Reasonable Anti-Gypsyism in Europe', in T. Agarin (ed.), *When Stereotype Meets Prejudice: Antiziganism in European Societies.* Stuttgart: ibidem-Verlag, pp. 27–44.
———. 2015. 'The Perpetual Mobile Machine of Forced Mobility: Europe's Roma and the Institutionalization of Rootlessness', in Y. Jansen, R. Celikates and J. de Bloois

(eds), *The Irregularization of Migration in Contemporary Europe*. Lanham, MD: Rowman & Littlefield, pp. 71–86.

———. 2017. 'Evictability and the Biopolitical Bordering of Europe', *Antipode* 49(1): 212–30.

Von Hagen, K. 2009. *Inszenierte Alterität: Zigeunerfiguren in Literatur, Oper und Film*. Munich: Wilhelm Fink.

PART II

❋ ❋ ❋

SOCIETY, HISTORY AND CITIZENSHIP

CHAPTER 2

❄ ❄ ❄

The Impact of Multifaceted Segregation on the Formation of Roma Collective Identity and Citizenship Rights

Júlia Szalai

Segregation stands out as a most pervasive trait of ethnic relations in Central and Eastern Europe. It affects Roma first and foremost. Despite the criticisms and long-standing claims of the European Union (EU) to launch policies and measures that effectively combat forced ethnic separation, and despite the spread of civil initiatives for desegregation in local communities, enforced isolation of Roma from the majority communities and their frequent concentration into Roma enclaves remain distinctive characteristics of interethnic relations in the region. Furthermore, the ethnic content of separation is underscored by important implications of class. Efforts to draw clear demarcation lines between the non-poor and the poor are easily argued for by cultural and behavioural traits that are most tellingly demonstrated by the 'otherness' of Roma. In addition to these multiple implications, segregated arrangements in housing, education or work are considered 'normal': for large groups of society – be they teachers, employers, doctors or simply fellow citizens in the neighbourhood – enforced separation and its implied downgrading of Roma are self-evident. A vast array of ideologies and moral reasoning is at play to strengthen convictions about the 'well-deserved' forcing aside of those who are said not to contribute to the social good, or who at best do so to a significantly lesser degree than the majority.

At the same time, there are signs of increasing awareness in Romani communities of structural embeddedness and, thus, structurally conditioned damages of segregation: a growing number of local NGOs engage in innovative anti-segregation programmes, while others initiate movements to expose the devastating implications of segregation on human and minority rights. Although thus far these civil initiatives have not been strong enough to secure meaningful changes in the political domain, their impact on developing a politicized language of segregation and on partially reframing the public discourse on class and ethnicity should not be underestimated (Vermeersch 2006).

While segregation undeniably provides a convenient framework for organizing and controlling the relationship between ethnicity and poverty, there are still important interests and arguments for countervailing and ultimately eliminating it. Obviously, the strongest interests, whether manifested or yet in passivity, are of those Roma who currently pay the biggest price. But beyond this, the majority also have important interests in undoing these devastating relationships. It is worth mentioning a few straightforward associations. The overall potency and efficiency of education would be enhanced by inclusive schooling: survey results show that segmentation and its accompanying deep inequalities have an adverse impact on the performance and general worldview of even those in the top echelons (Kézdi and Surányi 2009). Likewise, greater mobility, better adjustment and more efficient production could be attained by dismantling profound segmentation in the labour market: research shows that the deep divisions – usually justified by inequalities in knowledge and skills – block the potential of cooperation and hinder the application of modern technologies (Bauder 2001). And the list goes on. Desegregation in housing could make for greater geographical mobility for all, as well as increase safety and improve general health conditions for entire communities (Huttman, Saltman and Blauw 1991; Maloutas 2004; Maloutas and Fujita 2016).

While these and similar interests in desegregation are certainly at play, those for maintaining segregation seem stronger and more widespread; this is clearly demonstrated by the many variations and the powerful institutionalization of the phenomenon. Why is this the case? In light of the manifold important interests disbanding segregation, one has to ask: what are the social mechanisms that hinder desegregation and keep reproducing various forms and frames of forceful separation along lines of ethnicity with all the inescapable social class implications? Is this merely a matter of conflicting interests of lesser or greater potency, or are there certain traits of segregation that make it an outstandingly convenient way of expressing and reproducing social inequalities? If so, what are these implied gains, and who are the winners?

These questions and considerations call for a closer look at segregation from some important perspectives. The first among these relates to structural implications. While, overall, segregation tends to turn prevailing ethnic inequalities into marginalization and social exclusion, the various patterns of social segmentation are not uniform in this regard. This calls for a closer look at the different manifestations of segregation, and invites comparisons across the various institutional settings and domains of daily life where it takes place. In simple terms, we have to ask questions about the peculiarities of the segregating mechanisms and also find the intersecting associations between them.

The second perspective puts identity into focus. In addition to the deprivation that segregation induces in the social position and social belonging of Roma, the questioning of their personal and collective integrity and imbuing their collective self-evaluation and identity with self-depreciation, are, perhaps, the most dangerous consequences. Accumulated experience of devaluation and personal questioning and frequent ad hominem criticism grow into a built-in trauma of the personality that often becomes the source of troubled relationships within and outside the community. While exposition is widespread, the sources of resilience and self-protection are weak. Close parental relationships and strong ties within the community might help, but immediate calls for labour at distance, other sudden drives to leave and the challenges of poverty might suspend the protective ties together with the shield of self-reliance (Miller-Karas 2015). By undermining integrity and self-esteem, the roots of belonging are slashed and membership of the collective becomes a shame that one has to deny. However, without supportive ties to the community, Roma (and also the poor sharing their fate) are incapable as individuals of struggling for mere subsistence, let alone for an improvement in their condition and status. Notwithstanding, hacking away at the identity of the collective has further implications. This process erode notions of social belonging that, in turn, provide the basis for citizenship. Dismantling the unifying and universal contents of citizenship generates secondary status that leads to a differentiated understanding of basic rights and dangerously affects national cohesion, while preventing Roma from participating in fundamental social practices and accessing fundamental provisions. One of my primary aims is to show that probably the most severe straightforward consequence of segregation is fracturing citizenship rights and, thereby, eroding unity and a universal belonging to the nation.

The discussion that follows, by presenting the variegated manifestations of segregation and the drives that make for its interminable reproduction, is based on a vast array of empirical evidence that is drawn from several recent studies. Two sources are of key importance in introducing some most powerful forms of segregation and for demonstrating intersectionality. The first is the comparative European research project 'Ethnic Differences in Education and Diverging Prospects for Urban Youth in an Enlarged Europe' (EDUMIGROM) that investigated, among other things, the varied formations of inequalities and the ways in which these produce segregation in the Czech Republic, Hungary, Romania and Slovakia. The discussion below builds on evidence that this study brought up about the clashing interests of families representing the non-Roma majority and the Roma in their diverging approaches to schooling, which manifested in a great variety of segregating currents in urban communities (Szalai and Schiff 2014).

My second key source is the comparative study 'Faces and Causes of Roma Marginalization in Local Contexts: Hungary, Romania, Serbia' (Szalai and Zentai 2014), which looks at the formation of segregated arrangements in clusters of settlements by focusing on the emerging associations in education, labour relations, housing and the relations of local politics and policymaking. This study provides important insights into intersectionality and the impact of erecting walls along racial/ethnic lines that give rise to extreme deprivation in terms of a sharply reduced share and participation of Roma in the community's life. Besides these studies, lessons and examples are taken from the recent literature that has evolved in the region to understand and critically analyse the various forms and manifestations of racial/ethnic segregation.

The Manifold Manifestations of Segregation

Segregation embraces a great number of phenomena. It is an overarching concept that covers acts and processes of forceful separation directly initiated or indirectly developed on grounds of unequal distribution of power. In other words, those with power over those who are deprived of it are inclined to cement this state by drawing visible or invisible demarcation lines between themselves and those whom they consider 'other'. In this sense, segregation primarily denotes processes, acts and inclinations for constructing such lines of difference. Yet, acts and efforts of expressing difference can be rather impartial, without implications for differences in status, value contents and meaningful representations. Therefore, it is important to see that, besides expressing difference, there have to be additional implications that transform impartiality into hierarchical categories and deprive the subordinated and/or powerless group of sharing equal values and norms. There are further important distinctions on the map of segregation: firstly, if turning the difference into forceful separation is temporary or terminal; and secondly, if it bears on the basic rights of those affected or, while maintaining a certain degree of equity, it limits their scope of participation with a potential for later correction. These differences have important implications on whether the options for countervailing forceful separation remain open or whether segregation becomes an all-inclusive state of degradation and exclusion.

An example in the field of education illustrates these differences. Up until recently, it has been a widespread practice throughout Central and Eastern Europe to enrol Roma children in so-called 'special schools'. These schools apply special curricula with limited contents, and those concluding primary education in them can, at best, continue studying in the lowest-ranked special vocational units, and are deterred 'by definition' from applying to ordinary secondary schools. Such a separation has an enormous impact on the entire adult career and, thus, represents a form of segregation that automatically results in exclusion. In Hungary, special schools were closed down a few years ago, and a new definition of 'special educational needs' (SEN) has been used to channel selection towards a reduced curriculum. Although children with SEN are still often educated in separate settings, nevertheless, they are part of the same school and their teaching is based on extra provisions, but driven by the routine of ordinary instruction. It is not to say that the change erased segregation (it did not), but it turned the terminal into temporary, and washed away straightforward institutional distinctions. As a result, despite still important inequalities in performance and the continuation of studies, the rates of participation of Roma students in secondary education and their performance scores have been improving substantially. And what is perhaps even more important: while Roma children's forceful placement in special schools offered an institutional base for all-round exclusion and deprivation of the right to study and work, their still widespread categorization as SEN-students lacks such institutional frameworks and thus, on its own, leaves the door ajar for corrective measures towards inclusion.

Similar examples of differences in the depth and scope of impact can be seen when looking at employment. It is true that, when employed at all, Roma tend to work in the least protected and physically most exhausting segments of the labour market. This is a clear case of segregation keeping Roma employees away from other groups and also limiting co-operation with them. Nevertheless, their status as employees, the calculation of their remuneration, their vacation and union membership rights are kept within the framework of general rules that apply at a given firm. Even the potential for participating in training and, thereby, aspiring to better and higher positions remains open, although actual access to these channels proves limited.

The rapidly spreading practice of squeezing Roma into public works represents another form of segregation that has powerfully institutionalized 'otherness' and has led to exclusion. As an alternative to unemployment and as a scheme of regulating access to welfare provisions, public works offer very limited earnings for a limited time, and despite the governmental rhetoric of improving employability, participation in these schemes acts as a straightforward route to enduring exclusion (Albert 2015). By making it compulsory as a precondition for accessing welfare, by disregarding distinctions of vocation and qualification, by predetermining the length of participation, and by openly denying the opportunity to appeal, these programmes directly institutionalize 'otherness', define it as a basis for behavioural corrections, and practically shut the door that leads to the world of 'ordinary' labour – that is, it turns their case into exclusion (van Baar 2018). As the data show, public works easily become a self-sustaining, distinct domain from where people have no paths that might lead out (Bokov, Csoba and Hermann 2014).

The list of examples could easily be extended. Yet, the above amply demonstrate that there are important variations among the forms of segregation with regard to their impact on exclusion. The potency of the different forms, ranging from exhibiting distinctions while maintaining Roma social membership to producing all-round deprivation and exclusion, can be considered a key dimension to understanding the phenomenon.

The difference is important for two reasons. On the one hand, it suggests that not all forms of segregation are at the point of entering intersectional relations. As a tendency, the 'lighter' procedures of distinction leave the door open for changing individual situations and escaping unfavourable classification brackets. After all, aspirations and efforts to continue education away from segregated vocational training or investment in changing jobs for more rewarding constellations are clear demonstrations of two things simultaneously: that routes exist for escaping segregated arrangements, but that access to these routes is always individualized. The examples all tell the same story: outstanding individual effort, dedication and smartness provide the energy needed for entering alternative pathways, and, while such individual performances deserve acknowledgement and appreciation, it is important to note that the devastating collective implications of segregation remain entirely unaffected. Nevertheless, the partial permeability of the segregated constructs implies that these arrangements are usually too weak to be merged with other forms of segregation, and generate a complexity of exclusionary associations. Hence, they generally remain open to questioning and withdrawal.

At the same time, by leaving some room for individual manoeuvring, the above-mentioned 'lighter' forms of segregation have a dual message with regard to collective identity. While they do not differ from harsher forms in applying deeply personalized ideologies that address the behavioural deficits, bad habits and questionable values of Roma, such negative arguments are intermingled with recognition of individual efforts, dedication and performance (all of which are utterly lacking in the ideological underpinning of more abrasive forms of segregation). The mixture carries the message of 'developmental potentials' and implies, however hesitantly, the majority's openness to making compromises. In this second sense, there remains some room for reconstructing collective identity and for building it on reassured self-esteem and further efforts for recognition.

The distinction between the 'lighter' and 'harsher' forms of segregation leads us to a closer look at intersectionality. It seems the 'lighter' forms remain lighter because of their preserved potential for individual escape, which usually aims to leave behind all negative evaluations and categorizations. This is possible precisely because of the one-dimensional character of the categorization, which does not engage with other aspects regarding distinct spheres and domains of life. In contrast, the harsher forms could easily grow to all-encompassing degradation, driven by forming a chain of depreciations in fields that are principally independent. And this is how we arrive at intersectional forms of segregation that best provide for the majority's needs and interests by keeping Roma at bay.

It could be argued that intersected segregation is the true and most prevalent form of the phenomenon. This is less the case because of the nature of prejudices that tend to extend devaluation from childbearing to work or to the running of the household. The primary reason behind this form of segregation is the structural nature and related institutional arrangements of non-Roma/Roma relations. Indeed, these structures are constructed as manifestations of separation. Let us have a look at them.

The most obvious and visible domain is housing. The spread of Roma settlements, slums and even racially ghettoized villages have implications for schooling and work. It is easy and pretty straightforward to designate a primary school for children who come from a Roma neighbourhood. Their teaching in Roma classes simply appears as a natural extension of their home conditions. Even if prejudices do not play a role, it is easy to say that, on the ground of their neighbourhood relations, these children will help and support each other, thus keeping them together makes teaching easier, and perhaps less discipline is needed than if they were mixed up with other groups of the community-at-large. However, such dual segregation – at the intersection of housing and schooling – enlarges risks of exclusion. Children from the Roma segment (slum, village) are deprived of entering into peer relations with those outside their neighbourhood, and are also prevented from observing different models of behaviour, different values and different cultures. This way, the strong foundations of forceful separation, accompanying them well into adulthood, are developed through forms of intersectionality that seem self-evident but actually provide a strong basis for unbroken reproduction. In addition, these institutionalized patterns of segregation feed into the majority's prejudices. Run-down conditions and serious infrastructural shortages are interpreted as manifestations of Roma carelessness and neglect, which is then extended to the children who do not value school and do not aspire to better themselves through actual effort. These prejudices reinforce the widespread conviction that it is proper to keep Roma schooling apart. At the same time, the accompanying complex ideology is powerful enough to hide the interests maintaining the arrangements of multifaceted segregation, by combining the domains of housing and schooling. At the same time, these interests are of great importance and feed intersectionality. Primarily, there is generally great competition for resources in the locality (the municipality), and so the maintenance of a separate Roma segment – which has often come about after evicting Roma from their earlier placement – simply reduces the number of groups involved in the competition. Secondly, status implications are also important. The visibly poor conditions of the Roma neighbourhood increase the relative value of the other ones, including even those of the poor among the non-Roma community. These conditions are simply reinforced by segregating the schooling of young inhabitants inside the Roma segment. The message is that it is viable to construct an entire Roma life according to segregated conditions that make their living more organic and, at the same time, noticeably different from that of the majority community. And, despite the widespread insecurity of daily living, gradual impoverishment, frequent unemployment and unsatisfactory conditions in work, this marked separation provides telling evidence of the higher status and social involvement of even the poorer groups of the majority.

Similar examples can be identified when housing and work enter intersectionality; their tight relations produce virtually inescapable, new qualities of segregation. The key issue here is unemployment: be they urban slums, separated segments on the outskirts of cities and towns, or ghetto-villages populated almost exclusively by Roma, all such communities experience high rates of unemployment that distinguish them from communities dominated by the majority. The 40 to 90 per cent rate of unemployment in these ethnic communities has several corollaries: it (re)shapes household economies and makes them dependent on welfare; it pushes members of the community into the uncontrollable relations of the informal economy; it invites child labour and thus breaks young people's educational career; and in general, it removes contact and cooperation with the outside world. Intersectionality between housing and labour makes it very easy for the non-Roma to find and identify the potential subjects for extending or, for that matter, limiting labour market participation according to the changing needs the market generates. The recently launched and expanding public works programmes give a formalized framework to such never-ending fluctuation. By being frequently tailored for the local Roma community, these programmes help local businesses by providing cheap labour, while reducing competition by adjusting the length and frequency of participation to the needs of the local production. It is easy to see that the availability of large groups of Roma workers reduces the cost and time of seeking employees for certain tasks – and so it is the advantages of intersectionality of housing and labour, which neither factor could provide alone, that make access so attractive and straightforward. At the same time, the interests of the majority are not restricted to advantages in employment. Partly by saving expenditure, and partly by direct control over what Roma should perform, the vast array of personal and domestic services that they offer in the informal economy make an important contribution to the household economies of the local middle class. But one should emphasize that organizing Roma into 'shifts', according to their collective geographic availability and their shared compulsion due to unemployment, brings cheap labour into local development schemes, and makes these schemes appear truly collective initiatives. Finally, disciplinary implications should be mentioned as well. The collective appearance that Roma poverty is generated by widespread unemployment (what is more, by long-term unemployment), adds visible evidence to the widely held conviction that Roma are uncivilized, lack inspirations for decency, are lazy and negligent at work, and are unreliable employees. These arguments are accentuated by assumptions that Roma abuse the welfare system and get unjustifiable access to its provisions. With all these implications, public works are considered as 'Roma terrain', to be avoided by all means, even by poor non-Roma. This way, again, the impoverished lower-middle class is strengthened in its position, and gains access to additional clear distinctions that separate their poverty from that of Roma, the latter being something utterly different in both roots and appearance.

The above examples put housing into the focus of intersectionalities. However, it would be misleading to assume that it is only housing that enters into intersecting relations: if interests behind them are strong enough, and if intersectionality brings about new, powerful manifestations of separation, then new associations can be developed across any of the spheres and institutions of daily life. As we saw earlier, certain types of segregation are weaker than others and, thus, are less likely to enter intersectionality. However, there are no domains in which only weak formations would occur. Their stronger counterparts are ready to enter intersecting relations across different areas and, thus, to draw the entire domain under powerful manifestations of forceful separation. At the same time, these strong formations of segregation cannot be 'created' at will. As the various examples indicate, massive collective interests are assumed to enter the stage where intersecting arrangements can provide outstandingly potent manifestations of the distinction between 'us' and 'them', and expect no additional investment to maintain established distinctions and separations.

A telling example of energetic efforts to draw up lines of separation is provided by the intersecting relations between education and work, where intersectionality has developed a new institutional framework of ghetto-like segregation across the expanding schemes of public works. In this context, we have to look at two, initially independent processes: the deepening segmentation of secondary-level education, and new responses to long-term unemployment by organizing a new work segment. Apart from the growing inequalities in the quality and the cultural contents of education in both theoretical and technical secondary schools, recent years have also brought about a deep hierarchization in vocational training that is meant to offer meaningful responses to the deepening differences between professions and occupational qualifications. By applying ever-stricter entrance examinations and performance requirements in earlier education, differentiated enrolment has become the rule in this domain as well. It follows that poorly performing Roma students – who usually come from weak segregated primary schools – are almost automatically referred to the lowest-ranked segments of vocational training that many leave prior to gaining a certificate that would, anyway, be of limited use. With no access to the more rewarding segments of the system, many of them drop out and seek work either in the household or in the informal economy. Their road to public works is straightforward: either as young unemployed, or young people with low 'employability', public works remain the only 'visible' domain of their existence. Intersectionality between the low segments of vocational training and public works creates a unifying framework that keeps poor Roma youth under control, and utilizes their work according to the changing needs of the regular labour market. The association between education and work is reinforced by the concomitant ideologies: harsh segregation of these young people is argued by parental failure to teach them the necessary values and behavioural norms and, thereby, exposing them to the corrective measures of the community at large. This way, intersectionality appears as a natural and, at the same time, most effective response of society.

So far, the emergence of the varying strong, multifaceted manifestations has been discussed. It is, however, equally important to look at the ways in which such intersecting formations become the dominant manifestations of segregation, and how they can be perpetuated undisturbed. For a better understanding, we now have to turn to the ways in which Roma communities respond to segregation, and how their potential for self-defence and independence are affected.

The Sources of Community Self-Protection and Identity

While segregation in its manifold manifestations is a shared experience for Roma communities, there are great differences regarding the ways they protect themselves against the damage and disadvantages that segregation causes, both to them as individuals and to the community as a whole. These differences partly follow from the diverse histories and internal structures of the communities that, in turn, designate the positions of their members, and are partly influenced by the ways different communities construct their identity – a component that usually turns out to be the strongest constituent of the strategies that they apply and cultivate in their external contacts. These differences become particularly important in informing self-protection against extra-strong forms of segregation generated by intersecting relations of exclusion and appearing in forceful separation from the outer world. As we will see, relatively strong and intact communities are usually potent enough to avoid subordination to such terminal and inescapable forms of deprivation, while internally divided and weaker communities often lose the battle against such external pressure and become hopelessly submerged in harsh subordination.

Differences in cohesion and capacity for self-protection emerge along various dimensions. The traditions of working relations with non-Roma, the adjunct internal division of tasks and roles, common memories of the genesis of the community and of ancestry, sub-ethnic divisions, religiosity and the unifying/dividing impact of church membership, success in finding ways to reduce poverty, and records of individual members who have successfully broken out with the help of the community – all of these matter.

For the most part, the case studies of communities that were visited in the framework of the two above-mentioned cross-country comparative studies revealed the extent of destruction that segregation exerted on the Roma collectives. Yet, examples demonstrating the power of the community to develop self-protection and to attain certain acknowledgement of their status could be found in all the participating countries. These exceptional cases had a similar history and some similar traits in all places. The strongest element of the more or less intact functioning of these potent Roma communities is usually their massive embeddedness in the community at large, developed over the preceding decades. Most frequently, it was cooperation between non-Roma and Roma in mining, construction and, less frequently, agriculture that was practised long enough to strengthen and organize relationships well beyond work, by reaching out to housing and education as well. Despite the closing down of the mines and agricultural cooperatives, which played a similar role apparently, the structures that were developed – most notably in housing and the use of the communal infrastructure – remained in place for a long time. One-time Roma workers are also keen to maintain them and friendly relations with their old companions. As the interviews showed, these relations were often transmitted to the children, who learn early enough to value them with regard to their own perspectives. In this framework, they accept parental authority, and follow without objection the rather rigid division of roles within the family. Independence from parental control is usually less important for them than for the majority of youth in their generation. Paternalism appears in their eyes as an asset that provides models and protection, and, in this regard, they do not differentiate between the patterns in the interethnic relations and the organizing principles of their own family.

Owing to their exceptionally strong ties with the majority, and also to the unconditional acceptance of inbuilt paternalism in these relations, these Roma communities demonstrate a good deal of resistance to the devastating impact of segregation. Of course, they are not entirely free from segregation: the children do not escape it in education, and those seeking employment do not escape it on the labour market. Nevertheless, the presence of past fellow workers or neighbours with whom Roma have a friendly relationship always provides a reference, and this is sometimes enough for protection. Although these background relationships are individual in nature, their density in the community makes it better and more acknowledged than other Roma associations in the village/town or in the wider region. This feeling of superiority feeds a rather high degree of cohesion which is explained, in turn, by the good qualities and externally acknowledged values of the community, and which is backed by a good deal of self-assurance and self-esteem. High collective self-esteem and strong cohesion are rare assets for members of the community: outward migration is rather infrequent, whilst the community protects itself by building thick walls against immigration. Because of an overarching approach to maintain self-defence on a collective basis, these communities are very stable in number and internal composition. Whilst this is an advantage in the short run, it might risk the ability to respond properly to new challenges and new forms of segregation in the long run. It is enough to think of the latest developments on the labour market to see that, all of a sudden, members of such communities lose the backing of former non-Roma co-workers, and find themselves unprotected amidst the conditions of public works that do not acknowledge such precedence.

Although the dense supportive network built with the active and enduring participation of non-Roma provides the strongest protection and also a firm basis for a positive self-evaluation of the community, the case studies revealed a similar role for religious alliances, as well as preserved memories of substantial associations and feelings of belonging, as part of the old history of the community. Religion develops and maintains strong ties; it organizes the practices, locations and expressions of togetherness, while providing hope and offering assistance in attempts to break out of poverty. At the same time, such communities are deeply structured by hierarchies according to the rule of the church. The designated roles towards the lower end of the scale underscore diminished value and subordination, and thus often reinforce the secular relations of discrimination and deprivation while adding the powerful notion of divine will to their acceptance. In communities where all families belong to the same church, religiosity assists members in their fights against segregation; and a charismatic leader may often offer extra help to young people in promoting their education. Furthermore, the social services field in the name of the churches is on the rise, and offers highly respected roles and tasks, especially to women. Because of all these advantages, religion becomes a strong base of cohesion and of positive values that members see in their community. At the same time, religiosity can also be a source of cleavage: when different parts of the community belong to different churches, or some refuse it altogether, the differentiation may give rise to destructive competition or openly unequal support for members of the different groups. Such ruptures increase the vulnerability of the entire Roma community and undermine the foundations of an all-encompassing collective identity. Holes in this fragile wall of protection affect primarily the weakest and least-protected members, but in the longer run can also erode the strength of the entire community. Weakened solidarity increases the defencelessness of all members, and opens platforms for separation and selectivity. The increased risk of external interventions strengthens segregational pressures, which then break up even the remnants of cohesion and mutual support. In retrospect, it is easy to see that unquestioned collective identity, and the all-embracing cohesion built on it, are the primary sources of self-defence and the strongholds for collective protection against segregation.

Consequently, in communities that are incapable of developing a uniting collective identity, exposure to segregation is high. As empirical evidence shows, such cases outnumber those that are built on solid foundations of cohesion and shared values of a strong collective identity (Virág 2010; Szalai and Zentai 2014). In addition to the many transient constellations, two types of collectives, prone to the lack of all-embracing identity and cohesion, can be distinguished: those with internal ruptures along sub-ethnic lines, and those with large groups of newcomers who do not become integrated into the host community. The first type usually grows out of preceding enforcements: in the name of urban renewal or development, a group of Roma is evicted and 'relocated' in an already existing community. Besides all the involved injustices in the process, the authorities have no sensitivity at all for sub-ethnic or cultural differences; 'Roma are Roma' in their eyes. However, the two communities find the enforced togetherness perhaps the greatest injustice. They close doors to each other, and refuse to accept representation by the others. Members of both groups hope to maintain their distinct entity and overlook any advantage of building up a shared collective. It goes without saying that acts of cohesion do not develop and that there are no common values that would appear as potential bases for a shared collective identity. These communities are exposed to hostility and a disruptive functioning to pass everything down to the individuals and their families. Such a breakdown of in-group solidarity exposes the community, and its individual members, to all forms of segregation, though some occur more frequently than others. Given the deep differences in the internal geography, arrangements founded on multifaceted enforcement in housing, education and/or work give rise to the most frequent collective forms of exclusion, with lasting implications by loosening the ties of collective self-protection.

The story is not so different in cases where a dividing line develops between the 'old' inhabitants and the 'newcomers'. The achievements of the 'old' community fade in the course of a transformation that the arrival of the 'new' group initiates. However, this change is perceived as a deep insult: the 'old' members see it as a form of degradation and a profound questioning of their rights. Mutual hostility between the two groups deepens the divide, whilst making the entire community prone to forces of segregation and exclusion. Furthermore, the multiplication of actors competing for employment, enforced share in the distribution of scarce services, and a much-criticized lack of modesty on the part of the 'newcomers' can contribute to frequent clashes between the two groups. Again, it is lack of cohesion and pervasive incapability to reshape collective identity by embracing now both groups, that are the unavoidable consequences. Without such protective constituents, the involved groups – both the 'old' and the 'new' – are easily exposed to segregation in all its malevolent, multifaceted forms.

While it makes a great difference whether cohesion and a self-assuring collective identity, with predominantly positive contents, can be constructed and/or maintained, it is important to underline the fragility of these traits. The most sensitive constituent is the relationship with the non-Roma, especially engaging in cross-ethnic neighbourhood contacts. Because of historical experience, which is continuously reinforced by contemporary encounters, Roma desires and claims for recognition belong to the deeply ingrained wishes and ambitions of their community. Acceptance and recognition by the 'other' is the most closely observed aspect of dealings with the majority. Such longing becomes even stronger as it turns into shaping individual aspirations and begins to function as the organizing principle of everyday life. In addition to all the negative aspects and consequences of segregation, some of the greatest damage it can do to Roma collectives is to question their recognition, and to replace self-assuring arguments with disparaging contents and evaluations. As we know from classical works on identity formation (Turner 1975; Tajfel 1981), the ways in which people see themselves and assess their place in their immediate and wider worlds easily absorb external contents, identify with their truth, and integrate them into their self-conceptualization. If these contents tend to devalue the person, then self-hatred and punitive tendencies towards the self become built into one's identity, and create the soil for even more destructive and negative conceptualizations. The process is similar on the collective level. Negation or withdrawal of recognition, and all the blaming for inaptness and a lack of proper values and skills, enter the community as pieces of an unquestionable truth, and slowly start to occupy the place of earlier positive contents that then fade away. Gradually, the community's self-image gets synchronized with external disparagement and, at this point, the collective is ready to internalize segregation, with all its ills, as something deserved. The mechanisms of internalization help to smooth the process of accepting segregation as the only viable arrangement for interethnic living, and may also help to maintain cohesion, despite the breakdown of a self-assured collective identity. However, communities deprived of trusting their own strength, and being denied recognition as equal partners in negotiations on the common issues of the community at large, lose much potential in their fight for equality and the observance of minority rights. In other words, the construction of a healthy and combatant collective identity directly impacts the contents of citizenship rights of all individual members.

Political Participation and Citizenship Rights

As we have seen, there is a direct relationship between the quality and contents of collective identity and the construct of individual identities. However, equally important are the implications for the politicization of the Roma cause that, in turn, shape the place of Roma in the national community as reflected in their citizenship rights. Politicization of the 'Roma issue' is a rather controversial process for three, partly interrelated, reasons. The first is widespread poverty, as the dominant status in the Roma community that fosters claims to reduce inequality and develop efficient anti-poverty programmes. This framing pays little attention to ethnic aspects, positions the Roma among a larger category of the poor, and identifies social policy as the main area where improvements could and should be attained. A second distinct strand puts emphasis on the harm and deprivations that Roma suffer on grounds of their ethnic minority status. In this approach, the focus of political claims is minority rights and their institutionalization. In this framework, the strengthening of the legal regulations of minority rights takes precedence above all other developmental aspects, and issues of inequality and poverty are left to general politics. The third source of ambiguities relates to the issue of representation. The question is always that of authenticity: given the weakness of Roma political participation, can non-Roma actors appear on the political stage on behalf of the Roma community? The varied reactions to this question influence the militancy of Roma politics and, thus, deeply impact the responses to the challenges of the first two strands.

No doubt, these broad currents have importantly influenced macro-level politics in shaping the national programmes of the Decade of Roma Inclusion or in informing the new, EU-instigated national Framework Strategies for governmental managing of the 'Roma problem'. However, macro-level negotiations took place far away from the Roma communities and gave but limited scope to any viable forms of Roma representation. These large-scale programmes and plans became the acknowledged products of dedicated professionals, experts and practitioners who often knew little about Roma, but who had decades-long experience in early childhood education, urban development, or the planning and management of anti-poverty programmes.

All this means is that we do not get any closer to the political interests or participation of rank-and-file Roma by looking at macro-level developments. It is not an exaggeration to say that the far-off daily forms of Roma involvement belonging to another world are not sensed by the larger community, which regards Roma political participation and action as practically non-existent. In fact, the reasoning goes further than that: the widespread conviction is that the ills and disadvantages that Roma suffer follow from their political disinterest. If they were more active, and took representation seriously, they could achieve more, simply because their presence and participation could not be circumvented.

And here we are back at segregation. In regard to the visibility of political participation, segregation means cutting off the possibilities of uniting forces with even neighbouring communities. Roma are often confined to small circles of parents struggling for better schooling for their children, of workers making efforts for decent employment, or of fellow inhabitants trying to gain a portion of local development funds to pave muddy streets in their poor and devastated neighbourhoods. Cohesive Roma communities engage in such struggles, but, at best, it is only the mayor and the local administrators who hear anything about their efforts. Roma are aware of the political dimension of their struggle. However, with no formal representation, all such politics become part of informal negotiations and, as such, the results can always be questioned and even negated. Of course, maintaining this informality is in the strong interest of the majority: it is exactly this and the concomitant invisibility of Roma as political actors that guarantees that 'doing good' and meeting the claims of the Roma community always appear as concessions that back prevailing paternalistic relations. And lessons from widespread practices show that segregation proves the best and safest arrangement to maintain and reproduce informality. It goes without saying that this truth is even more powerful in the case of weaker communities, which, if rarely united around certain collective claims, are easily broken up by internal divisions and vicious competition. In these cases, segregation works as a reflection of the internal divisions that do not help – in fact, they hinder – attempts at unity and cohesion, and at gaining recognition through representation. It follows that the political efforts of these communities languish before even becoming articulated.

The goals set by Roma political endeavours on the local level could, in principle, find their way to national politics. However, enclosure, in tight circles of segregation, often blocks such possibilities. The claims of the community appear disjointed from the demands and efforts of other communities, and are perceived by the public as non-embedded, exceptional cases. It is easy to see that the walls of separation are safeguarded by segregation, which blocks permeability and any attempts at uniting. A further consequence is the questioning of actions at the personal level. Apart from the exceptional cases of a few successful Roma mayors, emerging leaders of local mobilization are rarely considered by the community at large as being true representatives. For the most part, as long as they agree to control their people in exchange for meeting the claims of their community, they are accepted as 'representatives'. However, they are easily squeezed out when more powerful groups come to an agreement that better forgets Roma. At this moment, it turns out that representation is in vain (that it never was assumed with any sincerity); moreover, the frustrated Roma community can easily turn against its leader for failing to fulfil his envisioned mission.

Despite all the in-built weaknesses and limitations, the gradual politicization of claims and needs has implications, even within the confines of segregation. The first important aspect is collectivism. Be it a small local movement for desegregating the school where Roma children study, or the drafting of a claim for cleaning the waterpipes of the Roma settlement, these small movements always involve larger groups of the community, and the spontaneously emerging division of roles leads to larger-scale actions, movements and cooperation. The second important implication relates to language. Lacking a general vocabulary and deliberating of politics, the communities are left on their own to find the phrases that best express their claims and underlying arguments. Such exercises conclude in the gradual development of a peculiar language for Roma politics. Although these linguistic achievements and innovations remain confined, a potential is still there for them to enter the general linguistic discourse on representation. Third, the emergence of local-level Roma politics assumes new divisions of roles and duties. This might lead to strengthened cohesion, while, at the same time, adding to individual skills and behavioural routines. This way, participation in local politics, even amidst segregated conditions, involves an important learning process, concluding in new contents and skills that can be usefully transferred to other spheres of public appearance.

By considering these aspects and advantages, Roma political participation does not differ in any measure from the general trends: Roma do not exhibit indifference in politics, nor do they refuse opportunities for getting involved. Yet, very little of their endeavours appears in the public domain, and most of their initiatives and actions remain hidden and unremarked, even in the locality. The clue, as mentioned above, is the deep deconstruction of the Roma political body through segregation. It breaks up unities and potential alliances, and tends to organize the Roma community into miniscule units that are dressed up with some meaning. In this sense, segregation is a deeply political matter that has to be fought in the political arena. However, it is difficult to identify the actors whose ambition and goal would be desegregation in the political sense. Such interests should be framed by striving for strengthening national unity and the universality of citizenship rights.

National unity is a topic frequently referred to nowadays, but mostly in talks and actions against migrants and refugees. It is meant to denote the universal nature of values within the national framework, but cohesion and the overarching character of the political institutions of the nation are also implied. Roma always have an ambivalent position in the rhetoric: as parts of the universal political framework, they are acknowledged; yet, at the same time, their cultural 'otherness' sweeps them to the margins of a society embodying national unity, and imbues their national standing with ambiguities. Hostility towards 'cultural otherness' easily translates to accentuated estrangement of Roma that, in turn, inspires the withdrawal of independent Roma politics, and develops new patterns of opportunistic accommodation.

The situation is more complex with regard to citizenship rights. By considering them in the triad as developed by T.H. Marshall some sixty years ago (Bottomore and Marshall 1992), we recognize multiple ruptures. As to the practising of political rights, above we have seen abilities to develop forms of collective representation and participation, but have also seen the severe limitations and structurally created hindrances that reduce, if not wash away, any Roma political endeavours. In this sense, we can say that segregation is a barely visible, but most powerful measure of political disenfranchisement that does not need additional interventions to limit Roma participation in matters of politics and that works as an efficient arrangement for controlling the articulation of claims of the Roma community.

However, the most destructive impact of segregation can be seen in limiting and reducing the social rights of Roma. These rights, as components of citizenship, assume a common understanding of basic human values that involve, among others, an unconditional acknowledgement of togetherness, as well as a recognition of cultural differences. Furthermore, social rights encompass access to the provisions and services that society renders and guarantees to its members as equal constituents of the nation and the state. It is by acknowledging their belonging that entitlement to basic provisions and services is universally defined, and access to them is usually made easy by applying a few uniform rules and categorizations.

A closer look at these contents of social rights reveals severe Roma disadvantages and deprivations. The issue of broadly conceived 'culture' is at the heart of differentiating between the majority and the Roma minority, and of arguing for segregation. Roma culture is considered inferior and incapable of internalizing the values of modernity. It follows that, in the majority's eyes, this culture reproduces backwardness, and hinders the rise of the individual as the key actor of modern society. This reasoning calls for separation along cultural lines: Roma are forced to accept their 'otherness' and also the frameworks offered for practising their culture away from the majority. It is not by accident that it is education that provides the primary domain for such forceful separation. Segregated schools and classes not only reflect otherness, but also act as agents of socialization and, thereby, assist the undisturbed reproduction of contents that are denoted as 'inferior'. It is easy to see that segregation on cultural grounds devalues the entire Roma community and, consequently, deprives it of the foundations of self-esteem and a self-respecting identity. On its own, this seems enough to limit any politicization on cultural grounds that, more or less automatically, blocks any claims for equal value for different cultures or for diminishing their hierarchization.

It has to be added that segregation in education contributes not only to the devaluation of Roma culture, but also seriously affects a set of further basic rights. The forceful separation of Roma in poor-quality segments of the school system limits their right for free choice in education. As we saw above, these segregated segments practically shut the door in the face of young Roma seeking to continue their studies. Furthermore, the poor quality of teaching in segregated units, away from the mainstream, deprives Roma students of useable knowledge and contributes to early unemployment and exclusion from the labour market. Again, it is important to emphasize that these consequences grow out of segregation, without additional interventions. This is why segregation proves to provide a cheap and powerful social arrangement for fixing differentiations and turning them into exclusion as an ultimate form of social rights deprivation.

However, education is not the only domain with serious challenges to the notion of equal citizenship rights. As we have seen, housing is yet another important domain where segregation is flourishing. Let us now consider the implications for citizenship rights. Expropriation of land and the eviction of Roma to make room for more potent interests are clear examples of not only limiting but also cutting off the rights of the involved community. A further case of severe rights violations is the denial of ownership, which is equal to exclusion from the housing market, and also results in a stark limitation on the free right of Roma to move. In this way, Roma are forcefully designated to certain low-standard areas, while the maintenance of such segregated units reinforces the lack of mobility and keeps them under the strict control of the authorities. In this way, the right to decent housing simply does not work, and collective confinement to dilapidated areas just underscores the lack of opportunities for local improvement or change.

Segregation in housing and its implied collective deprivation lead to 'self-explanatory' exclusion from the distribution of developmental resources. Enforced acceptance of conditions is interpreted by the local authorities as a sign of consent, and, thus, housing segregation is extended to denying a share of collective resources or a serious undervaluation of the assigned amount. In this way, deprivation of rights to decent housing and unrestricted movement is extended by their exclusion from access to the collective assets and resources for improvement, which are often distributed without any preliminary deliberation of the needs of local Roma. In this process, the segregated units appear as if they were in their deplorable state by their own will. An unhealthy environment, the run-down state of the houses, the dusty roads and the lack of pretty gardens are conceived as the 'culture' of Roma, who would pay no attention to shared common areas and would neglect caring for them. Such arguments, then, are considered strong enough reasons to exclude Roma territories from a share of public funds and developmental resources.

Segregation also deeply affects the welfare rights of Roma, and does so in several ways. First, the welfare implications of long-term and terminal unemployment should be considered. Although there are important variations in the preceding employment histories, their impact fades as time passes. Instead, enduring joblessness becomes the shared experience that defines and homogenizes the statuses of the members of the Roma community. The most painful and endangering aspect of the new, homogenized status is collective detachment from social security that implies the loss of one's entitlement to a pension. Deprivation appears as fully justified. Since the whole build-up of social security is based on employment and the involved capacity of the employee to pay contributions that 'buy' later provisions, those lastingly out of employment lose the foundations of membership and become excluded after a while. Deprivation of the benefits under the umbrella of social security – ranging from sick pay to public provisions for childcare and various forms of pension – implies severe financial insecurity. But it is equally important that exclusion from social security concludes in losing membership in society at large, thus inducing the erosion of the foundations of citizenship rights. Those 'expelled' from social security become invisible, and invisibility is transferred to the entire community: what appears before the public is poverty, but the reasons for this state remain in the dark.

Yet, the story does not end here. Being cut off from gainful work and access to social security simultaneously means exclusive dependence on public funds in the form of means-tested welfare provisions. However, entitlement to these benefits is not automatic, and nor at all guaranteed. Being jobless and out of social security makes it seem that Roma are lazy and unorganized, and that their poverty follows from personal ineptitude and failures that appear uncorrectable due to their embeddedness in collective practices. In this domain, such depreciating arguments serve two simultaneous goals: they justify the majority's authority over Roma and also assist in economizing with the local resources. Their ideological foundations make the various welfare provisions easily questionable, and shaky in their content and magnitude. The arising uncertainties have their own function: they maintain relations of paternalism and subordination, and justify any disciplining. A further consequence is the emergence of 'welfare ghettos'. The Roma community, thus far enclosed into the multiple segregated segments of schooling, work and housing, now appears endangering public funds – that is, not only representing 'otherness', but creating adversities by their very existence. In this way, welfare rights are turned upside down: share in welfare becomes a source of shame, and, by its collective extension, welfare becomes a most criticized aspect of how the majority perceives Roma. This negativity was recently accentuated by associating entitlement to welfare with participation in public works. Enforced involvement in these schemes takes away any remnant of rights. Work becomes a duty in exchange for public money for a mere livelihood: choice and individual decision are missing at all points of the process. Furthermore, the earlier described segregated nature of the public works schemes extends the depriving implications of work and welfare to the entire community, and thus represents it as a specificity of the Roma collective. The resulting dual depreciation brings about a further serious curtailment of citizenship rights, also involving a questioning of the basic right to work.

Our overview of the manifold impacts and lasting implications of segregation on Roma citizenship rights concludes in asserting deep structural deviations: there are not only inequalities in accessing and practising these rights, but one can also speak of the manifestations of second-class citizenship.

Second-class citizenship involves separate spaces and distinct routines reasoned by distinct ideologies and notions detached from the respective fields and practices of the majority. Moreover, second-class citizenship expresses and fixes exclusion, and maintains an unbridgeable demarcation line between the two groups – non-Roma and Roma. Furthermore, second-class citizenship invokes legal regulations and the institutionalization of 'otherness'. Strengthened and reinforced by these rights of a secondary order, the exclusion of Roma becomes an organic part of the dynamics of the social order.

Conclusions

When the issue of segregation comes up in public discourse, it is mostly framed in terms of clashing values, habits and behaviours – that is, it appears as a cultural matter. Although the cultural aspects are important, the above discussion has shown that significant interests and struggles for power acquire comfortable expression in segregation, representing a structural force with great potency. What is more, there are strong tendencies for multiplying and fixing the impacts of segregation by emerging domains of intersectionality that tend to provide institutional frameworks for playing out the forced separation of Roma, and serve the unbroken reproduction of a given status quo. As we saw, there are multiple interests at play here. Segregation and the involved manifestation of the degraded social status of the 'other' help to strengthen feelings of superiority and success in broad circles of the majority who face lasting insecurities and risks of impoverishment. At the same time, the constant threat, which segregation implies, works as an efficient warning for those just above the verge of poverty: it reminds them of the importance of discipline and close observance of socially expected and sanctioned norms. In this sense, segregation not only implies direct control over the minority, but also helps the practising of power over large segments of society.

Segregation also serves important interests of production. By providing a 'reserve army' of people who can be drawn into employment if needed, but who can be forced out with equal ease, segregation greatly helps to even out the fluctuations of the labour market, while minimizing adaptation costs. In addition, segregation contributes to the informalization of labour, whereby it expands the sources of adaptability. With the recent spread of public works as a powerful institutionalization of inferior status while multiplying usage of Roma labour, a new contribution of segregation has arisen: the strengthening of often weak and shaky local businesses. But above all, political interests have to be considered: segregation breaks the Roma community into fragments and provides a self-perpetuating arrangement for keeping all efforts at Roma mobilization within limited circles, as if attempts to articulate collective needs were always particular and exceptional. The deep segmentation along lines of segregation not only hinders any powerful representation of the Roma minority, but also guarantees the invisibility of all such attempts. In this way, segregation effectively blocks any arising solidarity across ethnic lines, and silences the articulation of common interests between the Roma and non-Roma poor. The additional disciplining implications help to erase poverty from the political agenda and reduce the importance of the phenomenon, while keeping it away from the responsibility of those groups in society who are actually privileged actors in the prevailing state of affairs.

Given this multitude of interests in support of segregation, the prospects of meaningful change are rather gloomy. Even if attempts at desegregation appear on the professional and political landscape in education or housing, the dominantly experienced intersectional arrangements can hardly be challenged this way. Such arrangements would require multiple responses founded on complex policies, however the power and dedication behind them are usually weak, and solidaristic initiatives easily die out. In other words, despite all the goodwill and smartness, segregation cannot be erased through local action. It follows that true and lasting desegregation requires elevating the issue to the stage of macro-level politics.

Although the above enumerated important interests in the maintenance of segregation are powerful, there is perhaps one domain where the countering trend might be even stronger: this is the issue of citizenship. Indeed, segmentation of citizenship rights and the emergence of a distinct second-class order for Roma imply dangers for the entire society. First and foremost, the mere existence of such an order breaks up the unity that universal rights are meant to guarantee and represent. By taking away these rights from a part of society, unity itself becomes seriously questioned and a breaking up of society appears on the horizon. But, beyond this, by defining reduced citizenship rights for Roma, it is suggested that anybody's rights could be questioned and restricted. In this way, all the social institutions providing and guaranteeing people's social rights might become delegitimized, or reduced in scope and quality.

Owing to these severe implications, which might endanger the very foundations of a democratic society, renewal of universal contents of citizenship may be an overarching interest that brings together the political efforts of both the majority and the Roma minority. As soon as claims for reconstructing the unified content of citizenship appear on the political agenda, a critical review of segregation as the major framework for creating and maintaining second-class citizenship cannot be circumvented any longer. And this will be the moment when Roma minority interests meet important majority interests to engage together in a powerful deconstruction of segregation and in efforts towards Roma inclusion in full citizenship.

Júlia Szalai obtained her PhD in Sociology in 1986 and her Doctor of Science in Sociology in 2007, both from the Hungarian Academy of Sciences. She is Senior Research Fellow at the Center for Policy Studies and Visiting Professor at the Romani Studies Program of the Central European University, Budapest. Her fields of research include: comparative studies of the social status and political participation of Roma in Central and Eastern Europe; gender and race/ethnicity informing old and new poverty amidst post-communist transformation; comparative welfare state studies; and recognition struggles and social movements of ethnic minorities in contemporary Central, Eastern, and South Eastern Europe. She has led a number of cross-country comparative studies of ethnic/racial discrimination and inequality by class, race and gender across Europe. Her publication list includes some 260 articles in peer-reviewed Hungarian-, English-, French- and German-language academic journals, and 32 monographs and edited volumes.

Note

Let me express my sincere gratitude to Slobodan Cvejić, Ágnes Kende, Vera Messing, Mária Neményi, Enikő Vincze, Violetta Zentai and Jenő Zsigó for their rich insights and precious comments that helped me in developing my ideas about the complexities of racial/ethnic segregation in Central and Eastern Europe.

References

Albert, F. 2015. *Public Works in Hungary: An Efficient Labour Market Tool?* Brussels: European Commission ESPN.

Bauder, H. 2001. 'Culture in the Labor Market: Segmentation Theory and Perspectives of Place', *Progress in Human Geography* 25(1): 37–52.

Bokov, V., J. Csoba and P. Hermann (eds). 2014. *Labour Market and Precarity of Employment.* Vienna: Wiener Verlag für Sozialforschung.

Bottomore, T., and T.H. Marshall. 1992. *Citizenship and Social Class.* London: Pluto Press.

Huttman, E., J. Saltman and W. Blauw. 1991. *Urban Housing Segregation of Minorities in Western Europe and the United States.* Durham, NC: Duke University Press.

Kézdi, G., and É. Surányi. 2009. *A Successful School Integration Program*. Budapest: Roma Education Fund.
Maloutas, T. 2004. 'Segregation and Residential Mobility', *European Urban and Regional Studies* 11(3): 195–211.
Maloutas, T., and K. Fujita (eds). 2016. *Residential Segregation in Comparative Perspective*. London: Routledge.
Miller-Karas, E. 2015. *Building Resilience to Trauma*. London: Routledge.
Szalai, J., and C. Schiff (eds). 2014. *Migrant, Roma and Post-Colonial Youth in Education: Being 'Visibly Different'*. Basingstoke: Palgrave Macmillan.
Szalai, J., and V. Zentai (eds). 2014. *Faces and Causes of Roma Marginalization in Local Contexts: Hungary, Romania, Serbia*. Budapest: Center for Policy Studies, Central European University.
Tajfel, H. 1981. *Human Groups and Social Categories*. Cambridge: Cambridge University Press.
Turner, J.C. 1975. 'Social Comparison and Social Identity', *European Journal of Social Psychology* 5(1): 5–34.
van Baar, H. 2018. 'Contained Mobility and the Racialization of Poverty in Europe: The Roma at the Development Security Nexus', *Social Identities* 24(4): 442–58.
Vermeersch, P. 2006. *The Romani Movement: Minority Politics and Ethnic Mobilization in Contemporary Central Europe*. Oxford: Berghahn Books.
Virág, T. 2010. *Kirekesztve: Falusi gettók az ország peremén* [Being Excluded: Rural Ghettos Near the Borders]. Budapest: Akadémiai.

CHAPTER 3

❀ ❀ ❀

REFLECTIONS ON SOCIALIST-ERA ARCHIVES IN HUNGARY AND SHIFTING ROMANI IDENTITY

Nidhi Trehan

This chapter examines socialist-era ethnographic materials in Hungary with a view to revisit and elucidate the complexities of Romani collective identity formation in Central and Eastern Europe. To a significant extent, Romani identity has been influenced by various forces such as state policy interventions, as well as displays of both social prejudice and social solidarity by the majority. What is striking about the record – based on an interrogation of socialist-era archives[1] from the 1950s to the 1980s as sites of the epistemological enterprise and state ethnography (Stoler 2002) – are continuities and discontinuities, at times ruptures, with postsocialist regimes. In other words, during the various phases of the socialist experiment in Hungary, from the post-Second World War totalitarian Stalinist puppet state, to the 1956 Revolution and Kádárist policy 'reform' mechanisms of the 1960s and 1970s, to the postsocialist liberal democratic SZDSZ/MSZP[2] coalition government of the 1990s and the present-day autocratic regime of Viktor Orbán, we can observe similar preoccupations of the Hungarian state vis-à-vis Romani communities.

However, there are noticeable ruptures as well: the Hungarian socialist state would not have countenanced the openly anti-Gypsy racism that is often instrumentalized by democratically elected postsocialist populist leaders seeking to gain electoral advantages by employing the race card.

This contemporary resurgence of exclusionary ideologies, which has not been seen in Europe since the 1930s, certainly constitutes a rupture from postsocialist liberal democratic ideals based on constitutional protections of minority citizens across the European Union (EU), dating back to the adoption of the norms of the Copenhagen Criteria, even before the 2004 accession of Hungary and other postsocialist countries.

With respect to tackling antigypsyism – that is, deeply entrenched prejudices in society against Romani people, reinforced by linguistic cues and ethno-cultural practices of stigmatization that Roma faced during socialist regimes – it is important to note that Roma continue to face these prejudices in postsocialist democracies, which today in Hungary has been labelled by some as 'illiberal democracy'. Antigypsyism has often had violent manifestations, which have resulted in the murder, displacement and forced migration of Roma, thereby perpetuating age-old mythologies both about 'shiftlessness' and inherent nomadism.

In this chapter, I offer an analysis of how, from the 1970s onwards, scholars, journalists and policymakers, including Hungarian Roma, have dealt with the so-called 'Gypsy Question' – a common term at the time, *cigánykérdés* in Hungarian. I suggest that a more nuanced, historicized approach to the socialist-era experience of Romani communities – including the question of Romani identity – is empirically, methodologically and conceptually necessary to arrive at a richer understanding of the socialist and postsocialist experience for Roma. I then connect this to the contemporary context of rising majoritarian nationalist, populist 'illiberal democracies' in Europe, developments that are exacerbating anti-Roma and anti-migrant sentiments on the continent, thereby furthering the divide between Roma and non-Roma. Finally, I elaborate on what this means for the Romani identity struggle today, even as the attempts of the EU to keep a check on these xenophobic impulses and dangerous developments appear to be woefully inadequate.

Revisiting the Socialist Era: Post-1968 Kádárist Hungary

In much of the popular literature on socialist-era policies and practices regarding Roma, there appears to be a trend to consider these approaches as monolithically authoritarian and repressive. The conventional undifferentiated narrative is that, after a promising period of a few years marked by the repudiation of fascism and National Socialism, and of relative openness during the parliamentary republics just after the Second World War, dictatorial communist regimes swept across the Central and East European countries that came under the watchful gaze of the Soviet Union.

The narratives of multi-ethnic coexistence in the Socialist Federal Republic of Yugoslavia during the time of Josep Broz Tito, for instance, and the experiences of Romani communities within its various republics remains under-researched, and this is a lacuna in Romani studies scholarship. This is especially true with reference to the lack of general knowledge of a 'Roma awakening' in the arts and literature as well as the consolidation of Romani identity and language standardization within socialist Yugoslavia (Djurić 1990; Hancock, Dowd and Djurić 1998; Acković 1994; Friedman 1999). Moreover, if one reads the poetry and prose of Romani intellectuals who were published authors themselves during the 1970s – here one can refer to the works of Ilona Lacková, Choli Daroczi József, Menyhért Lakatos, Lajos Bogdán, Károly Bari, Rajko Rjurić, Dragoljub Acković and dozens of others – we see a critical piece of the puzzle, as these writings give us a window onto the richness and complexity of Romani identity in these times. Moreover, the contributions of numerous socialist-era artists and musicians must also be recognized from the perspective of Romani cultural expression. Another scholar, whose recent historical work has paid close attention to the dialogic nature of socialist-era policy regarding Roma – and in turn, the complex agency and identity of Romani interlocutors themselves – is Celia Donert (2017), who has written on the Czechoslovak Romani experience.

For inasmuch as Romani lifeworlds were crafted and framed by socialist-era government directives or policies, the formation of Romani identity was always dialogic and syncretic. There was a constant interplay of resistance and acceptance and adaptation in terms of what it meant to be a Hungarian Romani citizen or, for that matter, a Czechoslovak Rom or Bulgarian Romni. The lifeworlds of Roma were also informed by a diversity of integration experiences mediated through class, gender and sexuality, and a contemporary wave of Romani feminist scholarship has brought this to light (Kóczé 2009; Oprea 2017; Schultz, this volume).

Thus, contrary to the reductionist narrative on the broader socialist experience for Roma, which emphasizes repression of identity and traditional economic practices, a deeper analysis of various documents from the socialist-era archive allows for a far more heterogeneous and ambiguous assessment of Romani lifeworlds. Here, one can think particularly of publications within (state-controlled) newspapers, sociographic writings of the time, films such as *Cseplő Gyuri* (1978) by filmmaker Pál Schiffer, or other societal reflections, such as statements by an incipient democratic Romani leadership on the socioeconomic and human rights conditions of their communities.[3] In this respect, authors such as István Pogány (2004) have brought the diversity of experiences of Roma to the fore more prominently.

Socialist-Era Silences: Roma in Footnotes or the Missing Roma

Traditional historiography in Europe has given little voice to Roma. Indeed, masterful works of the Hungarian socialist experience and labour class identity formation rarely delved into the experiences or narratives of Roma in Hungary (Swain 1992; Pittaway 2012). That is why recent scholarship like that of Csaba Dupcsik (2009) as well as Bálazs Majtényi and György Majtényi (2016) is important. They have been reflective of this point and used earlier historical works and socialist-era government policy directives, among other sources, on the issue of Roma, extensively. According to Majtényi and Majtényi, the fundamental goal of 'counter histories [is to] uncover the memories of oppressed and excluded groups and to criticize state power ... [this] provides an opportunity for moral reflection on past and current issues of human social existence' (ibid.: 4).

However, in their history of the exclusion of Roma in socialist and postsocialist Hungary, Majtényi and Majtényi have primarily analysed official Hungarian government policy documents and few newspaper articles from the socialist period. Unlike Donert (2017), they do not focus as much on the experiences of exclusion from the point of view of the Roma themselves, or on how such an account could perhaps offer a more complex picture of the ways in which exclusion was often negotiated and thus also more ambiguous during socialism. Indeed, my own interpretation of the socialist-era records – and particularly regarding Romani identity – is perhaps not as pessimistic about the socialist state and its motivations as Majtényi and Majtényi (2016) suggest. According to their research, assimilation of Roma was the main goal of the socialist government. However, apart from the official socialist government directives that they analysed, I would emphasize as equally important newspaper articles, sociographic texts and popular works, such as novels by Romani authors and cultural entrepreneurs who displayed solidarity with Roma. These forms of cultural production that comprised representation of Roma did not reduce Romani citizens to some trope, but humanized Roma and included them in the broader Hungarian 'socialist project' as citizens of Hungary (*magyar polgárok*), perhaps for the first time in Hungarian history. This is significant, as post-Second World War rebuilding was underway, and although there were noticeable gaps in state policies intended to include Roma, state policies actively sought to offer socioeconomic integration through education, employment and housing;[4] it was then envisioned that, ultimately, Roma would form an integral part of the Hungarian socialist body politic. For this reason, it is also important to begin the analysis of the impact of socialism from the basis of post-Holocaust rebuilding. Scholars must also acknowledge the sheer devastation that characterized postwar Europe and the position of Romani communities in the aftermath of the Holocaust. Indeed, the renewal and reconstruction of postwar societies was the primary objective of the socialist regimes at this time, and the conditions of absolute deprivation in which Roma lived and survived in Europe during the Second World War, the Holocaust and its aftermath, need to be contextualized further (Kallai 2002; Bársony and Daróczi 2008; Hancock 2010).

The repudiation of European fascism and Nationalist Socialist regimes of the past did offer hope to working-class Hungarians, and among this cohort were significant numbers of Roma. Under the surface, however, the popular prejudices remained – for instance, of Roma being criminals, of not 'being worthy' perhaps of various rights, and of being 'incapable' of certain responsibilities. These were ingrained prejudices that brought into sharp relief the roadblocks to the socialist ideals of equity and social integration of 'Hungarians of Gypsy ethnicity' as they were then formulated and referred to in official state documents.

As Judit Kármán Szabó's (2016, 2017) research on the participation and sacrifice of Hungarian Roma in the 1956 Revolution indicates, many Roma were consciously reflective of their dual identity and their allegiance to the 'Hungarian nation'. She cites an interview with Gábor Dilinkó, a 'tough Gypsy boy from Újpest' who received the award of 'Faithful Persistence' from the Hungarian Republic in 1991 for his role in the revolution and became a brigadier general; subsequently in 1998, he was granted the prestigious Knight's Cross of the Order of Merit. When asked about his experiences of torture while imprisoned for over twelve years (five months of which were in solitary confinement) on charges of 'armed insurgency and infidelity against the ruling regime', Dilinkó[5] had this to say:

> I do not complain. One must endure this for [one's] country. If I consider myself to be a Hungarian, I remain Hungarian in times like this as well. But I never denied being a Gypsy. That is not acceptable! (Varga 2006, cited in Szabó 2017)

In a telling commentary from a 1973 piece published in the journal *Forrás* (Source), novelist Menyhért Lakatos describes the lifeworld of urban Roma in Budapest who had achieved a modicum of 'integration' within Hungarian society, and whose identity reflected that reality:

> They send their children to school, and we find many skilled workers and white-collar workers among them. Over 30 per cent have some sort of secondary education, and their standard of living equals the general level attained by the non-Gypsy population. Nevertheless, they are immersed in permanent isolation. As regards their racial nature, external influences do not interrupt their everyday life; these people do not hide their Gypsy background, though they do not boast

about it either. These are the people who smile when praised and who do not fight against prejudice. Feeling at home in both worlds, they are reluctant to break with either. Their sole purpose in life is to create a petit-bourgeois existence for themselves. (Lakatos, cited in Crowe 1994: 94)

In order to understand Romani identity formation during socialism, it helps to put Dilinkó's statement of his identity and Lakatos's keen observations on upwardly mobile Roma in the context of the history of anti-Roma racism and that of the emergence of the 'Gypsy Question' during Hungarian socialism in particular. I will discuss these backgrounds in the next two sections.

The 'Gypsy Problem' in Europe: Historical Antecedents to the Racialization of Roma

The persistence of the corrosive 'othering' and marginalization of European Romani communities within European history are important to examine. A policy continuum, which perceived Roma as 'deviants' and 'problems', has persisted – albeit unevenly across regions and countries – since the Middle Ages, as various regimes sought to control peripatetic Roma, and in some cases, control their trades and economic interactions. The goal was to effectively assimilate Roma culturally and linguistically, thereby erasing their cultural distinctiveness, which was perceived as necessarily backward and primitive, even in need of 'Christianizing'[6] (Trehan 2009; Hancock 2010).

In modern times, under state socialist governments, some of these practices and policies have been characterized by genocidal and racialized practices, such as the coerced sterilization of Romani women in countries such as Czechoslovakia, as well as the racial profiling of Roma who were investigated by police crime units specializing in 'Gypsy crime' in Hungary (Tauber 1979: 49–57). However, one must note that in West Germany, the Nazi-era 'Gypsy crime' office based in Munich continued until 1965 (Margalit 2007), and in some Scandinavian democracies, sterilization of 'undesirable' groups also persisted in the 1960s and 1970s (Trehan and Crowhurst 2006). This suggests that whether the political system was state socialist or one characterized by multi-party democracy exhibiting a free press and transparent elections, Roma and other dehumanized groups continued to silently bear the brunt of egregious policies of genocide in post-Holocaust Europe.

The discursive construction of Roma as 'problems' has been deeply embedded in European popular and scientific discourses for several centuries. European history is replete with examples of customary and legal exclusion of Romani communities. Although perhaps not everywhere termed the 'Gypsy problem' or 'Gypsy Question', the use of this phraseology to describe how Roma are a priori perceived as incompatible with European society, and their perceived 'otherness', became amplified in the late nineteenth century, which was a time of empire for a number of European powers, including the Habsburg dual monarchy of Austro-Hungary.

In some discursive constructions by the intellectual classes of Europe, the term 'problem' was perhaps more of a synonym for the French noun *problématique*, especially as used by folklorists, 'Gypsylorists', and other Orientalists (Bussell 1919; Hancock 2000: 9). Although not 'overtly' racist perhaps, this type of usage was certainly pregnant with the power of 'othering' and objectification. Its usage implied the inferiority and deviance of Roma, and left a damaging legacy that reinforces the subaltern position of the Roma to this day (Trehan and Kóczé 2009). Although the Hungarian state was never a 'colonizer' of the Romani communities in the classical sense of the term, their governance and regulation has been a continuous reality throughout European history. Thus, the strong homogenizing aspects of various regimes of governmentality,[7] and the cultural subordination of Romani communities emanating from this, have contributed to a subalterity of Romani lifeworlds, as well as to diverse forms of violence (physical, genocidal, epistemic, etc.) directed squarely upon them (Spivak 1988; Zoltan 2006).

There are notable parallels with discourses constructed on European Jewry and that of European Roma; examples are the 'wandering Jew' stereotype of the Middle Ages; the 'Jewish Question' raised in debates about the integration of Jews in Europe; as well as the literature produced on Jewish 'emancipation', mainly by Jewish intellectuals themselves (McCagg 1989; Marx 1992; Felsenstein 1999). Yet, the critical difference between the Jewish and the Romani case is that, with respect to the latter, these mythical social constructions continue to be hegemonic in the contemporary European *imaginarium* of the Roma. Moreover, references to 'Gypsies' in Hungarian popular culture contribute to the reinforcement of particular stereotypes on the Roma. One example is Geza Gárdonyi's popular novel, *Egri csillagok* (The Stars of Eger or Eclipse of the Crescent Moon), a late nineteenth-century literary classic about the historical Battle of Mohács, fought in 1526 by the Hungarians against the Ottoman Turks. Read by Hungarian children in elementary school, the novel contains depictions of Roma as lazy, cunning and amusing buffoons (Gárdonyi 1991). General stereotypes and, thus, social labels about the Roma continue to range from the negative to the 'forgiving' in contemporary Hungary. The Roma are depicted as workshy, engaged in pickpocketing, robbing, burglaries and begging; they are seen as always looking for trouble and unrestrained ('hot-blooded'). Romani women are seen as prostitutes, while the men are thought to have voracious sexual appetites, and the Roma in general are seen as dirty. With respect to the more 'forgiving' or 'positive' side, Roma are seen as good musicians and entertainers. In Hungary, the use of colloquialisms in daily speech persists, such as, for example, 'swallowing the wrong way' (*cigányútra ment*, translated literally as 'went down the Gypsy alley') (see Stewart 1997: 113–14; Trehan 2009: 88).

More analysis of these types of diffuse and persistent popular prejudices or 'everyday racism' (Essed 1991) – mapped onto Hungarian culture for generations, including during the socialist era – is required. In order to understand how, despite clear Hungarian Socialist Workers' Party (MSzMP)[8] objectives to the contrary, Roma marginalization persisted within state socialist structures well into the 1980s – albeit to a lesser extent than previously, as evidenced by data such as child mortality, literacy and employment – it is important to contextualize Hungarian politics at the time, and in addition, to examine the 'Gypsy Question' at the level of popular culture and everyday society. Here, I cover a history of ideas and ideologies, including a discursive overview of the 'Gypsy problem' or 'Gypsy Question'.

Policy on the 'Gypsy Question' during State Socialism

Együtt dolgoztunk, együtt buliztunk! (We worked together, we partied together!)
—Blanka Kozma, Romani women's activist in Budapest[9]

The post-Stalinist state socialist period in Hungary is identified closely with the Kádár years, named as such for the key political figure who was to become the architect of so-called '*gulyás* [goulash] communism' in Hungary. János Kádár came to power after the defeat of the 1956 revolution, and the subsequent execution of its communist reformer leader Imre Nagy by the Soviets in the summer of 1958. It was during this climate of harsh political repression, in the early days of Hungarian Socialist Workers' Party rule in Hungary, that 'official' social science research came to be marked by the work of state bureaucrats, who produced ethnographies influenced by Marxist-functionalist theoretical approaches on the 'Gypsy Question' (Pogány and Bán 1958; Stewart 2001).

In June 1961, the MSzMP adopted a decree that emphasized the 'backwardness' of Roma and effectively called for their total assimilation so that 'the improvement of the situation of the Gypsy population' would be a success (cf. Majtényi and Majtényi 2016). However, over the next decade there would be evolving developments within the MSzMP, the Hazafias Népfront (Patriotic People's Front),[10] and amongst Hungarian social scientists who began qualitative and quantitative research on Roma in earnest.

Party functionaries of the time wrote reports on the 'progress of Gypsies' in the fields of education, employment and housing, as well as some studies on the phenomenon of 'Gypsy crime' (Trehan 2009). Many of these official discourses on the 'Gypsy Question' were then picked up by Hungarian broadsheets, a few articles from which I highlight below.

By the late 1960s, with the introduction of the New Economic Mechanism (NEM), the economic system of Hungary gradually moved towards a mix of socialist and small-scale market-oriented policies, with increasing, but proscribed, liberalization (Swain 1992). Nonetheless, the socialist period was marked by strong social control, engineered by the state. Although Roma were encouraged, much like other Hungarians living in predominantly rural areas, to join the industrial proletariat by becoming miners and construction or railway workers, there were also state policies that targeted Roma specifically. Particularly after the adoption of the June 1961 decree on 'The problem of Gypsy integration', the 'Gypsy Question' was constructed as a 'social problem' devoid of any ethnic component; thus, socialist policies focused on the provision of jobs, housing and education for Roma (Stewart 2001: 82–85). Nevertheless, the socialist state did not adequately acknowledge the barriers connected to the 'customary' exclusion of Roma – antigypsyism – which posed a significant obstacle to their integration. Thus, in the educational system, there was de facto segregation, on the basis of 'customary', decades-long spatial segregation (each village had its own Romani quarter or settlement, *cigánytelep*), and many community schools that catered to Romani pupils were also built upon this de facto 'separate but equal' precept under socialism. In this manner, large numbers of Romani children became tracked into substandard schools, including schools for children with learning disabilities.[11] In the area of housing, Roma were subjected to the 'separate but equal' principle in the form of the '*cs lakás*' (cs = *csökkentett értékű, csökkentett komfortfokozatú*, or so-called 'reduced-comfort' housing) built specifically in Romani 'settlements'. By contrast, in urban areas, there were some achievements in housing integration for Roma, as Romani families in Budapest and other cities were allocated flats in the city centres.

With respect to the criminal justice system, by 1970 the police had established a special department in Budapest for the express purpose of studying 'Gypsy modes of criminality', and these included the fingerprinting of approximately two thousand Romani people, the vast majority of whom resided in state juvenile institutions and did not have prior criminal records (Noszkai 1987, cited in Kóczé and Versitz 1997: 24). These fingerprints were also used to assess whether or not 'criminogenic behaviour' of Roma could be detected from dermatoglyphics. Thus, from 1974 to 1989, the Hungarian Socialist Republic kept separate, official statistics on Romani prisoners, and developed special police units and methodology concentrating on 'Gypsy crime' (Kóczé and Versitz 1997: 24).

Concurrent to government demographic surveys, the folklorist tradition of modern 'Romologia' was propounded by Kamill Erdős. As a member of the Gypsy Lore Society, he was a prolific ethnographer fascinated by Romani linguistic and cultural diversity, publishing much of his influential work in the 1950s and 1960s (Macfie Archives 2007). Nonetheless, Erdős himself ultimately believed that assimilation was the only future for Roma (Stewart 2001: 81–82).

Social Science, Dissident Politics and the 'Gypsy Question'

In order to highlight both the continuities and discontinuities in socialist discourses on the Roma in Hungary, I will analyse the key role of prominent intellectuals and human rights dissidents who participated in the construction of public narratives on Roma. Alongside the 'folklorist' tradition led by Erdős in the postwar period, there was another type of discursive framework on the Roma that emerged in the socialist era, particularly from the 1970s onwards. This framework becomes prominent through the works of Hungarian social scientists and social workers, such as those of István Kemény, Zsolt Csalog, Katalin Pik, Gábor Havas, Ottilia Solt and Anna Csongor, in which they examined the presence of poverty in their country. In doing so, some of them became particularly interested in Roma and began to conduct extensive demographic surveys on each Romani community's status in terms of employment, education and health. In some respects, they were 'pushing the envelope' at that time, as these research subjects were not held in high regard by the socialist state: indeed, by discussing the poverty that they encountered in Romani communities, they were – directly or indirectly – highlighting substantial criticisms of the regime.

During the early transition period, social scientists – and, frequently, dissidents – who engaged with the subject of 'poverty and Gypsies', including Gábor Havas, János Ladányi and István Kemény, conducted a pioneering demographic survey on Roma in 1971. In Hungarian, the question about the relation between poverty and the Roma has always been articulated rather provocatively: *cigánykultúra vagy szegénykultúra?*, which is 'Gypsy culture or poverty culture?' As Angéla Kóczé (2009) points out, this binary clearly indicated a lack of intersectional thinking which suggested exclusive categories, instead of an analysis of Romani lifeworlds which could incorporate (at least) both class and ethnicity.

Social workers and educators such as Anna Csongor (former director of the Autonomia Foundation, a development NGO working in Romani communities), Ágnes Diósi (pedagogue), and the late Zita Reger (linguist) were also influential figures in the sphere of education of Romani children in Hungary. Journalists, such as the late Pulitzer prizewinner Zsolt Csalog, raised the public's consciousness in the 1980s about the entrenched discrimination and racism that Roma experienced in Hungary, despite their socioeconomic and cultural contributions to wider society.

These very same people were affiliated with the *demokratikus ellenzék* (democratic opposition) in Hungary, when it began to become more visible in the 1980s, having created 'alternative' institutions such as the political movement which then transformed into the Free Democrats party, the SZDSZ; the magazine *Beszélő*; as well as SZETA, a foundation that assisted the poor. As Ferenc Kőszeg, the former director (and founder) of the Hungarian Helsinki Committee, shared with me, this had an adverse impact on their career prospects, and many, including Kemény, suffered professionally as a result of pursuing their research interests on the prevalence of poverty amongst Roma (Trehan 2009).

The Hungarian Press and Discourses on the Roma

A survey of local and national broadsheets, as well as more serious essays by Hungarian intellectuals in periodicals such as *Kritika*, suggests that during state socialist times, the 'Gypsy problem' occupied a significant place in Hungarian public discourse from the early 1950s onwards. For example, in the article 'Gypsies on the Road to Socialist Development' (Figure 3.1), published in a local paper from the city of Székesfehérvár, the journalist Péter Ruffy closes with a quote: '*egyik ember annyi, mint a másik, bár a böre barna vagy fehér*' or 'whether we have brown or white skin, we are all the same'.

Furthermore, contrary to some readings of the nature of socialist discourses on the '*cigánykérdes*' ('Gypsy Question') as primarily state propaganda (Majtényi and Majtényi 2016: 63–65), many of the articles examined suggest a surprising level of candour, understanding and even compassion for the socioeconomic problems and the challenges of integration faced by Roma during the Kádár regime, indicating a degree of salience given to the issue by the MSzMP. Moreover, there is also a sense of déjà vu as one goes through articles about employment, housing, education and health and sanitation of Roma, as the discourse on the Roma – particularly that taken up by Romani activists in postsocialist Hungary – concentrates on *the very same problems* that Romani communities struggle with in contemporary Europe. This suggests the strong continuities of structural exclusion from the past – a

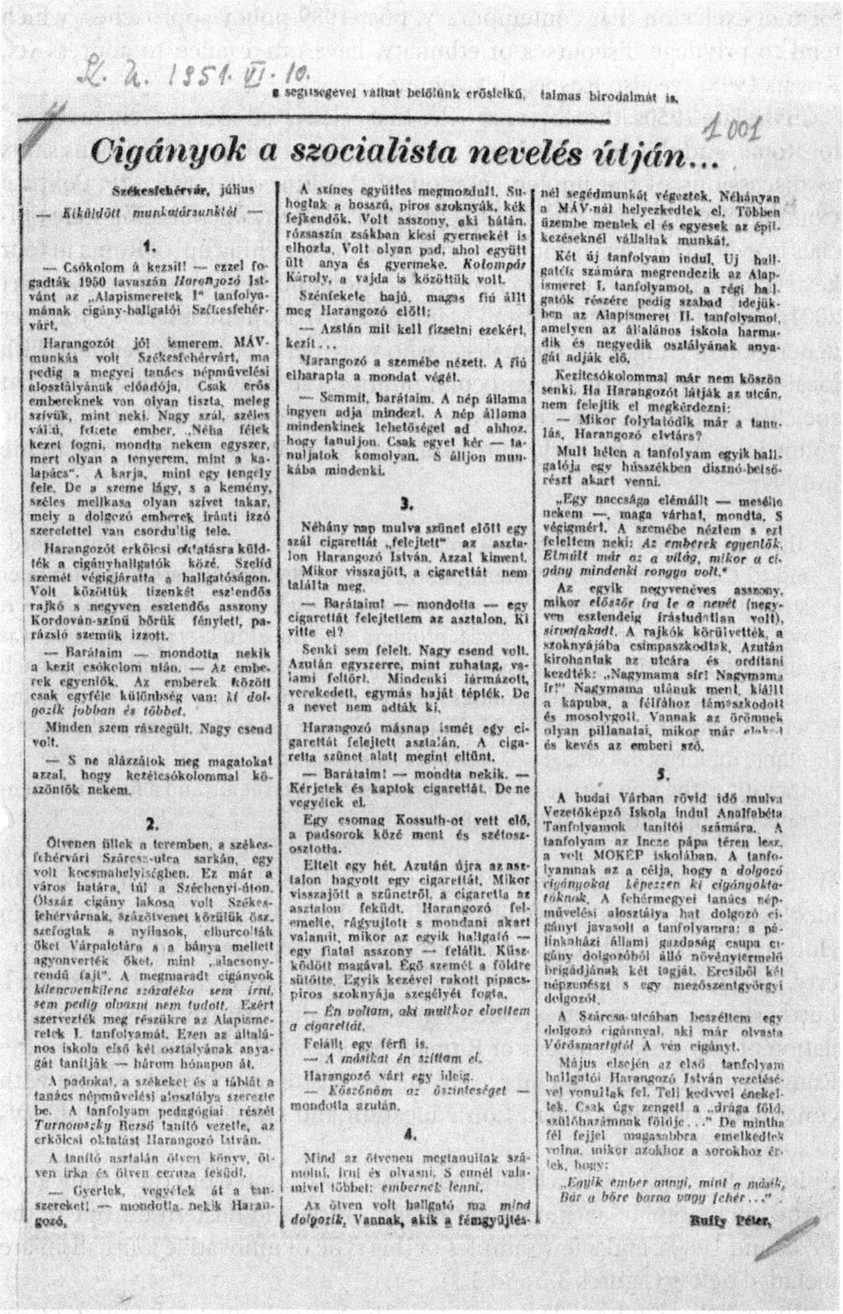

a segítségével válhat belőlünk erőslelkű, talmas birodalmát is.

1001

Cigányok a szocialista nevelés útján...

Székesfehérvár, július

— *Kiküldött munkatársunktól* —

1.

— Csókolom a kezsit! — ezzel fogadták 1950 tavaszán *Harangozó* Istvánt az „Alapismeretek I" tanfolyamának cigány-hallgatói Székesfehérvárt.

Harangozót jól ismerem. MÁV-munkás volt Székesfehérvárt, ma pedig a megyei tanács népművelési alosztályának előadója. Csak erős embereknek van olyan tiszta, meleg szívük, mint neki. Nagy szál, széles vállú, fekete ember. „Néha félek kezet fogni, mondta nekem egyszer, mert olyan a tenyerem, mint a kalapács". A karja, mint egy tengely fele. De a szeme lágy, s a kemény, széles mellkasa olyan szívet takar, mely a dolgozó emberek iránti izzó szeretettel van csordultig tele.

Harangozót erkölcsi oktatásra küldték a cigányhallgatók közé. Szelíd szemét végigjáratta a hallgatóságon. Volt közöttük tizenkét esztendős rajkó s negyven esztendős asszony. Kordován-színű bőrük fénylett, parázsló szemük izzott.

— Barátaim — mondotta nekik a kezit csókolom után. — Az emberek egyenlők. Az emberek között csak egyféle különbség van: *ki dolgozik jobban és többet.*

Minden szem rászegült. Nagy csend volt.

— S ne alázzátok meg magatokat azzal, hogy kezétcsókolommal köszöntök nekem.

2.

Ötvenen ültek a teremben, a székesfehérvári Szárcsa-utca sarkán, egy volt kocsmahelyiségben. Ez már a város határa, túl a Széchenyi-úton. Ötszáz cigány lakosa volt Székesfehérvárnak, százötvenet közülük összefogtak a nyilasok, elhurcolták őket Várpalotára s a bánya mellett agyonverték őket, mint „alacsonyrendű fajt". A megmaradt cigányok *kilencvenkilenc százaléka sem írni, sem pedig olvasni nem tudott.* Ezért szervezték meg részükre az Alapismeretek I. tanfolyamát. Ezen az általános iskola első két osztályának anyagát tanítják — három hónapon át.

A padokat, a székeket és a táblát a tanács népművelési alosztálya szerezte be. A tanfolyam pedagógiai részét *Turnowszky* Rezső tanító vezette, az erkölcsi oktatást Harangozó István.

A tanító asztalán ötven könyv, ötven irka és ötven ceruza feküdt.

— Gyerlek, vegyétek át a tanszereket! — mondotta nekik Harangozó.

A színes együttes megmozdult. Suhogtak a hosszú, piros szoknyák, kék fejkendők. Volt asszony, aki hátán, rózsaszín zsákban kicsi gyermekét is elhozta. Volt olyan pad, ahol együtt ült anya és gyermeke. *Kolompár* Károly, a vajda is közöttük volt.

Szénfekete hajú, magas fiú állt meg Harangozó előtt:

— Azstán mit kell fizetni ezekért, kezít...

Harangozó a szemébe nézett. A fiú elharapta a mondat végét.

— Semmit, barátaim. A nép állama ingyen adja mindezt. A nép állama mindenkinek lehetőséget ad ahhoz, hogy tanuljon. Csak egyet kér — tanuljatok komolyan. S álljon munkába mindenki.

3.

Néhány nap mulva szünet előtt egy szál cigarettát „felejtett" az asztalon Harangozó István. Azzal kiment. Mikor visszajött, a cigarettát nem találta meg.

— Barátaim! — mondotta — egy cigarettát felejtettem az asztalon. Ki vitte el?

Senki sem felelt. Nagy csend volt. Azután egyszerre, mint zuhatag, valami feltört. Mindenki lármázott, verekedett, egymás haját tépték. De a nevet nem adták ki.

Harangozó másnap ismét egy cigarettát felejtett asztalán. A cigaretta szünet alatt megint eltűnt.

— Barátaim! — mondta nekik. — Kérjetek és kaptok cigarettát. De ne vegyétek el.

Egy csomag Kossuth-ot vett elő, a padsorok közé ment és szétosztotta.

Eltelt egy hét. Azután újra az asztalon hagyott egy cigarettát. Mikor visszajött a szünetről, a cigaretta az asztalon feküdt. Harangozó felemelte, rágyujtott s mondani akart valamit, mikor az egyik hallgató — egy fiatal asszony — felállt. Küszködött magával. Égő szemét a földre sütötte. Egyik kezével rakott pipacspiros szoknyája szegélyét fogta.

— *Én voltam, aki multkor elvettem a cigarettát.*

Felállt egy férfi is.

— *A másikat én szíttam el.*

Harangozó várt egy ideig.

— *Köszönöm az őszinteséget* — mondotta azután.

4.

Mind az ötvenen megtanultak számolni, írni és olvasni. S ennél valamivel többet: *embernek lenni.*

Az ötven volt hallgató ma *mind dolgozik*. Vannak, akik a fémgyűjtésnél segédmunkát végeztek. Néhányan a MÁV-nál helyezkedtek el. Többen üzembe mentek el és egyesek az építkezéseknél vállaltak munkát.

Két új tanfolyam indul. Uj hallgatók számára megrendezik az Alapismeret I. tanfolyamot, a régi hallgatók részére pedig szabad idejükben az Alapismeret II. tanfolyamot, amelyen az általános iskola harmadik és negyedik osztályának anyagát adják elő.

Kezitcsókolommal már nem köszön senki. Ha Harangozót látják az utcán, nem felejtik el megkérdezni:

— Mikor folytatódik már a tanulás, Harangozó elvtárs?

Mult héten a tanfolyam egyik hallgatója egy hússzékben disznó-belsőrészt akart venni.

„Egy naccsága elémállt — mesélte nekem —, maga várhat, mondta. S végigmért. A szemébe néztem s ezt feleltem neki: *Az emberek egyenlők. Elmúlt már az a világ, mikor a cigány mindenki rongya volt.*"

Az egyik negyvenéves asszony, mikor *először írta le a nevét* (negyven esztendeig írástudatlan volt), *sírvafakadt*. A rajkók körülvették, a szoknyájába csimpaszkodtak. Azután kirohantak az utcára és ordítani kezdték: „Nagymama sír! Nagymama ír!" Nagymama utánuk ment, kiállt a kapuba, a félfához támaszkodott és mosolygott. Vannak az örömnek olyan pillanatai, mikor már elakad és kevés az emberi szó.

5.

A budai Várban rövid idő mulva Vezetőképző Iskola indul Analfabéta Tanfolyamok tanítói számára. A tanfolyam az Incze pápa téren lesz, a volt MOKÉP iskolában. A tanfolyamnak az a célja, hogy a *dolgozó cigányokat képezzen ki cigányoktatóknak*. A fehérmegyei tanács népművelési alosztálya hat dolgozó cigányt javasolt a tanfolyamra: a pálinkaházi állami gazdaság csupa cigány dolgozóból álló növénytermelő brigádjának két tagját, Ercsiből két népzenészt s egy mezőszentgyörgyi dolgozót.

A Szárcsa-utcában beszéltem egy dolgozó cigánnyal, aki már olvasta *Vörösmartytól* A vén cigányt.

Május elsején az első tanfolyam hallgatói Harangozó István vezetésével vonultak fel. Teli kedvvel énekeltek. Csak úgy zengett a „drága föld, szülőhazámnak földje..." De mintha fél fejjel magasabbra emelkedtek volna, mikor azokhoz a sorokhoz értek, hogy:

„*Egyik ember annyi, mint a másik,*
Bár a bőre barna vagy fehér..."

Ruffy Péter.

FIGURE 3.1 'Gypsies on the Road to Socialist Development', *Székesfehérvár Újsag*, July 1951. Folio no. 1001, Open Society Archives (HU OSA), Budapest.

form of exclusion that contemporary, post-1989 policy approaches, which tend to privilege discourses of ethnicity, have often failed to address (cf. Kovats 1998, see also Rostas, this volume).

In the late 1950s, there were articles that celebrated socialist 'engineering' for Roma, and this continued into the 1960s, but at this point the focus shifts to discussions of the implementation of the June 1961 MSzMP Political Committee's policy on the 'Gypsy Question', thereby encouraging state officials in every Hungarian county to embrace the 'catching up' of Roma in four key sectors: employment, housing, education and health policies (Stewart 2001; Trehan 2009; Majtényi and Majtényi 2016). Nonetheless, for a younger generation of Hungarian journalists, who were perhaps not too familiar with local press coverage of Romani communities, the conventional view is that socialist-era newspapers were almost devoid of discussions on Roma. As one young journalist in his early thirties and an NGO activist emphasized to me in 1999:

> Through the 1980s and before, Roma issues were not separated as such; according to the accepted government policy, and all the [news]papers were under strict governmental party control, there was no such thing as 'Roma issues' – it was considered generally as a social problem, and the ethnicity of the people was not an issue open to be discussed. It fits very well into the hypocritical approach with which the mainstream politics handled the entire Roma issue – not making a debate about it, and not working out an efficient policy in terms of the largest ethnic minority in Hungary ... [B]ut ... afterwards, in the early 1990s after the transition, the Roma issue became more of a centred theme and a focus of attention. (quote from Trehan 2009: 108–9)

While it is correct to suggest that ethnicity was not emphasized out of ideological pressures, journalists writing about Romani communities in Hungary clearly had much more freedom of expression to discuss poverty, marginality and societal exclusion than is commonly assumed. Furthermore, although the policies under socialism clearly favoured assimilation of Hungarian citizens of Romani background, the discourses on the Roma that had begun to emerge by the late 1970s and 1980s resonate with contemporary policy debates on education and employment as pathways to social integration.

István Pogány (2004), a legal scholar, has also pointed out the significance of the 'sociographic' writing tradition in Central and Eastern Europe of the 1970s and 1980s, and a few samples of this type of innovative journalism are included below (figures 3.2 and 3.3).

The article (Figure 3.2) begins with an extract from an evocative poem 'You Think' (*Azt hiszitek*) by Romani poet Károly Bari, from where the title of the article is also taken:

FIGURE 3.2 'Outside the Gate', *Magyar Hírlap*, 9 January 1972. Open Society Archives (HU OSA), Budapest, 2009.

You think that I am the only pilferer for light and love before the city gate . . .
many of us wait beyond the gates for you to gift us with engravings of your trust!
(HU OSA 1999; translation NT)

The 'city gate' is a very powerful symbol of an exclusionary boundary and, in this case, it epitomizes the centuries-long marginalization of the Roma, who were not allowed to settle within the boundaries of many European cities until the 1800s. Bari reminds us that 'engravings of trust' are a requirement for coexistence, and the Romani interlocutor awaits these.

My second example (Figure 3.3) is a sample article from the late 1970s. Featured in the bottom right-hand corner is Jószef Vekerdi,[12] a prominent linguist, Orientalist and Romologist, who, one year prior to this news report, had co-authored a seminal text for the Patriotic People's Front entitled 'Gypsies on the Road to Progress' (Vekerdi and Mészáros 1978). Amongst other participants were Romani intellectuals Gusztáv Balázs and Mrs Ottó Kovács, as well as government secretary Lajos Papp.

Moreover, although government censors were clearly in operation – especially after the defeat of the 1956 Uprising – some thought-provoking sociographic pieces of writing did appear, which invoked humanist perspectives in the discourse on the Roma, and discussed issues such as social stigma, discrimination and deprivation, as being at the root of the problems they faced. Although journalists and writers were monitored by the state, Hungarian citizens, along with others in the Eastern Bloc, used creative means to subvert governmental agendas and were able to discuss taboo subjects such as poverty, Gypsies and the declining income of workers, as well as the problems faced by Hungarians beyond the Hungarian borders. One outlet was the publication of *samizdat* (underground publications), often copied by cyclostyle machines and distributed through dissident networks.

Another sample of such work is the non-fictional monograph by journalist and sociologist Zsolt Csalog entitled *Kilenc cigány* (Nine Gypsies), based on the lives of nine Roma from Hungary in the 1970s, in a similar vein to the writings of the progressive American polemicist Studs Terkel, who tried to highlight 'the people's voices'. As Csalog noted himself, he wished to offer different representations of Hungarian Roma, thereby 'disputing prevalent stereotypical and mostly negative images of Roma . . . perhaps promoting solidarity and acceptance'. The work gives voice to the perspective of mostly young adults (both women and men) as they speak about their lives and work, touching upon interethnic relations, discrimination, poverty and integration into the new socialist society of the 1970s (Courage, Connecting Collections 2018).

Nonetheless, as the Hungarian Helsinki Committee's head, Ferenc Kőszeg, emphasized, this discourse remained limited to dissident circles in

FIGURE 3.3 'The Problems of Gypsies and the Society', *Népszava*, 5 August 1979. Open Society Archives (HU OSA), Budapest, 1999.

the 1970s and early 1980s and, understandably, had limited impact on the Hungarian government's policy approach to these sensitive issues at the time (Trehan 2009). Martin Kovats (1998) writes about the shift that took place after the legislation on minorities in Hungary in the 1990s, whereby an increasing liberalization of governance structures encouraged cultural and ethnic expression. It is possible that it was one way for the late socialist government to camouflage the failures of previous decades of integration policy for Romani communities.

Csalog's seminal sociographic text 'Nine Gypsies' was published in 1976, and an extract from it reads:

> 320,000 Gypsies live in Hungary today. This is indeed a large number, proportionally too – every thirtieth Hungarian is a Gypsy! After 15 years, every twenty-second Hungarian person will be Gypsy. This is a huge crowd, even without taking the proportion into account: if they all stood holding hands, they could form a chain, which would go from Mátészalka [eastern Hungary] to Sopron [western Hungary]. Do you think nine people can represent that many? (Csalog 1976)

Thus writes the author in the postscript of his book, citing a question from a friend. Csalog answers this question in the affirmative. Through the lives of nine Roma, he describes the contours of their life, family and work, especially of the younger generation of the Romani population.

The 'Kossuth Klub' Intellectuals: An Elite Romani Voice?

Another key question related to policy antecedents from the late socialist era is the role of urban Romani intellectuals, whom I refer to as the 'Kossuth Klub' crowd as they used to meet in this popular venue in central Budapest on a regular basis in the late 1980s and early 1990s.[13] Many of these intellectuals participated actively in debates on the 'Gypsy Question' in the 1960s and 1970s, and formed the first group of 'dissident' Romani intellectuals in socialist Hungary. Pál Farkas's article is one sample of their writing from the transition period in 1990 (Figure 3.4). He offers a polemic about how Roma have not been viewed as humans, how the Hungarian socialist state did not want to recognize them as a national or ethnic minority, and how the foundation of the Hungarian Gypsy Socialist Democratic Party – of which he became secretary in October 1989 – was a key development for the advancement of Romani people.

Figure 3.4 is an extract of Pal Farkas's article from the magazine *Élő Szó* of the Hungarian Gypsy Social Democratic Party. As secretary of the newly formed party, Farkas exhorts fellow Roma (he uses the Hungarian word *cigányok*) to understand that they are equal to other groups in Hungarian society and worthy of the same rights of citizenship as ethnic Serbs, ethnic Slovaks and others, and he promotes social democratic politics as the way

Figure 3.4 'Brothers, Gypsies!', *Élő Szó* (Living Word), 20 March 1990.

forward for his community. His party also cooperated with the Patriotic People's Front, a socialist-era quasi-state government body that engaged with citizens at the local level in order to bring 'cohesiveness to various classes and groups in society', effectively monitoring their activities (Trehan 2009).

Hungary in 'Transition'

Additional policy continuities from late socialism to the present day were noticeable in assessing the influence of government officials who began to specialize in minority affairs, especially those of the Roma. They included: Csaba Tabajdi, who was head of the state minorities office in the 1980s and early 1990s, and who, in addition, served as an MP for the Hungarian Socialist Party and as a representative for Hungary at the Council of Europe in 2001; Imre Pozsgay, head of the Patriotic People's Front in socialist Hungary (from 1982 to 1988); and János Báthory, an architect of the pivotal Law on Ethnic and National Minorities (1993), and head of the Office of Ethnic and National Minorities (under the purview of the Ministry of Justice) during the FIDESZ-led government from 2000 to 2002. Beginning in the mid-1990s, Hungary established a plethora of state offices and structures with the specific task to manage the Romani population and to implement related state policies.

With respect to discourses generated during late socialism, Wizner (1999) has identified interesting links between scholars, teachers and social reformers of the time, such as Ágnes Diósi (pedagogue), the late Ottilia Solt (sociologist and former MP) and Zsuzsa Ferge (sociologist), who engaged in 'poverty research', as well as Júlia Szalai and Gábor Havas who conducted earlier studies on Roma, both independent research and state-commissioned. This discursive emphasis on poverty and Roma resulted in, at least partially, the Romani population itself being considered as synonymous with 'the poor'.

In addition, ethnographers and social scientists Katalin Kovalcsik, Péter Szuhay and Michael Stewart generated further knowledge about Romani communities in Hungary during late socialism. 'Late socialism' was a period of increasing reforms in social policy areas such as education and healthcare. Within the economic sphere, international financial institutions such as the IMF and the World Bank encouraged shifts towards a more neoliberal direction (Haney 2002). Changes in the political sphere also transpired as the socialist state began to open itself up to more consultative mechanisms outside the party apparatus.

The Discursive Transformation of the 'Gypsy Question' in the 1990s: (Re)Surfacing Ethnicity

In postsocialist Europe, research on Roma has grown visibly, particularly in the areas of sociology, anthropology, political science and social policy. These studies are similar to those conducted during the previous socialist regimes, with the visible exception that Roma are now clearly viewed as *ethnic* minorities. In particular, social policy research on 'integration' has become popular with various governments in postsocialist countries, which have taken great pains to demonstrate within the halls of the EU their goodwill on what has now been termed the 'Roma issue' – even while references to the 'Gypsy Question' or the 'Roma problem' have never disappeared.

Moreover, the 'Gypsy Question' discourse continues to manifest itself in the print media, broadcast television, social media, public statements by politicians, crime control policies by the government, academic research by social scientists and, quite often, government policies themselves. An example of this was in January 1998, when – at the congress of the Lungo Drom National Gypsy Interest Association in Szolnok – Prime Minister Gyula Horn of Hungary made a statement urging Roma to distance themselves from 'those who live off crime' in their community (see Human Rights Watch 1999). Another example, published on the internet – and, interestingly, disseminated by the Commission on Security and Cooperation in Europe's Helsinki Commission – was by Géza Jeszenszky, the Hungarian ambassador to the United States. In an open editorial to *The Washington Post* in July 1999, Jeszenszky complained of Hungary's misrepresentation in the Western media:

> Before you think that, as the ambassador of Hungary, I feel compelled to whitewash the problems in my country, let me state a few facts. Hungary has a large Gypsy minority with serious social problems deriving mostly from poverty, poor education and, *in many cases, an inherited lifestyle that lacks any incentives to break out and do better*. It is also a fact, however, that the Hungarian government, and society in general, recognizes this problem and accepts responsibility for its amelioration. The reporter blames 'institutional racism' for the problems of Hungarian Gypsies. I find it reassuring that he cannot provide a shred of evidence to prove this point. What is 'institutional' in Hungary is that we have a national government agency established specifically to deal with the problems and aspirations of national and ethnic minorities. It spends most of its budget on programmes for the Gypsies, our largest minority. It is presently headed by a member of our Bulgarian minority. Earlier, however, its head was a highly educated woman from the Gypsy minority. Hungary has one of the most enlightened minority laws in the world. This makes it possible for Gypsies to elect their own self-governments, even in those places where they are dispersed among the general population and, consequently, cannot form a majority. (Jeszenszky 1999, emphasis added)

There are two points to note about this statement. First of all, Jeszenszky attributes 'serious social problems' to an 'inherited lifestyle' of the Roma and, thus, in a classic example of cultural determinism, renders complex socioeconomic problems 'natural' and 'private' (see Introduction, this volume). Secondly, he categorically denies the possibility of 'institutional racism' in

Hungary, and instead, deflects the issue of structural disadvantage that confronts Roma by highlighting Hungary's minorities legislation as a positive step taken by the government, which, at the time, was one of Europe's most far-reaching and seemingly progressive laws. Such discourses emanating from national politicians and published in the media are examples of what Teun van Dijk refers to as 'elite racism', which he qualifies as follows: '[N]ot only [do] various elites have a special set of racist ideologies and practices... their position [also] allows them to 'preformulate' those of the population at large, and thus to produce and reproduce the white consensus (van Dijk 1991: 43).

By the late 1980s, and continuing into the transition period, Hungarian state policy towards Roma became increasingly characterized by 'ethnic coupling' and the 'politics of difference', as demonstrated by the growing number of 'Gypsy-specific' programmes (Havas, Kértesi and Kemény 1995; Kovats 1998; Stewart 2001). Therefore, the socialist era notion of Roma as a class fraction devoid of any 'cultural capital'[14] was already being challenged within Hungarian government circles, well before powerful NGO human rights entrepreneurs began promoting the recognition of Romani ethnicity. Viewing Romani communities as having contributed cultural capital, including their knowledge and skills to Europe across the centuries, is equally difficult for European society to recognize, let alone acknowledge – say, through the inclusion of their role in European lifeworlds, whether it was in the countryside as artisans or in urban centres as musicians – as there is only a superficial understanding of their historical contributions (see also Magazzini, this volume).

During the post-1989 transition period, the expectation that the state should be held accountable for alleviating poverty and socioeconomic problems in postsocialist Hungary began waning as neoliberal policy agendas became more prominent. Thus, one ongoing peril in the postsocialist era is that the 'plight of the Roma' can, therefore, be mistakenly read by the majority society as resulting from their 'different' (read 'inferior') ethnicity – a racialized trope – rather than, for example, from the chronic cycle of poverty in which many Romani communities have been trapped for decades, without the benefit of sustainable policy interventions by the state.

This polarization is also evident in much of European policy towards Roma (Acton 1998). The postsocialist version of the 'culture/poverty' debate has been discussed by Szuhay (1995) and Noszkai (1995) in the Hungarian journal *Társadalmi Szemle* (Social Bulletin), as well as in various articles in the *Amaro Drom* (Our Way) magazine, which covered Romani issues during the 1990s. From 1998 to 2002, the right-of-centre, nationalist-leaning FIDESZ government led by Viktor Orbán tended to avoid discussions of the growing marginalization in Romani communities, choosing instead to focus on ethnic difference. In April 2002, parliamentary elections brought a socialist–liberal coalition government to power. The postsocialist pendulum had now swung in the other direction: whereas during the previous communist regime, Romani *ethnicity* per se was not a large part of the discourse and focus was placed upon building the material circumstances of Romani families to working-class standards, postsocialist administrations have tended to downplay the rising impoverishment of Romani communities, and have instead created institutions resulting in the highlighting of ethnic difference to Hungarians at large (Kovats 1998; Wizner 1999).

From a Politics of 'Dialogue' to a Politics of 'Declaration'

During the 1990s, the expansion of third sector influence and imminent EU accession resulted in greater pressure on Central and East European states to place a stronger priority on the integration of their Roma vis-à-vis the minority rights framework, since one of the explicit requirements for EU membership included an improvement in the treatment of minorities (Kovats 1997, 1998).[15] With respect to the influence of Hungarian civil society at this time, the National Soros Foundations began compiling reports on their Roma-related activities, particularly in the areas of education and culture. Furthermore, George Soros's Open Society Institute established and funded regional organizations in Budapest, such as the Educational Policy Institute (EPI), the Constitutional and Legislative Policy Institute (COLPI) and the Local Government and Public Service Reform Initiative (LGPSRI). All of them participated actively in various Roma-related projects throughout the region. In addition, the Roma Participation Program (RPP) was seen as a special effort on the part of Soros and his colleagues to increase Romani participation *within* the Soros network itself, and by extension, within the developing civil societies of Central and Eastern Europe.

What is important to note here is that although Hungary's legislative achievements were initially seen as a model for minority policy in the region in the 1990s, popular disaffection with the implementation of the Minorities Law of 1993 and with the Hungarian government's policies led to a reassessment of the socialist–liberal coalition (1994–1998) government's 'multicultural' approach towards Roma. One activist from the Roma Press Centre, Gábor Miklósi, assessed the situation in 1999 as follows:

> The state policy remains very hypocritical. This is the most tragic aspect of the entire problem, because there is no willingness from any of the [political] parties to deal with this Gypsy issue in depth... so state policies remain at a very surface level. Because of this integration towards the European political organizations,

and NATO and the European Union . . . there is an external pressure on the government to deal with this issue – and for this reason, shop window-like organizations and shop window-like measures are being introduced, but the internal willingness to deal with this issue and to work out long-term plans with short-term exact measures is still missing . . . so, very low budgeted mid-term government programmes are being worked out, the deadlines keep being missed, and I can say that on a mainstream level, the politicians are doing a very bad job and they will have a lot to be ashamed of in twenty years; but, on the other side, as you pointed out, civil society is getting better, and I think it will be the Gypsies themselves who will force the prevailing governments or politicians or political powers to deal with them. (Trehan 2009: 108)

Looking at socioeconomic indicators within Romani communities, such as rates of employment, educational achievement, health and housing from 1999, and comparing them to 1989, is sobering (Kállai and Törszök 2005). Although official socialist policy did not strengthen Romani identity directly – indeed, it tended to discourage its overt development – by providing for the basic material needs of Roma and by discouraging ethnic chauvinism in the public sphere, Romani citizens enjoyed a modicum of economic integration into mainstream Hungarian society as they were encouraged to join the working class (Pogány 2004).[16]

It should be noted that policies relating to Romani communities have historically been mostly generated by non-Romani elites. This continues to the present day, where in both the governmental sphere and civil society, the participation of the Hungarian intellectual class dominates. As a result, the influence of Hungarian elites who frame policy on Roma, such as social scientists, social reformers, so-called 'Roma experts' and consultants, civil servants, as well as Romani intellectuals, is worthy of scrutiny (Higley, Pakulski and Wesolowski 1998). Government policymakers and prominent intellectuals were in favour of fostering the development of a middle-class Romani intelligentsia, and the foundation of the Gandhi Gimnázium (Gandhi Secondary School) in Pécs in 1994 was one concrete expression of this, as dedicated pedagogues garnered private funding as well as financial support from the Hungarian state. Incorporating insights from research on Roma politics after socialism, I emphasized the post-1995 era in Hungarian policy vis-à-vis Roma, suggesting that the previous 'policy of dialogue' – as coined by Kovats (1998) – has been replaced by intransigence and attempts at power consolidation on the part of the state, in which 'declarations of progressive intent' serve as substitutes for structural investments in ameliorating Roma marginalization (Trehan 2009: 109).

Whether the 'Decade of Roma Inclusion' policy reforms or the EU-instigated 'National Roma Integration Strategies' (NRIS) and its successor policies will be successful through its proposals for socioeconomic integration of Romani communities remains an open question (see also Rostas, this volume). Indeed, subaltern voices from within the Romani movement – those that are seeking to unapologetically express their Romani identity (whether it be through the Romani language or other forms of cultural reproduction), while at the same time striving to be recognized as part of the European fold – are challenging these complex, paradoxical processes and, thereby, perhaps contributing to the fundamental reshaping of contemporary European identity.

Conclusion: The Contentious State and Romani Identity

In discussing the relationship between the state, Romani communities and national identity, Majtényi and Majtényi posit that the 'state pushed Roma communities in Hungary to the periphery, later blaming Roma for social problems and, then, presenting them as an antagonistic minority' (2016: 205). They accurately emphasize the agency of Roma who were viewed 'not just as victims throughout history, but also ... as active participants – for example, as defenders of freedom against the dictatorial state' (ibid.). Nonetheless, in the 1980s, during the one-party, state-socialist era in Central and Eastern Europe, both policy discourses and news articles framed Roma as 'compatriots' and discussed the poverty and lack of educational opportunities they seemed to be mired in, despite attempts to integrate them into the labour market. Even if, at times, the tone of the debate was distinctly patronizing and racialized towards Roma, one could detect the simultaneous coexistence of empathy towards Romani citizens of these states, as a result of the prevailing ethos of the socialist project. Indeed, Majtényi and Majtényi also contrast the socialist era to the situation today, which they suggest is far more polarized, as social scientists are perceived as biased in favour of Roma and minorities: '[U]nlike in the Kádár era, sociology is unable to have a direct dialogue with the political sphere' (2016: 169). The above highlights the ambiguity and the complexity of Romani lifeworlds in the era of state socialism in Central and Eastern Europe.

Beginning in the late 1980s – when progressive, socialist-era, pro-democracy activists started to embrace the universal language of human rights – the discourses on the region's Romani communities began to shift perceptibly (Trehan 2009). These discourses challenged the prevailing essentialist discourses on the 'Gypsy problem'. The collective work of a diversity of human rights entrepreneurs – ranging from NGO activists to Romani intellectuals, including pro-Roma media outlets – along with some notable forward-thinking government bureaucrats in the last decades of transition, planted the seeds to found the ubiquitous movement for the rights of the

Roma. In other words, the roots of the exposure to contemporary human rights issues in Europe can be traced back to the impact of the work of an earlier generation of Romani activists and public intellectuals in Central and Eastern Europe, who were already engaged in these issues at the local and national levels back in the 1970s and 1980s. For them, 'socialist solidarity' and 'dignity for all' were important and salient values (Solt 1998).

From the 1990s onwards – during the transition and, subsequently, in the postsocialist era – liberal NGOs and governments in Europe began to discuss the scale of the challenges posed by the past decades of neglect and poor policy interventions vis-à-vis Romani citizens in Europe. As civil, political and cultural rights came to the fore during the period of 'democratic transition', Central and East European states had to meet the Copenhagen Criteria for gaining the prized membership of the EU. However, it appears that the policymaking elite in postsocialist Europe concentrated their interventions on (largely) US-inspired 'democratization' programmes – that is, a clear preference for civil and political rights enhancement via legislative and 'rule-of-law' reforms – while the social and economic rights and conditions of Roma communities were gradually neglected.

The advent of neoliberalism and a reductionist interpretation of human rights that privileged civil and political rights and their impact on Romani communities suggests the coexistence of both progressive and regressive tendencies in these newly democratized regimes – what some scholars have aptly referred to as 'ambiguous' outcomes for Roma (van Baar 2011). In other words, despite the existence of so-called 'Roma rights' – inclusive of EU human rights norms and protections – and the significant efforts of a diverse set of 'rights entrepreneurs' working for over two decades in Europe at both the national and European level, Romani communities continue to be problematized in new forms, as they work to overcome socioeconomic marginalization within a 'free market' economic system.

As alluded to early on in this chapter, Hungary, under the increasingly authoritarian leadership of Prime Minister Viktor Orbán, is characterized by a radical rupture with liberal democratic norms wherein the state acts to safeguard basic constitutional principles such as the rule of law and protection of minorities. Instead, the construction of illiberal, 'majoritarian' democratic institutions is in full swing, whereby 'state policies and the attitudes of the representatives of the state are increasingly similar to those of the dictatorial past' (Majtényi and Majtényi 2016: 209).

What remains to be seen is how Roma will respond to these new challenges, which seem to be contesting their allegiance to the state as the borders around identity harden. Certainly, the rich archival narratives of the Romani subaltern (about the subaltern and from the perspective of the subaltern) are still being assembled. These will shed further light on the complexity and fluidity of Romani collective identity formation during the socialist and postsocialist eras, and in modern times and beyond.

Nidhi Trehan is currently a Faculty Fellow to the Bentsen Chair of the Lyndon B. Johnson School of Public Affairs, and Visiting Scholar at the Romani Archives and Documentation Center at the University of Texas at Austin. She is a Fellow at the Institute of Social Sciences in New Delhi and holds a PhD from the London School of Economics and Political Science. She was a Postdoctoral Research Fellow at University College London from 2008 to 2010. Active in the areas of human rights and social policy as a practitioner and academic since 1996, she has published on human rights, identity politics, NGOs/social movements and migration, with a focus on the Romani communities of Europe. Nidhi Trehan was based in India from 2010 to 2017, where she worked in the management of the American Montessori Public School, a senior secondary school close to New Delhi.

Notes

This chapter is based on some of the materials in my PhD dissertation (Trehan 2009), and I would like to thank the editors for their insightful feedback and comments. I also would like to thank Júlia Szalai for her valuable comments.

Every effort has been made to obtain permission for the materials used in this chapter. In the absence of any response to the enquiries, the author and publisher would like to acknowledge the following Hungarian periodicals for use of their material: *Magyar Hírlap* and *Népszava*.

1. Here, I utilize the word 'archives' in the way that Stuart Hall (2001) used it when describing the 'living archive of the diaspora' as a discursive formation. More specifically, this is an ongoing project whereby materials and artefacts from the socialist era continue to be assembled by researchers, shedding light on the complexity of Romani identity and agency under state socialism.
2. This was a coalition of the Szabad Demokraták Szövetsége – a Magyar Liberális Párt (Alliance of Free Democrats – Hungarian Liberal Party) and the Magyar Szocialista Párt (Hungarian Socialist Party).
3. This leadership ultimately became part of the democratic opposition in the late 1980s.
4. This is not to suggest that access to social services of the state were on par for Roma – classrooms and even student mealtimes were often segregated for Romani children; housing was substandard, especially in rural Hungary, and access to healthcare had its own set of problems. Rural Roma were often targeted in 'forced hygiene' campaigns.

5. Gábor Dilinkó began to paint in the 1970s, eventually becoming a successful artist with a unique style (he painted with his fingers because of serious injuries he had sustained during the revolution). In 2018, the Government of Hungary recognized him posthumously with a 100 HUF commemorative postage stamp in his honour.
6. Ironically enough, under Orbán's regime, Hungary has added explicit references to the 'Christian identity' of the Hungarian nation in constitutional amendments promulgated in 2011. See https://www.constituteproject.org/constitution/Hungary_2013.pdf?lang=en.
7. In connection to this, the Habsburgs also enacted strong regulatory measures targeting Roma within their territories, and in addition, although the socialist regime renounced national or ethnic feeling, the institutions within the purview of the Hungarian socialist state – the schools, hospitals, factories, orphanages and prisons – nevertheless all served to stamp a particular 'Hungarianness' on its diverse Romani communities (Kállai and Törzsök 2005).
8. Magyar Szocialista Munkáspárt (MSzMP).
9. Quoted in Trehan 2009: 85. Blanka Kozma is a Romani women's activist and a former member of the Budapest City Council.
10. The Hazafias Népfront was a quasi-state body which published in 1978 *A cigányság a felemelkedés útján* [Gypsies on the Road to Rising], an influential booklet at the time. By the 1980s, the term *beilleszkedés* (integration) also emerged in public discourse.
11. This de facto segregation has been challenged in several jurisdictions across the region by human rights organizations conducting legal interventions (ERRC 2000, 2002).
12. By the early 1990s, Vekerdi's earlier work was being denounced by Romani activists and their supporters, who exposed the racist overtones of his work. Indeed, earlier, in the 1980s, the Communist Party had taken administrative action against him, denouncing his racism. He had been a member of the Hungarian Academy of Sciences' Orientalist Studies Council.
13. The Kossuth Klub was a popular cultural/political venue located in Budapest's VIII District, on Múzeum Street.
14. Notably, the Hungarian state did promote numerous Romani cultural activities, including the world-famous '100 Member Gypsy Orchestra', which even performed in such far-flung places as Australia during the 1980s.
15. Martin Kovats (1997: 55, see also 1998) probes the 'relationship between increasing Roma poverty and the policy of "dialogue"'.
16. Conversely, state dependency was fostered in a number of Romani communities, particularly those that had become 'proletarianized' (this was true for Hungarian citizens of other ethnicities as well).

References

Acković, D. 1994. *Istorija informisanja Roma u Jugoslavii 1935–94* [History of Roma Information in Yugoslavia 1935–94]. Belgrade/Novi Sad: Romski Kulturni Klub & Društvo Vojvodine za jezik i književnost Roma.

Acton, T. 1998. 'Authenticity, Expertise, Scholarship and Politics'. Professorial inaugural address. University of Greenwich. Retrieved 28 November 2018 from http://www.gypsy-traveller.org/pdfs/acton_article.pdf.

Bársony, J., and Á. Daróczi (eds). 2008. *Pharrajimos: The Fate of the Roma during the Holocaust*. New York: IDebate Press.

Bussell, F. 1919. 'The Problem of the Gipsies: Sigynnæ, Sequani, Zigeuner', *Folklore* 30(2): 103–29.

Courage, Connecting Collections. 2018. 'Zsolt Csalog Collection'. Retrieved 8 October 2018 from http://cultural-opposition.eu/registry/?uri=http://courage.btk.mta.hu/courage/individual/n1540.

Crowe, D. 1994. *A History of the Gypsies of Eastern Europe and Russia*. New York: St. Martin's Press.

Csalog, Z. 1976. *Kilenc cigány* [Nine Gypsies]. Budapest: Koszmosz.

Djurić, R. 1990. *Bi Kheresqo Bi Limoresqo* [Without a Home, Without a Grave]. Paris: L'Harmattan.

Donert, C. 2017. *The Rights of the Roma: The Struggle for Citizenship in Postwar Czechoslovakia*. Cambridge: Cambridge University Press.

Dupcsik, C. 2009. *A magyarországi cigányság története: Történelem a cigánykutatások tükrében, 1890–2008* [The History of the Hungarian Gypsies: History Reflected in Gypsy Research, 1890–2008]. Budapest: Osiris.

Essed, P. 1991. *Understanding Everyday Racism*. London: Sage.

European Roma Rights Centre (ERRC). 2000. *Focus: Roma in Hungary*. Budapest.

———. 2002. 'Extreme Poverty'. Special issue, *Roma Rights* 1: 1–168.

Felsenstein, F. 1999. *Anti-Semitic Stereotypes*. Baltimore, MD: Johns Hopkins University Press.

Friedman, V. 1999. 'The Romani Language in the Republic of Macedonia', *Acta Linguistica Hungarica* 46(3–4): 317–39.

Gárdonyi, G. (1899) 1991. *Egri csillagok* [Eclipse of the Crescent Moon]. Budapest: Corvina.

Hall, S. 2001. 'Constituting an Archive', *Third Text* 15(54): 89–92.

Hancock, I. 2000. 'The Consequences of Anti-Gypsy Racism in Europe', *Other Voices* 2(1). Retrieved 29 November 2018 from https://www.othervoices.org/2.1/hancock/roma.php.

———. 2010. *Danger! Educated Gypsy. Selected Essays*. Hatfield: University of Hertfordshire Press.

Hancock, I., S. Dowd and R. Djurić (eds). 1998. *The Roads of the Roma: A PEN Anthology of Gypsy Writers*. Hatfield: University of Hertfordshire Press.

Haney, L. 2002. *Inventing the Needy*. Los Angeles: University of California Press.

Havas G., G. Kértesi and I. Kemény. 1995. 'The Statistics of Deprivation: The Roma in Hungary', *Hungarian Quarterly* 36(3): 67–80.

Higley, J., J. Pakulski and W. Wesolowski. 1998. 'Introduction', in J. Higley, J. Pakulski and W. Wesolowski (eds), *Postcommunist Elites and Democracy in Eastern Europe*. London: Macmillan, pp. 1–33.

Human Rights Watch. 1999. *Human Rights Watch World Report 1999: Hungary*. Retrieved 29 November 2018 from https://www.hrw.org/legacy/worldreport99/europe/hungary.html.

Jeszenszky, G. 1999. 'Story on Hungary's Gypsies "ill-informed, malicious"', *The Washington Times*, 12 July: A14.

Kállai, E. 2002. 'The Hungarian Roma Population During the Last-Half Century', in E. Kállai (ed.), *The Gypsies/The Roma in Hungarian Society*. Budapest: Teleki László Alapítvány, pp. 35–50.

Kállai, E., and E. Törzsök (eds). 2005. *A Roma's Life in Hungary*. Budapest: Bureau for European Comparative Minority Research.

Kóczé, A. 2009. *Missing Intersectionality: Race/Ethnicity, Gender and Class in Current Research and Policies on Romani Women in Europe*. Budapest: Center for Policy Studies, Central European University.

Kóczé, A., and P. Versitz. 1997. 'Juvenile Justice and Rromani Youths in Hungary', in A. Patrignani and R. Villé (eds), *Rromani Youths*. UNICRI publication series No. 59. Rome.

Kovats, M. 1997. 'The Good, the Bad and the Ugly: Three Faces of "Dialogue"', *Contemporary Politics* 3(1): 55–71.

———. 1998. 'The Development of Roma Politics in Hungary 1989–1995', PhD dissertation. Portsmouth: University of Portsmouth.

Macfie Archives. 2007. University of Liverpool, see Archive Hub at http://www.archiveshub.ac.uk/news/0606gls.html

Majtényi, B., and G. Majtényi. 2016. *A Contemporary History of Exclusion: The Roma Issue in Hungary from 1945 to 2015*. Budapest: CEU Press.

Margalit, G. 2007. 'Zigeunerpolitik und Zigeunerdiskurs im Deutschland der Nachkriegszeit', in M. Zimmermann (ed.), *Zwischen Erziehung und Vernichtung*. Stuttgart: Steiner Verlag, pp. 483–509.

Marx, K. (1843) 1992. 'On the Jewish Question', in K. Marx, *Early Writings*. London: Penguin, pp. 211–42.

McCagg, W. 1989. *A History of Habsburg Jews 1670–1918*. Bloomington: Indiana University Press.

Noszkai, G. 1995. 'Nemzet? Értelmiség? Értelem! Nemzetiség!' [Nation? Intelligentsia? Intelligence? National/ethnic minority?], in P. Szuhay et al. (eds), *Cigány kultúra* [Gypsy Culture]. Nyár: BUKSZ.

Oprea, A. 2017. 'Toward the Recognition of Critical Race Theory in Human Rights Law', in J. Bhabha, A. Mirga and M. Matache (eds), *Realizing Roma Rights*. Philadelphia: University of Pennsylvania Press, pp. 39–56.

Pittaway, M. 2012. *The Workers' State: Industrial Labor and the Making of Socialist Hungary, 1944–1958*. Pittsburgh, PA: University of Pittsburgh Press.

Pogány, G., and G. Bán. 1958. 'A magyarországi cigányság helyzetéről' [On the situation of Hungarian Gypsies], *Munkaügyi Szemle* 5: 42–45.

Pogány, I. 2004. *The Roma Café*. London: Pluto Press.

Solt, O. 1998. 'Solt Ottilia: Interjúzni muszáj' [Ottilia Solt: Interviewing is necessary], in K. István, F. Eörsi János and F. Havas Gábor (eds), *Méltóságot mindenkinek. Összegyűjtött írások I* [Dignity for all. Collected works]. Budapest: Beszélő, pp. 29–48.

Spivak, G. 1988. 'Can the Subaltern Speak?', in C. Nelson and L. Grossberg (eds), *Marxism and the Interpretation of Culture*. Urbana: University of Illinois Press, pp. 271–313.

Stewart, M. 1997. *The Time of the Gypsies*. Oxford: Westview.

———. 2001. 'Communist Roma Policy 1945–1989 as Seen through the Hungarian Case', in W. Guy (ed.), *Between Past and Future*. Hatfield: University of Hertfordshire Press.

Stoler, A.L. 2002. 'Colonial Archives and the Arts of Governance', *Archival Science* 2: 87–109.

Swain, N. 1992. *Hungary: The Rise and Fall of Feasible Socialism*. London: Verso.
Szabó, J. 2016. '1956 cigány narratívái' [1956 Gypsy Narratives], in F. Vitéz Ferenc (ed.), *Mediárium X*. Debrecen: DRHE Kölcsey Ferenc Tanítóképző Intézet, pp. 14–24.
———. 2017. 'The Forgotten Gypsy Heroes of the Hungarian Revolution of 1956'. Retrieved 29 November 2018 from https://www.szabonekarmanjudit.hu/publikaciok.
Szuhay, P. 1995. 'Constructing a Gypsy National Culture', *Budapest Review of Books* 5(3): 111–20.
Tauber, I. 1979. 'A cigányok által elkövetett bűncselekmények kriminológiai kutatása' [Criminological Research of Crimes Committed by Gypsies], *Belugyi Szemle* 5: 49–57.
Trehan, N. 2009. 'Human Rights Entrepreneurship in Post-Socialist Hungary: From "Gypsy Problem" to "Roma Rights"'. PhD dissertation. London: London School of Economics and Political Science, University of London.
Trehan, N., and I. Crowhurst. 2006. 'Minority Groups and Reproductive Rights: Coerced Sterilisation and Female Genital Mutilation in Europe', in H. Widdows, I. Alkorta-Idiakez and A. Emaldi-Cirion (eds), *Women's Reproductive Rights*. New York: Palgrave Macmillan, pp. 88–108.
Trehan, N., and A. Kóczé. 2009. 'Racism, (Neo-)Colonialism and Social Justice: The Struggle for the Soul of the Romani Movement in Post-socialist Europe', in G. Huggan and I. Law (eds), *Racism, Postcolonialism, Europe*. Liverpool: Liverpool University Press, pp. 50–73.
van Baar, H. 2011. *The European Roma: Minority Representation, Memory and the Limits of Transnational Governmentality*. Amsterdam: F&N.
van Dijk, T. 1991. *Racism and the Press*. London: Routledge.
Varga, I. 2006. 'Szerettem a szabadságot' [I Loved Freedom], *Barátság* 13(5): 5132–33.
Vekerdi, J., and G. Meszáros. 1978. *A cigányság a felemelkedés útján* [Gypsies on the Road to Rising]. Budapest: Hazafias Népfront Országos Tanácsa.
Wizner, B. 1999. 'The Development of the Romany National Movement in Hungary'. Unpublished MA thesis. Budapest: Central European University.
Zoltan, F. 2006. 'Citizens or Denizens? The Future of Romani Integration in Europe'. Panel presentation, Centre for the Study of Human Rights, London School of Economics, June.

CHAPTER 4

❀ ❀ ❀

GENDERED AND RACIALIZED SOCIAL INSECURITY OF ROMA IN EAST CENTRAL EUROPE

Angéla Kóczé

This chapter contributes to the analysis of gendered and racialized poverty of Roma in East Central Europe (ECE). Gender and racial inequalities certainly existed under state socialism, but since its fall at the end of the 1980s, neoliberal market capitalism has contributed considerably to the reproduction and reinforcement of the racialization of poverty, and given it a different, more intense scope and depth. The region's welfare restructure, from welfare to workfare, has had a devastating impact on the material lives of particular social classes and ethnic/racialized groups. In post-1989 scholarship, scholars working on Roma-related issues, and feminist scholars in Eastern Europe, have respectively added Roma and women separately to the list of the main 'losers' of the welfare transition. Both groups of scholars have independently come to the conclusion that, because of the narrowing of social rights and political guarantees, Roma as well as women have become increasingly excluded and marginalized in the region's newly established democracies.

Most scholars who have examined the transition of the political and economic restructure in ECE, and particularly the shift from protective welfare regimes to punitive workfare ones, have largely overlooked the underlying feminization and racialization of social security that have become key characteristics of neoliberal capitalism. One of its main critics, the sociologist

Loïc Wacquant, has underscored the structural changes that are associated with neoliberal capitalism, which include the decline of manufacturing, the elimination of traditional, factory or unskilled jobs, the rise of precarious employment, the erosion and/or privatization of welfare services, the polarization of wealth, and ghettoization and spatial segregation of certain racialized minorities who are governed through punitive apparatuses (legislation, policies, etc.) (Wacquant 2001, 2009). Even those who have critiqued neoliberal capitalism have frequently not or not adequately recognized the intersecting gendered and racialized effects of capitalist production that exemplify and reproduce exploitative relations and structural violence. In her seminal book, Adrienne Roberts (2017) demonstrates that she is one of the few scholars who do actually address the intersecting gender and racial aspects of neoliberal capitalism. She argues that the destruction of welfare through policing and penal regimes has been used to coercively discipline the poor and marginalized segments of society – something she considers as characteristic of the history of capitalism. She extends her argument and emphatically points out that the forms of legalized punishment and restructured welfare have resulted in a gendered and racialized institutionalized operation. According to her, gender and race are the key factors through which this operation has been constructed and regulated, partly as forms of disciplining and devaluing the labour associated with social reproduction (ibid.: 3). This chapter builds on her and other theorizations of welfare restructure, as well as on a review of and critical engagement with sociological debates on punitive welfare reforms in East Central European countries. By so doing, I will identify the intersecting gendered, racialized and classed mechanisms that have disproportionately disadvantaged Roma, and Romani women in particular. This is all the more important, since their situation has often not been incorporated in analyses of the region's main welfare reforms.

In this chapter, I follow Kimberlé Williams Crenshaw (1989), who coined the term 'intersectionality' to analyse the experience of black women who are not included in traditional scholarship focusing on gender or race. These divisive boundaries are currently established in welfare-gender and welfare-Roma studies as separate and largely exclusive realms of scholarship. Indirectly, this scholarly approach, which uses race, gender and sex as separate and exclusionary categories, has led to the further marginalization and invisibilization of racialized women such as the Romani, and their lived experiences. Intersectional theoretical and methodological paradigms are important to capture the complex intersecting structural and discursive inequalities based on race, gender and class, as well as to highlight the gendered and racialized experience of unemployed, low-income Romani women, who are differently positioned in ECE welfare reform from Romani men and non-Romani women. One profound difficulty in conducting the kind of analysis that I am calling for is that it requires cross-country, comparative, desegregated data based on both ethnicity and gender – and these data have rarely been collected.

I argue that social and political discourses on neoliberal welfare have generally become racialized and gendered, and have produced the categories of the 'deserving' (white) and 'undeserving' (racialized, Roma) poor, which have become implicit norms and tacit assumptions in the dominant modes of poverty governance. Moreover, these categories have become prominent tools of social control, such as policing, correcting 'behaviours' and improving 'work ethics', and have led to masking structural unemployment, poverty and inequality in East Central Europe. Poverty governance has emerged as part of a broader political and economic restructuring that some have described as the neoliberalization of welfare, although this term has been contested. One of my main arguments is that the neoliberalization of welfare has deepened the gendered racialization of Roma. This process requires scholars to rethink and reframe their theoretical and methodological interventions, which should go beyond the more established welfare-related scholarship on East Central Europe that tends to deal with gender and race in relative isolation.

In line with these required redirections, my aim is to contribute to the emerging literature on the gendered, racialized and classed welfare reforms in East Central Europe, which show the normalization of racialized practices of disciplinary and punitive poverty governance. Furthermore, this approach goes beyond the narrow economic conception of neoliberalism as a market ideology, and proposes a sociological conceptualization of the impact and logic of neoliberal poverty governance that includes gendered racialization, paternalization, workfare, penalization, social insecurity and spatial segregation through discourses of 'dependency' and 'individual responsibility'. This approach to neoliberalism implies that we have to theorize the welfare restructuring not only as an austerity measure to reduce public spending, but also as a core state mechanism that differentiates 'worthy' from 'unworthy' gendered and racialized citizens in the lower regions of social stratification. I will use both empirical evidence and several years of fieldwork in 'underdeveloped', micro-regions in north-east Hungary to clarify the operations and consequences of the gendered, racialized and classed regimes of poverty governance in East Central Europe.

Neoliberal Social Insecurity: From Welfare to Workfare

Neoliberalism as a contested, paradoxical practice seems to have spread all over the world and reconfigured itself into gendered, sexualized, racialized and classed 'local manifestations'. John Clarke (2008), for instance, has characterized neoliberalism as a 'pervasive' concept that is entangled with various theoretical frameworks ranging from classic and neo-Marxist engagements with class and political economy to hegemony and governmentality (see also van Baar 2011: 164). As a contested concept in which specific localized manifestations have been recognized, neoliberalism (mainly critique of neoliberalism) has also been mobilized as a productive explanatory framework regarding the post-1989 Europeanization of Roma affairs without focusing on the intersection of gender and race (Templer 2006; Sigona and Trehan 2009; van Baar 2011; Themelis 2016).

Several scholars have pointed out that the promise of social and economic prosperity with EU accession has failed and rather conveyed disillusionment and racial resentment (Templer 2006; Trehan and Sigona 2009; Kóczé 2012). Nando Sigona and Nidhi Trehan (2009) have discussed neoliberalism as an imported and externally imposed framework of policies that has increased the marginalization and precarization of large segments of the European population, including large numbers of marginalized Roma. Sypros Themelis (2016) highlights that the current socioeconomic crisis in a neoliberal Europe has further intensified the existing racial and social inequalities between Roma and non-Roma. He also maintains that the 'capitalist reintegration of Eastern Europe has had devastating effects for the Roma who, even before the transition, used to belong to the most vulnerable section of the working class in economic, cultural and political terms' (ibid.: 7). I follow Aihwa Ong's approach to neoliberalism who defines it as 'reconfiguring relationships between governing and the governed, power and knowledge, and sovereignty and territoriality' (Ong 2006: 3). Ong draws attention to the crucial issues of translation, articulation and discursive practices of neoliberalism. She argues for ethnographic attention to capture the local translation of neoliberalism into a historical spatiotemporal context. Her approach to neoliberalism opens up conceptual and political possibilities, and also poses an intellectual challenge, in terms of capturing hybrid assemblages of neoliberalism. Instead of using a monolithic and exclusionary concept of neoliberalism, several scholars (Ong 2006; van Baar 2011) have called for using a more innovative and productive reading of neoliberalism, and for understanding it along the lines of hybridity and assemblages of different styles and techniques of governing.

The Shift to Workfare

In post-1989 East Central Europe, there was a necessary shift to market-based economies, which have fundamentally restructured the system of social protection and welfare governance. Ever since, the countries in the region have periodically experienced economic ruptures and troubling social developments that brought enormous challenges, such as high unemployment, rising levels of poverty, social inequality and an increasingly ageing population. Indisputably, the changes in the region coincided with high expectations of the new political and economic systems, as well as with the hope that they would improve the situation of people living in extreme poverty, and protect middle and lower classes with a fragile socioeconomic status from pauperization (Tausz 2009; Ferge 2017). The region's drastic transformations from welfare to workfare started mainly in the 2000s and, thus, much later than in the UK or the US. One of the most radical interventions took place in Slovakia in 2004, where the government under Mikuláš Dzurinda introduced various cutbacks in social services. The most visible protest escalated into riots and the looting of shops by Roma and non-Roma in Eastern Slovakia. Nevertheless, politicians and the media immediately racialized the riots and lootings as 'Gypsy' riots (see van Baar 2011: 197).

Nicolette Makovicky explains the drastic change as the widely shared belief among people that they were 'living in a society where the state had abandoned its moral obligation to provide for its citizens: corporate tax had been lowered, but employment and inflation was on rise, welfare was being cut, and health insurance and pension schemes were being privatized at great cost to the individual citizen' (Makovicky 2013: 77). This was also the year in which the Slovak government introduced so-called 'activation work' policies that aimed to 'activate' long-term unemployed, who had lost their work ethic and, therefore, needed to be activated and turned into a productive wage-labour force (van Baar 2011; Grill 2018). In the longer run, however, in most East Central European countries, 'moderate' activation works rapidly changed into more punitive workfare schemes. The basic idea behind workfare (public works) is to make the delivery of social aid and assistance conditional on participation in publicly organized, communal work. In East Central Europe, workfare-based activation mainly involves low-skilled, low-prestige jobs provided by municipalities, which generally pay salaries below the minimum wage, and are financed from governmental budgets. The examples of the Czech Republic and Hungary are illustrative as well.

In the Czech Republic, the workfare version of activation was introduced in 2006 and gradually became more punitive. Tomáš Sirovátka (2014, 2016), who has extensively researched Czech activation policies, distinguishes three phases, which he qualifies as 'incentive reinforcement/work first' (2006), 'radical activation: workfare' (2007–08) and 'the failures of the activation reforms' (2012–13). The Slovak uprising of Roma in 2004 sparked by the shift to workfare was a warning sign for the neighbouring Czech Republic and

Hungary. Sirovátka succinctly points out that, 'until 2006, the social assistance scheme aimed at preventing poverty and social unrest, thus allowing for a peaceful transition to a market economy' (2016: 97). In the first phase, reforms mainly introduced a broad definition of suitable work (part-time, flexible, temporary jobs), conditionality as well as repressive sanctions (in the case of non-cooperation, existence minimum instead of living minimum, etc.), while in the second phase, activation work was increasingly radicalized and became a punitive tool. He also explains the 'failures' of the activation reforms owing to political and institutional factors. According to him, the government had several 'failures' caused by poor preparation, design and implementation of activation programmes, as the most important issue was to keep to the government's political commitment and cut public expenditures (Sirovátka 2016: 92).

In Hungary, the shift to workfare was solidified in 2009, when the socialist–liberal coalition introduced the 'Road to Work' programme (Szikra 2014; Szőke 2015). This programme was a culmination and extension of the previous public work programmes in which significantly fewer recipients of social benefits – only 10 to 15 per cent – were involved annually (Köllő 2011 cited in Vidra 2018: 76). The Hungarian 'Road to Work' programme increased and extended public works, first of all as a solution to long-term unemployment, by increasing the number of social aid recipients in public work. Until 2009, fourteen thousand people had been involved in public works annually. In 2009, this number increased to sixty thousand, and has grown progressively since (Scharle 2011: 14). However, the 'Road to Work' programme also serves two other aims. First, it has helped to provide a cheap, exploitable workforce for various public sectors, as well as for companies who face challenges due to a shortage of workers. Secondly, the programme has actively stigmatized, racialized and deepened the structural and discursive division between 'deserving' white poor and 'undeserving' Roma, while undermining the social citizenship of the beneficiaries of workfare (Szalai 2007, 2013, and this volume; van Baar 2011, 2012; Szőke 2015; Ferge 2017).

To a considerable extent, the reasons for the structural changes made to East Central European states and societies, such as the sweeping welfare reforms, have been attributed to the European integration and enlargement processes that took place throughout the 1990s and 2000s (Lendvai 2008; van Apeldoorn 2008). The European Union (EU) had the ambitious goal of becoming the 'most competitive' economy in the world by 2010. This strategic plan was set at the Lisbon summit of March 2000 (European Council 2000) and became known as the 'Lisbon Strategy'. Bastiaan van Apeldoorn (2008) has analysed what he calls 'embedded neoliberalism' in relation to Europe's multilevel crisis, and how it has been supported by the inherent contradictions within European governance: 'Drawing on Polanyi (1957), embeddedness here refers to the role of the state in sustaining and reproducing markets by in effect protecting society from the destructive effects of the self-regulating market' (van Apeldoorn 2008: 24–25). He also explains 'embedded neoliberalism' as that specific form of neoliberalism based on Polanyi's 'principle of social protection', which treats and protects humanity and nature as 'productive organization'. Embedded neoliberalism differs from what is commonly understood as neoliberalism, van Apeldoorn argues, since the latter is usually associated with the 'principle of economic liberalism' that aims to establish an unbridled self-regulated market. Van Apeldoorn argues that while these two contradictory principles are combined in the Lisbon Strategy, in the European project, the 'principle of social protection' has ultimately been fully subordinated to the 'principle of economic liberalism' (ibid.: 25). According to him, the Lisbon Agenda conceives social protection through the adaptability of the labour force in a competitive globalized world economy. He argues that when 'adhering to the notion that labour market flexibility can and should be combined with social security, the latter is made dependent on the former', and explains that the workfare state subordinates social protection, since 'work is the best way to prevent social exclusion and maintain social cohesion and that a recommodification strategy is the best way to get people back to work' (ibid.: 29).

Beyond the Dominant Analysis of the Shift to Workfare

When we combine a conceptualization of 'welfare to workfare' that is regionally specific with a feminist perspective of intersectionality, the ways in which the gendered, racialized and classed neoliberalization of welfare have significantly affected Romani women in East Central Europe come fully into view. In 2013, the European Union Agency for Fundamental Rights (FRA) published an analysis of data collected in eleven EU member states that is desegregated by gender, and covers primarily the core areas of employment, education, housing and health. This analysis shows, for instance, that only 21 per cent of Romani women are in paid work, compared to 35 per cent of Romani men. By comparison, to emphasize the precarious situation of all Roma in the EU: in 2017, in the twenty-eight EU member states, the average female (paid) employment rate was almost 67 per cent, while that of men was just over 78 per cent (European Commission 2018). The vulnerable status of Romani women can also be demonstrated by means of the survey's 'household poverty indicator'. According to the analysis, '87 per cent of Roma households have an income below the national at-risk-of-poverty level compared to 46 per cent of non-Roma households surveyed and compared to 17 per cent for the EU's population in general' (European Union Agency for Fundamental Rights 2013). The report also shows that families with four or more children are more likely to have the highest at-risk-of-poverty rate. As many as 90 per cent of Roma families with four or more children are below the at-risk-of-poverty threshold.

In fact, women in these families have become a primary target of welfare services in ECE. These women are overrepresented among those who rely on welfare benefits, and their existence is largely if not entirely dependent on them. When they are employed, many of them are actually offered a paid job in the social services sector, or a sector of the social services, including NGOs focused on services such as education and health. Moreover, these women are the wives, mothers and daughters whose unpaid household, care work and obligations are redefined by the shift in the welfare state. Romani women as beneficiaries, care givers and social workers are constitutive and indispensable actors of the welfare regime. Moreover, in many localities, Romani women work as mediators between Roma communities and various welfare institutions (Kóczé 2018).

Below, I argue why at least three analytical perspectives are essential to adequately discuss the East Central European gendered, racialized and classed neoliberal governance of poverty. First, we have to reframe welfare reform in East Central European countries; second, we should fundamentally problematize the discourse of 'welfare dependency'; and third, we have to critically analyse the discourse on the empowerment of Romani women. Let me first outline what these three perspectives imply before I further explain and analyse them in the remainder of this chapter.

The first perspective involves framing welfare reform in East Central Europe differently – namely, relinking social welfare and penal policies with intersecting racial, class and gender inequalities that have significantly shaped the structure of redistributive policies. Several studies show that millions of people have been pushed to the verges of societies, mainly those whose education and work experiences were not 'compatible' with the new competitive market economy. Postsocialist regimes, increasingly constrained by both domestic and international forces, have diminished state redistribution, restored privileges to specific institutions (such as church- or state-supported foundations), promoted private education, and excluded discursively and structurally those who are deemed as worthless or unproductive, such as gendered and racialized Roma groups. The shift to workfare-based welfare services significantly relies on a behaviourist philosophy. Some specific segments of public works have become a symbol of deterrence, surveillance and stigma that are particularly attached to Roma in segregated areas. Indeed, long-term unemployed, unskilled groups have become 'surplus' or 'problem' populations. They are under lock and key through punitive workfare, and forced into informal and often illegal 'culturalized' and racialized grey and black markets, as well as into illegal money lending (usury), trafficking and prostitution.

The second analytical perspective involves questioning the discourse of 'welfare dependency', which stigmatizes welfare recipients through an intensive discursive campaign, feeding into a racist mindset. The more symbolic discourses of 'welfare dependency' have significantly merged with the material conditions that justify the punitive measures of truncated welfare. The discourse that legitimizes the shift from welfare to workfare contains several underlying assumptions. It is reasonable to pose questions such as: 'Why are debates about poverty and racial/ethnic inequality in ECE framed in terms of welfare dependency?;' 'How and why has the term "welfare dependency" become racialized?'; 'Why have Romani women become the epicentre of social reproduction in the context of "welfare dependency"?'; and 'What are the racial and gender subtexts of this discourse, and what are the core assumptions?' The racialization of 'welfare dependency', constructed as a gendered and racialized biopolitical boundary between white deserving poor and non-white undeserving poor, ultimately hampers class solidarity among subordinated, precarious populations (see also van Baar, Chapter 5, this volume). Instead of solidarity and defending public welfare institutions, the system covertly promotes the racialization and collective scapegoating of Roma to obstruct or even criminalize resistance to neoliberal structural oppression. The term 'welfare dependency' has negative connotations, and also evokes the strong emotive image of the 'welfare mother', which has often been used to describe young Romani women who are over-supported and have lost their motivation to work. This trope of the 'underserving poor' is repeatedly used in social and political discourses.

The third perspective required for an adequate analysis is related to how women are supposedly empowered through undoing welfare. Many Romani women in ECE are employed by various NGOs under the banner of 'women's empowerment'. Aradhana Sharma persuasively argues that in the 'contemporary neoliberal era, empowerment has emerged as a keyword, effectively replacing the now much-maligned term welfare' (Sharma 2008: 15). The opposite of the 'end of welfare' or 'welfare dependency' has become coded as 'empowerment', Sharma argues, and we see something similar in the case of Romani women. This approach instrumentalizes women in the name of 'empowerment' to provide the largely absent or reduced welfare services, either on a voluntary basis or in the context of precarious working conditions.

Framing Matters: Gendered and Racialized Poverty Governance of Roma

The account by Dorothee Bohle and Béla Greskovits of the East Central European version of neoliberalism is depicted as 'an embedded neoliberal regime' coupled with the support of indigenous capitalists, increased employment mainly via state-financed public works, reduced social welfare expenditures and oppression of the socially and economically large populations who are viewed as 'incompatible' with their social and economic politics (Bohle and Greskovits 2007: 444). Statistical data show that Roma are one of the prominent, statistically overrepresented groups amongst the most disadvantaged populations who are most likely to be socially, economically and politically excluded and spatially segregated (European Union Agency for Fundamental Rights 2014). Despite the measurable exclusion and marginalization of Roma, there is a dominant diagnosis with regard to structural changes and subsequent framing that undermines the theorization of how gendered and racialized inequality impacts social stratification and social redistribution. Various scholars who have interpreted and discussed the consequences of global economic restructuring and the current financial crisis in ECE use some of the following phrases regarding the racial exclusion of Roma.

Dorottya Szikra (2014), for instance, has concisely elaborated on the reactions of Hungarian governments to the global economic crises and their social and political consequences since 2010. Through an analysis of three case studies, she illustrates the neoliberal, *étatist* and neoconservative turn of social policies in Hungary. Her first case study concerns reforms to the pension scheme and the drastic limitations of social insurance rights, while in her second case study she analyses the recent welfare reform that replaced unemployment benefits and activation policies with compulsory public works and workfare programmes. Her third and final case study critically examines the new family policy, which supports rich, productive families through a generous tax-credit system, instead of investing in the most disadvantaged families. Although it is not her central focus to provide an intersectional analysis of welfare restructuring, she timidly neglects to complicate her analysis through an interrogation of the intersections of race, gender and class. She uses the same phrase that many scholars have used when they talk about the ways in which structural and welfare reform have impacted Roma, and why they are overrepresented in the socially excluded and most marginalized population groups. Indeed, she concludes that the societal changes have contributed to 'the polarization of society and an increase in deep poverty, *especially, but not only among Roma*' (Szikra 2014: 488, emphasis added). Her article focuses on the welfare reform in Hungary, in particular during the Orbán government between 2010 and 2014. However, the framing of her article – thus, without a distinction between welfare beneficiaries – obscures the racialization and institutional racism against Roma in the welfare system.

Zsuzsanna Vidra has also recently analysed the sociopolitical context of the shift towards punitive workfare in Hungarian social policies. She disagrees with those scholars who have primarily explained the emergence and reinforcement of the Hungarian workfare regime as caused by processes of neoliberalization that have been both encouraged and supported by international organizations (Vidra 2018: 74). She argues that the welfare transformation towards punitive workfare took place in the mid-2000s and intensified with both the 2008 global financial crises and growing political populism. Her analysis primarily focuses on the workfare system, but tends to neglect the social and political factors behind the shift to punitive workfare. In her analysis, she accepts that the high and steadily increasing percentage of 'inactive' people of working age has been one of the most pressing issues in Hungary:

> [This percentage] rose from 23 per cent in 1990 to 35 per cent in 1996 (Fábián et al. 2014). The high rate of inactivity is linked to the low education level of this population. For example, in 2010 the employment rate of those with only primary education was 28 per cent for males and 24 per cent for females; among the skilled workers the rate was 68 per cent for males and 56 per cent for females (Messing 2012; Messing et al. 2013). (Vidra 2018: 75)

First of all, Vidra's uncommented use of the phrase 'inactivity' is problematic, for this terminology is an integral part of the neoliberal newspeak that has invisibilized the racializing contexts in which social policies have been articulated on the ground and, thus, this discourse and its implications should be critically discussed as well (van Baar 2011, 2012). Later, Vidra refers to János Ladányi's research to admit that the problem of the poorly educated, 'inactive' population in Hungary remained unresolved, despite the 'solidarity type of social policy instruments' of the early 1990s. Her line of reasoning continues as follows:

> In sum, the economy has been incapable of absorbing this surplus of manpower since the early 1990s. The most vulnerable among the low-educated group is the Roma. *This is, however, far from being a Roma-specific problem: it affects about 700–800 thousand people, of which 'only' about one-third is Roma*. However, they are overrepresented in this socially excluded group by four or five times, while about 40 per cent of all Roma belong to this population (Ladányi 2012). (Vidra 2018: 75, emphasis added)

In this line of argumentation, Vidra isolates postsocialist legacies from the hybrid local articulations of neoliberal welfare and, at the same time, does not discuss or even acknowledge the consolidation of gendered and racialized stratification. However, as I have argued above, framing the neoliberal restructuring of both welfare and poverty governance *without* linking these processes to the gendered and racialized impact of redistributive policy is highly problematic. Most notably, discussing the restructure of social policies primarily or even strictly in their economic context results in neglecting to address the long-term structural generational violence against Roma, and Romani women in particular. Vidra's argumentation that the discussed problem is '*far from being a Roma-specific*' one is similar to the destigmatizing efforts in the United States in the 1960s, when leading advocates emphasized the fact that white recipients comprised the majority of the welfare recipients (Schram, Soss and Fording 2003: 196–221).

In the literature, a direct connection between welfare reforms and gendered racialization in East Central Europe is rarely made and, consequently, the impact and reproduction of marginalized/excluded positions in societal structures remains largely unnoticed. A notable example is Júlia Szalai, one of the few sociologists in the region who has connected welfare distribution with ethnic subordination, and qualified this relationship as a key factor leading to societal stratification (Szalai 2007, 2013, and in this volume). She has carefully explained the ethnic subordination of Roma in the Hungarian process of welfare restructuring. According to her, 'the indicated processes [welfare reform in postsocialist Hungary] concluded in the evolvement of a bifurcated welfare system with hermetically separated structures of services for the well-integrated and the marginalized groups of society, respectively' (Szalai 2013: 13). She has discussed what she calls the 'highly segregationist world of local welfare assistance', which functions differently for the presumably 'well-integrated' and the needy, who are further divided from the former along a tangible colour line that traverses Hungarian society. Szalai has argued that the separated welfare system for the marginalized is vindicated by the notion of 'cultural otherness' (ibid.: 14).

János Ladányi has articulated the racialization of Roma even more explicitly. He recognizes the existence and continued reproduction of ethnic disadvantages affecting Roma that have accumulated throughout history. In other words, the structural disadvantages of Roma were not a newly emerging phenomenon in postsocialist Hungary but, as he underlines, the poverty of Roma has intensified during the rapid market reforms and the development of the neoliberal state, leading to a situation in which the Roma have become a highly racialized underclass (Ladányi 2001: 67–79).

Hitherto, there has been limited comparative statistical evidence that reveals the *gendered* racialization of poverty. Iván Szelényi and Donald

TABLE 4.1 Poverty rates among the Roma population in three countries, 1992 (age range 20–57).

	Bulgaria		Hungary		Slovakia	
	Men	Women	Men	Women	Men	Women
ROMA	40.4	55.3	41.4	44.3	32.1	35.8
NON-ROMA	10.0	12.5	7.0	10.6	9.4	13.3
RATIO OF ROMA	1.37		1.07		1.11	
N* (ROMA)	61	46	42	49	57	48

*N = Number

Source: Szelényi and Treiman (1992).

Treiman's (1992, cited in Emigh, Fodor and Szelényi 2001) comparative and cross-country study of Bulgaria, Hungary and Slovakia provides some evidence of the gendered racialization of Roma. Based on the data they collected, almost half of the Roma live in poverty, compared to only 10 per cent of the non-Roma population. In these three countries, desegregated data are available that are based on gender and ethnicity (Emigh, Fodor and Szelényi 2001: 22–23), and this illuminates the intersecting gendered racialization between the Roma and non-Roma populations.

Based on the significant differences between Roma and non-Roma, as well as between men and women, Rebecca Jean Emigh, Eva Fodor and Iván Szelényi have argued that 'one of the characteristics of the newly emerging poverty in Central and Southern Europe is that important differences are created among women' (Emigh, Fodor and Szelényi 2001: 22). Contrary to other scholars, they have also noted that the significant discrepancy – or, as they have called it, the 'bifurcation' – between Romani and non-Romani women is structured along racial lines: '[W]omen at the very bottom of the social hierarchy are minority women, in particular, of Roma ethnicity' (ibid.). Contrary to white non-Romani women in the working class, Romani women did not collect significant resources or hoard opportunities as beneficiaries of the 'exploitative emancipation' during the era of state socialism; instead, they were primarily treated as 'welfare problems' (ibid.: 23). In her seminal study *Inventing the Needy*, Lynne Haney describes how Romani women were mainly identified as 'bad mothers' by welfare institutions during state socialism. She explains that, '[w]hile good mothers manoeuvred through the maternalist welfare apparatus, bad mothers were more confined in their movements . . . They had a harder time passing welfare workers' domesticity tests, and their failure to do so left them more vulnerable to the coercive arm of this welfare apparatus' (Haney 2002: 149). Thus, Romani women accumulated gendered and racialized disadvantages that were later reproduced and rearticulated during postsocialist welfare reforms.

There was an *'ingénue'* hope in East Central Europe during the transitional period that the countries involved would not just go through political and economic changes, but that these changes would be accompanied by the development of a new 'progressive' welfare system. Katalin Tausz has evaluated the new welfare system in ECE in the following way: these countries 'fell into the trap of creating a welfare system while making cuts in social expenditure required in order to mitigate budgetary crisis. These activities took place during a period of high unemployment, of rising levels of poverty and social inequality' (Tausz 2009: 245). While there was hope that the new, reformed welfare system would improve the social well-being of millions of people, prevent the pauperization of middle classes and provide the basic needs for those living in extreme poverty, the system finally resulted in new racialized forms of exclusion, intensified by the market-based economy and the neoliberalization of welfare. In most analyses related to welfare reform, Roma are mentioned – usually only in a few sentences – when these analyses discuss how social inequalities and poverty rates have changed during welfare reforms. For instance, Tausz refers to Roma as a factor that increases the risk of poverty without further analysis: 'Unemployment, especially long-term unemployment, the lack of appropriate qualifications, the type of settlement (e.g. village or small town) and being Romany – all these significantly increased, and continue to increase, the risk of poverty' (ibid.: 256). In the same *Handbook of European Welfare Systems* (Schubert, Hegelich and Bazant 2009) to which Tausz contributed, the chapter on Slovakia says a bit more about Roma; the high percentage of Roma receiving benefits, for instance, would have become one of the persistent problems of the Slovak welfare system. The chapter also mentions that Roma have been discriminated against for decades and that the vast majority of them are uneducated; they are 'low skilled and living in territorial *seclusion*' (Wientzek and Meyer 2009: 463, emphasis added). The authors' choice of the term 'seclusion' tends to suggest that Roma *chose* to live in 'solitude', whereas their isolated living in segregated settlements has obviously been the result of intersecting social, political, economic and territorial exclusion (see also Szalai, this volume). Later in the text, the authors address the exclusion of Roma from the labour market (ibid.: 464), but this mere acknowledgement does not argue in favour of the *structural* links between income inequality, welfare redistribution and gendered and racialized disadvantages.

The chapter on the Czech welfare system in the same handbook also dedicates a short part to 'Roma communities' (Ripka and Mareš 2009: 116). It acknowledges that Roma live under difficult social and economic conditions. The chapter also highlights that there are approximately four hundred segregated communities in various Czech towns, and that the situation of Roma is characterized by high unemployment, often between 90 and 100 per cent. Voitech Ripka and Miroslav Mareš state that the vast majority of Roma are living in *'dependency on social assistance benefits* and state social support benefits' (2009: 116, emphasis added). Furthermore, they argue that there are two principal stances towards Roma, one centred on culture and the other on social exclusion. The chapter reflects neither on the gendered racialization of 'culturally centred' policy, nor on how Roma are excluded from insurance-based welfare services. Instead, the authors use a vocabulary that tends to further stigmatize Roma, by using terms such as 'dependency on social benefits' to legitimize the introduction of activation policies or other techniques developed in the context of the neoliberal governance of poverty.

I have argued that in order to analyse welfare reforms in East Central Europe critically and to interrogate the gendered racialization involved, we should approach these reforms differently and use both intersectional desegregated data (ethnicity, gender, class) and intersectional analyses. This shift requires an analysis that explains how the structures of redistribution have changed and how the poor have been governed by various governmental techniques. Moreover, the proposed redirecting of the analysis of welfare reforms will also contribute to a significant extension of the space for specifying a critique of contemporary institutional racism, paternalistic practices and (perhaps) well-intentioned gender and colour-blind academic discourses.

Gendered and Racialized Discourse of 'Welfare Dependents'

I have already touched upon how Romani women were perceived and treated as 'bad mothers' by welfare institutions and workers (Haney 2002). However, Romani women have always borne the labour of social reproduction to maintain and reproduce the working Romani population. Barbara Laslett and Johanna Brenner (1989) have defined social reproduction as activities and attitudes, behaviours and emotions, responsibilities and relationships that are directly involved in the maintenance and reproduction of life on a daily and generational basis. Much of the literature on social reproduction is embedded in a feminist political economy framework that mainly focuses on unpaid domestic labour, women's economic roles in capitalist societies and how various social institutions (state, market, civil society, households and the like) contribute to social reproduction.

However, the social reproduction of racialized poor women has historically always been connected with their relationship to 'worthiness', as defined through social, economic and political discourses. Bridgette Baldwin (2010) has explored how economic 'worthiness' has defined welfare policy discourse on black women throughout the history of welfare in the United States. She has convincingly shown that despite the economic activity of poor black women, they were often described as 'welfare queens', labelled as 'underserving and unworthy' of any social welfare programme. She also underlines that in US history, despite the changing economic role of black working-class women, they were always stripped of 'respectability'. The latter qualification was mainly reserved for white women who were served by black female domestic workers. Baldwin argues that poor black women were 'consistently deemed to be the negation, the opposite of compensatory worthiness within the poor for contradictory reasons' (Baldwin 2010: 5). Thus, following Baldwin's line of argumentation, regardless of whether poor black women were historically framed as 'employable workers' or 'welfare queens', their representations within welfare policies and related discourses have served as a classifying gendered and racialized meta-narrative to regulate who deserves and who does not deserve to be (fully) supported by the welfare regime.

In spite of the growing literature on the neoliberal restructuring of welfare in East Central Europe (Lendvai 2008), there is not much scholarly work that explicitly centres on gender and racialization. Nevertheless, racism and racialization continue to limit the life opportunities of racialized populations, while enforcing the structural advantage and privilege of being white. The feminist activist-scholar Silvia Frederici (2018) argues that capitalism has normalized structural violence in various forms of disciplining women of the lower classes, and in particular women who are targets of racial discrimination, to legitimate their subordination to a patriarchal capitalist order. She also highlights that there is currently an escalation of violence against racialized women. She considers 'globalization' as a political restructuring, a 're-colonization' process, in which capital has an uncontested dominance to control and rearrange various resources, wealth and labour. This process cannot be achieved without discursively and materially violating women who are directly responsible for social reproduction and have the gendered capacity to keep their communities together (Frederici 2018: 2). In relation to welfare restructuring and redistribution in the neoliberal era, Frances Fox Piven has argued that redistribution is no longer taking place from the rich to the poor, but rather from the bottom and middle to the top (Piven 2015: 3). The Hungarian sociologist Zsuzsa Ferge calls this mode of operation a 'perverse' welfare redistribution (2017: 87) that increases wealth and social benefits at the top (insurance-based social benefits, unequal tax system, etc.) at the expense of basic welfare for the lower classes, and in particular for racialized poor Roma in East Central Europe. This unequal and unjust welfare redistribution has perpetuated and normalized structural violence.

The stigmatized representation of racialized populations as 'welfare dependents', 'lazy', 'sexually promiscuous', 'reproducers of a dangerous population' or 'lacking a work ethic' supports practices of welfare reform that reduce the social benefits of the 'underserving' poor (Gilens 1999; Schram, Soss and Fording 2003). Moreover, this kind of symbolic (gendered and racialized) discourse has been used to legitimize welfare restructure and the devastation of the material conditions of the racialized poor. Reflecting on the situation in East Central Europe, similar kinds of representations of poor Romani women have served as iconic images in the shift of social policy to workfare. On the one hand, poor Romani women are constructed as 'welfare dependents' and situated at the epicentre of the social reproduction of undesired/unwanted Roma (Kóczé 2014). On the other hand, however, they are also perceived as 'change-makers' by recognizing and institutionalizing their social reproductive role in the course of dismantling welfare. First, I will analyse the impact of the symbolic discourse that constructs Romani women as 'welfare dependents', and then discuss their role in undoing welfare.

The iconic representation of Romani women as 'bad mothers', 'welfare dependents' and 'welfare mothers' is a fundamental part of the social narrative that depicts women of low morale and uncontrolled sexuality. With the shift to workfare, welfare policies – although technically 'a-racial' – have, even more problematically, been articulated racially. There are various largely institutionalized aspects that have contributed to the gendered racialization of Roma, including historical legacies, media discourses, public opinion, policy articulations and, last but not least, discourses of welfare reform that have centred on work ethics and duties.

In 2013, the *Slovak Spectator* reported that there was a well-known public myth, according to which 'Roma abuse the social benefits system by having many children, refusing to work and boosting their incomes from state contributions, while making more money than many who are actually working' (Cuprik 2013). This myth captures the essence of the racialization of welfare. First, this myth illustrates that welfare has become equivalent to support for an 'underserving' part of the population that allegedly lacks any responsibility and work ethos. Second, the myth depicts Roma as an inferior group that strategically produces children to abuse public resources, which have been indirectly supported by ostensibly hard-working, non-Roma taxpayers. A similar myth encouraged the Hungarian far-right political party Jobbik to propose the elimination of the so-called *megélhetési gyermekvállalás* ('children for cash' or 'having children for strategic, opportunistic reasons') policy.[1] Without mentioning the Roma – but using a clearly racializing subtext connected with them – Jobbik advocated the following in its 2014 general election manifesto:

We would transform the family welfare benefits system by putting a brake on having children for cash, and supporting responsible family planning. We would transform the [child] benefit system so that parents aged over 18 would, from the third child onwards, only receive child benefit through tax reduction. Those families raising children while on social benefits [the unemployed, long-term unemployed and public workfare participants] will receive social and child benefits via transfer to a social services card.[2] (Jobbik 2014. Program for the National Election, my translation)

The fertility of Romani women and their problematization as a threat to the nation are recurrent themes in and around welfare policies. In 2009, Oszkár Molnár, the mayor of Edelény in Northeast Hungary, claimed that Romani women deliberately harmed their unborn children. He stated that they hit their bellies with rubber hammers and took medicines to give birth to children with disabilities in order to be entitled to higher social benefits. Even though Molnár was a representative of Fidesz – at that time the ruling party at the national level – Fidesz did not condemn his statements, suggesting that they represented only a 'local issue' (Hungarian Helsinki Committee 2011). However, his racist statements evoked one of the biggest protests of Romani women in recent history. They requested that he quit his position as mayor.[3] Another 'incident' took place in a hospital in the large north-eastern city of Miskolc in February 2016. A Romani woman who was giving birth claimed that she had been subjected to verbal harassment and racist remarks, including 'You Gypsies give birth only for the money!' (Balogh 2017).

In the midst of the profound welfare restructuring, in 1998, the sociologist Márta Gyenei published an article in the Hungarian daily newspaper *Népszabadság* that supported the idea of 'children for cash'. Basically, her research shows that Romani women's reproductive practices contribute strategically to the income of their families through child benefits (Gyenei 1998). Gyenei considers this as one of the economic survival strategies of poor Roma and non-Roma families who were radically affected by structural unemployment in the 1990s. In those days, she was criticized for using the terms 'children for cash' and the 'strategic reproduction' of Romani women. Currently, however, political parties and media have used and nurtured these cultural scripts to legitimize the shift to workfare, and support the idea of the 'underserving' poor.

The rage over minorities, even though they are numerically smaller, constitutes a problematic 'we-making' process (Appadurai 2006: 49–50). Arjun Appadurai has eloquently addressed the need for some majorities to set in motion an 'us-and-them dialectic', which would be key to the consolidation of their majoritarian identities, and which could even lead to what he calls 'predatory identities' (ibid.: 51, see also van Baar with Kóczé, this volume). He defines as 'predatory those identities whose social construction and *mobilization require the extinction of other, proximate social categories, defined as threats* to the very existence of some group, defined as a "we" (ibid.: 51, emphasis added). In a similar vein, Romani women who embody the social reproduction of Roma have been defined as threats to majoritarian identities in East Central Europe. Gendered antigypsyism has been 'reawakened' and thus become manifest through these discourses related to welfare benefits and social reproduction, in which Roma as a minority group are strictly perceived as fundamentally different from those who are members of the majority.

Empowerment of Romani Women by Undoing Welfare

The restructuring of welfare in East Central Europe has created some conflicting arrangements. As described above, in the context of newly arranged welfare policies, Romani women have started to embody the social reproduction of undesired/unwanted Roma who 'illegitimately' take advantage of welfare. At the same time, however, and seemingly in contradiction with this role, these women have also become the target of various development programmes that conceptualize Romani women as 'change-makers' in their communities. Mainstream feminists have usually celebrated the empowerment and emancipation of racialized women. However, there is an emerging critical feminist scholarship that contests the empowerment and emancipation of women (particularly working-class and racialized women) in the era of global capitalism. Currently, social citizenship has been undermined and welfare has been restructured by an instrumentalization of women's social reproductive role in their communities. Nancy Fraser (2009), Hester Eisentein (2010) and other scholars have critiqued the mainstream feminism that has become co-opted by the ideology of advanced capitalism and consumerism. Zuzana Uhde (2016) calls this situation, in which feminist publics and political issues are considerably commodified and marketized, 'distorted emancipation'. According to Uhde, most feminist achievements remain rather private and contribute to the private economy by neglecting or further stigmatizing 'public goods' or 'public services'. Similarly, Aradhana Sharma has persuasively argued that in the 'contemporary neoliberal era, empowerment has emerged as a keyword effectively replacing the now much-maligned term welfare' (Sharma 2008: 15). The mechanisms of the 'end of welfare' or 'welfare dependency' have become recoded or reframed as 'empowerment' in a development world, similar to the use of 'empowerment' regarding Romani women in East Central Europe. This specific reframing of the capacities of Romani women in terms of empowerment reflects the Foucauldian conceptualization of neoliberalism as both an economic-political and a sociocultural project. In this respect, neoliberalism is 'premised upon a shift towards governmentalities that merge market and state imperatives and which produce self-regulating "good subjects" who embody ideals of individual responsibility' (Bernstein and Jakobsen 2013).

Most Romani women's 'empowerment' projects are related to Romani women's social reproductive role, making them responsible for their community/family welfare while also making them compensate for the lack of welfare services in their own communities. As I have discussed elsewhere (Kóczé 2016), in 2011, there were several Roma Mother Centres in Hungary that were supported financially and professionally by the Roma Initiatives Office of the Open Society Foundation (OSF). The main aim of these centres was to act as a kind of 'self-help' mothers' group that had to facilitate access to services (healthcare, childcare, education etc.), and play an important role in mobilizing their communities through the organization of common activities. The aim was that, in the long run, these centres might contribute to Roma self-organization and political mobilization processes, and promote the growth of advocacy skills and social inclusion. The Colourful Pearls Association (Színes Gyöngyök Egyesület) and SZIROM, a Roma women's organization located in Pécs and Szikszó, managed these Roma Mother Centres. After approximately three years, all Roma Mother Centres closed owing to the lack of funding from OSF's Roma Initiatives Office.

Based on my observations, the concept of the programme was built on the logic of a neoliberal state that considerably privatizes and philanthropizes social services and, thus, through undoing public welfare, deprives in particular the poorest citizens. With good intentions, the organizers wanted to create a self-sustaining community and day-care centre, based on the active involvement of mothers and their (unpaid) voluntary work. By so doing, the organizers aimed to improve social, health and educational services for Roma families. However, one of my first questions relates to the material reality in these poor marginalized communities, and whether they actually allow for such initiatives. Indeed, how can we expect 'low-income' mothers – in actual fact, mothers without income – to do voluntary work sustaining the operation of a day-care centre that was previously provided as a welfare service? Notwithstanding all the good intentions of and behind the programme, it tended to further isolate Roma from non-Roma communities, and to racialize social services at the local level. The programme promoted the responsibilization of Roma communities and individuals, and indirectly maintained or even reinforced structurally racialized and gendered oppression. As in the Foucauldian conceptualization of neoliberalism as a form of governmentality that aims at producing 'self-responsible', self-regulating neoliberal subjects, this programme did not substantially reflect the shrinking role of the government in the delivery of welfare, but instead assumed, claimed and recreated the self-responsible neoliberal Romani mothers as part of the charity programme.

Conclusion

In mainstream studies that discuss welfare reform in East Central Europe, it is common to talk about poverty and income inequality without adequately reflecting on the deeply entrenched gendered and racialized social structures that perpetuate structural violence, particularly against racialized women. In this chapter, I have proposed the adoption of three analytical perspectives that should lead to addressing more thoroughly and more comprehensively these deeply entrenched gendered and racialized social structures. The first perspective requires a significant reframing of welfare transformations in postsocialist East Central Europe. Instead of viewing income inequality and poverty as distinctly class- or economy-related issues, I have argued that we should take into account the gendered and racialized divisions as social structuring factors that reproduce inequalities. My second analytical perspective critically reflects on the discourse of 'welfare dependency' that has stigmatized and racialized welfare recipients, and contributed to the production of what Appadurai has called 'predatory identities' (2006). The third analytical perspective I have advocated relates to the problematic neoliberal discourse of emancipation and empowerment of women who have been considerably instrumentalized to actively participate in dismantling public welfare. In this context, under the banner of 'empowerment', Romani women have been encouraged – mostly on a voluntary or low-income basis – to fulfil a role in welfare delivery that was previously organized as a social service. Much more research will be required to review and analyse how gender and racialization have shaped seemingly neutral welfare/ workfare policies in East Central Europe; yet I hope that the three analytical perspectives that I have introduced in this chapter will contribute to the development of a sharper vision and articulation of the roles of gender and racialization.

Angéla Kóczé is an Assistant Professor of Romani Studies and Academic Director of the Roma Graduate Preparation Program at Central European University in Budapest, Hungary. In 2013–2017, she was a Visiting Assistant Professor in the Department of Sociology and Women's, Gender and Sexuality Studies Program at Wake Forest University in Winston Salem, NC, USA. She has published several peer-reviewed articles and book chapters with various international presses, including Palgrave Macmillan, Ashgate,

Routledge and CEU Press, as well as several thematic policy papers related to social inclusion, gender equality, social justice and civil society. In 2013, the Woodrow Wilson International Center for Scholars in Washington, DC, honoured Kóczé with the Ion Ratiu Democracy Award for her interdisciplinary research approach, which combines community engagement and policymaking with in-depth participatory research on the situation of the Roma. She is a co-editor of *The Romani Women's Movement: Struggles and Debates in Central and Eastern Europe* (Routledge, 2018, with Violetta Zentai, Jelena Jovanović and Enikő Vincze).

Notes

The writing of this chapter would not have been possible without the critical comments of Huub van Baar and the careful editing of Gwen Jones.

1. The idea behind this problematization is that women give birth to children primarily to contribute to the income of the family through receiving child-specific welfare benefits.
2. The Hungarian version of the text: 'Átalakítanánk a családi pótlék rendszerét, megfékezve a megélhetési gyermekvállalást és támogatva a felelős családtervezést. A pótlék rendszerét oly módon alakítjuk át, hogy a szülőnek csak 18 éves kortól folyósítanánk, a 3. gyermek után már csak adókedvezmény formájában. Azok a gyermeket nevelő családok, akik szociális támogatásban részesülnek, a segélyt és a családi pótlékot egyaránt szociális kártyára utalva kapják meg'. Retrieved 19 December 2018 from https://jobbik-hu-static.azureedge.net/sites/default/files/cikkcsatolma ny/kimondjukmegoldjuk2014_netre.pdf, p. 28, point 5.
3. For more information about the protest, see https://index.hu/belfold/2009/09/07/ edelenyi_pm_nyugtatoval_bolonditottak_a_roma_gyerekeket/.

References

Appadurai, A. 2006. *Fear of Small Numbers*. Durham, NC: Duke University Press.
Baldwin, B. 2010. 'Stratification of the Welfare Poor: Intersections of Gender, Race and "Worthiness" in Poverty Discourse and Policy', *The Modern American* 6(1): 4–14.
Balogh, L. 2017. 'Az Egyenlő Bánásmód Hatóság határozata szerint roma nemzetisége miatt zaklattak egy szülő nőt a B.A.Z. Megyei Kórházban' [The Equal Treatment Authority concluded that Romani woman who gave birth was harassed in B.A.Z. County Hospital, based on her Roma minority affiliation], JTI Blog, 6 February. Retrieved 6 December 2018 from http://jog.tk.mta.hu/blog/2017/02/az-egyen lo-banasmod-hatosag-roma-zaklattak-szulo-not.

Bernstein, E., and J. Jakobsen. 2013. 'Introduction', *S&F Online* 11.1–11.2. Retrieved 11 December 2018 from http://sfonline.barnard.edu/gender-justice-and-neoliberal-transformations/introduction/.

Bohle, D., and B. Greskovits. 2007. 'Neoliberalism, Embedded Neoliberalism and Neocorporatism: Towards Transnational Capitalism in Central-Eastern Europe', *West European Politics* 30(3): 443–66.

Clarke, J. 2008. 'Living With/in and Without Neoliberalism', *Focaal* 51: 135–47.

Crenshaw, K. 1989. 'Demarginalizing the Intersection of Race and Sex: A Black Feminist Critique of Antidiscrimination Doctrine, Feminist Theory and Antiracist Politics', *University of Chicago Legal Forum* 140(1): 139–67.

Cuprik, R. 2013. 'Busting the Roma Welfare Myth', *The Slovak Spectator*, 28 October.

Eisenstein, H. 2010. *Feminism Seduced: How Global Elites Use Women's Labor and Ideas to Exploit the World*. Boulder, CO: Paradigm Publishers.

Emigh, R., E. Fodor and I. Szelényi. 2001. 'The Racialization and Feminization of Poverty?' in R. Emigh and I. Szelényi (eds), *Poverty, Ethnicity and Gender in Eastern Europe during the Market Transition*. Westport, CT: Praeger, pp. 1–32.

European Commission. 2018. 'The EU in the World – Labour Market'. EUROSTAT. Retrieved 3 September 2019 from https://ec.europa.eu/eurostat/statistics-explained/index.php/The_EU_in_the_world_-_labour_market.

European Council. 2000. 'Presidency Conclusions', Lisbon European Council, 23 and 25 March. Brussels.

European Union Agency for Fundamental Rights (FRA). 2013. 'Analysis of FRA Roma Survey Results by Gender'. Retrieved 6 December 2018 from http://fra.europa.eu/en/publication/2013/analysis-fra-roma-survey-results-gender.

———. 2014. 'Roma Survey: Data in Focus. Poverty and Employment: The Situation of Roma in 11 EU Member States'. Retrieved 6 December 2018 from http://fra.europa.eu/en/publication/2014/poverty-and-employment-situation-roma-11-eu-member-states.

Fábián, Z., et al. 2014. 'Hungary: A Country Caught in its Own Trap', in B. Nolan et al. (eds), *Changing Inequalities and Societal Impacts in Rich Countries*. Oxford Scholarship Online. Retrieved 6 December 2018 from http://www.oxfordscholarship.com/view/10.1093/acprof:oso/9780199687428.001.0001/acprof-9780199687428-chapter-14.

Ferge, Z. 2017. *Magyar társadalom – és szociálpolitika (1990–2015)* [Hungarian Social Politics 1990–2015]. Budapest: Osiris Kiadó.

Fraser, N. 2009. 'Feminism, Capitalism and the Cunning of History', *New Left Review* 56: 97–117.

Frederici, S. 2018. 'Globalization, Capital Accumulation and Violence against Women'. Lecture, 16 February, Duke University. Retrieved 6 December 2018 from https://gendersexualityfeminist.duke.edu/sites/gendersexualityfeminist.duke.edu/files/Silvia%20Federici%20Reading%20-%20Violence%20againstwomen.pdf.

Gilens, M. 1999. *Why Americans Hate Welfare*. Chicago, IL: University of Chicago Press.

Grill, J. 2018. 'Relearning to Labour? "Activation Works" and New Politics of Social Assistance in the Case of Slovak Roma', *Journal of the Royal Anthropological Institute* 24(s1): 105–19.

Gyenei, M. 1998. 'A "stratégiai gyerek", avagy miért növekszik nálunk a csecsemőhalandóság' ['Strategic children' or why does the child mortality rate increase?], *Népszabadság*, 14 November, 24–25.

Haney, L. 2002. *Inventing the Needy: Gender and the Politics of Welfare in Hungary*. Berkeley: University of California Press.
Hungarian Helsinki Committee. 2011. 'General Climate of Intolerance in Hungary'. Retrieved 6 August 2019 from https://www.helsinki.hu/en/general-climate-of-intolerance-in-hungary/.
Jobbik. 2014. *Kimondjuk. Megoldjuk: Választási program 2014* [Expressing and resolving: Election programme 2014]. Retrieved 6 December 2018 from https://www.jobbik.hu/hireink/kimondjuk-megoldjuk-valasztasi-program-2014.
Kóczé, A. 2012. 'Civil Society, Civil Involvement and Social Inclusion of the Roma', in A. Ivanov and J. Kling (eds), *Roma Inclusion Working Papers*. Bratislava: United Nations Development Programme. Retrieved 6 December 2018 from https://issuu.com/undp_in_europe_cis/docs/cso_for_web_18-01.
———. 2014. 'A rasszista tekintet és beszédmód által konstruált roma férfi és női testek a médiában' [Construction of Romani male and female bodies by racist gaze and discourse in the media] *Apertúra* (Summer–Fall). Retrieved 6 December 2018 from http://uj.apertura.hu/2014/nyar-osz/kocze-a-rasszista-tekintet-es-beszedmod-altal-konstrualt-roma-ferfi-es-noi-testek-a-mediaban.
———. 2016. 'Romani Women and the Paradoxes of Neoliberalism: Race, Gender and Class in the Era of Late Capitalism in EastCentral Europe', in E. Kovats (ed.), *Solidarity in Struggle Feminist Perspectives on Neoliberalism in East-Central Europe*. Budapest: Friedrich Ebert Stiftung, pp. 42–54.
———. 2018. 'Illusionary Inclusion of Roma through Intercultural Mediation', in H. van Baar, A. Ivasiuc and R. Kreide (eds), *The Securitization of the Roma in Europe*. New York: Palgrave Macmillan, pp. 183–206.
Köllő, J. 2011. 'A munkaerőpiactól elszakított közfoglalkoztatás reprodukálja önmagát' [Unrelated to the labour market, public work reproduces itself], *Beszélő* 16(7). Retrieved 6 December 2018 from http://beszelo.c3.hu/cikkek/%E2%80%9Ea-munkaeropiactol-elszakitott-kozfoglalkoztatas-reprodukalja-onmagat%E2%80%9D.
Ladányi, J. 2001. 'The Hungarian Neoliberal State, Ethnic Classification and the Creation of a Roma Underclass' in R. Emigh and I. Szelényi (eds), *Poverty, Ethnicity and Gender in Eastern Europe during the Market Transition*. Westport, CT: Praeger, pp. 67–82.
———. 2012. 'A magyarországi "romapolitika" csődje' [Breakdown of the Hungarian 'Roma Politics'], *Le Monde Diplomatique Magyar Kiadás*. Retrieved 6 December 2018 from http://www.magyardiplo.hu/kiutak-konferencia-cikkek/951-amagyarorszagi-romapolitika-csdje.
Laslett, B., and J. Brenner. 1989. 'Gender and Social Reproduction: Historical Perspectives', *Annual Review of Sociology* 15(1): 381–404.
Lendvai, N. 2008, 'EU Integration and the Transformation of Post-communist Welfare', *Social Policy & Administration* (42)5: 504–23.
Makovicky, N. 2013. '"Work Pays": Slovak Neoliberalism as "Authoritarian Populism"', *Focaal* 67: 77–90.
Messing, V. (ed.). 2012. 'Overview of the Labour Market Situation of Low-Educated and Roma Population and Regulations Affecting their Employment'. Neujobs State of the Art Report No. D19.1. Retrieved 6 December 2018 from http://www.neujobs.eu/sites/default/files/publication/2013/02/NEUJOBS_D19.1_February2013.pdf.
———, et al. (eds). 2013. '"From Benefits to Brooms": Case Studies Report on the Implementation of Active Labour Market Policies for Roma at Local Level'. Neujobs

Working Paper No. 19.3. Retrieved 6 December 2018 from http://www.neujobs.eu/sites/default/files/Del.19.3_22012014_0.pdf.
Ong, A. 2006. *Neoliberalism as Exception*. Durham, NC: Duke University Press.
Piven, F. 2015. 'Neoliberalism and the Welfare State', *Journal of International and Comparative Social Policy* 31(1): 2–9.
Polanyi, K. 1957. *The Great Transformation*. Boston, MA: Beacon Press.
Ripka, V., and M. Mareš. 2009. 'The Czech Welfare System', in K. Schubert, S. Hegelich and U. Bazant (eds), *The Handbook of European Welfare Systems*. London: Routledge, pp. 101–19.
Roberts, A. 2017. *Gendered States of Punishment and Welfare*. London: Routledge.
Scharle, Á. 2011. 'A közcélú foglalkoztatás kibővülésének célzottság, igénybevétele és hatása a tartós munkanélküliségre' [The targeting, use and effects of the growing public work programme on long-term unemployment]. Research Report with the contributions of G. Balás, A. Csite, N. Németh, Zs. Cseres-Gergely, J. Köllő and B. Váradi. Budapest Intézet and Hétfa. Retrived 11 December from http://www.budapestinstitute.eu/uploads/BI_kozcelu_kut_jelentes_2011aug30.pdf.
Schram, S., J. Soss and R. Fording (eds). 2003. *Race and the Politics of Welfare Reform*. Ann Arbor: University of Michigan Press.
Sharma, A. 2008. *Logics of Empowerment: Development, Gender and Governance in Neoliberal India*. Minneapolis: University of Minnesota Press.
Sigona, N., and N. Trehan (eds). 2009. *Romani Politics in Contemporary Europe: Poverty, Ethnic Mobilization, and the Neoliberal Order*. New York: Palgrave Macmillan.
Sirovátka, T. 2014. 'From Protection towards Activation', in I. Lødemel and A. Moreira (eds), *Activation or Workfare? Governance and the Neo-Liberal Convergence*. Oxford: Oxford University Press, pp. 256–88.
———. 2016. 'When Workfare Fails: Post-Crisis Activation Reform in the Czech Republic', *International Journal of Sociology and Social Policy* 36(1–2): 86–101.
Szalai, J. 2007. *Nincs két orszag...? Társadalmi küzdelmek az állami (túl)elosztásért a rendszerváltás utáni Magyarországon* [No two countries? Social struggles for state (over) redistribution in post-transition Hungary]. Budapest: Osiris.
———. 2013. 'Hungary's Bifurcated Welfare State: Splitting Social Rights and the Social Exclusion of Roma'. Adam Smith Research Foundation, Working Papers Series No 5. Glasgow: University of Glasgow.
Szelényi, I., and D. Treiman. 1992. 'Social Stratification in Eastern Europe after 1989', NSF Grant Proposal.
Szikra, D. 2014. 'Democracy and Welfare in Hard Times', *Journal of European Social Policy* 24(5): 486–500.
Szőke, A. 2015. 'A "Road to Work"? The Reworking of Deservedness, Social Citizenship and Public Work Programmes in Rural Hungary', *Citizenship Studies* 19(6–7): 734–50.
Tausz, K. 2009. 'From State Socialism to a Hybrid Welfare State: Hungary', in K. Schubert, S. Hegelich and U. Bazant (eds), *The Handbook of European Welfare Systems*. London: Routledge, pp. 244–59.
Templer, B. 2006. 'Neoliberal Strategies to Defuse a Powder Keg in Europe', *New Politics* X(4). Retrieved 6 December 2018 from http://newpol.org/content/neliberal-strategies-defuse-powder-keg-europe-decade-roma-inclusion-and-its-rationale.
Themelis, S. 2016. 'The Time of the Roma in Times of Crisis', *Ethnicities* 16(3): 432–51.

Uhde, Z. 2016. 'From Women's Struggles to Distorted Emancipation', *International Feminist Journal of Politics* 18(3): 390–408.
van Apeldoorn, B. 2008. 'The Contradictions of "Embedded Neoliberalism" and Europe's Multi-Level Legitimacy Crisis', in B. van Apeldoorn, J. Drahokoupil and L. Horn (eds), *Contradictions and Limits of Neoliberal European Governance*. New York: Palgrave Macmillan, pp. 21–43.
van Baar, H. 2011. *The European Roma: Minority Representation, Memory and the Limits of Transnational Governmentality*. Amsterdam: F&N.
———. 2012. 'Socioeconomic Mobility and Neoliberal Governmentality in Post-socialist Europe', *Journal of Ethnic and Migration Studies* 38(8): 1289–304.
Vidra, Z. 2018. 'Hungary's Punitive Turn: The Shift from Welfare to Workfare', *Communist and Post-Communist Studies* 51(1): 73–80.
Wacquant, L. 2001. 'Deadly Symbiosis: When Ghetto and Prison Meet and Mesh', *Punishment & Society* 3(1): 95–133.
———. 2009. 'The Body, the Ghetto and the Penal State', *Qualitative Sociology* 32(1): 101–29.
Wientzek, O., and H. Meyer. 2009. 'The Slovak Welfare System: Neo-liberal Nightmare or Welfare Pioneer of Middle-Eastern Europe?', in K. Schubert, S. Hegelich and U. Bazant (eds), *The Handbook of European Welfare Systems*. London: Routledge, pp. 462–77.

PART III

❀ ❀ ❀

EUROPE AND THE CHALLENGE OF 'ETHNIC MINORITY GOVERNANCE'

CHAPTER 5

✽ ✽ ✽

GOVERNING THE ROMA, BORDERING EUROPE
Europeanization, Securitization and Differential Inclusion

Huub van Baar

The post-1989 situation of Europe's minoritized Romani groups has been much debated in, but also increasingly beyond, Roma-related scholarship. Repeatedly, studies and reports have focused on the precarious status of Romani minorities and migrants across Europe and discussed the ongoing violation of their rights, the persistence of poverty in which many Roma live, their politicized appearance at supranational policy- and decision-making institutions and, to a lesser degree, the diverse roles that Roma themselves and organizations that support them have played in and beyond what has been called 'the Romani movement' (Puxon 2000; Vermeersch 2006).

Among the various recurrent themes, perspectives and concepts used to examine the situation of Romani minorities are: human rights, social justice and rights discourses more generally; inclusion and exclusion mechanisms, practices and policies; redistribution, recognition and representation; cultural memory and remembrance (particularly of the Nazi genocide); Europeanization; citizenship; Romaphobia, antigypsyism, racism and discrimination; Romani mobilization and social movements; and, last but not least, identity and alterity, including subjects ranging from ethnicity, class, gender, culture, community, kinship, sociality and nationality to agency, subalternity, grass roots, heterogeneity and hybridity. In this chapter, I directly or indirectly discuss several of these topics from the angle of what I have called 'the Europeanization of the representation of Roma representation' (van Baar 2011a). I will demonstrate that this viewpoint of Europeanization closely relates to and fundamentally affects most of the lenses through which Roma have thus far been analysed.

In various literatures that have discussed the post-1989 situation of Roma, the notion of Europeanization has also popped up, most notably in the contexts of policy, identity, rights, discourse, European Union (EU) citizenship and supranational governance at the European level (see, for instance, Cruickshank 2012; Ram 2012, 2014; Vermeersch 2012). These debates have largely taken place against the background of analyses of how the situation of Roma has changed since the end of the Cold War and, in particular, of how these changes have coincided with the emergence of European and other transnational policies, networks and discourses dealing with those who are called, or call themselves, Roma.

Some have suggested that these perspectives of Europeanization are largely similar, and point to 'the process of Roma inclusion in European institutions', where these institutions have identified Roma 'as a priority issue' of their policies (Matras 2013: 232, 243). However, I will explain that while my notion of the Europeanization of Roma representation overlaps in some ways with its use elsewhere, it profoundly departs from how the notion is used in most of these studies. In order to clarify this divergence and the way in which I have aimed to redirect the debate, I will address some of the key problems concerning how the notion of Europeanization has often been used, implicitly or explicitly, in debates about the European Roma.

First, I will explain that despite the suggestion that analyses in terms of Europeanization critically discuss the role of European institutions, they frequently remain expressions of various forms of methodological Eurocentrism and, most notably, do not adequately examine how novel and reshaped processes of bordering Europe have affected Roma and their representations and self-representations. Secondly, I will discuss the limits of the currently dominant uses of 'Europeanization' for a critical interrogation of Roma-related policies, programmes and discourses. I will show how and why even the more critical approaches to the situation of Roma have often remained essentially Roma-centric, and to an extent that significantly reduces the potential scope of these critiques.

In the context of these and similar debates assessing the current situation of Europe's Roma, I return to the notion of the Europeanization of Roma representation that I introduced to the debate in 2011. I will show how this perspective helps to redirect critically Roma-related scholarship, and move beyond the Eurocentric and Roma-centric parameters of many current debates about their position. I will explain why and how my interpretation of the Roma's Europeanization, considered as a form of transnational governmentality, critically develops these debates beyond the currently prevalent domains of policy or discourse formation and transformation. My approach will help to historicize the ways in which Roma are governed and to rethink the prevailing ways of discussing Roma in relative isolation from profoundly changing security, development, citizenship, border and migration regimes within, at and beyond Europe's contested borders. In doing so, I will show that it becomes possible to rethink the binary scheme of inclusion and exclusion that has dominated analyses of the ways in which many of Europe's Roma have been marginalized and displaced. Towards the end of this chapter, and on the basis of a reassessment of the current position of Roma from the angle of Europeanization and 'differential inclusion' (Mezzadra and Neilson 2012), I will propose a research agenda beyond the existing preponderance of Eurocentric and Roma-centric approaches.

The Europeanization of 'the Roma Issue': Policy, Identity, Discourse

In line with a trend in European integration and governance studies, Roma-related scholarship has overwhelmingly used the notion of Europeanization to discuss how a particular issue – in this case 'the Roma issue' – has been constructed and discursively framed as a European policy or political issue, how it has been developed, disseminated and institutionalized at the European level and, subsequently, how it has impacted domestic environments, transforming national and subnational norms, attitudes, policies, structures and the like. To a large extent, this view fits Claudio Radaelli's influential definition of the term more than fifteen years ago:

> Europeanization consists of processes of (a) construction, (b) diffusion and (c) institutionalization of formal and informal rules, procedures, policy paradigms, styles, 'ways of doing things', and shared beliefs and norms which are first defined and consolidated in the making of EU public policy and politics and then incorporated in the logic of domestic discourse, identities, political structures and public policies. (Radaelli 2003: 31)

This concept of Europeanization has demonstrated its usefulness in analysing the construction and institutionalization of policies at the European level, and examining how, and to what extent, they have impacted on various domestic levels in and beyond the enlarging EU. In a similar way, some have discussed the emergence, consolidation and differentiation of Roma-related European or other transnational policies regarding topics such as human and minority rights, antidiscrimination and social inclusion (Kovats 2001; Klímová-Alexander 2005; Vermeersch 2006; Guy 2009; Cruickshank 2012;

Ram 2012; Goodwin and de Hert 2013; Bunescu 2014; Law and Kovats 2018). Several of these scholars have also combined these analyses with investigations into how these policies have impacted domestic arenas, most recently in the context of the 'ethnic turn' in EU policies and the development of the EU Framework for Roma (for the latter, see European Commission 2011; see also van Baar 2018b).

However, this 'top-down' approach to Europeanization, which analyses supranational policy and discourse formation and transformation, and moves on to examine their impact and transformation at 'lower' institutional levels, has been criticized for its unidirectional angle. Its critics have suggested that we also need to adopt a notion of Europeanization that takes into account the 'bottom-up' dimension – or, to put it more generally, a politics of scaling that includes the ways in which different kinds of actors, and nation-states in particular, try to 'upscale' their individual interests to the European level (Jones and Clark 2010; see also van Baar 2008). Peter Vermeersch (2003: 894–95; 2012: 1203–9), for instance, has illustrated that states or state-related actors have tried to Europeanize 'the Roma problem' in attempts to address its alleged Europeanness, and to shift responsibilities for solving it to the European level (see also Ram 2012; van Baar 2011a, 2011b). More generally, several studies on the position of Europe's Roma have clarified that various actors, including national authorities and civil society organizations, have attempted to put 'the Roma' on the European agenda (Vermeersch 2006; McGarry 2010; Ram 2010; Sobotka 2011; Law and Kovats 2018) and thus contributed to a sort of Europeanization from below. Yet although this approach seriously complicates top-down readings of Europeanization, the latter has nonetheless remained the most prevalent in the debate about Europe's Roma, even among scholars who have shown receptiveness to the ways in which state and non-state actors try to influence the European Roma agenda from 'below'.

This dominance has become particularly clear when scholars discuss the relationships between European and (sub)national policies and discourses about Roma, such as in the case of an EU member (or candidate member) state's compliance (or a lack thereof) with EU laws and rules, or their adoption of 'Roma integration strategies' vis-à-vis the EU Framework for Roma. The majority of analyses discuss these relations in terms of discrepancies between what has been institutionalized at the European level – political debates, policies, governance structures, discourses or normative frameworks – and what has been achieved at national or subnational levels throughout Europe. These discrepancies are presented in terms of those between policy formation and transfer, between policy development and implementation, between discourse and practice, between legislation and law enforcement or, last but not least, between (well-meant) intentions at the supranational level and (troublesome) actions, attitudes or behaviours at the domestic level.

Melanie Ram (2014: 18), for instance, suggests that European endeavours to improve the situation of Roma at the domestic level have 'facilitated a landscape of progressive sounding programmes on paper, supportive statements and even many positive actions, but a lack of significant tangible results'. To illustrate the fact that serious and sustainable changes and results in the situation of Roma have never really been achieved in most Central and East European countries, Ram uses the telling metaphor of Potemkin villages, erected during the enlargement process, that today, at a time of ongoing inclusion policies and programmes, 'still stand' (ibid.). Referring to the facades that these Potemkin villages represent, she argues that, at domestic levels, we have frequently been faced with 'a significant discrepancy between transposition of legislation and enforcement or application' (Ram 2012: 418). Consequently, the Europeanization of Roma policy, Roma identity or discourses regarding them has primarily been evaluated in terms of its 'positive and negative implications' (ibid.: 420, 431; see also Guy 2009).

In his welcome discussion of the framing of Roma as a European public policy issue, Vermeersch (2012: 1204) has similarly suggested that we need to take into consideration the 'potential dangers of Europeanizing the Roma' (see also Kovats 2003). He gives several examples of how the European Parliament has recently started functioning as a platform for some of its members to mobilize the Europeanization of Roma identity, policy or discourse to make divergent and mutually conflicting claims. These range from calls to improve the status, inclusion and situation of Roma, and pleas for the joint responsibility of European institutions and states to do so, to attempts at shifting national responsibilities to the European level and blaming Roma for 'their own' problems. Thus, Vermeersch illuminates how the Europeanization of 'the Romani issue' has been mobilized for various political reasons, including by those who have, 'rather paradoxically, opened up new opportunities for nationalist politicians to plead against new national measures to help the Roma' (2012: 1297).

These analyses that assess the Roma's Europeanization in terms of advantageous and disadvantageous implications, or potentially beneficial or risky consequences, help to critically evaluate the ways in which old and new member states of European institutions, and of the EU most notably, have dealt with internationally or Europe-wide debated, adopted or recognized rules, norms or discourses. These analyses are critical of European institutions to the extent that they reveal several of the tensions, contradictions and challenges central to the relationships between those institutions, their member states and state-related actors. These examinations have also been critical of the character of European Roma-related measures, such as the lack of political will to effect change, or the non-binding character of soft governance instruments like the EU's Open Method of Coordination and the correlated EU Framework for Roma.

At the same time though, these and similar analyses of the Europeanization of 'the Roma issue' or European Roma-related policies more generally have remained largely Eurocentric to the extent that their primary point of reference is 'the Roma', or how they are framed, and not 'Europe' – at least not to a significant degree. Consequently, discussions about European policies have often remained limited to suggestions that laws, treaties, rules, measures, norms or policies have been implemented and articulated inadequately or – when institutionally incorporated or ratified – have not (effectively) been mobilized to improve the situation of Roma. While these conclusions are valuable insofar as they reveal policy discrepancies and norm deviances, such analyses primarily mirror the norms and standards of European or international institutions, without seriously questioning the principles and values, such as freedom, security, citizenship, rights, justice and development, or the ways in which they have been embedded and normal*ized* within the very tissue of minority-related governance and the conceptual frameworks of liberal democracies. Consequently, such analyses result in calls for more adequate and more reflective policy formation, transfer and implementation, and for greater or more adequate pressure on the executing actors at both European and domestic levels. In response to the ways in which reinterpretations of the Europeanized Roma issue have 'diverged' from initial European institutional framings, Vermeersch, for instance, concludes that European 'institutions . . . need to be *mindful* of the problems of political *re*interpretation' and that they 'need to continue to *respond forcefully and cleverly* to attempts at political *re*interpretations' (2012: 1208, 1209, emphasis added).

Any plea for more reflection and political action regarding the ways in which sociopolitical actors within and outside European institutional arenas have mobilized 'the Roma issue' for their own political agenda – whether liberal, neoliberal, populist, nationalist or extremist – is welcome. Yet by focusing too much on the uses and abuses, or the chances and risks of the Europeanized 'Roma issue', such pleas remain Eurocentric and Roma-centric to a significant extent. Indeed, the empirical or methodological concentration on those policies that directly relate to the situation of Roma – human and minority rights, antidiscrimination, social inclusion and the like – tend to underrepresent the profound impact that significant changes in Europe's institutional, political and social infrastructures have had on Roma. Observations that deal at the European institutional level with programmes that sound positive or progressive 'at least on paper' tend to assume that, once again, the crucial problem is one of discrepancies between discourse and practice, or between policies and their application or implementation. As I explain below, these and similar assumptions do not sufficiently take into account that the troublesome ambiguities regarding the contemporary position of Roma are structurally and inherently related to European institutional, political, governmental and socioeconomic architectures and infrastructures, and that they considerably affect Roma, as well as several other groups in Europe and on its fringes.

The Europeanization of Roma Representation

The reason I have introduced the notion of the Europeanization of Roma representation (van Baar 2011a) relates to the pressing issues discussed above, and aims to enable a debate about the fundamental shifts and ambiguities regarding the contemporary position of Europe's Roma and the ways in which Europe has been bordered. The notion of the Europeanization of Roma representation is not situated at the same conceptual or methodological level as that of the Europeanization of Roma policy, identity or discourse. Analysing the Roma's position from the angle of the Europeanization of their representation involves a critical interrogation of the various conditions under which the Europeanization of Roma policy, identity or discourse has become possible in the first place. Three closely interrelated analytical dimensions – an epistemological, a governmental and a geneaological one – characterize this investigation.

The Epistemological Dimension: From Problem to Problematization

The epistemological dimension of analysing the Europeanization of Roma representation entails a shift from a focus on 'problems' to one on 'problematizations' (van Baar 2011a: 8–12, 153–63, 321–23, 2011b). Problematizations do not primarily concentrate on emerging or identified problems and possible answers to them, nor on something considered 'problematic', but rather, on why and how certain things, such as behaviour, phenomena, processes or groups, have become a 'problem' to be solved, managed and regulated in certain ways:

> To one single set of difficulties, several responses can be made. And most of the time different responses actually are proposed. But what must be understood is *what makes them simultaneously possible*: it is the point in which their simultaneity is rooted; it is the soil that can nourish them at all *in their diversity and sometimes in spite of their contradictions* . . . Problematization . . . develops the *conditions*

in which possible responses can be given ... This development of a given into a question, this *transformation of a group of obstacles and difficulties into problems* to which the diverse solutions will attempt to produce a response, this is what constitutes the point of problematization. (Foucault 1997: 118, emphasis added)

Accordingly, if we look at the case of the European Roma through the lens of problematization, we can interrogate a key epistemological question: how could the existence of various so-called Romani groups in many different countries in Europe actually develop into a question and be transformed into a 'European issue', or a specific set of 'European problems', to which diverse and often mutually conflicting policies, tools, interventions, measures and processes attempt to answer? This question and viewpoint significantly differ from the ways in which the Europeanization of Roma policy, identity or discourse have been discussed. In those cases, the focus is still primarily oriented towards the posing of a political or policy problem, and the diverse ways in which related actors and agencies could or should respond to it, or have to improve or redirect their responses. Accordingly, we can distinguish between various responses or solutions to the issue and continue to qualify them as (potentially) beneficial or risky, or advantageous or disadvantageous, vis-à-vis the improvement of the situation of Roma. Instead, problematization interrogates the conditions under which the multiple configurations of the problem-response relationship have entered into play in the first place. In other words, the focus on problematization makes something which has become normal(ized) unfamiliar again, and interrogates the question of and process towards this normalization or even naturalization. Last but not least, this shift towards analysing the situation of Roma in terms of problematization is also linked to a focus on the importance of knowledge formation – an issue to which I will return below.

The Governmental Dimension: Europeanization as Transnational Governmentality

The epistemological, analytical layer is intertwined with the governmental dimension of the Europeanization of Roma representation, which relates, firstly, to the ways in which, since the collapse of socialism, Roma have been increasingly problematized and governed in terms of their 'Europeanness'. Secondly, this dimension involves the classifying and governing of a variety of groups, living all over Europe, under the umbrella term 'Roma' – a categorization that is a precondition for any top-down or bottom-up kind of Europeanization. Thirdly and most significantly, this dimension entails devising and assembling various large-scale, Europe-wide governmental programmes and instruments that are dedicated to, most notably, the inclusion, participation, recognition, (human) development, security and empowerment of Roma. I have referred to this third dimension as that of 'institutional developmentalism' (see van Baar 2018a, 2019).

This viewpoint departs from approaching Europeanization primarily in contexts of policy, discursive, ideological or normative frameworks (Risse-Kappen, Cowles and Caporaso 2001; Featherstone and Radaelli 2003; Schimmelfennig and Sedelmeier 2005; Graziono and Vink 2006; Cruickshank 2012; Ram 2012, 2014), even though it also involves the formation of political and administrative structures and the dispersal of norms and values at European level. However, the governmental viewpoint shifts the focus to Europeanization as a form of governmentality (Walters and Haahr 2005). As I have explained extensively elsewhere (van Baar 2011a), considering Europeanization, and that of Roma representation in particular, as a form of transnational governmentality has several implications, the most important of which I will discuss here.

The Foucauldian notion of governmentality can be considered, as Judith Butler has succinctly stated, as a 'mode of power concerned with the maintenance and control of bodies and persons, the production and regulation of persons and populations, and the circulation of goods [and people, HvB] insofar as they maintain and restrict the life of the population' (Butler 2004: 52). Over the course of modern European history, Foucault (2007) argued, liberal ways of governing have been increasingly articulated as the government of populations, rather than territories, aiming at improving these populaces' well-being – their welfare, health, fertility, safety, wealth, productivity, security, longevity and the like – through the social production of freedom and the shaping and regulation of the conditions in which one can be free. Central to this view is that the state and other institutionalized forms of political government, such as the EU, have neither a core nor a substance, but are to be considered as relational, and linked to heterogeneous practices and styles of articulating the activity of governing.

The advantage of a governmentality approach is that it deconstructs the state or 'Europe' as a pre-given, 'natural' centre of power that embodies a relatively coherent set of rules, norms or institutions that it disseminates across a governed space. A governmentality approach analyses both the state and the EU as historically specific assemblages that codify and annex locally devised mechanisms of power to regulate populations. Thus, state and supra-state institutions need to be understood as materialized intersections of various technologies and strategies of power that merely bring these institutions, as well as the legitimization of their power and the normalization of their discourses and practices, into existence. Put differently, diverse governmental technologies, such as social inclusion and other development programmes, benchmarking and the Open Method of Coordination (OMC), or EU rules regarding migration, labour, antidiscrimination and free movement, need to be assembled to codify and normalize the functioning of institutions (such as the EU), and to naturalize their authority. Thus, central to my approach is not so much the Europeanization of Romani minority governance, but rather the governmentalization of Europe through the elaboration, rationalization and centralization of diverse power relations and technologies, and their assemblage under the auspices of European institutions (van Baar 2011a: 27–73, 153–89).

How could this reading of Europeanization as governmentality help to understand the position of Roma in Europe? First of all, seen from this angle, both 'Europe' and 'the Roma', rather than only the latter, are the objects of the Europeanization of Roma representation. Indeed, 'Europe' and institutions such as the EU are not a priori given centres of rule that mobilize or disseminate power; rather, they have been authorized through a relatively stable, although contingent and contestable assembling of power relations and technologies in which 'Europe' and 'the Roma' are enacted simultaneously. Secondly, understanding Europe-wide, Roma-related development programmes, such as those of social inclusion, community development, activation or human security as 'governmentalizing technologies', enables us to see them not so much in terms of their benevolence or good intentions. Rather, we can understand them as mechanisms that also control, classify and manage the minoritized (Romani) groups involved. Finally, concentrating on the latter, and thus on the ways in which these mechanisms are vital parts of European political and institutional architectures and infrastructures, enables us to reveal their limits and ambiguities. The contingency and contestability of how technologies of quasi-neutral 'ethnic minority governance' are assembled also allow for critique and openings for their alternative (or even reverse) redirection or reassemblage. These latter possibilities are involved, for instance, in how diverse actors – ranging from those who encounter or circumvent development programmes locally, or those who securitize regimes, to the key figures and agencies of the heterogeneous Romani movement – have tried to repoliticize or appropriate these programmes and to challenge their supposedly natural, benign, benevolent, politically neutral or socioeconomically inevitable character.

The Genealogical Dimension: Historicizing Minority Governance and Knowledge Formation

The implication of the simultaneous de-reification of 'Europe' and 'the Roma' is that we must be fully aware of their historical specificity and connection: thus, we also need to historicize our understandings of their present-day relationship, and the practices from which it has emerged. On several occasions, I have proposed that historically shifting Roma representations and self-representations have been closely related to the shifting ways in which they are governed, and govern themselves, and to changes in how the relation between 'Europe' and 'the Roma' is made intelligible through the formation of expertise and knowledge (van Baar 2011a: 75–231, 2013). For instance, I have explained how, in the late eighteenth century, the problematization of Roma in terms of a minority part of the population, and the simultaneous emergence of something like 'Gypsy Studies' in the German and Habsburg academies, occurred alongside the rise of assimilationist and proto-liberal forms of minority governance. The Gypsies or *Zigeuner* – as they were commonly called then – were rendered a 'non-European' minority, for their allegedly homogeneous people, culture, language, traditions and customs were supposed and imagined to originate outside Europe – in Egypt or India – thus endangering 'progress' and 'civilization' in Europe.[1]

Through a close and correlated reading of these events, I have shown that the first historical problematization of Romani or Gypsy groups in *minority* terms in the eighteenth century emerged alongside the development of novel practices of governmentality, knowledge formation and minority self-articulation and agency. Reading these histories genealogically, rather than as a kind of logical, linear, progressive or regressive development towards the present – as, for instance, Wim Willems (1997), Ian Hancock (2002) and Yaron Matras (2004) have done in significantly different ways – helps to critically historicize this triangular relationship between Roma representations, practices of minority (self-)governance and forms of knowledge formation (van Baar 2011a: 75–149; see van Baar with Kóczé, Introduction, this volume).[2] In line with the present argumentation, I have contended that the current problematization of Roma as a 'European minority' has coincided with the rise of new articulations of minority governance, and with novel forms and sites of knowledge and expertise formation. Formerly dominant forms of governing Roma – such as those based on liberal, welfarist and policing types of rule – have currently been assembled in manifold ways with neoliberal forms of governance, and resulted in a hybrid form of transnational governmentality (van Baar 2011a).[3] Much more than in the past, Roma-related expertise has been developed in the contexts of intergovernmental and non-governmental organizations, such as the World Bank, United Nations agencies, the EU's Agency for Fundamental Rights (FRA), the Organization for Security and Co-operation in Europe (OSCE), the Open Society Institute (OSI) and many smaller NGOs and platforms. While some have suggested that these NGOs have been co-opted into a so-called 'Roma (development) industry' (Sigona and Trehan 2009) dominated by intergovernmental organizations (IGOs), others have stated that the expertise developed within civil society organizations has been presented problematically as scholarly evidence, and mobilized to legitimize policy transformations (Marushiakova and Popov 2011). Whereas these phenomena of 'NGO-ization' and 'NGO science' are undoubtedly related to several troublesome developments, in these analyses the role and scope of NGOs has been discussed one-sidedly, rather than *ambiguously* (for a more extensive discussion of these issues, see van Baar 2013, 2018b).

On the one hand, policymakers and those NGOs that predominantly function as a kind of service deliverer have been involved in processes of depoliticization, in which complex political problems are rendered 'technical', 'natural' or 'private' (Rose 1999), as if they were only of a non-political and neutral character. Consequently, primarily political problems are removed from the domain of political discourse and debate, reformulated in the 'objective' and 'neutral' language of expertise, policymaking or science, and relocated onto the allegedly neutral terrains of management, monitoring, development, community building, activation, empowerment and the like. At the same time however, processes of depoliticization have coincided with those of repoliticization in which various kinds of actors and agencies – including Roma, their advocates, activist networks, NGOs and scholars – have attempted to challenge the quasi-neutral 'nature' of policies, projects and measures, and turned them into 'public' issues and dilemmas to be debated.

More generally, central to the current articulation of the triangular relationship between Roma representations, governmentalities and knowledge formation is, thus, not a discrepancy between policy building and its implementation, or between supranational intentions and (sub)national nonconformities, but, much more fundamentally, a crucial ambiguity in the way in which populations are governed within Europe's contested borders. In what follows, I will try to make this ambiguity more tangible by exploring some of the intersections of security, citizenship and development in contemporary Europe.

Security at Its Nexus with Citizenship and Development

Two of the societal domains in which the position of Roma has been much debated are those of citizenship and development. In the case of citizenship, several of the ongoing debates concern the status of Roma as citizen, migrant, refugee or asylum seeker and the practices that they – advocacy groups and authorities at various levels and scales, including European institutions – have developed to address their political membership. In the closely related case of development, scholars have debated the impact of development programmes – dealing primarily, but not exclusively, with social inclusion, antidiscrimination, antiracism, human security, community or capacity building, activation, participation or empowerment – on the situation of the poorest Roma in particular. To show how these domains are integrally related to an analysis of the Europeanization of Roma representation, I will discuss them separately by first zooming out from the Roma's position and then, after a brief interrogation of the more general European context and its ambiguities, return to how these domains have profoundly impacted the situation of Roma.

The Security–Citizenship Nexus

Ideas of European unity, cohesion and integration have been closely connected to definitions of the EU in terms of its four central freedoms: the free movement of people, capital, goods and services. To promote these freedoms, the development of infrastructures that encourage mobility has become key to the promotion of European integration in and beyond the EU. The introduction of Schengen, for instance, can be regarded in light of such infrastructures and, in this case, as a governmental technology aimed at reducing barriers represented by national borders. Yet although the EU has been reconceptualized as an easily traversable space, and EU citizenship has been based on the paradigm of free movement, the relationship between freedom and security has been considerably redefined. The establishment of the EU's Justice and Home Affairs policy in 1992, the rearticulation of the EU as an Area of Freedom, Justice and Security and the correlated Europeanization of security, migration and border policies, have been closely accompanied by the securitization of migration and borders in Europe – that is, their problematizing in terms of threats to the Union's security and stability (Huysmans 2006; Bigo 2008).

These securitizing processes have not been limited to discursive framings. Rather, they have been fully incorporated into the EU's architecture and its technologies of governance.[4] Jef Huysmans (2006) has argued that the Europeanization and securitization of migration and border policies can be considered as a spillover effect of European economic integration, and particularly of the development of the EU's internal market. The largely economically inspired incorporation of the Schengen Treaty into the EU system in the 1990s, and thus the 'removal' of the EU's internal borders, have engendered a cycle of policy formations in which policies on migration, crime and terrorism have been conjointly communitarized. At this new institutionalized nexus of freedom and security, desired forms of circulation of people, capital, goods and services – such as those that are usually associated with business, tourism, student exchanges and high-skilled migration – are ambiguously distinguished from unwelcome and undesirable forms of circulation that endanger the smooth functioning of the EU's internal market and its correlated, socially produced freedom of movement. It is not only transnational crime, terrorism and trafficking that have been classified among these 'dangerous' forms of circulation, but also, and increasingly, irregularized migration, including that of the global poor (Duffield 2007; De Genova and Peutz 2010; Jansen, Celikates and de Bloois 2015; van Baar 2015, 2017a). This distinction has been articulated 'ambiguously', because through these policy formations, the EU's approach to migration has been institutionally assembled together with the combating of transnational crime, trafficking and terrorism. Migration policies have been directly linked with the EU's security policies and infrastructures. Thus, we can consider the problematization of migration in terms of security as a *direct* form of securitization, institutionally propagated at EU level – one that has profoundly intermingled with national and local forms of securitization involving various actors, ranging from state-related actors such as politicians, policymakers, the police and other security professionals, to the media, 'vigilant' citizen's groups, populists and extremists.

These processes of securitization bring us back to Roma. In the aftermath of 1989, the violation of the rights of Roma in Central and Eastern Europe, and their position as citizens and migrants more generally, have been central in the endeavours of advocacy groups to put 'the Roma' onto the European agenda, and they became key elements in EU reports on the progress made towards accession by the then EU candidate member states in the East. Yet even while the European Commission and human rights groups were unanimous in denouncing the rights situation of Roma in these countries, when Roma migrated westward and asked for asylum in EU member states, they were almost unconditionally denied or neglected – or, in the case of those fleeing the collapse of Yugoslavia, only conditionally 'tolerated' and faced with a precarious state of deportability (van Baar 2017a, 2017b). Several scholars have shown how the migration of Roma has indeed been problematized in terms of alleged threats to public order, social or even national security (Castle-Kaňerová 2003; Vašečka and Vašečka 2003; Guglielmo and Waters 2005; van Baar 2011b; Hepworth 2012; van Baar, Ivasiuc and Kreide 2019).

Securitizing trends towards Roma before the EU's eastward enlargement were not ancillary, but rather perfectly in line with the general tendency to securitize migration and borders in Europe, and were *central* to how EU member states treated them. These trends, not only towards Romani migrants, but also towards domestic Roma, are integral parts of a wider, ongoing trend to irregularize their status as citizens, migrants, asylum seekers or refugees (van Baar 2015, 2017a). Through traversing practices of orientalization, securitization and nomadization, Roma are problematized as 'backward' and 'inferior', as 'dangerous' and 'treacherous', as 'drifting parasites' and 'wilful wanderers' and, thus, as irregular in the diverse meanings of deviation from what is socially and culturally rendered 'normal', 'natural' and 'regular' (van Baar 2017a).

Put differently, the Europeanization and securitization of migration and borders have impacted on the conditions of mobility not only centrifugally, on non-EU migrants outside or already inside Europe, but also centripetally, on EU citizens such as Roma who have been faced with the persistent precarization of their societal position (van Baar 2014, 2017a). The case of Roma shows that these transnational governmentalities traverse Europe's populations themselves – or, argued conversely, that Roma often end up in the symbolic categories of 'non-' or 'not-yet Europeans', despite the EU citizenship that most of them hold, and despite the promise of their 'European integration'. Even after becoming EU citizens, their securitization has continued to reinforce their supposed 'illegality' and 'rootlessness', to legitimize treating them differently from others, and to demand from them additional efforts before they are regarded as full and equal members of the states in which they live, and the 'Europe' to which they belong (van Baar 2017a).

The Security–Development Nexus

Similarly, and closely related to how Roma have been faced with the institutionalized promise of their European citizenship, many of them have become the subjects of the institutionalized will to improve their situation through the devising and assembling of development programmes. More precisely, these programmes – so the arguments of intergovernmental, governmental and non-governmental development, inclusion and empowerment agencies usually go – would increase their capabilities and capacities, and gradually lead to the improvement of their situation and to the ability to exercise their citizenship more adequately. I have argued (van Baar 2011a, 2018a, 2019) that we should interrogate such developmental endeavours in view of both postcolonial developmentalism and the post-Cold War neoliberal merging of development and security regarding the global poor (Escobar 1995; Ferguson 2006; Duffield 2007).

Roma have not merely become a development or security issue within the new institutional commitment to them by various organizations, as some have suggested (see, for instance, Kovats 2001). Rather, they could appear at the institutional radar of agencies and actors such as the EU, the OSCE, the UN and the World Bank owing to a major transformation in how 'security' and 'development' have been comprehended and practised. A shifting problematization of security, development and their relation has led to a situation in which Roma could become subjects of development and security in these post-1989 institutional contexts. Let me outline the main parameters of this shifting problematization (for an extensive discussion, see Duffield 2001, 2007; van Baar 2011a: 153–89, 2018a, 2019)

Roughly speaking, until the final stage of the Cold War, security and development were primarily seen in the context of *national* states and economies. Security mainly meant 'national security' and the threat of *inter*-state conflicts. Accordingly, and particularly in the aftermath of postcolonial independence, the development of 'developing' 'Third World' countries was considered to be an issue of improving their national economies in order to incorporate them gradually in the global economies of the 'developed' 'First World' (for a critique of this view, see Escobar 1995). Yet since the 1980s, security and insecurity, but also poverty and underdevelopment, have increasingly been understood in the contexts of *intra*-state conflicts between ethnicized, religionized or culturalized groups that have to be solved through liberal and neoliberal, people-oriented developmental interventions that do not focus in the first place on anticipated changes in national economies, but rather on those at the level of communities, intergroup relations and the capacities and capabilities of individuals and groups to become self-reliant and enterprising. In the context of these shifts, notions of human security and human development, and of building human and social capital, have emerged and become key to how, most notably, UN agencies, the World Bank, the EU and the OSCE have extended and redirected their policies, revising their mandates to include ethnicized groups such as Roma. Thus, we have seen a biopoliticization of development (Mezzadra, Reid and Sammadar 2013) that comprises a governmental logic and mechanism of which the main object is the 'bios' of individuals and communities (their lifeworlds, health, human and social capital, means of subsistence, etc.), as well as a constellation of governmental technologies aimed at increasing, protecting and regulating life via government through community, collectives and minority–majority relations.

Yet at the juncture of security and development, Roma are faced with a grim deadlock. The fact that poverty and underdevelopment are considered dangerous, with the potential to result in conflict, instability and insecurity, has led to institutional practices of the securitization of Roma that, next to other, more visible societal forms of their securitization, seriously hamper their socioeconomic and migratory mobility (van Baar 2012, 2015, 2018a). The simultaneous neoliberalization of development programmes has led to a one-sided focus on Roma as a 'problem group' to be included, developed, empowered and activated. The culturalization, racialization and territorialization of the problems with which many Roma are confronted, alongside the profound biopolicitization and neoliberalization of development, have resulted in a situation where the complex socioeconomic, political and historical reasons for their current marginalization are considerably underrepresented or even neglected in the institutionalized commitment to the European Roma (van Baar 2011a, 2018a; van Baar, Ivasiuc and Kreide 2019).

Differential Inclusion as Bordering Practice: Roma as Europe's Internalized Outsiders

Elsewhere and above, I have suggested that the complex dynamics at the current junctures of security, citizenship and development cannot be considered in the context of a singular policy logic, a discursive structure or a hegemonic ideological framework, such as neoliberal capitalism, for instance (Harvey 2005; Wacquant 2009; cf. van Baar 2011a). Rather, this dynamic and its impact on the European Roma is characterized by a fundamental ambiguity. The Europeanization of Roma representation, seen as the effect of a hybrid, multiple kind of governmentality, involves a shift from problematizing Roma as externalized outsiders against whom Europe has defined itself, to considering them, since 1989, as the *internalized* outsiders to be included as productive, participating and 'true' Europeans. Ongoing practices such as the expulsion of Roma from France, but also the articulation of social inclusion and other development programmes throughout Europe, show that we are dealing here with a highly ambiguous shift, characterized not so much by the emergence of regimes and mechanisms of exclusion – as if dealing with a clear and rigid distinction between inside and outside – but by practices of 'differential inclusion'. Sandro Mezzadra and Brett Neilson have introduced this notion to point to a 'substitution of the binary distinction between inclusion and exclusion with continuous parametric modulations – that is, processes of filtering and selecting that refer to multiple and shifting scales, ratings and evaluations' (Mezzadra and Neilson 2012: 68).

This notion is also relevant in the case of Roma because, albeit ambiguously and through enduring states of deportability (De Genova 2002) and evictability (van Baar 2017a), Roma are included in spaces of labour and citizenship and have substantially contributed to the sphere of production. At the same time, these contributions are rarely recognized or publicly discussed. The notion of differential inclusion underlines the variegated nature of contemporary regimes of labour and citizenship, in which spatial differentiations frequently correspond with divergent, yet overlapping types of governing, such as those related to policing, disciplinary, pastoral, liberal, welfarist or neoliberal practices (Ong 2006; van Baar 2011a, 2012). Along conceptual and methodological lines similar to those of differential inclusion, an analysis of the Europeanization of Roma representation avoids situating challenges and contestations of Roma displacement and marginalization outside these intersecting governmentalities, as if an improvement to their position were largely or even entirely external to these realities, positioned in the field of, for instance, local knowledge, grassroots communities, religious groupings, or the inventive tactics of those who try to circumvent or challenge securitization (van Baar 2011a, 2013, 2018b). Considering the Roma's position as 'internalized outsiders' – and thus through a lens of differential inclusion – contributes in at least three different 'programmatic' ways to unfolding research and knowledge formation beyond the methodologically Eurocentric and Roma-centric parameters discussed earlier.

First, the notion of differential inclusion departs from the idea that borders are merely obstructing or blocking devices that divide already existing or created worlds. Rather, it considers borders as 'world making', and irregularized people and groups as central, rather than marginal, 'to the fundamental transformations that have reshaped citizenship and labour, culture and space over the last two decades' (Mezzadra and Neilson 2012: 59, 63). Thus, in line with critical security, border, citizenship and migration studies, irregularized subjects are not only placed at the heart of analyses of present-day border, security, citizenship and migration regimes, but also, and more fundamentally, of interrogations of how these regimes are or can be challenged, redirected and changed. Similarly, examining Roma from the angle of the Europeanization of their representation makes it possible to move beyond Eurocentric analyses and to interrogate the ways in which Roma are ambiguously governed in terms of their Europeanness and European identity. To make such an interrogation possible, I have suggested, we need to embed the Europeanization of Roma representation in a genealogy of how Roma have been governed at the biopolitical borders of Europe and how, simultaneously, they have contributed to the contestation of these bordering regimes, rationales, technologies and epistemologies (van Baar 2011a, 2013, 2017b).

Mezzadra and Neilson have clarified that, for them, the border is 'not so much a research object as *an epistemological viewpoint* that allows an acute critical analysis not only of how relations of domination and exploitation are being redefined at the present time but also of the struggles that take shape around these changing relations' (Mezzadra and Neilson 2012: 66–67, emphasis added). In Foucauldian fashion, they also and importantly extend their epistemological perspective to include the cognitive borders involved in 'the scientific division of labour associated with the sectioning of knowledge into different disciplinary zones' (ibid.: 65). I would like to connect this welcome extension to my idea that in order to critically interrogate the ways in which 'Europe', 'the Roma' and their complex relationship have currently and historically been made intelligible through knowledge and expertise formation, we need to challenge the (at least methodologically) Eurocentric and Roma-centric focus of many scholarly approaches to Roma, including those of newly established academic forums funded by European or non-profit organizations. While these approaches have often been critical of trends towards ethnicization or racialization, they remain Roma-centric to the extent that their approaches ethnographically and one-sidedly concentrate on practices, programmes, tactics, discourses or policies that directly and primarily relate to Roma. Therefore, there is a need to seriously diversify – beyond ethnic boundaries and demarcations – the scholarly lenses through which we study Roma and their realities.

The recent introduction of notions such as intersectionality (Kóczé 2009; Greenfields 2011; Brooks 2012; Smith and Greenfields 2013), hybridity and superdiversity (Tremlett 2009, 2014; Silverman 2012, this volume) to scholarship on Roma is to be welcomed, for these are potentially useful tools to interdisciplinarize Roma-related research beyond one-sided, ethnically trained lenses. These and similar new-fangled notions are important, and not only in terms of revealing the discrepancies between the daily realities of cultural difference and governmental endeavours to manage 'cultural diversity' or – relevant here – 'heterogeneity' among and across Romani groups. They are also important to challenge what, twenty years ago, Willems (1997: 305) called the 'splendid isolation' of scholarship on Roma that, despite or maybe even because of the gradual disciplinarization and integration of 'Romani Studies' into the academic world, has not yet come to an end. Those who study the situation of Roma have to avoid the disciplinarization of Roma-related scholarship, equivalent to academic isolation, purification or even ghettoization, be it from a desire to maintain preserved power positions or reproduce scholarly capital, or for other, more or less understandable reasons. To be sure, this is a serious risk that accompanies every attempt to challenge the persistent trend of treating national or regional (European, American, etc.) history in disciplinary isolation, and to render minority histories and experiences marginal and insignificant. This risk has also become manifest in scholarly fields such as African American Studies, Diaspora Studies and Jewish Studies, which have emerged precisely to dispute self-contained national and regional histories (Buck-Morss 2009: 21–23).

This issue leads me to discuss one final way in which a focus on differential inclusion helps in overcoming the centrisms discussed above. Considering Roma as Europe's internalized outsiders, and analysing their situation through a lens of differential inclusion, offer methodological contributions that connect their societal position to that of other irregularized minority and majority groups beyond ethnic difference and space, including illegalized migrants, Muslim minorities, minority women or youth and the working poor (De Genova and Peutz 2010; Stenning et al. 2010; Szalai and Schiff 2014; Jansen, Celikates and de Bloois 2015). Enabling these relational investigations, and those of minoritizing and majoritizing processes, implicates firstly a call for comparative research among and between ethnicized, racialized, culturalized, religionized and otherwise minoritized groups (even though comparative perspectives of, for instance, antisemitism, Islamophobia and antigypsyism or Romaphobia have hitherto been radically underrepresented); and secondly, particularly now that European citizenship tends to be increasingly 'stripped of any social and progressive meaning' (Mezzadra 2015: 132), we need to reflect on how the differentiated systems of bordering Europe affect human subjects beyond the contested binaries of 'authorized' and 'unauthorized', 'regular' and 'irregular', 'legal' and 'illegal', 'EU' and 'non-EU' migrants.[5] Mezzadra touches on this sore point when he emphasizes the importance of not isolating the struggles and movements of the irregularized and unauthorized from 'other conflicts involving "legal migrants" and even autochthonous populations in order not to replicate the language and taxonomies of migration policies and governance' (ibid.: 124). Similarly, we should avoid using positivist framings of Roma as 'ethnic groups' that, in recent in history, have become the targets of transnational 'ethnic minority governance' in Europe. Indeed, if we reproduce understandings of ethnic identity and ethnicity that have significantly contributed to highly ambiguous outcomes on the ground, through all sorts of developmentalist programmes for instance, we likewise replicate 'the language and taxonomies' of European minority policies and practices of minority governance that we should critically interrogate and challenge.

Relating Mezzadra's idea to scholarly investigations of the position of Roma has important consequences. Goffman-inspired analyses of stigmatization (e.g. Lucassen, Willems and Cottaar 1998) have argued that any serious lack of everyday social interaction between minoritized groups and their neighbours, and thus the existence of an enduring social distance between majorities and minorities, considerably impacts on the effectiveness of stigmatization and mutual distrust. Following Mezzadra's idea, I call for translating such findings to the ethnographical level of scholarly work to discuss critically how and to what extent disciplinary isolation as well as methodological Eurocentrism and Roma-centrism tend to result in a troublesome scholarly alienation from gaining insight into the *common* conditions under which precarious lives continue to be produced and reproduced in contemporary Europe.

Huub van Baar is an Assistant Professor of Political Theory at the Institute of Political Science at the Justus-Liebig University of Giessen in Germany. He is also a Senior Research Fellow at the Amsterdam Centre for Globalisation Studies (ACGS) at the Faculty of Humanities of the University of Amsterdam, and an affiliated researcher at the Amsterdam Centre for European Studies (ACES). He coordinates a research project on the formation and transformation of Romani minorities in modern European history, which is part of the research programme Dynamics of Security: Forms of Securitization in Historical Perspective (2014–2021), funded by the German Research Foundation (DFG). He has published widely on the position and political and cultural representation of Europe's Romani minorities, predominantly from the angle of how their situation has changed at the nexus of citizenship, security and development. He has published peer-reviewed articles in, for instance, *Social Identities, Antipode, Journal of Ethnic and Migration Studies, City, Third Text, Citizenship Studies, International Journal of Cultural Policy* and *Society and Space*. He is the author of *The European Roma: Minority Representation, Memory and the Limits of Transnational Governmentality* (F&N, 2011) and the main co-editor of *Museutopia: A Photographic Research Project by Ilya Rabinovich* (Alauda, 2012, with Ingrid Commandeur) and *The Securitization of the Roma in Europe* (Palgrave Macmillan, 2019, with Ana Ivasiuc and Regina Kreide). He is currently finalizing a monograph entitled *The Ambiguity of Protection: Spectacular Security and the European Roma*.

Notes

I would like to thank all the participants at the international symposium 'Global Governance, Democracy and Social Justice', held on 7–8 April 2015 at Duke University and Wake Forest University in North Carolina, for their valuable comments. I would particularly like to thank Angéla Kóczé for making this event, and therefore this book, possible. The research from which this chapter is drawn was funded by the German Research Foundation (DFG), grant SFB/TRR 138, entitled 'Dynamics of Security: Forms of Securitization in Historical Perspective'.

1. In his groundbreaking study of Europe's historical construction of the 'Gypsies', Klaus-Michael Bogdal (2011: 173) discusses what I call 'the representation of Roma as a *non-European minority*' in terms of a 'de-Europeanization' (*Enteuropäisierung*). Although Bogdal explains the exclusion of Roma from European cultures and its 'civilizational' imagination along lines similar to mine, his notion of the Gypsies' *de*-Europeanization implicitly suggests that prior to the end of the eighteenth century they were seen as Europeans, which I want to question.

2. Hancock has discussed (at least rhetorically) the history of Roma primarily in terms of a continuous history of persecution (van Baar 2011a: 86–87, 118, 305), while Willems, particularly from the Enlightenment onwards, perceives this history as a regressive one of permanent stigmatization without much, if any, room for Roma agency or the historicization of its articulation (van Baar 2011a: 87–99, 140–49). Matras, on the other hand, reads this history as a bifurcated one in which regressive trends can be strictly separated, through a scientist method, from progressive, positive ones (van Baar 2011a: 99–105, 140–49). See also the discussion on essentialism versus constructivism in the Introduction to this volume.
3. Contrary to what Zsuzsanna Vidra (2018) has suggested and to what Nando Sigona and Nidhi Trehan (2009) have argued, I do not consider postcommunist regimes, nor the transitions towards them, as fully motivated by practices or policies of neoliberalization. Understanding neoliberalism as a hybrid form and practice of governmentality, rather than as an ideology or a set of policies, helps to avoid several of the pitfalls that have become manifest in analyses of neoliberalization. As I have extensively argued (van Baar 2011a: 163–74, 191–231), neoliberalism as governmentality avoids, most notably, the understanding of neoliberalism as something that comes from 'outside' (e.g. from the United States), or to read it along the lines of functionalism and periodization (as if economic systems succeeded one another). In my approach to governmentality as a form of power that has been articulated *topologically*, neoliberal policies, programmes or techniques are never articulated 'purely', but always in a hybrid way, and are thus fundamentally intermingled with other styles and techniques of governing, including welfarist, policing and liberal ones.
4. An analysis in terms of governmentality and problematization, therefore, goes further than discourse and frame analyses. The former involves not only an analysis of discourses and discursive practices, but also that of non-discursive practices and the co-constitutive role that techniques and technologies play in regimes of rule (van Baar 2011a: 35–41).
5. The current Brexit impasse has perhaps contributed to an unexpected revaluation of European citizenship, but if it does materialize, it will probably only lead to more rather than fewer heated debates about practices of differential inclusion and exclusion at the contested borders of and within the EU.

References

Bigo, D. 2008. 'Globalized (In)Security', in D. Bigo and A. Tsoukala (eds), *Terror, Insecurity and Liberty*. London: Routledge, pp. 10–48.

Bogdal, K.-M. 2011. *Europa erfindet die Zigeuner: Eine Geschichte von Faszination und Verachtung*. Frankfurt am Main: Suhrkamp.

Brooks, E. (ed.). 2012. 'Comparative Perspectives Symposium: Romani Feminisms'. Special issue, *Signs* 38(1): 1–46.

Buck-Morss, S. 2009. *Hegel, Haiti and Universal History*. Pittsburgh, PA: Pittsburgh University Press.

Bunescu, I. 2014. *Roma in Europe: The Politics of Collective Identity Formation*. Farnham: Ashgate.

Butler, J. 2004. *Precarious Life: The Power of Mourning and Violence.* London: Verso.
Castle-Kaňerová, M. 2003. 'Round and Round the Roundabout: Czech Roma and the Vicious Circle of Asylum Seeking', *Nationalities Papers* 31(1): 13–25.
Cruickshank, N. 2012. 'Perspectives on Europeanization: Roma and Integration', *L'Europe en formation* 364(2): 401–16.
De Genova, N. 2002. 'Migrant "Illegality" and Deportability in Everyday Life', *Annual Review of Anthropology* 31: 419–47.
De Genova, N., and N. Peutz (eds). 2010. *The Deportation Regime: Sovereingty, Space and the Freedom of Movement.* Durham, NC: Duke University Press.
Duffield, M. 2001. *Global Governance and the New Wars.* London: Zed Books.
———. 2007. *Development, Security and Unending War.* Cambridge: Polity.
Escobar, A. 1995. *Encountering Development.* Princeton, NJ: Princeton University Press.
European Commission. 2011. 'An EU Framework for National Roma Integration Strategies up to 2020'. Brussels.
Featherstone, K., and C. Radaelli (eds). 2003. *The Politics of Europeanization.* Oxford: Oxford University Press.
Ferguson, J. 2006. *Global Shadows: Africa in the Neoliberal World Order.* Durham, NC: Duke University Press.
Foucault, M. 1997. 'Polemics, Politics and Problematizations', in P. Rabinow (ed.), *Ethics: Subjectivity and Truth.* New York: The New Press, pp. 111–19.
———. 2007. *Security, Terrritory, Population. Lectures at the Collège de France 1977–1978.* New York: Palgrave Macmillan.
Goodwin, M., and P. de Hert (eds). 2013. *European Roma Integration Efforts.* Brussels: Brussels University Press.
Graziono, P., and M. Vink (eds). 2006. *Europeanization: New Research Agendas.* New York: Palgrave Macmillan.
Greenfields, M. 2011. 'What Makes a Gypsy or Traveller Vulnerable?', in M. Greenfields, R. Dalrymple and A. Fanning (eds), *Working with Adults at Risk from Harm.* Maidenhead: Open University Press, pp. 207–30.
Guglielmo, R., and T. Waters. 2005. 'Migrating towards Minority Status', *Journal of Common Market Studies* 43(4): 763–86.
Guy, W. 2009. 'EU Initiatives on Roma', in N. Sigona and N. Trehan (eds), *Romani Politics in Contemporary Europe.* New York: Palgrave Macmillan, pp. 23–50.
Hancock, I. 2002. *We Are the Romani People.* Hatfield: University of Hertfordshire Press.
Harvey, D. 2005. *A Short History of Neoliberalism.* Oxford: Oxford University Press.
Hepworth, K. 2012. 'Abject Citizens: Italian "Nomad Emergencies" and the Deportability of Romanian Roma', *Citizenship Studies* 16(3–4): 431–49.
Huysmans, J. 2006. *The Politics of Insecurity.* London: Routledge.
Jansen, Y., R. Celikates and J. de Bloois (eds). 2015. *The Irregularization of Migration in Contemporary Europe: Deportation, Detention, Drowning.* Lanham, MD: Rowman & Littlefield.
Jones, A., and J. Clark. 2010. *The Spatialities of Europeanization.* London: Routledge.
Klímová-Alexander, A. 2005. *The Romani Voice in World Politics.* Aldershot: Ashgate.
Kóczé, A. 2009. *Missing Intersectionality: Race/Ethnicity, Gender and Class in Current Research and Policies on Romani Women in Europe.* Budapest: Center for Policy Studies, Central European University.

Kovats, M. 2001. 'The Emergence of European Roma Policy', in W. Guy (ed.), *Between Past and Future: The Roma of Central and Eastern Europe*. Hatfield: University of Hertfordshire Press, pp. 93–116.
———. 2003. 'The Politics of Romani Identity', *Open Democracy*, 29 July.
Law, I., and M. Kovats. 2018. *Rethinking Roma: Identities, Politicisation and New Agendas*. New York: Palgrave Macmillan.
Lucassen, L., W. Willems and A. Cottaar. 1998. *Gypsies and Other Itinerant Groups*. Basingstoke: Macmillan.
Marushiakova, E., and V. Popov. 2011. 'Between Exoticization and Marginalization', *Behemoth* 2011(1): 51–68.
Matras, Y. 2004. 'The Role of Language in Mystifying and Demystifying Gypsy Identity', in N. Saul and S. Tebbutt (eds), *The Role of the Romanies: Images and Counter-Images of 'Gypsies'/Romanies in European Cultures*. Liverpool: Liverpool University Press, pp. 53–78.
———. 2013. 'Scholarship and the Politics of Romani Identity', in *European Yearbook of Minority Issues*. Leiden: ECMI, pp. 209–45.
McGarry, A. 2010. *Who Speaks for Roma? Political Representation of a Transnational Minority Community*. London: Continuum.
Mezzadra, S. 2015. 'The Proliferation of Borders and the Right to Escape', in Y. Jansen, R. Celikates and J. de Bloois (eds), *The Irregularization of Migration in Contemporary Europe*. Lanham, MD: Rowman & Littlefield, pp. 121–36.
Mezzadra, S., and B. Neilson. 2012. 'Between Inclusion and Exclusion', *Theory, Culture & Society* 29(4/5): 58–75.
Mezzadra, S., J. Reid and R. Sammadar (eds). 2013. *The Biopolitics of Development*. New Delhi: Springer.
Ong, A. 2006. *Neoliberalism as Exception*. Durham, NC: Duke University Press.
Puxon, G. 2000. 'The Romani Movement', in T. Acton (ed.), *Scholarship and the Gypsy Struggle*. Hatfield: University of Hertfordshire Press, pp. 94–113.
Radaelli, C. 2003. 'The Europeanization of Public Policy', in K. Featherstone and C. Radaelli (eds), *The Politics of Europeanization*. Oxford: Oxford University Press, pp. 27–56.
Ram, M. 2010. 'Interests, Norms and Advocacy: Explaining the Emergence of the Roma onto the EU's Agenda', *Ethnopolitics* 9(2): 197–217.
———. 2012. 'Lost in Transition? Europeanization and the Roma', *L'Europe en formation* 364(2): 417–34.
———. 2014. 'Europeanized Hypocrisy: Roma Inclusion and Exclusion in Central and Eastern Europe', *Journal on Ethnopolitics and Minority Issues in Europe* 13(3): 15–44.
Risse-Kappen, T., M. Cowles and J. Caporaso (eds). 2001. *Europeanization and Domestic Change*. Ithaca, NY: Cornell University Press.
Rose, N. 1999. *Powers of Freedom*. Cambridge: Cambridge University Press.
Schimmelfennig, F., and U. Sedelmeier (eds). 2005. *The Europeanization of Central and Eastern Europe*. Ithaca, NY: Cornell University Press.
Sigona, N., and N. Trehan (eds). 2009. *Romani Politics in Contemporary Europe*. New York: Palgrave Macmillan.
Silverman, C. 2012. *Romani Routes: Cultural Politics and Balkan Music in Diaspora*. Oxford: Oxford University Press.
Smith, D., and M. Greenfields. 2013. *Gypsies and Travellers in Housing: The Decline of Nomadism*. Bristol: Policy Press.

Sobotka, E. 2011. 'Influence of Civil Society Actors on Formulation of Roma Issues within the EU Framework', *International Journal on Minority and Group Rights* 18(2): 235–56.

Stenning, A., et al. 2010. *Domesticating Neo-Liberalism*. Oxford: Wiley-Blackwell.

Szalai, J., and C. Schiff (eds). 2014. *Migrant, Roma and Postcolonial Youth in Education across Europe*. New York: Palgrave Macmillan.

Tremlett, A. 2009. 'Bringing Hybridity to Heterogeneity in Romani Studies', *Romani Studies* 19(2): 147–68.

———. 2014. 'Making a Difference without Creating a Difference', *Ethnicities* 14(6): 830–48.

van Baar, H. 2008. 'Scaling the Romani Grassroots: Europeanization and Transnational Networking', in F. Jacobs and J. Ries (eds), *Romani/Gypsy Cultures in New Perspectives*. Leipzig: Leipzig University Press, pp. 217–42.

———. 2011a. *The European Roma: Minority Representation, Memory and the Limits of Transnational Governmentality*. Amsterdam: F&N.

———. 2011b. 'Europe's Romaphobia: Problematization, Securitization, Nomadization', *Environment and Planning D: Society and Space* 29(2): 203–12.

———. 2012. 'Socioeconomic Mobility and Neoliberal Governmentality in Post-socialist Europe', *Journal of Ethnic and Migration Studies* 38(8): 1289–304.

———. 2013. 'Travelling Activism and Knowledge Formation in the Romani Social and Civil Movement', in M. Miskovic (ed.), *Roma and Education in Europe*. London: Routledge, pp. 192–203.

———. 2014. 'The Centripetal Dimension of the EU's External Border Regime', *Etnofoor* 26(2): 87–93

———. 2015. 'The Perpetual Mobile Machine of Forced Mobility', in Y. Jansen, R. Celikates and J. de Bloois (eds), *The Irregularization of Migration in Contemporary Europe*. Lanham, MD: Rowman & Littlefield, pp. 71–86.

———. 2017a. 'Evictability and the Biopolitical Bordering of Europe', *Antipode* 49(1): 212–30.

———. 2017b. 'Boundary Practices of Citizenship: Europe's Roma at the Nexus of Securitization and Citizenship', in R. Gonzales and N. Sigona (eds), *Within and Beyond Citizenship*. London: Routledge, pp. 143–58.

———. 2018a. 'Contained Mobility and the Racialization of Poverty in Europe: The Roma at the Development–Security Nexus', *Social Identities* 24(4): 442–58.

———. 2018b. 'Neoliberalism and the Spirit of Nongovernmentalism: Towards an Anthroposociology of Roma-related Engagement and Activism', in S. Beck and A. Ivasiuc (eds), *Roma Activism: Reimagining Power and Knowledge*. Oxford: Berghahn Books, pp. 25–44.

———. 2019. 'From "Lagging Behind" to "Being Beneath"? The De-developmentalization of Time and Social Order in Contemporary Europe', in H. van Baar, A. Ivasiuc and R. Kreide (eds), *The Securitization of the Roma in Europe*. New York: Palgrave Macmillan, pp. 159–82.

van Baar, H., A. Ivasiuc and R. Kreide (eds). 2019. *The Securitization of the Roma in Europe*. New York: Palgrave Macmillan.

Vašečka, I., and M. Vašečka. 2003. 'Recent Romani Migration from Slovakia to EU Member States', *Nationalities Papers* 31(1): 27–45.

Vermeersch, P. 2003. 'Ethnic Minority Identity and Movement Politics', *Ethnic and Racial Studies* 26(5): 879–901.

———. 2006. *The Romani Movement: Minority Politics and Ethnic Mobilization in Contemporary Central Europe*. Oxford: Berghahn Books.
———. 2012. 'Reframing the Roma', *Journal of Ethnic and Migration Studies* 38(8): 1195–212.
Vidra, Z. 2018. 'Hungary's Punitive Turn: The Shift from Welfare to Workfare', *Communist and Post-Communist Studies* 51: 73–80.
Wacquant, L. 2009. *Punishing the Poor: The Neoliberal Government of Social Insecurity*. Durham, NC: Duke University Press.
Walters, W., and J.-H. Haahr. 2005. *Governing Europe: Discourse, Governmentality and European Integration*. London: Routledge.
Willems, W. 1997. *In Search of the True Gypsy: From Enlightenment to Final Solution*. London: Frank Cass.

CHAPTER 6

ETHNIC IDENTITY AND POLICYMAKING
A Critical Analysis of the EU Framework for National Roma Integration Strategies

Iulius Rostas

After the fall of communism, the situation of the Roma in Europe became an issue of concern for many European institutions dealing with human rights, such as the Organization for Security and Co-operation in Europe (OSCE), the Council of Europe and the European Union (EU). Since the early 1990s, Roma rights advocates and human rights groups have succeeded in placing Roma on the agendas of national governments and international organizations and institutions. As a result, governments in countries with significant Romani populations, mostly in Central and Eastern Europe, have adopted national programmes for Roma integration, elaborated action plans under the Decade of Roma Inclusion 2005–2015 and complied with the EU's Framework for National Roma Integration Strategies (EU Framework for Roma).[1]

Despite the numerous programmes, policies and projects adopted and implemented by different actors throughout Europe, the situation of most Roma has continued to worsen. A 2009 survey conducted by the European Union Agency on Fundamental Rights concludes that Roma are the most vulnerable group to discrimination; every second 50 per cent of those Roma questioned declared they had been subjected to discrimination in the last twelve months (EUFRA: 2009: 1). Similarly, a 2012 survey conducted by the United Nations Development Programme (UNDP), the World Bank and the European Commission shows that in addition to discrimination, those officially defined as Roma live in significantly worse conditions than the non-Roma in their proximity, and face limited access to preschool education as well as a high rate of school dropout, segregation in education, improper housing conditions (about 45 per cent of Roma live in households lacking basic facilities) and extreme poverty (about 90 per cent of Roma live below national poverty lines) (EUFRA and UNDP 2012: 12). The situation of the Roma seems paradoxical: the more attention it receives and the more measures targeting Roma are adopted and implemented, the worse the situation seems to become. This paradox urges us to look for explanations and solutions. In this chapter, I will explore several causes of this troublesome state of affairs.

My aim is to analyse the process and content of EU public policies towards Roma as part of the EU Framework for Roma. I will examine the ways in which policymakers and Romani activists have categorized Roma as a target group, the problems Roma face, and the policy answers that have been provided on these issues. In doing so, I will propose an operational definition of ethnic identity that could be measured within the policymaking processes and, as my main case study, I will analyse the EU Framework for Roma through the lens of Romani identity. The main research question for my investigation is why the EU Framework and policies on Roma fail to produce the expected social change that inspired these policy initiatives.

My research hypothesis is that one of the most important causes for this limited impact is a policy failure to adequately take Romani ethnic identity into consideration. How do policymakers define 'the Roma'? Who exactly is part of the group that these policies target? How are their 'problems' defined? Who instigates these definitions of 'the Roma'? What are the constraints in defining Roma? How are they categorized within the processes of policymaking? These are important questions that influence the design and potential outcome of policies. In my approach, I combine policy design theory, policy analysis and critical race theory (CRT): the first analyses the content of policies and the social construction of the target group, the second considers the policymaking process, and the third examines the role of racism in shaping Romani ethnic identity and, consequently, in informing policy processes.

Ethnic Identity and Policy Studies

Over the last three decades, the literature on ethnic identity and ethnicity has developed significantly. Despite the predictions that ethnicity will disappear due to its limited relevance for the class struggle (Marx) or the triumph of liberal values and liberal democracy (Fukuyama), over the last three decades one has been able to witness a process of ethnic revival among different groups, which has led in some cases to exacerbated nationalism, with consequences such as violent conflicts, redrawing of state borders and even genocide. In this context, the interests of researchers in issues connected to ethnic identity and ethnicity could be regarded as a development of the interconnection between theory and praxis. Yet anthropological, cultural, psychological and sociological approaches have dominated the literature on ethnic identity and ethnicity, while approaches from political science and, to an even larger degree, policy studies, have so far been underrepresented.

My theoretical starting point is Rawi Abdelal's work on identity. The research team led by Abdelal has attempted to develop a unifying theory of collective identity (ethnic, religious, social, and so on) considering that the absence of such a theory has resulted in conceptual and methodological perplexities in the study of identity (Abdelal et al. 2001, 2006, 2009). I critically build on the theory developed by Abdelal and his colleagues, and use it to examine the situation of the Roma in Europe. Methodologically, I test this theory by applying it to the Roma, a heterogeneous ethnic group highly stratified along multiple lines and spread throughout Europe, who have no kin state and are regarded as the 'most vulnerable' group in the EU (Toritsyn 2009: 10).

Based on the analysis of thousands of articles and books on identity, Abdelal and his colleagues (Abdelal et al. 2001) have proposed the following definition:

> We define a collective identity as a social category that varies along two dimensions – content and contestation. Content describes the meaning of a collective identity. The content of social identities may take the form of four, non-mutually-exclusive types:
> - Constitutive norms refer to the formal and informal rules that define group membership;
> - Social purposes refer to the goals that are shared by members of a group;
> - Relational comparisons refer to defining an identity group by what it is not – i.e. the way it views other identity groups, especially where those views about the other are a defining part of the identity;
> - Cognitive models refer to the worldviews or understandings of political and material conditions and interests that are shaped by a particular identity;
> - Contestation refers to the degree of agreement within a group over the content of the shared identity. (Abdelal et al. 2006: 696)

This definition has several weaknesses. The issues overlooked by Abdelal's team are the role of the out-group in defining identity, the group's representation in the public sphere – especially the societal problems faced by the group – and the causal relationships in public policymaking. Abdelal and colleagues limit the relational dimension of identity to comparison, without considering power relations among groups. For example, Group A might use its power to impose a certain image or narrative about Group B. In my opinion, a distinction should be made between the perception of a group by the larger public, especially in terms of the problems it faces, and the causes of problems that governmental policies aim to solve. These weaknesses can be considerably mitigated when we bring the definition of Abdelal's team into dialogue with critical social studies, and critical race theory in particular, and the ways in which these fields of study have significantly contributed to debates about identity.

In order to deal adequately with the situation of the Roma, therefore, I want to extend Abdelal's definition of identity in several ways. First, I include the perception of others as a key defining element of my extended definition. The case of the Roma shows that the ways in which outsiders define, identify and categorize a group directly impact on how that group perceives and defines itself. In addition, if identity is relational, as Abdelal suggests, and if we subscribe to this perspective, one cannot limit the definition of identity to the in-group only. As Henri Tajfel and John Turner (2004) have shown, the out-group is also an important reference point for both the self-esteem and collective identity of the in-group. Secondly, I want to go further and add power relationships as a specific element to the definition of identity in policy studies. Power relationships are key to understanding the social position of a group, the mechanisms of exclusion, and the challenges faced in bringing about social change. Thirdly, inspired by critical race theory scholars, I consider racism towards Roma as part of their everyday experience, and as yet another critical component of Romani identity (Bell 1992; Delgado and Stefancic 2001; Gillborn 2015).

Finally, two further elements should also be taken into consideration in developing an adequate approach to the relevance of identity in policy studies. The first relates to the need for a further contextualization and understanding of policymaking processes. Often, the end results of policymaking alone do not inform us sufficiently on the situation prior to government intervention, and therefore we should focus more specifically on policymaking processes and how they take place. Experiences with policymaking regarding the Roma from Central and Eastern Europe, for instance, underline the importance of minority participation in these processes; thus, an analysis of how, and to what extent, identity plays a role in these participation practices is required in order to shed more light on the complex *process* of policymaking.

The second element to be included is the role of experiential knowledge in shaping our understanding of policymaking processes. As CRT scholars have argued (Gillborn 2008), experiential knowledge expressed through counter-stories provide the interpretive frameworks to make sense of the lived experience of people who have experienced racism themselves. The lived experiences of processes of policymaking towards Roma, and my involvement in different capacities in these processes, provide a valid perspective on the challenges that different stakeholders face during each stage of policymaking.

Therefore, to analyse the role played by Romani identity in policymaking processes, I use the following definition of ethnic identity:

> Ethnic identity is a social category, as well as a process, organized along four dimensions:
> (1) Ethnic group participation in the policymaking process;
> (2) Ethnic claims and grievances expressed formally by social actors who speak on behalf of the group;
> (3) Representation of the group or the problems they face in the public sphere through the involvement of different social actors – policymakers, researchers, representatives of the group, etc. – in the policymaking process, and
> (4) Causal relationships that determine the current state of affairs identified by analysing public policy documents.

Participation means giving a 'voice' to the target group. Through participation in the policymaking process, the ethnic group can express its preferences, define interests and negotiate priorities in relation to other groups and institutions. When a vulnerable group is the target of the policy, participation is of even greater importance, since the group's vulnerability stems from the fact that their voice was not heard during policymaking through the classic channels of representative institutions in a democratic society. In other words, the interests of this group were not included in the democratic machinery of interest aggregation that sets the public interests of society and the governmental agenda. Unlike the European Commission, which sees vulnerability as being a result of poverty and social exclusion, I understand vulnerability to be a result of the unequal distribution of power and opportunities within the larger social and political system.[2]

Ethnic claims are those demands made by actors who pretend to speak on behalf of the ethnic group. In addition to the issue of the legitimacy of actors making such claims, a further significant aspect to consider is the correlation between the grievances of the target group and the claims made by those who speak on its behalf – that is, the ways in which claims are made and framed as larger societal problems, and how these claims are articulated as public interests and placed on the political agenda. From a political point of view, Roma are treated as politically insignificant actors, perceived by mainstream political actors as an electorate that can be easily manipulated and corrupted. All over Europe, and with only a few exceptions, the rule is that mainstream political parties refuse to put Roma-related issues on their agenda. They usually refuse to do so on the grounds of alleged ethnic bias, possible electoral costs determined by the strong antigypsyism among the electorate, or their inability to represent the interests of vulnerable groups more generally. This practice places Roma in a unique position in terms of their limited capacity to put relevant topics on political agendas or to influence policy decisions.

Concerning agenda setting, one important issue is the way in which majority groups perceive an ethnic group and the problems its members face. Thus, the ways in which Roma have been problematized in media and policies often differ from, for instance, the higher number of socioeconomic barriers they face in everyday life. This discrepancy could serve as an indicator of the chances of success for those policies. As part of this dimension of ethnic identity in policymaking, one has to consider how policymakers and political elites have presented these problems, the inputs to which they have reacted, the responses and types of documents that codify the adopted measures, and their correlation with other mainstream policies.

An analysis of causal relationships provides a deeper understanding of policymaking towards Roma. Identifying the root causes of the problems that many Roma face is key to any adequate understanding of the policy objectives, implementation structures, policy tools employed, and resources allocated for implementation. It is important to mention that the 'causal relationships' (see my definition above) are a *reflection* of the ways in which those with a key role in policymaking processes frame cause and effect. How stakeholders explain certain situations indirectly influences the identification of those considered responsible for the situation, as well as the kinds of intervention deemed to be required for its improvement. The stakeholders' approach, and how they propose solutions to the identified problems in particular, also determines to a great extent the way in which actors are positioned. As Deborah Stone puts it: 'Problem definition is the active manipulation of images of conditions by competing political actors. Conditions come to be defined as problems through the strategic portrayal of causal stories' (Stone 1989: 299). Causality, mostly identified through discourse and text analysis, should be correlated with ethnic claims and the representation of problems faced by the group, to which competing causal story governmental actors respond.

Policy Studies and Collective Identity

The advantage of the approach introduced above is that it allows us to analyse policies towards Roma both as content and as process. For example, it is important to see how policymakers, experts and Romani social actors have categorized the Roma as a social category, thereby determining who is included and who is not part of the group targeted by policymaking. Moreover, this approach also helps us to see how these processes have influenced Romani self-identify and the ways in which Roma communicate their ethnic identity in the public sphere. Yet to adequately understand policymaking towards the Roma, one also has to examine the ways in which Roma participate in this process, since in some cases the processes behind the emergence and materialization of policy documents may influence their success more than their explicit content. For example, in an attempt to increase school participation and to combat dropout, it makes sense to involve Romani parents in designing such policies, as it is they who are primarily responsible for the education of their children, sending them to school and providing the resources that enable them to attend school. Considering Roma parents' opinions on both the education of their children and the obstacles they and their children encounter in accessing quality education would help policymakers to design more effective measures. Most importantly, such an approach avoids simply consulting experts on education or implementing an existing programme or 'best practice' that may have had positive results elsewhere. One option does not necessarily exclude the other, but too often, the position of Roma is disregarded and the role of experts 'on Romani issues' overestimated in policy interventions regarding Roma.

Policy design theory seems to be the most appropriate conceptual frame for understanding both policymaking towards Roma and the impact of such policies so far. Anne Schneider and Helen Ingram, who are among the founders of policy design theory, have suggested that this theory 'is important because it helps explain why some groups are advantaged more than others independently of traditional notions of political power, and how policy designs can reinforce or alter such advantages' (Schneider and Ingram 1993: 334). Representatives of this theory have analysed not only the efficiency and effectiveness of public policy, but also taken into account: dimensions such as support for specific policies; responsiveness to the interests and needs of citizens; the capacity to generate consensus and agreement; relations between implementing agencies and how they relate to those targeted by the policy; and ways in which policies produce a more just society (Ingram and Schneider 2006: 169; Howlett, Mukherjee and Woo 2015). Accordingly, policy analysts are able to focus on both the content of the policy as well as the policymaking process.

One key element of the policymaking process is the social construction of target populations:

> Social construction is a process through which values and meanings become attached to persons and groups that provide rationales for how they are treated. The combination of power and such social construction frequently shapes policies in ways that send damaging messages, because those with certain power characteristics and positive images always get benefits while others almost never do. That in turn encourages or discourages the fight for people's own interests and beliefs. (Ingram 2016)

Hence, scholars using policy design theory understand policymaking as a way to promote certain values and interests, a particular social construction of knowledge and groups, and power relations in society.

With reference to policy consequences, scholars have analysed the ways in which policymakers have constructed their target groups, and the impact on democracy. Using entitlement and deservedness as dimensions of policy impact analysis, Ingram and Schneider (2005, 2006) argue that governments usually differentiate target populations along the lines of power and the social construction of these groups, and distinguish between those who deserve benefits and those who do not. Schneider and Ingram also explore how governments and their policies create and maintain 'systems of privilege, domination and quiescence among those who are the most oppressed' (Schneider and Ingram 1997: 53). They understand policymaking as an arena in which different values and interests compete, and thus articulate existing and evolving power relations among different groups. In this sense, policies not only deliver benefits/resources and burdens/sanctions – who gets what, when and how from their government – but they also constitute discourses about who deserves what and who counts as worthy. In addition, policy design impacts on the implementation of policies, mobilization and the quality of democracy (Ingram 2016).

Critical race theory has inspired my work in answering the question of policy failure when it comes to policymaking towards Roma. The ways in which Romani identities were perceived and the ways in which 'Roma' have historically been constructed as a social group indicate continuity between past and current policies. Racism towards Roma – antigypsyism – was and continues to be part of everyday experiences for Roma, irrespective of educational level, income, place of residence or gender. Intersectionality, as one of the tenets of CRT, is a key concept in understanding how different identities and inequalities are related. Because of the belonging to diverse groups, people experience racism differently, based on different intersecting grounds. Romani women might experience racism differently from Romani men or Romani LGBTIQ. However, the primacy of antigypsyism is key in understanding the oppression of Roma. The survival strategies developed by Roma have been built in reaction to the racism and exclusion they have faced. Moreover, antigypsyism has inculcated prejudices and a lack of self-esteem in many Romani individuals and communities. Thus, antigypsyism is part of how Romani identities have been constructed, and should also be considered during processes of policy formation.

Defining and Categorizing the Roma

For centuries, Roma have been misrepresented in the public imagination. All over Europe, Romani culture and identities have been excluded from mainstream cultural and educational institutions. They have not been part of the mainstream curricula in any European educational system, and Romani artists have been excluded from mainstream cultural spaces. The representation of Romani identity in the public sphere was the privilege of non-Romani writers, artists and scholars (Hancock 1987). Historically, policies towards the Roma were an attempt to assimilate them, to get rid of their 'Gypsiness' and transform them into peasants, Christians, members of the working class, sedentarized taxpayers, or just invisible individuals. The Roma were perceived as a danger, and policies targeting them were designed with the specific aim of changing their very nature (van Baar 2011: 77–149). Research suggests that the Roma are currently among the most hated minority groups in Europe.

One of the significant challenges that scholars face when analysing Romani groups and identities is the understanding of diversity among Roma. Internal stratification does not follow the classical cleavages that sociology students learn, such as gender, level of education, residence and income. In the case of the Roma, there are other cleavages at work as well, which can better explain the situation of different communities. As well as the more classical cleavages, these include, for instance, lineage or ancestry, the degree of integration/assimilation, the ability to speak the Romani language, family customs, the type of community in which they live, and the place of residence. Lineage or ancestry is often translated into English as 'kinship', even though not all members of a Romani subgroup are related by 'blood'. In fact, members of a Romani subgroup might be 'blood'-related, but define themselves (or are usually categorized as belonging to a group) based on their ancestors' profession transmitted from generation to generation, including horse traders, blacksmiths, gold and silver workers, spoon-makers and cauldron-makers.

Other scholars have identified similar cleavages relevant to the analysis of diversity in Romani groups. According to Delia Grigore and Gheorghe

Sarău (2006: 35), the most important criterion for classifying Roma is 'kinship' (*neamul*), which 'does not relate to blood kinship, but [to] the classification of Romani groups according to the following elements: traditional craftsmanship, social organization structures, family customs and calendar holidays' (Grigore and Sarău: 2006: 35, translation IR). These criteria differ significantly from the usual criteria of societal stratification such as education, religion, place of residence and gender.

These diverse Romani groups have, similar to other professions, also developed their own professional language, one that is difficult for outsiders to understand. This might explain why linguists who study the Roma mistakenly talk about a myriad of Romani dialects.[3] Living in different countries, Romani-speaking Roma have borrowed words from majority languages and incorporated them into their own; this can also explain some of the differences between the Romani language spoken in and across different countries (Hancock 2002: 142). Nevertheless, with few exceptions, most Roma who speak Romani use it as the base for communication among themselves, even when they are from different countries. There are a number of words and formulations that might be unknown to interlocutors, but this does not mean that they speak different languages. The differences might come especially from the professionalization of language, the number of borrowed words from other languages, and the degree of assimilation of the interlocutors.

Who is Roma and who is not, and the actual number of Roma, have constantly preoccupied scholars and authorities alike. It is self-evident that the number of Roma depends on the definition adopted. János Ladányi and Iván Szelényi (2001) have suggested that the definition of who is Roma (and who is not) depends on the classifiers, those who do the classification. On the contrary, Acton and his colleagues suggest that the enumeration depends on the situation of the person questioned (Acton, Cemlyn and Ryder 2014). Nevertheless, the number of Roma or the accuracy of estimates is important for policy design.

While Roma have come to the attention of international organizations such as the Council of Europe, the OSCE and the EU, the denominations these institutions use to refer to Roma have varied over time. Katrin Simhandl (2009) has analysed the developments in these discourses and the denominations used by various institutions. She shows how Council of Europe and EU documents first used the terms 'itinerant', 'travelling people' and 'people with nomadic origins' before using the ethnic term 'Gypsy', then shifting to 'Roma/Gypsy/Traveller', and later moving towards using 'Roma/Sinti/Traveller' or only 'Roma/Traveller'. More recently, their documents have been using 'Roma' as the dominant term.

Since 2010 the Council of Europe has used 'Roma' to refer to all these groups: 'The term "Roma" used throughout the present text refers to Roma,

Sinti, Kale, Travellers and related groups in Europe, and aims to cover the wide diversity of groups concerned, including groups [that] identify themselves as Gypsies' (Council of Europe 2010). The Council of Europe defines the Roma in a broad, generic way, incorporating all relevant groups, but failing to mention what exactly keeps all these diverse groups together.

In the EU Framework for Roma, on the other hand, the European Commission uses a definition of the Roma as an umbrella term that covers a whole variety of groups:

> The term 'Roma' is used – similarly to other political documents of the European Parliament and the European Council – as an umbrella which includes groups of people who have more or less similar cultural characteristics, such as Sinti, Travellers, Kalé, Gens du voyage, etc., whether sedentary or not; around 80% of Roma are estimated to be sedentary. (European Commission 2011)

The commission does not elaborate on what kinds of shared 'cultural characteristics' it considers as the basis for membership of the larger group of Roma. Moreover, both the general formulation of 'people who have more or less similar cultural characteristics', and the non-exhaustive list of groups covered by the definition, leave room for speculation, since many other groups in Europe might share some of the cultural characteristics of people who define themselves as Roma. In such an important definition of the group targeted by 'Roma policy', the reference to the sedentarization of these groups and the estimated percentage of 'sedentary' Roma could be regarded as indicators of the confused situation in which policymakers find themselves when it comes to Roma-related policies.

In another document, the European Commission incorporates terms used by both international organizations and representatives of Romani groups, yet it fails to mention which groups are involved, or provide information on whether or how consensus on the discussed issues has been established among these representatives. Thus:

> The term 'Roma' is used here, as well as by a number of international organizations and representatives of Roma groups in Europe, to refer to a number of different groups (such as Roma, Sinti, Kale, Gypsies, Romanichels, Boyash, Ashkali, Egyptians, Yenish, Dom, Lom), and also includes Travellers, without denying the specificities and varieties of lifestyles and situations of these groups. (European Commission 2012)

In this definition, the reference to lifestyle and living circumstances of the enumerated groups is supposed to bring clarity. Nevertheless, the lifestyle spectrum among members of this group is actually quite wide. What seems to bring them together in the current definition is their marginal positioning in relation to those in power, and the societal exclusion they face. The groups involved have not been part of the discussion of this definition, nor does the term 'Roma' reflect their choice (Rostas 2014).[4]

The broad understanding of Roma implied in this definition makes the term 'Roma' politically charged. Indeed, the definition imposes the inclusion of groups that, in national and regional contexts, refuse to be associated with Roma. Ashkali and Egyptians from Albania, Kosovo and Macedonia, for instance, have persistently refused to be associated with the term 'Roma'.

In contrast with these definitions, the European Roma and Traveller Forum (ERTF) defines Roma by focusing on three elements: self-declaration, the ability to speak the language, and respect for the *Romanipen*: 'A Roma is an individual who avows oneself [*sic*] to the common historical Indo-Greek origin, who avows oneself to the common language of Romanes, who avows oneself to the common cultural heritage of *Romanipen*' (European Roma and Travellers Forum 2009: Article 1). The merit of this definition is that it spells out what unites those defined as Roma. However, it is very narrow, since in practice, many Roma do not meet the conditions it sets. Rather than empathizing with those individuals who have encountered such intensive oppression that they no longer speak the language, the definition excludes them. In addition, *Romanipen* has a complex and different meaning for different Romani groups, and therefore presents a problematic criterion for identifying Roma.

The categorization of Roma adds up to the difficulties in defining them. In most EU member states, Roma are recognized as a national minority – a condition deriving from the affiliation of these states with the Council of Europe. As a result, they enjoy certain rights regarding language use and the protection of their identity, including the right to participate in decision making concerning the rights of national minorities. However, the EU does not recognize specific national minorities, and therefore no specific policies exist that target national minorities. Until 2004, the European Commission was reluctant to adopt any political measure based on ethnicity. Only after agreeing to set up a special internship scheme for Roma did the commission become more open to adopting 'ethnic' policies – in other words, policies targeting a specific ethnic group. At the EU level, Roma are categorized as a vulnerable group at risk of poverty and social exclusion, and are thus subjected to social inclusion policies together with other groups. The categorization of Roma as a vulnerable group is highly troublesome, as it presupposes that all Roma are at risk of poverty. While a significant proportion of Roma do face poverty, the European Commission's categorization presupposes that this is the main cause of Roma exclusion. This categorization runs the risk of racializing poverty, and thus reinforces the stigma associated with Romani identity.

The debate over the definition and categorization of Roma is of crucial importance, as it sets not only the target population of the policies – who is included within their scope – but also determines policy design: problem definition, setting objectives, choice of policy tools, implementation structures, and monitoring the evaluation of progress and impact. Moreover, the debate over the definition and categorization of Roma constructs in particular ways those regarded as 'Roma', and sends out messages of worthiness, as Ingram (2016) has shown.

The EU Framework for Roma and the Debate about Romani Identities

In this section, I will use the four elements of the definition of ethnic identity introduced above to analyse the context in which the EU Framework for Roma was adopted, as well as its content. I will examine how Roma participated in the elaboration of the EU Framework; what ethnic claims and grievances were made by different actors on behalf of Roma; the ways in which Roma were problematized within public discourse; and how the causes of the current situation of Roma were framed (and what effects this has had).

On 5 April 2011, as a follow up of the Council of the European Union Conclusions from December 2007 and December 2008, the European Commission adopted a Communication – An EU Framework for National Roma Integration Strategies up to 2020 – through which member states were asked to adopt or to revise their National Roma Strategies by the end of 2011. The EU Framework is the most complex policy arrangement for Roma in Europe and is part of the Europe 2020 strategy of the EU. It aims at smart, sustainable, inclusive growth with greater coordination of national and European policy. The EU Framework for Roma was complemented by the December 2013 European Council Recommendation on effective Roma integration measures in the Member States (Council of the European Union 2013).

Previous initiatives targeting Roma were national policies, strategies and/or programmes, which had a lower degree of coordination. The first round of policymaking towards Roma was constituted by national strategies, adopted by EU candidate countries from Central and Eastern Europe in the second half of the 1990s as part of their accession process. The second round of policymaking took place in the context of the Decade of Roma Inclusion 2005-2015. As part of the decade, and with the support of the World Bank and the Open Society Institute, prime ministers from nine countries pledged to close the gap between Roma and non-Roma over the following ten years. As a result, participating governments designed national action plans aiming to achieve the stated objective in four areas: education, employment, health and housing.

The adoption of the EU Framework for Roma was preceded by two EU Roma summits – in Brussels in September 2008, and in Cordoba in April 2010. Prior to adoption of the EU Framework, the European Parliament adopted several resolutions that recommended that the European Commission and member states adopt measures for addressing the diverse problems that Roma were facing. On the eve of the EU Roma summit, the Roma Platform was set up. This is a structure that brings together EU and national bureaucrats and officials, academic experts and civil society representatives. At its second meeting in April 2009 in Prague, the Roma Platform adopted the ten 'Common Basic Principles on Roma Inclusion' as a guidance document when formulating policies towards Roma.[5] Following the 2010 European Commission Communication, in September 2010 the commission established a Roma Task Force to assess member states' use of EU funds for Roma integration. According to some scholars, these structures first and foremost focus on the use of EU financial instruments for Roma, but do not include Romani institutions (Sobotka and Vermeersch 2012).

The EU Framework was adopted without Roma taking any active part in defining the problems they faced, in setting priorities or in the course of action through negotiations with other stakeholders. A close look at the preparatory phase of the EU Framework reveals the rush to adopt such a document. The framework is based on a study conducted in 2010 and published in January 2011 (Bartlett, Benini and Gordon 2011). Based on this study, on 21 February 2011, Lívia Járóka, a Hungarian MEP with a mixed Romani and non-Romani family background, presented a motion for a resolution to the European Parliament (Járóka 2011). Following discussions and several amendments by different committees, the European Parliament adopted the resolution on 9 March 2011. Less than two months after Járóka's motion, and under a month since the EP resolution, the European Commission adopted the EU Framework. It is important to note that other EP resolutions, including calls from member states and the conclusions of the European Council, did not trigger such a quick reaction from the commission. What exactly explains this rush?

The EU Framework was adopted during the Hungarian presidency of the EU – an important factor in the rush to adopt a policy document on Roma. Viktor Orbán, Hungarian prime minister and leader of the FIDESZ party, wanted to leave a legacy of his cabinet holding the rotating EU presidency. Járóka, a member of the European People's Party group of which FIDESZ is a part, became the spokesperson for the project, filling a symbolic role considering her mixed ethnic background. However, this symbolism cannot compensate for the lack of Roma participation. There were no open consultations with Romani groups, and no Roma members in the research team led by Bartlett, Benini and Gordon. One of the European commissioners in charge of the Roma portfolio, László Andor, does not mention any consultation with Romani groups in preparation of the EU Framework, and none of his three advisors working on Roma were of Romani origin (Andor 2018).

The EU Framework did not stimulate Roma participation at national or local levels either. Officially, the European Commission encouraged the development of individual national strategies in cooperation with Roma and local authorities. Some member states (among them France, Greece and Malta) objected to the proposal as they did not recognize national minorities. Other countries objected on the basis that they already had their own arrangements (Czech Republic and UK), while some were very keen to comply (Hungary, Romania and Bulgaria). In practice, by setting a relatively short deadline for submitting their strategies, the European Commission put pressure on national governments to adopt and submit their national strategies and thus to comply with the EU Framework. As a result, with less than nine months left for compliance, member states adopted national strategies with limited or no Roma participation in the design of these policies. In addition, in most member states, local authorities were not included in policy design, a fact that explains their limited enthusiasm for implementing measures required by the national strategies.

The EU Framework for Roma brought nothing new in terms of Roma participation. Among the structures set up at EU level, it is only the Roma Platform that includes representatives of Romani civil society. However, it is unclear how these representatives are selected, as there are no publicly defined criteria for selection. At the national level, Romani participation takes place through national minority representation mechanisms, structures that were generally designed to be more limited in scope than those proposed by policies targeting Roma. In some instances, Romani NGOs are consulted but their participation is not institutionalized. No structures with clear rules and procedures exist in which authorities, Roma and other stakeholders can negotiate and agree on proposed measures or projects. The network of National Roma Contact Points (NRCP) was set up in 2012 as a coordination mechanism within governments, aiming to facilitate dialogue among and between member states, as well with the European Commission. The NRCP are understaffed and lack effective tools to evaluate policy implementation. The network meets twice a year, but the lack of transparency is an issue of concern for civil society organizations (Mirga-Kruszelnicka 2017: 14).

A close look at the work of, and claims made by, Roma rights groups in Europe reveals the grievances and ethnic claims made by Roma, or on behalf of them. Since the early 1990s, Roma rights groups in Europe have complained about the systemic discrimination and exclusion that Roma face in everyday life. The European Roma Rights Centre, a Budapest-based human rights NGO advocating for and defending the human rights of Roma, has produced a series of reports documenting human rights violations in a number of countries. The European Roma Information Office, a Brussels-based advocacy NGO, was very active in advocating for a European Union policy for Roma, especially after its founding in 2003. Following informal gatherings of such groups concerned with the situation of Roma, a decision was taken in 2008 to form the EU Roma Policy Coalition (ERPC) as a network of national and international NGOs working on Roma-related issues and aiming for the adoption of an EU Framework Strategy on Roma Inclusion.[6] These groups called for a strong antigypsyism component as part of the EU Framework, and for a powerful rights-based approach to Roma policy, inspired by the EU Charter on Fundamental Rights (ERPC 2010). For the ERPC, the key priorities for any EU Roma policy were: non-discrimination, gender equality, children's rights and citizenship; social inclusion, including in particular equitable access to education and vocational training, employment, housing, health and social services; freedom of movement, access to justice, prevention of anti-Roma crimes, ethnic profiling and child protection. The ERPC emphasized policy design – division of responsibilities between different governance levels, strong governance mechanisms, complementary approaches, data collection, monitoring and evaluation, and funding allocation – and Roma and civil society participation as key ingredients for successful policy.

Poverty has been identified by researchers and development organizations as a major challenge faced by significant proportions of Roma wherever they live. Unemployment, exclusion from quality education, poor housing conditions and limited access to healthcare services were documented by NGOs and international organizations, as already agreed upon by governments participating in the Decade of Roma Inclusion. In addition, throughout Europe, Romani organizations claimed political representation in order to address the problems faced by Romani communities effectively.

In 2007, a group of Romani artists formulated claims for Romani cultural and identity representation institutions at the national and international level (Junghaus and Székely 2007). In the past, these claims by activists and artists were only made at the national level. The Romani artists involved in the first Romani pavilion at the Venice Biennale of 2007 – a world-renowned cultural event – made it clear that there is no socioeconomic inclusion without cultural inclusion. The same group of artists, including several Romani activists and academics, pushed for a European Roma Institute to promote

Romani culture and identity, an initiative that was realized in June 2017 (see Magazzini, this volume).

The representation of Roma and problems faced by members of this minority indicate the gap between Roma grievances and ethnic claims, and the construction of these problems by policymakers. In addition, it reveals the challenges in designing policies targeting Roma. Research data clearly indicates that Roma are the most hated group throughout Europe. Antigypsyism is thus not a phenomenon limited to Central and Eastern Europe, where most Roma live and where democratic institutions are believed to be weaker than in Western Europe. Antigypsyism is a Europe-wide issue, deeply embedded in political practices, structures and competition, all of which increase the exclusion and vulnerability of the Roma.

The 2007–2008 anti-Roma campaign that culminated in a policy of fingerprinting Roma in Italy's 'nomad camps', the mass expulsion of Roma from France that was heavily reported in 2010, the serial shootings of Roma in Hungary in 2008–2011, the mob violence against Roma in Romania, and the skinhead attacks in the Czech Republic and Slovakia are just a few examples of the extreme violence that Roma have faced in recent years across Europe. There are other practices, more subtle and sometimes hidden, that reproduce inequalities between Roma and majorities in European societies: segregation, especially in housing and education; ethnic profiling, violence and raids by law enforcement agencies; and structural and institutional discrimination in accessing public services (see also Kóczé, this volume; Szalai, this volume). In addition, different obstacles to exercising political rights, including the right to vote, make Roma feel second-class citizens in their countries, where migration represents an exit strategy from oppression.

In the public imagination, from innocent games to children's books and films, from popular sayings to discourses of top politicians and high-ranking officials, Roma are considered lazy, uneducated, criminal and uncivilized people who are unwilling to work, who do not value education, and who undermine majoritarian institutions.

Public discourse on the problems faced by Roma has been almost entirely shaped by development agencies, international organizations and experts. According to the European Commission (2010), the Roma are a group at risk of exclusion and poverty, who face issues in access to education, employment, housing and health. Not surprisingly, these were the sectors on which governments participating in the Decade of Roma Inclusion pledged to focus in order to close the gap between Roma and non-Roma. In a way, the EU Framework could be regarded as an extension of that Decade of Roma Inclusion to EU member states.

An analysis of the causal relationships provides us with the main premises and assumptions behind policies aimed at Roma. The EU Framework is based on economic determinism, with the difficult situation of Roma determined by their economic situation. In his analysis of European inclusion policy on Roma, Marek Szilvasi distinguishes three types of inclusion discourses, each of which relates to a different approach to Roma inclusion policies: liberal anti-discrimination, multiculturalism and socioeconomic inclusion (Szilvasi 2015: 13). However, he emphasizes 'the centrality of the labour market and the performance of economies to Roma inclusion policies' (ibid.: 251). As other scholars have also pointed out, social inclusion is regarded mostly as economic (or labour market) inclusion, the assumption being that once Roma have jobs, all their other problems will be solved:

> We have attempted to show how, instead of an integration model based on mutual respect and recognition of shared existence within a defined social space, the integration model proposed in the Framework is narrowly defined as economic integration of individuals into the formal market economy. Integration is thus an economic process, rather than a never-ending course of social and cultural interaction; that is, that although social cohesion may be an end goal or by-product of integration within the Framework, the means and primary ends are economic. (Goodwin and Buijs 2013: 2052)

Thus, despite the calls for a strong antigypsyism component, the EU Framework falls short of that, an aspect heavily criticized by Roma rights groups (ERPC 2011). The EU is concerned with discrimination against Roma, but its antidiscrimination discourse is part of its broader antidiscrimination legal framework, whose efficiency is questioned when considering the extent of discrimination faced by the Roma. The EU Race Equality Directive, for instance, does not mention segregation among different forms of discrimination, and deals in a limited way with structural, institutional and intersectional discrimination (Rostas 2012; Schiek 2016).

Having defined the problems faced by Roma in terms of poverty and economically driven inclusion, the EU Framework sets policy objectives in four areas: 'ensuring that Roma children achieve at least primary education'; 'reducing the employment ratio between Roma and non-Roma'; 'reducing the gap between Roma and non-Roma population' in health; and lastly, in terms of housing, 'closing the gap between Roma and non-Roma access to basic public services such as water, electricity and gas' (European Commission 2011). Not only have these objectives been formulated in ambiguous terms, without precise targets or time frames, they are also minimal in effect, with a negligible impact on improving Romani people's lives in Europe. Most probably, they also reflect a certain bias in portraying Roma. For example, in all member states, education is mandatory beyond the primary level. As such, establishing an objective that is already an obligation of the state, as stipulated in national legislation, is an illogical act and an expression of the belief that Roma cannot be educated to the degree provided by national legislation. Moreover, a person with only primary education has limited employability. As a result, Roma will most probably be blamed for failing to find a job. A second observation is that the educational and employment objectives are not correlated in the EU Framework. In fact, the weak correlation and compatibility of Framework policy objectives with mainstream policies, such as those on poverty reduction, stimulation of economic growth, reduction of unemployment, educational or health system reform, infrastructural development and agriculture, represent strong arguments for questioning the EU and members states' commitments to tackle the problems faced by many Roma.

One of the most striking absences from the EU Framework is the scarcity of data regarding the societal situation of the Roma. Reliance on estimates of the number of Roma and the failure to include a mechanism for monitoring and evaluation of progress might be regarded as an indicator of the policymakers' commitment to improve the situation of Roma. Hence, one should not be surprised that the responsibilities are diffuse, with no concrete budgets assigned, unclear implementation structures, and very limited policy tools. Using the diagram proposed by Schneider and Ingram (1993), one might see exactly what happens when governments intend to distribute benefits to those with no power, who are negatively perceived by the public and categorized as deviants: the policy design is so poor that the impact of distributing benefits to the 'undeserving' becomes negligible.

Conclusion

In this chapter, I have attempted to provide an answer to the question of why policies towards Roma in Europe fail to bring the expected social change. I have analysed the EU Framework for Roma using the definition of identity in policy studies developed in the first part of the chapter. I have shown how different definitions and categorizations of Roma by policymakers and Roma themselves provide different understandings of who the target group of policies is, and how these different understandings of who Roma are and the problems they face influence the design of policies aimed at Roma: problem definition, setting the objectives, choice of policy tools, implementation structures, and monitoring the evaluation of progress and impact.

By using policy design theory, policy analysis and critical race theory, I have shown that one of the primary causes of the limited impact of policies towards Roma is the lack of their ethnic relevance: their failure to take Romani ethnic identity into consideration. I have done so by analysing the content of the policies and the social construction of the target group, the policymaking process, and the role of ethnic identity in informing policy processes.

Based on my analysis, I expect that the impact of the EU Framework on the situation of Roma will be negligible. However, such foreseeably insignificant outcomes could be highly significant and impactful for the Roma, but only in a negative sense, since they are more than likely to reinforce the already ubiquitous antigypsyism. First, populist politicians and the public alike will blame Roma for 'their' failure to integrate, citing the high figures of funding allocated for Roma inclusion while neglecting the poor design of such policies. A second consequence will be that the failure of the EU Framework to bring the social change expected in these societies will send out the message that Roma are unworthy, and do not deserve to be treated as full citizens.

One of the relevant questions regarding the EU and Roma is whether the reforms promoted at EU level to become more interventionist and redistributive in its policies will have a positive impact on the situation of Roma. My answer is in line with CRT and the analysis in the present chapter: the barrier to improving the situation of Roma depends mostly on tackling antigypsyism effectively, including the use of transitional justice tools such as truth and reconciliation processes. As my analysis has shown, the policy tools used by states or by a supranational entity like the EU would most probably be impeded primarily by the policy design rather by any limitations in the regulatory powers at their disposal.

Iulius Rostas is the Chair of the Romani Studies Program and an Assistant Professor at the Central European University (CEU) in Budapest, Hungary. He was an Affiliated Fellow of the Institute for Advanced Studies at CEU, a Senior Fellow at the Open Society Foundations Roma Initiatives Office and a Visiting Lecturer at Corvinus University of Budapest. He has worked for the Open Society Foundations, the European Roma Rights Centre (ERRC) and the Government of Romania, and consulted for the Organization for Security and Co-operation in Europe (OSCE), the World Bank, the European Commission and the Roma Education Fund. Rostas is the editor of *Ten Years After: A History of Roma School Desegregation in Central and Eastern Europe* (CEU Press, 2012), and the author of *Social Inclusion or Exclusion: The Rights of Persons Living with HIV in Moldova* (Cartier Publishing, 2011) and *A Task for Sisyphus: Why Europe's Roma Policies Fail* (CEU Press, 2019).

Notes

I would like to thank Huub van Baar and Angéla Kóczé for their comments and suggestions on the text.

1. Faced with intense international criticism of the situation of Roma in their countries, governments in Central and Eastern Europe – the region where most European Roma reside – adopted national programmes for Roma inclusion. These programmes or strategies were adopted in the context of EU enlargement, in which the protection and recognition of minorities, and especially of Roma, was an official political criterion for joining the EU, as part of the Copenhagen criteria. In the context of OSCE activities on the Roma, participating member states have adopted the 'OSCE Action Plan on Improving the Situation of Roma and Sinti within the OSCE Area' (2003), a political document promoting specific intervention in areas such as education, health, employment, housing, public and political participation, combating racism and discrimination, and cooperation with Romani organizations. At a 2003 conference on the situation of the Roma in Europe, at the initiative of the World Bank and the Open Society Institute (OSI), nine governments from Central and Eastern Europe – those of Bulgaria, Croatia, Czech Republic, Hungary, Macedonia, Montenegro, Romania, Serbia and Slovakia – launched the Decade of Roma Inclusion (2005–2015). These governments, later joined by those of Albania, Bosnia and Herzegovina, Spain, Slovenia and the United States (the latter with observatory status), committed themselves to implement, over a period of ten years, national action plans designed to improve the situation of the Roma in four specific, wide-ranging areas: education, employment, housing and health.
2. The European Commission (2010) defines vulnerable groups as those that 'face higher risk of poverty and social exclusion compared to the general population'.
3. In a comment on an earlier version of this chapter, Thomas Acton suggested that it is common for any language to have different dialects. He also emphasized the need to study both divergent and convergent dialectical cleavages of the Romani language. One has still to recognize that the divergent cleavages in the study of the Romani language are so dominant that someone who is not familiar with Roma could easily misunderstand and challenge the very existence of the Romani language as a unifying factor of different Romani subgroups.
4. No meeting with Roma groups was recorded in 2012 on the agendas of the European Commission units dealing with Roma. The Council of Europe organized the sole meeting bringing together diverse groups in 2003. The author participated in that meeting. See Council of Europe 2012.
5. These principles are: (1) Constructive, pragmatic and non-discriminatory policies; (2) Explicit but not exclusive targeting; (3) Inter-cultural approach; (4) Aiming for the mainstream; (5) Awareness of the gender dimension; (6) Transfer of evidence-based policies; (7) Use of European Union instruments; (8) Involvement of regional and local authorities; (9) Involvement of civil society; and (10) Active participation of the Roma.
6. The members of the coalition were: Amnesty International (AI); European Network Against Racism (ENAR); European Roma Grassroots Organizations Network (ERGO); European Roma Information Office (ERIO); European Roma Rights

Centre (ERRC); Minority Rights Group International (MRGI); Open Society Foundations (OSF); Policy Center for Roma and Minorities (PCRM); Roma Education Fund (REF) and Fundacion Secretariado Gitano (FSG). It is interesting to note that while most of these organizations had a good reputation, Roma were poorly represented. Only two organizations were Roma-led (ERIO and PCRM), and only three could claim that they were networks of, or included, Romani organizations from different European countries (ERIO, ERGO and ENAR).

References

Abdelal, R., et al. 2001. 'Treating Identity as a Variable: Measuring the Content, Intensity, and Contestation', Paper presented at APSA Annual Convention, 30 August – 2 September, 2001, San Francisco.
———. 2006. 'Identity as a Variable', *Perspectives on Politics* 4(4): 695–711.
———. 2009. *Measuring Identity: A Guide for Social Scientists*. Cambridge: Cambridge University Press.
Acton, T., S. Cemlyn and A. Ryder. 2014. 'Conclusion: In Search of Empowerment', in A. Ryder, S. Cemlyn and T. Acton (eds), *Hearing the Voices of Gypsy, Roma and Traveller Communities*. Bristol: Policy Press.
Andor, L. 2018. 'EU Policy and Roma Integration (2010–14)', *Journal of Poverty and Social Justice* 26(1): 113–26.
Bartlett, W., R. Benini and C. Gordon. 2011. *Measures to Promote the Situation of Roma EU Citizens in the European Union*. Brussels: European Parliament.
Bell, D. 1992. *Faces at the Bottom of the Well: The Persistence of Racism*. New York: Basic Books.
Council of Europe. 2010. 'The Strasbourg Declaration on Roma'. CM(2010)133. 20 October. Strasbourg.
———. 2012. 'Descriptive Glossary of Terms Relating to Roma Issues'. 18 May. Strasbourg.
Council of the European Union. 2013. 'Council Recommendation on Effective Roma Integration Measures in the Member States'. Employment, Social Policy, Health and Consumer Affairs Council Meeting, 9–10 December, Brussels.
Delgado, D., and J. Stefancic. 2001. *Critical Race Theory: An Introduction*. New York: New York University Press.
European Commission. 2010. 'Inclusion of Vulnerable Groups'. Retrieved 27 September 2018 from http://ec.europa.eu/employment_social/2010againstpoverty/extranet/vulnerable_groups_en.pdf.
———. 2011. 'Communication "An EU Framework for National Roma Integration Strategies up to 2020"'. COM(2011)173. 5 April. Brussels.
———. 2012. 'Communication "National Roma Integration Strategies: A First Step in the Implementation of the EU Framework"'. COM(2012) 226. 21 May. Brussels.
European Roma Policy Coalition (ERPC). 2010. 'Essential Elements of the "EU Framework for National Roma Integration Strategies"'. 2 November. Brussels.
———. 2011. 'EU Framework Weak on Discrimination against Roma'. 5 April. Budapest.
European Roma and Travellers Forum. 2009. *Charter on the Rights of the Roma*. Strasbourg. Retrieved 3 September 2019 from http://a.cs.coe.int/team20/cahrom/5th%20

CAHROM%20plenary%20meeting/Item%206.%20ERTF%20Charter%20on%20 the%20Rights%20of%20Roma.pdf.
European Union Agency on Fundamental Rights (EUFRA). 2009. 'EU-MIDIS Data in Focus Report 1: The Roma'. Vienna.
European Union Agency on Fundamental Rights (EUFRA) and United Nations Development Programme (UNDP). 2012. 'The Situation of Roma in 11 EU Member States: Survey Results at a Glance'. Retrieved 11 April 2015 from http://fra.europa.eu/sites/default/files/fra_uploads/2099-FRA-2012-Roma-at-a-glance_EN.pdf.
Gillborn, D. 2008. *Racism and Education*. London: Routledge.
———. 2015. 'Intersectionality, Critical Race Theory, and the Primacy of Racism', *Qualitative Inquiry* 21(3): 277–87.
Goodwin, M., and R. Buijs. 2013. 'Making Good European Citizens of the Roma: A Closer Look at the EU Framework for National Roma Integration Strategies', *German Law Review* 14(10): 2041–56.
Grigore, D., and G. Sarău. 2006. *Istorie și Traditii Rrome* [Roma history and traditions]. Bucharest: Salvati Copiii.
Hancock, I. 1987. *The Pariah Syndrome*. Ann Arbor, MI: Kamora.
———. 2002. *We Are the Romani People – Ame Sam e Rromane Džene*. Hatfield: University of Hertfordshire Press.
Howlett, M., I. Mukherjee and J. Woo. 2015. 'From Tools to Toolkits in Policy Design Studies', *Policy & Politics* 43(2): 291–311.
Ingram, H. 2016. 'The Subliminal Effects of Policy Messages on the Democratic Exercise', *Revista Envío* 420. Retrieved 27 September 2018 from http://www.envio.org.ni/articulo/5217.
Ingram, H., and A. Schneider. 2005. 'Introduction: Public Policy and the Social Construction of Deservedness', in A. Schneider and H. Ingram (eds), *Deserving and Entitled: Social Constructions and Public Policy*. New York: State University of New York Press, pp. 1–28.
———. 2006. 'Policy Analysis for Democracy', in M. Moran, M. Rein and R. Goodin (eds), *The Oxford Handbook of Public Policy*. Oxford: Oxford University Press, pp. 169–89.
Járóka, L. 2011. 'Report on the EU Strategy on Roma Inclusion'. 18 February. Brussels: European Parliament.
Junghaus, T., and K. Székely. 2007. *Paradise Lost: The First Roma Pavilion*. Budapest: Open Society Institute.
Ladányi, J., and I. Szelényi. 2001. 'The Social Construction of Roma Ethnicity in Bulgaria, Romania and Hungary during Market Transition', *Review of Sociology* 7: 71–89.
Mirga-Kruszelnicka, A. 2017. *Revisiting the EU Roma Framework: Assessing the European Dimension for the Post-2020 Future*. Budapest: Open Society Foundations.
Rostas, I. 2012. 'Judicial Policy Making: The Role of the Courts in Promoting School Desegregation', in I. Rostas (ed.), *Ten Years After: A History of Roma School Desegregation in Central and Eastern Europe*. Budapest: CEU Press, pp. 49–90.
———. 2014. 'Identitatea etnică și elaborarea politicilor publice: cazul romilor în Europa Centrală și de Est' [Ethnic identity and policymaking: The case of the Roma in Central and Eastern Europe]. PhD dissertation. Cluj-Napoca: Babes Bolyai University.
Schiek, D. 2016. 'Revisiting Intersectionality for EU Anti-Discrimination Law in an Economic Crisis', *Sociologia del Diritto* 2: 23–44.

Schneider, A., and H. Ingram. 1993. 'The Social Construction of Target Populations', *American Political Science Review* 87(2): 334–47.

———. 1997. *Policy Design for Democracy*. Lawrence, TX: University of Kansas Press.

Simhandl, K. 2009. 'Beyond Boundaries? Comparing the Construction of the Political Categories "Gypsies" and "Roma" before and after EU Enlargement', in N. Sigona and N. Trehan (eds), *Romani Politics in Contemporary Europe*. New York: Palgrave Macmillan, pp. 72–93.

Sobotka, E., and P. Vermeersch. 2012. 'Governing Human Rights and Social Inclusion: Can the EU be a Catalyst for Local Social Change?', *Human Rights Quarterly* 34(3): 800–22.

Stone, A. 1989. 'Causal Stories and the Formation of Policy Agendas', *Political Science Quarterly* 104(2): 281–300.

Szilvasi, M. 2015. 'Roma and the Contradictions of European Inclusion Policies: Citizens Associated with European Societies'. PhD dissertation. Aberdeen: University of Aberdeen.

Tajfel, H., and J. Turner. 2004. 'The Social Identity Theory of Intergroup Behavior', in J. Jost and J. Sidanius (eds), *Key Readings in Social Psychology*. New York: Psychology Press, pp. 276–93.

Toritsyn, A. 2009. *Ex-ante Policy Impact Assessment vis-à-vis Vulnerable Groups in South Eastern Europe*. Bratislava: UNDP.

van Baar, H. 2011. *The European Roma: Minority Representation, Memory and the Limits of Transnational Governmentality*. Amsterdam: F&N.

PART IV

GENDER AND SOCIAL MOVEMENTS

CHAPTER 7

❊ ❊ ❊

INTERSECTIONAL INTRICACIES
Romani Women's Activists at the
Crossroads of Race and Gender

Debra L. Schultz

In the late 1990s and early 2000s, a critical mass of Romani women activists emerged in Central and East European (CEE) countries. They laid the foundations for a Romani women's movement within the democratic experiments of post-Soviet civil society. Civil society development in postcommunist European countries was not uniform, but it was sufficient to allow the development of Romani rights activism, which became particularly strong in Hungary, Romania, Bulgaria, the Czech Republic, Slovakia and the former Yugoslav states. European Union enlargement also played a significant role in the Romani politics of this period, presenting strategic entry points for Romani women's activism. Yet in this complex region, the civil society movements that were most strongly connected to transnational civic networks have been the most enduring (Foa and Ekiert 2017). This has been true of the Romani rights movement in general, and of Romani women's activism in particular. The relationship between the local and the transnational is what has enabled a vibrant Romani women's activism to develop in less than a decade.

This chapter examines how Romani women's activism, as specifically but not exclusively embodied in the Roma Women's Initiative (RWI) of 1999–2006, influenced individual and collective Romani identity formation in post-Soviet and civil society space in Central and Eastern Europe. Through individual life stories from the first wave of feminist-inspired activists and the history of the RWI, I will document how Romani women's activism, specifically the feminist claims they made on the Romani movement, women's movements, nation-states, multilateral institutions, donors, partners and, mostly importantly, on themselves and each other, impacted individual and collective Romani identity quests. The term 'first wave of feminist-influenced Romani women's activists' honours the fact that some of the most active women leaders did not and will not choose to label themselves as feminists. In turn, a small but influential group of still active and much-loved Romani women activist pioneers, who were even less inclined to identify as feminists, blazed important trails and served as activist role models.

Based on research with and about Romani women's activists, and on participant observation in a regional initiative to build a network for Romani women's activism, I demonstrate how Romani women's activism emerged when a small but influential group of Romani women, empowered by earlier efforts to develop pro-Roma consciousness, encountered the failure of the Romani rights movement to integrate Romani women's issues and the failure of CEE women's movements to address racism against Romani women and their communities. Simultaneously, Romani women's exposure to the global feminist movement and transnational feminist frameworks inspired their own creative thinking about issues affecting Romani women, through which they attempted to theorize political activism and translate them into policy change.

Librarians would categorize most of the early publicly available writing by Romani women involved in the RWI as 'ephemera', which connotes any written or printed matter not meant to be preserved. This includes speeches, programme brochures, essays and dialogues reprinted in the European Roma Rights Centre (ERRC) journal, as well as policy documents (Kurtić and Vasić 2002; Kóczé 2004; Bițu 2004; Memedova 2004, 2006a, 2006b; Schultz 2005b; Eminova 2006; Maya 2006a, 2006b; Járóka 2006). Derived from the Greek *ephēmeros* – 'lasting only a day' – this aptly characterizes these early testimonies of Romani women's issues to wider publics. At the time, many wished these speech acts *would* last only a day, because some Romani advocates (men and women) viewed Romani women raising women's issues as divisive to the larger Romani rights and identity project. An early roundtable on Romani women's rights organized in Budapest in 2000 with male and female Romani activists illustrates this tension (Bițu 2000). Yet Romani women activists' persistence in publicly claiming political space for themselves affirmed the identity 'Romani woman activist' and put forth a set of issues that could not ultimately be ignored.

The theory of 'intersectionality' was one of the major intellectual and political influences on Romani women's activism in the early 2000s (Kóczé

2009, 2011). European Romani women, particularly those from postsocialist states, clearly embodied unique forms of oppression based on the combined effects of race, gender, ethnic and class oppression, exacerbated by local specificities of transition (see also Szalai, this volume). Although the concept of multiple dimensions of oppression existed before, African American feminist and critical race legal scholar Kimberlé Crenshaw's (1989) article coining the term 'intersectionality' seemed to have a catalytic effect on critical antiracist feminist thinking (Collins and Bilge 2016). Crenshaw's groundbreaking work demonstrated how law and public policy had utterly failed African American women because of the law's inability to conceptualize and remedy harms based on both racial and gender discrimination.

The postsocialist European context remains very different, yet the theory of intersectionality provides a powerful framework for understanding Romani women's experiences. Looking at race, anti-Roma prejudice is clearly one of the few remaining 'respectable' forms of racism in Europe (McGarry 2017). While socialist ideals artificially suppressed public expression of such racism, the transition unleashed both anti-Roma racism and a kind of retrograde sexism. In addition, Romani gender politics and the invocation of the need to protect 'Roma culture' – for example, through the virginity cult and early marriage – challenged Romani women activists (see also Zentai, this volume). Looking at class, socialist ideals of equality encouraged the hiring of Romani workers, but the transition removed social constraints from latent racism, which often took the form of unabashed firing of Romani workers. This reinforced poverty among Roma and the perception of Roma as 'inassimilable'.

When Romani women tried to introduce the idea of 'multiple discrimination', they faced epistemological, legal and political roadblocks. This required Romani women advocates to educate the European Roma rights, women's rights, and human rights communities, while trying to promote real change on the ground that would tangibly improve the lives of Romani women, their families and communities. Intersectionality theory inspired Romani women to find a unique conceptual place in Romani identity debates, while at the same time exploring how to operate within existing human rights frameworks and machineries. Angéla Kóczé (2009) has written about the limits of human rights frameworks for Romani women's activism, with their impoverished analysis of 'power, resistance and identity'. In addition, the hegemonic focus of the international human rights community on civil and political rights foreclosed any discussion of economic, social and cultural rights. Discussion of those rights, most relevant to Romani women, veered dangerously close to potential critiques of capitalism. Such critiques were unwelcome in a region embracing neoliberal economic systems. Therefore, Romani women's activism has done much to expose the contradictions and limits of CEE's 'democratic transition', human rights frameworks, neoliberal economics, contemporary Romani politics and women's intersectional activism. Romani women, most intimately affected in families, may be the truth tellers who transform policy discourse on Roma away from 'social integration' paradigms to systemic analyses of poverty.

Romani women's activism arose in this period through a unique encounter between the extremely local (grassroots community-based activism) and the transnational (global feminist ideas and methodologies, and international funding networks) on the ground of post-Soviet European experiments with democracy and civil society. It was a form of politicization that bypassed the pitfalls of two CEE identity-based struggles: the extreme marginalization of Romani people because of racism, and post-Soviet ambivalence about gender issues. In addition, the intersectional nature of Romani women's agendas required them to reach across sectors and movements, avoiding the insularity sometimes endemic in purely identity-based struggles. The intersection of racism and sexism was a sensitive barometer of democratic transformation.

In classic feminist style but within Romani contexts, Romani women's gender-specific politicization occurred first out of women's individual experiences of violence or sexism, whether in the family, school, workplace or the Romani movement itself. Once a few brave women pioneers, like Letitia Mark in Romania and Blanka Kosma in Hungary, had dared to start Romani women's organizations, their existence validated the idea that Romani women needed their own space to talk, identify problems, strategize and find practical solutions. Even if the wider Romani movement did not want to address Romani women's issues, they had to take notice of women who led.

After a few early regional convenings of Romani women in the 1990s, the RWI began to structure programmes so that Romani women could convene nationally, identifying and prioritizing issues specific to each country. National connections allowed for more intimate relationship building, national campaign development and mentorship of younger women. This was classic movement building. Later, around 2005, when the RWI had identified the policy agendas and institutions they wished to impact, the RWI experimented with national 'focal points'. This somewhat bureaucratic framework, adapted from multilateral institutions, did not work very well because the most powerful RWI programmes were the ones that enabled diverse Romani women to explore their issues and ideas together.

This chapter first documents the development of the Roma Women's Initiative as an intersectional feminist project and then explores how key Romani women leaders developed their activist identities through local-level 'apprenticeships', emerging as leaders particularly at transnational levels. Finally, it assesses the impact of Romani women's activism and intellectual production, proposing that Romani women's activist experiences and insights provide a vital resource in Europe's current political climate.

The Roma Women's Initiative: Building towards an Intersectional Central and East European Romani Women's Agenda

Between 1998 and 2007, I was a participant observer in the efforts to build a network of Romani women activists in CEE as one of the founders of the Soros Foundation's Network Women's Program (NWP), which helped to create the Roma Women's Initiative. The RWI was a semi-autonomous, but NWP-affiliated project led by Romani women in alliance with non-Romani women working within national Soros foundations and a variety of Soros-affiliated programmes. Once introduced to Romani women activists through the Soros network's vibrant Romani rights programmes, it was immediately clear to me that the Romani women's activism arising in post-Soviet civil society was an important historical phenomenon, analogous to African American women's civil rights activism and Black feminist thought. This activism, nurtured by different traditions and impacted by unique historical circumstances in the region, called out for recognition, documentation and analysis. Within and beyond the above-stated period, I conducted oral history interviews with fifteen Romani women activists from across the CEE region, as well as from Spain and Scotland.

As an anti-racist feminist historian and Soros Foundation programme director, I was keenly aware of the methodological and ethical challenges involved in conducting and interpreting oral history interviews with Romani women activists, many of whom were my colleagues at the time. I sought to mitigate potential pitfalls of intellectual appropriation by using the self-reflexivity modelled in such classics as *Women's Worlds: The Feminist Practice of Oral History* (Gluck 1991), and debates around the relative added value of racial insiders and outsiders conducting research on race, first discussed in *Racing Research, Researching Race: Methodological Dilemmas in Critical Race Studies* (Twine and Warren 2000). The RWI also encouraged Romani women to document their own work and create new knowledge through Romani gender studies mini-schools.

Much of my work – academic, professional and activist – has been about how to best serve as an anti-racist feminist ally, a topic still under-theorized in US and global feminist literature. Going to college and graduate school when women of colour were challenging white feminists on their racism, I thought a lot about *how* to be an anti-racist feminist ally. I did not see Black feminist theorists as critics of the feminist scholarly canon; their writings *became* the canon because their truth claims were the most sound, and superseded what had come before.

From this body of theory and practice, I internalized certain feminist maxims. Feminist standpoint theory required interrogation of my own 'positionality'. My keen desire for anti-racist white women role models and my own identity issues as a secular/progressive Jew led me to focus my doctoral dissertation and book on Jewish women civil rights activists (Schultz 2001). Yet even within the feminist movement, there were already models of multivalent feminist conversations among differing allies that would still prove useful today. I saw Audre Lorde (1984) and Adrienne Rich model cross-racial feminist dialogue during a national speaking tour in the 1980s. I voraciously read books like *Yours in Struggle: Three Feminist Perspectives on Anti-Semitism and Racism* (Bulkin, Pratt and Smith 1988).

As I have written elsewhere (Schultz 2012), the moment I met Romani women activists in 1998, I knew I wanted to work with them. The women were incisive and bold, but equally compelling was the idea of Romani women as the potential embodiment of intersectionality. Here was a group marginalized on the basis of gender, race, class, ethnicity, and national original or lack of it – inassimilable and generally seen as Europe's most reviled 'other'.

When the RWI actually began, anti-racist feminism could no longer be a theoretical construct, but a set of best practices. To oversimplify, these included things to do and things to avoid. The negatives came first: do not romanticize Romani women, do not dominate by imposing your own vision of how they should organize and do not appropriate the voices or work of Romani women. The affirmative actions were to understand and constantly re-interrogate: the context in which I worked; how I entered that context and what assumptions (conscious or unconscious) I brought with me; my own motives (what did I wish to contribute and what did I get out of it?); arrogance versus humility in how I communicated; and most of all, what should principled practice look like?

As the editors of *The Romani Women's Movement* note, 'the experience and social position of Romani women are often seen as quintessentially subaltern'; yet equally relevant is their caution that not 'all Romani women feel comfortable with such characterization of their societal presence' (Kóczé et al. 2018: 9). Yet Kóczé posits Romani women's activism 'as a voice challenging societal hierarchy in general' (2011: 52), and Alexandra Oprea proposes that Romani women's experiences are the 'quintessential foundation' (2012: 19) for both anti-patriarchy and anti-racist politics. This idea excited me twenty years ago but I feared that writing or speaking about it then might be giving the wrong answer to postcolonial critic Gayatri Spivak's (1988) famous question 'Can the subaltern speak?' Clearly Romani women should speak for themselves – first.

Some things need be stated first in the interest of contextualization. In the ten years that I worked for the Soros Foundation's NWP (1997–2007), I earned a generous salary while working on issues I truly cared about with inspiring colleagues. Although I had subject expertise and professional experience, I was an American hired to work in a region not my own, speaking English, the hegemonic language. Western foundations and institutions like the World Bank operated as if they had the technical solutions to the region's problems. Their frameworks were the default assumptions, which only needed to be adapted to the region's specificities. My employer was a global capitalist who then posited the market as morally neutral – an analysis with which I disagreed – because it did not address the structural nature of income inequality. Nonetheless, in addition to investing millions in Roma rights advocacy, I also witnessed George Soros taking a personal interest in the development of young Romani leaders, asking them about their strategic approaches and listening attentively to their answers. The foundation sought to operate in many admirable ways, valuing local knowledge and building local leadership, but contradictions persisted. I took the privilege and responsibility of having (modest) power and (extremely modest) resources through my work to help to create spaces where women of the region, including Romani women, could genuinely speak, think and strategize together. This was basic feminist practice, so why should Romani women not have this opportunity? Yet if Roma rights activists still feel the need to say 'nothing about us without us' in 2020, many of the Roma programmes and institutions created earlier did not provide sufficient leadership by Romani people. However, when the RWI began and we invited Nicoleta Bițu and Azbija Memedova to join the staff, they both declined, citing their desire to maintain political independence from the foundation, and the need to have time for their roles as mothers. As feminist allies, that seemed perfectly reasonable. They worked as consultants, later joined by Enisa Eminova.

A key methodology at the beginning was simply to enable Romani women from across the region to come together in spaces separate from both Roma rights and women's rights events. As noted in a longer history of the RWI:

> After time for reflection, an agenda was shaped with a number of layers: to capacitate and empower Romani women activists to address inequalities within both the Romani movement and feminist movements, and the second layer was to put questions related to Romani women's needs on the political agendas at national and international levels. These layers were addressed while members of the network continued their work in Romani associations and communities at the local level. (Schultz and Bițu 2018: 29–50)

In the eight years between 1999 and 2006, the RWI and NWP supported more than fifty projects, trainings and events that reached hundreds of Romani activists and their allies. RWI projects provided information, learning experiences, policy data, leadership development and opportunities for collaboration among Romani women activists, and with many social movement actors, including national, regional and international institutions.

The 2003 Roma Women's Forum represented a pivotal moment. In the early 2000s, a small group of seasoned Romani women activists were increasingly called upon to contribute their expertise to rapidly developing European politics around Roma integration. Catalysed by the EU accession process, a number of emerging CEE countries sought to demonstrate commitment to minority rights and inclusion, one of the key criteria for EU admission. The Roma Women's Initiative was among many NGO and donor efforts to leverage that opportunity to push forward Roma rights issues.

The Roma Women's Forum, held on 29 June 2003 in Budapest, brought together leading Romani women activists from across the region with major donors, human rights leaders and representatives from CEE governments. The forum marked one of the first times that Romani women presented their own comprehensive policy agenda to high-level officials from regional governments and international agencies, including the World Bank and the European Commission. The goal was to ensure that Romani women's issues would be part of large-scale efforts to infuse money and policy support for a rapid turnaround in the condition of Romani people and politics throughout the region. This would soon come to be known as the 'Decade of Roma Inclusion 2005–2015'.

Romani women activists had worked for several years to broaden and deepen their leadership, to develop new skills and to put on the table several very challenging issues that touched on cultural sensitivities for Romani communities. These included early and arranged marriages, the cult of virginity before marriage, girls' education, domestic violence, trafficking and prostitution, coerced sterilization and gender politics within the Roma movement. Using 'multiple discrimination' as a conceptual framework, the RWI worked hard to articulate Romani women's concerns as policy issues.

Despite intensive lobbying efforts, and to the RWI's great disappointment, the Roma Women's Forum was not included in the high-level conference 'Roma in an Expanding Europe', which launched and structured the Decade of Roma Inclusion in 2003. The Decade eventually sought to demonstrate improved conditions for Roma in the areas of education, health, housing and employment, the four 'pillars' of programming approved by funders and organizers. Those who institutionalized the Decade declared 'gender' a 'cross-cutting issue', rather than one of the key focal points of its programmes. The difference between 'pillars' and 'cross-cutting issues' was not merely conceptual, but material. The 'pillars' had funding, staff, institutional support, legitimacy and accountability mechanisms; cross-cutting issues did not.

Margareta Matache, the first Romani woman to direct the historic organization Romani CRISS and currently a Harvard University postdoctoral research fellow, assessed the Decade. In a publication that looks critically from within the Soros foundation, she wrote: 'Overall, gender equality was the weakest point or the greatest failure of the Decade, in terms of ambitions, dialogue and results' (Matache 2015: 42). She cited the Decade's failure to implement the Roma Women's Forum policy platform, to provide funding to address discrimination against Roma women and to identify goals, actions, indicators and benchmarks for attention to gender equality. Matache nonetheless highlights the inclusion of Romani women's issues in the Decade's regional framework as an important and legitimizing first step.

Given the limits of advancing Romani women's rights at the national and European levels, the RWI turned to the international arena. The RWI prepared and supported Romani women to present their issues at the United Nations World Conference Against Racism in Durban in 2001 and at the UN Commission on the Status of Women 10th Anniversary Review of the Beijing Platform for Action in 2005. These UN conferences represented the most comprehensive efforts to assess, progress and plan global strategies for racial and gender discrimination respectively. Romani women introduced their intersectional issues at both conferences for the first time (see also Zentai, this volume).

At a high-level session of the Beijing Plus 10 conference, young activists Kerieva McCormick of the ERRC and RWI's Enisa Eminova pointed out that the situation of Roma and Gypsy/Traveller women across Europe was being almost completely ignored by women's groups regionally, internationally and at the United Nations. They wanted to make visible once and for all the extreme marginalization and vulnerability that European Romani women faced due to social exclusion, poverty and harmful community practices. Eminova issued an even more provocative challenge to the global women's movement to root out its own racism and classism when she was the first Romani woman to give a plenary speech – to two thousand people – at the Association for Women's Rights in Development (AWID) conference in Bangkok in 2005 (Eminova 2006). AWID is one of the largest global feminist gatherings in the world.

When Romani women spoke out at these historic global gatherings, they were claiming space on global social transformation agendas in ways they could not do at that time at the European level. This required them to see themselves as part of global women's movements and to experiment with using international human rights mechanisms. They were also initiated into a global feminist activist community that provided its own methodologies and a sense of connection with women's movements around the world. Romani women could observe, adapt and influence these feminist methodologies, adding the identity of global feminist to their Romani political identities. While UN mechanisms have their own limitations, making Romani women's issues visible at high-level policy institutions and global feminist organizations was a historic move. In other words, young Romani feminist activists used global feminist arenas to make public the recognition struggles of Romani women (Williams 2003).

Activist Identities and Apprenticeships

In 1997, Nicolae Gheorghe and Andrzej Mirga published an influential essay arguing that Romani identity was socially constructed, not an essentialized ethnicity, and that Romani people should more actively shape Romani identities. It is no wonder that Gheorghe, who would both mentor and marry Nicoleta Bițu, would be supportive of theory that posited Romani women's subordinate position as socially constructed. Their socially constructed identities, like those of women from many non-dominant cultural and religious groups, met the historical needs of a marginalized and despised community. A focus on 'purity' – maintained mostly via women – was one of the few defences they had against dominant societies who reviled them.

More recently, scholars have written about Romani identity as a political identity mostly defined by external actors such as international NGOs, national policymakers, the dominant societies in which they live and, to a lesser extent, by Romani activists themselves. With relatively little control over their representation in the public sphere, the multiplicity of representations hinders the political aspirations of Romani people (McGarry 2014). Romani intellectuals have also criticized the idea of the NGO-ization of Romani politics and an uncritical focus on social integration (Rostas, Rövid and Szilvási 2015). If misrepresentation for various political ends is true of Romani people in general, it is at least doubly true of Romani women. For example, Alexandra Oprea (2005) has dissected the exoticized media coverage of the arranged marriage of the twelve-year-old Romanian Romani girl Ana Maria Cioaba. She also tackles the seemingly intractable association of Romani women with fortune-telling and other criminal ventures (Oprea 2013). Given the hyper-visibility of Romani female victimhood or criminality in the media and public consciousness, it is particularly challenging to craft a positive public identity as a Romani woman, let alone a Romani woman activist.

Within Romani movements, women activists – particularly those who identify as feminists – also have to contend with the accusation that they are the dupes of white feminists or insufficiently committed to Roma rights activism. Biţu and others have been contesting this perception for years. The ongoing challenge of raising Romani women's issues alongside racial issues was recently articulated by Rita Izsák-Ndiaye – former UN Special Rapporteur on Minority Issues (2011–2017) and currently Rapporteur of the UN Committee on the Elimination of Racial Discrimination – at a conference at Harvard University on 5–6 April 2019 on "Neglected Voices: The Global Roma Diaspora" (Izsák-Ndiaye 2019). At that conference, fifteen out of the twenty-five main presenters were Romani women, but, with the exception of Angéla Kóczé, none centred Romani women's activism or included gender analyses in their remarks. While individual Romani women activists' voices may no longer be neglected, the focus on Romani women's issues has not yet been fully integrated into the discourse of Romani rights struggles.

Given all the pressures to construct a political identity as a Romani woman and activist, how did the small group of European Romani women who dared to identify as Romani leaders interested in women's issues develop a sense of self as a leader? What enabled them to succeed and become active in the public realm when few of their peers were able to do so?

Several consistent themes emerge in Romani activist women's lives. They come from families proud of their Romani identities, yet exposed to the complexities of those identities. They have received support and encouragement for high achievement, despite the society's low expectations for Roma. They have advanced professionally and socioeconomically, but continue to support their families and communities. They have witnessed the suffering of women at an early age and had a sense of being different in both Romani and non-Romani worlds, but they also have demonstrated an ability to cross boundaries and mediate those worlds. Last but not least, they have earned respect among male Romani leaders for their obvious ability to work successfully both with Romani communities and larger national, European and international structures (Schultz 2005a).

Family pride in Romani identity created an awareness of the complexities of those identities. Some Romani women activists, like Ostalinda Maya (born in Granada, Spain in 1982), came from families with mixed heritage: her mother was Mexican and her father, an activist and flamenco artist, was fiercely proud of his Romani identity. Maya has spent much of her adult life studying and working on Romani issues in Central Europe. Nicoleta Biţu (born in Constanta, Romania in 1970) watched her father navigate between Romani and non-Romani worlds as one of the relatively few Romani police officers in Ceausescu's Romania. Azibija Memedova (born in Dracevo, Macedonia in 1971) grew up in a multicultural neighbourhood and was told she was Turkish, but when she entered school, all her teachers and classmates perceived her as Roma. Alexandra Oprea (born in Bucharest, Romania in 1980) lived with her father in Romania until the age of eight, when they joined her mother who had migrated to the United States as a refugee. Also told she was Turkish as a young girl, she characterizes her family policy about Romani identity as 'don't ask, don't tell' (Schultz 2004b).

Oprea, Kóczé and Eminova were able to use education to mitigate the effects of poverty and marginalization. Despite anti-Roma prejudice and low expectations for Romani students, all their families had encouraged high achievement. Although Kóczé (born in Fehérgyarmat, Hungary in 1970) and Eminova (born in Skopje, Macedonia in 1981) were the only Romani students in their classes, they did not experience anti-Roma feeling until secondary school. Those moments of contradiction led to more proactive reflections on Romani identity. However, all the women felt some sense of 'otherness' in Romani communities as well. Their ability to cross borders – of family, ethnicity, language, nationality, race, gender, class and geography – remind us to 'valorize the capacities, skills and experiences of border crossing, of organizing life across borders' (Mezzadra and Neilson 2013: 8). But as the experience of most first-generation university students demonstrates, crossing borders out of the class into which one is born does not come without a price – ambivalence and struggle at the very least.

Many of the women activists had strong female role models in their families. Memedova's mother was the only one of four sisters to finish secondary school, despite her family's pressure to leave, and she raised two children on her own after her husband died. Eminova's grandmother travelled throughout Macedonia and Serbia, selling products created by her husband. Oprea's mother migrated to the United States alone and then brought her husband and daughter over to join her. Marika Palmái (born in Pécs, Hungary in 1980) came from what her community considered a very traditional Romani family and got married at fourteen. Yet she remembers admiring a slightly older Romani woman activist, Szilvia Lakatos: 'She is the only woman from the Romani community in Pécs who could make it and is still doing this, and this is why she was very important for me' (Schultz 2004a). With Lakatos as a role model and the support of her husband, Romani activist Gyula Vámosi, Pálmai started ARANJ, which translated from Hungarian means 'the Romani Wives and Women's Rights Association'. This was a self-described effort to involve married Romani women and mothers in Romani women's rights activities. As such, it was probably the first group to reach out explicitly to Romani women who may not have felt comfortable with feminist-identified agendas, but who nonetheless wanted to improve the lives of Romani women, their families and their communities.

Romani women activists also witnessed the keen suffering of women in their families. Bițu disliked her father's disrespectful treatment of her mother, but was driven to speak out directly as a teenager after watching several of her aunts' husbands beat them. Kóczé witnessed her mother's abuse at her father's hands before she died from asthma in Kóczé's arms when Kóczé was only seventeen. This close attention to the sufferings of their own families and communities later shaped the way Romani women would frame their activism in terms of an ethics of care for their communities. Like women activists in other times and places, they drew strength and motivation for activism from the connections among motherhood, politics and the urgent needs of racialized communities facing poverty (Naples 1998).

From Grassroots Apprentices to Activists

The Romani women profiled in this chapter have confidently navigated national, European and global networks to promote Romani women's issues for well over a decade. Yet their early connection to Romani activism is deeply rooted in local communities and their personal struggles with Romani identities. While experiences with strong women and gendered oppression in their families provided important role models, and sensitized Romani women activists to issues they would raise in the future, most learned the arts of activism at very local, intimate levels.

Nicoleta Bițu became an activist in 1991, just after the transition, when interethnic conflicts roiled a nearby local community. Romani houses were burned, and Bițu was then involved with a company helping to rebuild them. In 1992, she graduated with a social work degree from the University of Bucharest. She was just one of three Romani students in the whole university at that time, given an opportunity because of positive discrimination ('affirmative action' in the US context). She became a local mediator (fieldworker) with a Romani school in a Romanian village, dealing with health issues and other practical matters. As she noted: 'What is great about my involvement in the Romani movement is that I was not a kind of a star from the beginning. I've done everything very slowly and step by step. I was not discovered immediately and for four years I didn't speak in public'. Although Bițu had known Nicolae Gheorghe since she was seven because he knew her father, it was only after 1991 that she was among the promising young Romani people he mentored. In 1994, Gheorghe, Bițu and Nora Costache established the NGO Romani CRISS (Roma Centre for Social Intervention Studies), which was unique, because it had a full Romani staff and served as a kind of incubator for Romani activists. Among the most satisfying experiences during her early time with Romani CRISS was conducting leadership training for young people.

Azbija Memedova worked as a volunteer for a women's anti-violence hotline before she started working on Romani issues in the mid-1990s. Her mother had been involved in the first post-Yugoslav women's organization in Macedonia, and Memedova was much more attuned to women's issues than any ethnic ones, she recalls. One day, she was watching television and a Romani politician challenged Romani people to both 'come out' as Roma and also to contribute to their communities. Reluctantly, she took up that challenge and started an organization for Romani students. In 1997, two representatives of the Open Society Institute's Roma Participation Program came to Skopje, and asked her to start a Romani community centre in the Romani neighbourhood Shuto Orizari. Memedova had the support of Skopje's mayor, who knew her through her mother's political activism. The Roma Centre of Skopje opened in 1998, focusing on meeting the community's basic needs: 'We started with very concrete things, making very concrete things visible', Memedova emphasized; 'We provided water to one part of Shuto Orizari where fifty houses didn't have clean drinking water. We built a playground. We took thirty elementary school kids to summer camp, the first time they went outside of Skopje'. After establishing a track record of accomplishments with the Romani community, Memedova started working on interethnic relations, the issue most compelling to her, and one that continues to fuel Macedonian politics. Her goal was to help Romani youth integrate into Macedonian society.

Like Memedova, Enisa Eminova did not experience anti-Roma prejudice in primary school, attributing this to the fact that her country, then still part of Tito's Yugoslavia, had a strong ethic of solidarity across ethnic differences. However, once in secondary school, as the only Romani student in her class, she encountered anti-Roma racism from teachers and students, which accelerated as she became more involved in competitive sports. Her first coach refused to allow her to join the national team, because he felt those representing the country should be 'Macedonian'. He expressed this using very derogatory language. Later, she found another coach and did join the national team.

Because she did not speak Romanes, Eminova did not connect well with her Romani relatives, nor particularly with the Romani community. However, she applied to a Roma Junior Achievement Program at the Soros Foundation Macedonia, where she met her first mentor, a young Romani activist Elvis Ali. Later, Azbija Memedova became her mentor, introduced her to the young people in her organization, and eventually recommended her to join the Roma Women's Initiative. While first working with Romani communities, Eminova quickly learned Romanes and many local dialects. She also sensitized herself to Romani traditions as these communities interpreted them. These skills enabled her to navigate encounters with male Romani community leaders when introducing such sensitive topics as the virginity cult and encouraging community discussion about it. This became the nucleus of the Virginity Project, a very successful national and regional project led by young Romani women (Young Leaders 2001; Schultz 2005a).

Kóczé and Oprea, both of whom came from very challenging childhood circumstances, used education as a means to develop skills to contribute to their Roma communities. Kóczé, who started out as an elementary school teacher, quickly decided that higher education would be more empowering. When she left her small hometown to come to Budapest, she helped to establish and direct the Romaversitas Scholarship Program in 1996. Oprea continually sought higher education despite many obstacles, eventually becoming a lawyer to help the Romani community.

The Impact of Romani Women's Activism and Discourse

The conservative backlash of the most recent decade demonstrates the fragility of gains for both Romani rights and women's rights, leaving Romani women's issues still marginalized. Nonetheless, I also argue that early efforts to build a regional Romani women's movement had a greater impact on the lives of Romani women and a younger generation of Romani activists than can be quantified by mere policy change or the negative context of political backlash.

Poised between Roma rights and women's movements, Romani women activists exemplify the possibilities and limits of identity-based politics. Their empowerment comes from their cultural identity and connection to local communities. At the same time, efforts to articulate their intersectional issues in both the Roma rights and women's movements have been somewhat frustrating. Translating their issues into public policy has been even more difficult, as attested by encounters with national governments, the structures of the Decade of Roma Inclusion and the European Parliament.

The Romani women's movement arose at a very specific moment of democratic experimentation in post-Soviet CEE. When the NWP convened non-Romani post-Soviet women, there was mistrust, a resistance to the idea of women's solidarity and a lack of desire to articulate gender-based claims. This may have been due to Soviet historical trauma in general and women's 'forced emancipation', which offered little liberation and a double or triple work shift.

Romani women's early gatherings showed no such hesitation. During the Soviet era, Romani people's physical, economic and political isolation had insulated them to some extent from certain kinds of Soviet dynamics. For people living under what purported to be socialist 'egalitarianism', identity politics were for the most part taboo. But Romani families and communities had to develop strong senses of group identity in order to survive. Romani women activists could build on intra-community support. Women were neither community leaders nor heads of the early major Roma rights organizations, so their marginality allowed them to sidestep – to some degree – some of the internal movement conflicts.

A major critique of identity politics is that it requires forced homogenization of identity in order to present a united front. Yet as noted earlier, the founding Romani women leaders were already boundary-crossers by the time they encountered Romani politics. This may have engendered a certain confidence and a sufficiently strong Romani identity to enable them to jump forward and embrace strategic alliances with other movements more easily, marshalling non-Romani allies in effective ways and making more demands for conceptual, political and institutional autonomy.

Feminist-influenced Romani women activists benefited from the 'Romani ghetto' and were then among the first to venture outside it. Romani women were also among the most prominent spokespeople of the Romani movement, so when Romani men and women saw them speak at venues such as the European Parliament, the United Nations, the World Bank and the inaugural conference of the Decade of Roma Inclusion, their identities as leaders were reinforced to themselves and to national, regional and global leaders. The intense focus of funders and NGOs on Roma rights issues in the early 2000s helped to support the development of a cadre of Romani leaders and intellectuals, including some of the leading Romani women activists. When the opportunity arose to create separate spaces for Romani women, they used them for movement building, intellectual exploration and knowledge creation. This assertive subjectivity and intellectual inquiry is itself evidence of the impact of nascent Romani feminism in CEE's democratic experiments.

The Romani women's movement was and will be most powerful when sustaining a dialectical relationship between local communities and national, regional or transnational institutions. The future of the Romani women's movement depends upon sharing these histories with young Romani women, but at the same time giving them the space to articulate the issues that matter most to them. As with all social movements, leadership transitions involving founders are always challenging. The Romani women's movement has made a point to respect and involve older women leaders, and to seek to create cross-generational alliances.

Impact on Regional and Global Women's Movements

The effort to introduce Romani women's issues into regional women's movements was not initially successful because the effort to organize women's movements was so challenging. When Western feminists started exchanging ideas with post-Soviet feminists in the early days after the fall of the Soviet

Union, it became clear that there were many political, intellectual and epistemological differences that would take time to understand and bridge. Therefore, the ideas of intersectional feminism were particularly beyond reach in most of those early conversations. And despite a few stalwart non-Romani feminist allies, there was undeniable ignorance and racism on the part of some women's movement activists when first introduced to Romani women's issues.

Regional women's movements later made modest attempts to address the experiences of women in racial/ethnic minority groups, but those efforts never fundamentally transformed their agendas. Furthermore, despite some efforts by the European Women's Lobby and the International Roma Women's Network – a group of Romani women from eighteen countries who formed a loose network in 2003 focused more on legislative change than movement building (Izsák 2013) – the EU has never been able to develop policy based on intersectional analysis of women facing multiple forms of discrimination in Europe, including Romani women (Verloo 2017).

The global feminist movement is open to Romani women's issues, but has made little effort to theorize or integrate them into ongoing global feminist agendas. When Romani women took the initiative to speak at global feminist meetings and/or to use UN mechanisms for women's rights, there was acceptance, but perhaps a benign tokenism that still needs to be challenged.

Impact on the Roma Rights Movement, Roma Discourse, Roma Movement Theorizing and Romani Studies

Despite the lack of institutional and policy change, Romani women's activism and a discourse about Romani women's issues have been unleashed in the region. Discussion of Romani women's agendas is more evident in the Roma rights movement than in the regional women's movement. Romani women's activism has influenced the Roma rights agenda, but it has not yet transformed it to be fully inclusive of Romani women's leadership and social change agendas (see also Zentai, this volume). Admittedly, Roma rights and human rights activists were able to coalesce around, most notably, cases of coerced sterilization of Romani women. In landmark 2011 and 2012 cases, the European Court of Human Rights ruled against Slovakia for sterilizing Romani women without informed consent (Center for Reproductive Rights 2012). This is a positive development for Romani women's rights, but it is less threatening than other issues articulated by Romani feminists because it posits and protects the construct of Romani women as reproducers of the Romani people and culture. Yet attitudes are changing. Even in the early 2000s, the Virginity Project documented the openness of young Romani men in several countries to rethink gender norms. As Jelena Jovanović and

Violetta Zentai (2018) suggest in their recent research, this is particularly true of young educated Romani men.

Some older Romani men leaders were always supportive of Romani women's leadership and activism on women's issues; but most were not. Yet in recent years, even some of the Romani and non-Romani male allies who had shown little interest in supporting Romani women's feminist-oriented activism and thinking in the early 2000s seem to be adopting gender analyses in their writings (Kyuchokov 2011). This suggests recognition that some gender discourse is now de rigueur in progressive Romani politics.

Romani women's political and conceptual challenges to Romani gender politics paved the way for preliminary acceptance of Romani LGBTQI theory and identity development. In the early period of Romani women's activism, it was extremely taboo to challenge traditional gender roles by exploring gender-different identities. The space in between the Romani and women's movements was not comfortable for Romani LGBTQI people. Homophobia was rife in both movements. With the exception of brave pioneers like Vera Kurtić in Nis, Serbia, who was out as a lesbian, Romani LGBTQI activists kept a low profile concerning that part of their lives. The greatest support for Romani lesbian feminists probably came through global feminist connections, but they were less accessible on a regular basis.

Evidence of greater acceptance of LGBTQI Romani people, and concrete evidence of the radical influence of Romani feminist thinking, can be found among Romani activist intellectuals and in Romani Studies. Iulius Rostas, who was the founding chair of the new programme in Romani Studies at the Central European University in Budapest, together with non-Romani allies Márton Rövid and Marek Szilvási, articulates this new integration of intersectional thinking in activist Romani intellectual production:

> Nonetheless, we do advocate for dismantling the 'Roma ghetto'. The narrow focus on 'Roma inclusion' has diverted attention from questions of social justice, welfare, democracy and diversity. Anti-racist, feminist LGBT and leftist movements can be neither credible nor successful without incorporating Romani activists and organizations. In turn, Roma and pro-Roma organizations, institutions and networks cannot be successful without developing alliances with progressive social movements. (Rostas, Rövid and Szilvási 2015: 7–10)

Fremlová and McGarry (2018) even suggest that Romani LGBTQI people and LGBT movement strategies may invigorate Romani politics. The desire to think intersectionally and build coalitions across social movements suggests both the impact of Romani feminists and the potential maturing of the Romani movement.

Returning to the Roots, Building Institutions and Carrying Legacies Forward

Romani women leaders grew up in Soviet societies, experiencing oppression but also the first stirrings of Romani national and social movements. They navigated the post-Soviet transition, which awakened a belief in the possibility of social transformation and the universal values of human rights, only to confront the current rise of right-wing movements in Europe. But their early exposure to the extreme suffering and marginalization of Romani people may make them less naive and better prepared to deal with these trends.

The times may simply require progressive coalition building – skills Romani women activists have already practised. In the increasingly conservative climate of contemporary European politics, with some extreme right-wing elements, anti-Roma racism is taking virulent forms. Oprea (2012) has expressed the difficulty of pursuing Romani feminist agendas when Romani people are under racist siege, suggesting that Romani women activists may need to focus on basic community survival issues. Recent research with migrant Romani women in Spain suggests the formation of very informal grassroots networks that are enabling Romani women to access institutions to provide for their basic survival needs, while at the same time challenging racist discourse that dehumanizes Romani migrants (Sordé et al. 2014). This manifestation of intersectionality, combining survival needs with awareness-raising, may provide a model of multiple practices and sites for Romani women's activism.

Romani women activists' consciousness was forged at the local level and provides ongoing sustenance. Bițu, invoking the self-reflexivity that is a hallmark of both feminist epistemology and her core political values, feels that the privileges accorded her and other leading Romani activists engender a responsibility to address the continuing suffering and marginalization of the vast majority of Romani people. Bițu's recent work exemplifies this moment perfectly. She is helping to create a museum honouring the work of her late husband, Nicolae Gheorghe. She recently worked with evicted Romani families in Bucharest, and 'was in the streets' demonstrating again. She wrote on 4 February 2017: 'I have lived to see this around me again. I can't believe it. It's like going back twenty-five years' (personal communication). What gives her the most joy lately, she said, is running a small, informal school for young Romani people in her house.

Yet Bițu is also part of building European (transnational) institutions that will enable Romani people to preserve and share their own history and culture. She was on the board of the organization that helped to create the new European Roma Institute for Arts and Culture (ERIAC), which opened in

Berlin in June 2017, directed by leading art historian and Romani woman cultural activist Tímea Junghaus (see also Magazzini, this volume).

Similarly, Kóczé celebrated the opening of the Romani Studies Program at Budapest's Central European University (CEU) in October 2017. She was recently named as assistant professor for the CEU's 'Roma in European Societies Initiative', a 5-million-euro effort to improve the situation of Roma in all sectors at local, national and regional levels through teaching and research, leadership development and community outreach. She will also serve as academic director of the related Roma Graduate Preparation Program. Seeing Romani Studies established as an academic discipline in her native Hungary must feel extremely gratifying to Kóczé. As founding director of the Romaversitas Program, Kóczé is also experiencing the fruition of over twenty years work promoting the higher education of young Romani people. Reflecting intense intellectual exploration of the movement they were part of, both Kóczé and Bițu wrote their doctoral dissertations on Romani women.

The two other primary leaders of the Roma Women's Initiative have also experimented with a local/transnational model for their work. Memedova has returned to the local level as Macedonian representative of the Pestalozzi Children's Foundation, a transnational effort to promote children's rights. Eminova recently worked with migrant refugees in Greece and Macedonia. Prior to that, she worked for the International Rescue Committee to empower Muslim women in Chechnya and later with Muslim women in Iraq. Truly an intersectional global feminist practitioner, she is using her knowledge of how to promote women's empowerment in culturally conservative societies to focus particularly on Muslim women refugees and Muslim women in conflict contexts. In a different way of linking local and global, former European Roma Rights Centre Program Office for Women's Issues, Kerieva McCormack of Scotland, is pursuing her doctorate while working to build alliances for Romani women with indigenous women in the global feminist movement.

Transnational feminist solidarities have enabled Romani women activists to operate at times in spheres beyond limited (and frustrating) nation-state politics, building comprehensive movements for inclusion. These movements provide hope and vision, as they remain alert and sensitive to shifting exclusionary impulses, such as European responses to refugees from Africa and the Middle East. The earlier movement-building efforts of Romani women activists addressing multiple dimensions of discrimination offer a history and model that should help to integrate gender-related concerns into ongoing European minority and migration politics.

The Soros Foundation and its partners identified a critical mass of young Romani women and men as 'Young Leaders'. They were given resources, special opportunities, access and some power to craft their own programmes. While Romani feminist activism is quite a recent phenomenon, two mini-cohorts have already emerged. The slightly older cohort was born around 1970–71 and the younger around 1980–81. Although still quite young, women like Bițu, Memedova and Kóczé now have at least two decades of Romani activism behind them. As mothers, they have raised children who are poised to go out into the world on their own. As mentors of younger women like Eminova, McCormack, Matache and Oprea (most born in the early 1980s), they are supportive of emerging women's leadership, but also interested in theorizing from their own experiences, creating lasting Roma-led institutions and pushing the boundaries of theoretical frameworks that will move future Roma rights agendas forward in much more complex, inclusive and intersectional ways. The next generation of young Romani women may express similar frustrations about Romani gender politics, but they have role models, allies, discourses and concrete victories to undergird their efforts. They cannot take leadership in either the Romani or women's movements for granted, but they know they are entitled to lead.

The Roma Women's Initiative, active from 1999 to 2007, generated tremendous intellectual and political resources. Although its original institutional form no longer exists, the RWI's legacies live on in many forms at local, national, regional and transnational levels. It is particularly important to document these and other Romani women's activist efforts so that subsequent generations do not feel that they are the first to struggle with these issues, as is often the case in women's history. Future generations can learn from the strategies, tactics, victories and setbacks of earlier Romani women activists, as well as their intense feminist efforts to theorize from and beyond their own lives, to create vibrant and imaginative frameworks for Romani futures.

And the first generation of Romani feminists is not quite ready to retire. In a sense, they find themselves in the position that Hannah Arendt (2006) termed 'between past and future'. Arendt invoked the moral clarity of those who had the brief but intense experience of serving in the Resistance against Fascism in the Second World War, and who were then faced with the dual challenges of understanding the past and envisioning the future in an unstable Europe. Romani feminists and Romani women activists are also leading efforts to make visible the Romani Holocaust in a Europe that increasingly resembles and yet is different from the Europe about which Arendt wrote. Building on the advocacy of such pioneers as Agnes Daróczi of Hungary, US-based Romani women like Petra Gelbart and Ethel Brooks include in their work efforts to gain institutional recognition for the Romani Holocaust.

Romani women and their allies are in an excellent position to theorize the emerging connections between recent US and European forms of racism and right-wing totalitarian tendencies. In this era of Viktor Orbán and Donald Trump, perhaps Romani women on both sides of the Atlantic will be among the first to organize today's forms of anti-fascist resistance. I am looking forward to being on the same side.

Debra L. Schultz is an Assistant Professor of History at Kingsborough Community College of the City University of New York, where she teaches civil rights, women's and twentieth-century history, and co-directs the KCC Citizenship Academy. The author of *Going South: Jewish Women in the Civil Rights Movement* (New York University Press, 2001) and a founding programme director of the Soros Foundation's Network Women's Program, her work on the history, theory and practice of intersectional anti-racist feminisms encompasses both US women's civil rights activism and European Romani women's rights activism. Her current research examines public memorialization of the US civil rights movement within global human rights frameworks on historical, racialized memory, justice and reconciliation.

Note

I would like to thank my RWI co-conspirators Nicoleta Bițu, Azbija Memedova and Enisa Eminova for their trust, friendship, many hours of hard work, and most importantly, many shared moments of laughter. I am happy to collaborate again with colleagues I met through the Soros Foundation – Angéla Kóczé and Violeta Zentai – whose tenacity and long-term commitment I deeply admire. I am grateful for the innovative thinking and high-spiritedness of all the Romani and non-Romani women with whom I worked on Romani women's issues. Non-Roma women – the groundbreaking Slavicas – already working as allies to Romani women paved the way: Slavica Indveska of OSI-Macedonia and Slavica Stojanovic of OSI-Serbia. I thank my Network Women's Program colleagues, particularly founding director Anastasia Posadskaya-Vanderbeck and SEE coordinator Kimberly Middleton, for supporting my work on the RWI.

References

Arendt, H. 2006. *Between Past and Future*. New York: Penguin Classics.
Bițu, N. 2000. 'Roundtable: Romani Women in Romani and Majority Societies', *Roma Rights* 1. Retrieved 1 September 2018 from: http://www.errc.org/roma-rights-journal/romani-women-in-romani-and-majority-societies.

———. 2004. 'The Challenges Of and For Romani Women', *Roma Rights* 1. Retrieved 1 September 2018 from: http://www.errc.org/roma-rights-journal/the-challenges-of-and-for-romani-women.
Bulkin, E., M. Pratt and B. Smith. 1988. *Yours in Struggle: Three Perspectives on Racism and Anti-Semitism*. Ithaca, NY: Firebrand Books.
Center for Reproductive Rights. 2012. 'European Court of Human Rights Finds Slovakia Violated Romani Women's Rights in Another Involuntary Sterilization Case'. Retrieved 1 February 2017 from https://www.reproductiverights.org/press-room/european-court-of-human-rights-finds-slovakia-violated-romani-womens-rights.
Collins, P.H., and S. Bilge. 2016. *Intersectionality*. Cambridge: Polity Press.
Crenshaw, K. 1989. 'Demarginalizing the Intersection of Race and Sex', *The University of Chicago Legal Forum* 140: 139–67.
Eminova, E. 2006. 'Negotiations: Feminism, Racism and Difference', *Development* 49(1): 35–37.
Foa, R., and G. Ekiert. 2017. 'The Weakness of Postcommunist Civil Society Assessed', *European Journal of Political Research* 59: 419–39.
Fremlová, L., and A. McGarry. 2018. 'Negotiating the Identity Dilemma: Crosscurrents across the Romani, Romani Women's and Romani LGBTIQ Movements', in A. Kóczé et al. (eds), *The Romani Women's Movement: Struggles and Debates in Central and Eastern Europe*. London: Routledge, pp. 51–68.
Gheorghe, N., and A. Mirga. 1997. *The Roma in the Twenty-First Century: A Policy Paper*. Princeton, NJ: Project on Ethnic Relations.
Gluck, S.B. 1991. *Women's Worlds: The Feminist Practice of Oral History*. London: Routledge.
Izsák, R. 2013. 'The European Romani Women's Movement', in S. Batliwala (ed.), *Changing Their World: Concepts and Practices of Women's Movements*. Toronto: Association for Women's Rights in Development, pp. 59–60.
Izásk-Ndiaye, R. 2019. Keynote Address. Neglected Voices: The Global Roma Diaspora Conference, 5–6 April 2019. Cambridge, MA: Harvard University.
Járóka, L. 2006. 'Romani Women's Rights at the European Level', *Roma Rights* 4: 3–5.
Jovanović, J., and V. Zentai. 2018. 'Gender Relations and the Romani Women's Movement in the Eyes of Young Romani Men', in A. Kóczé et al. (eds), *The Romani Women's Movement: Struggles and Debates in Central and Eastern Europe*. London: Routledge, pp. 69–87.
Kóczé, A. 2004. 'Will Tomorrow Be A Better Day?' Speech. Brussels: European Parliament.
———. 2009. 'The Limits of Rights-Based Discourse in Romani Women's Activism', in N. Sigona and N. Trehan (eds), *Romani Politics in Contemporary Europe*. Basingstoke: Palgrave Macmillan, pp. 135–55.
———. 2011. 'Gender, Ethnicity and Class: Romani Women's Political Activism and Social Struggle in Post-Socialist Europe'. PhD dissertation. Budapest: Central European University.
——— et al. (eds). 2018. *The Romani Women's Movement: Struggles and Debates in Central and Eastern Europe*. London: Routledge.
Kurtić, V., and S. Vasić. 2002. 'Serbia: Roma Racial and Sexual Discrimination', in R. Raj (ed.), *Women at the Intersection*. New Brunswick, NJ: Rutgers University Center for Women's Global Leadership, pp. 21–26.
Kyuchokov, H. 2011. 'Roma Girls: Between Traditional Values and Educational Aspirations', *Intercultural Education* 22(1): 97–104.

Lorde, A. 1984. *Sister Outsider: Essays and Speeches by Audre Lorde*. Trumansburg, NY: The Crossing Press.
Matache, M. 2015. *A Lost Decade? Reflections on Roma Inclusion, 2005–2015*. Budapest: Roma Education Fund.
Maya, O. 2006a. 'The 10th Anniversary of the European Roma Rights Centre', *Roma Rights* 2/3: 15–17.
———. 2006b. 'Romani Women's Rights', *Roma Rights* 4: 1–2.
McGarry, A. 2014. 'Roma as a Political Identity: Exploring Representations of Roma in Europe', *Ethnicities* 14(6): 756–74.
———. 2017. *Romophobia: The Last Acceptable Form of Racism*. London: Zed Books.
Memedova, A. 2004. 'Romani Men and Romani Women. Roma Human Rights Movement: A Missing Element', *Roma Rights* 1. Retrieved 1 September 2018 from: http://www.errc.org/roma-rights-journal/romani-men-and-romani-women-roma-human-rights-movement-a-missing-element.
———. 2006a. 'UN Women's Discrimination Committee Reviews Macedonia', *Roma Rights* 1. Retrieved 1 September 2018 from: http://www.errc.org/press-releases/un-womens-discrimination-committee-reviews-macedonia.
———. 2006b. 'Shifting from Terminology to Substance', *Roma Rights* 4: 15–18.
Mezzadra, S., and B. Neilson. 2013. *Border as Method, or, the Multiplication of Labor*. Durham, NC: Duke University Press.
Naples, N. 1998. *Grassroots Warriors, Activist Mothering and the War on Poverty*. London: Routledge.
Oprea, A. 2005. 'The Arranged Marriage of Ana Maria Cioaba, Intra-Community Oppression and Romani Feminist Ideals', *European Journal of Women's Studies* 12(2): 133–48.
———. 2012. 'Romani Feminism in Reactionary Times', *Signs: Journal of Women in Culture and Society* 38(1): 11–21.
———. 2013. 'Psychic Charlatans, Roving Shoplifters, and Traveling Con Artists', *Berkeley Journal of Gender, Law and Justice* 22(1): 31–41.
Rostas, I., M. Rövid and M. Szilvási. 2015. 'On Roma Civil Society, Roma Inclusion and Roma Participation', *Roma Rights* 2: 7–10.
Schultz, D.L. 2001. *Going South: Jewish Women in the Civil Rights Movement*. New York: New York University Press.
———. 2004a. Interview with Marika Palmái. 30 June. In author's possession.
———. 2004b. Interview with Alexandra Oprea. 25 October. In author's possession.
———. 2005a. 'An Intersectional Feminism of Their Own: Creating European Romani Women's Activism', *Identities: Journal for Politics, Gender and Culture* 4(8/9): 243–77.
——— (ed.). 2005b. 'A Place at the Policy Table: Report on the Roma Women's Forum in Budapest, Hungary, 29 June 2003'. Budapest: Open Society Institute Network Women's Program.
———. 2012. 'Translating Intersectionality Theory into Practice', *Signs: Journal of Women in Culture and Society* 38(1): 37–43.
Schultz, D.L., and N. Bițu. 2018. 'Missed Opportunity or Building Blocks of a Movement? History and Lessons from the Roma Women's Initiative's Efforts to Organize European Romani Women's Activism', in A. Kóczé et al. (eds), *The Romani Women's Movement: Struggles and Debates in Central and Eastern Europe*. London: Routledge, pp. 29–50.

Sordé, T., et al. 2014. 'Solidarity Networks that Challenge Racialized Discourses: The Case of Romani Immigrant Women in Spain', *European Journal of Women's Studies* 21(1): 87–102.

Spivak, G.C. 1988. 'Can the Subaltern Speak?', in C. Nelson and L. Grossberg (eds), *Marxism and the Interpretation of Culture*. London: Macmillan, pp. 271–316.

Twine, F., and J. Warren (eds). 2000. *Racing Research, Researching Race*. New York: New York University Press.

Verloo, M. 2017. 'Multiple Inequalities, Intersectionality and the European Union', *European Journal of Women's Studies* 13(30): 221–28.

Williams, F. 2003. 'Contesting Race and Gender in the European Union', in B. Hobson (ed.), *Recognition Struggles and Social Movements*. Cambridge: Cambridge University Press, pp. 121–44.

Young Leaders. 2001. *On Virginity*. Skopje: Women's Action.

CHAPTER 8

❋ ❋ ❋

CAN THE TABLES BE TURNED WITH A NEW STRATEGIC ALLIANCE?

The Struggles of the Romani Women's Movement in Central and Eastern Europe

Violetta Zentai

The Romani women's equality agenda is embedded in practices of political intersectionality – that is, category-based political mobilization against subordination and exclusion produced through multiple and intersecting societal hierarchies. A while ago, I started drafting this chapter to study the opening and closure of opportunities to articulate the Romani women's equality agenda in Central and Eastern Europe; but by the time I had finished a first draft, important transformations were already in the making. Consequently, in the present chapter, I will take these transformations into consideration as well. I will investigate instances of intersectional politics that have taken shape along two axes of equality struggles and debates, related, firstly, to gender equality and women's rights, and secondly, to Romani empowerment and equality. I will also portray how Romani women's recent strategic moves have challenged my original double track inquiry. Meanwhile, Romani women have identified and organized themselves through new social and political affiliations, beyond the often contentious intersections of Roma rights and gender equality struggles, by moving from intersectionality to transformative anti-essentialism.

Conversations with the Literature

My inquiry has been inspired by Iris Marion Young's (1989) relational understanding of social groups composed by affiliations, identities and interests that converge in common experiences of marginalization for particular groups. The scholarship on Romani politics and participation also guides my reading of the political institutions in new, post-1989 Central and East European democracies, and various social movement formations based on the category of 'Roma' (Vermeersch 2006; Sigona and Trehan 2009; McGarry 2010; van Baar 2012; van Baar and Vermeersch 2017; Beck and Ivasiuc 2018). I rely on theories of collective identity that understand how cognitive, moral and emotional connections tie people to social groupings that are embedded in power relations, hierarchies and resistance to those hierarchies (McGarry and Jasper 2015). In these approaches, what differentiates identity from a social category is that it is both imagined and experienced in social interactions, and that identity may first have to be imagined so that it can be experienced. Francesca Polletta and James Jasper (2001: 294) comprehensively portray how social movements construct, deconstruct, celebrate and enact collective identities. Demanding recognition for new or cross-cutting identity constructions within a particular social movement may confuse or appear threatening for the collective (ibid.: 292). Identities play a critical role in mobilizing and sustaining participation, but they can also cause disappointment and departure from a movement.

My broader research agenda is influenced by various debates in critical gender scholarship, particularly by the pioneering way in which Kimberlé Crenshaw (1991) introduced the dual concepts of structural and political intersectionality, and by authors who discuss intersectionality as a compelling analytical framework to study the complexity of Romani women's political claims and participation (Bițu 1999; Oprea 2004; Schultz 2005; Popa 2009; Vincze 2010; Kóczé 2011; Gheorghe 2016). These scholars view injustices and power mechanisms, and their marked intersections, as the most important grounds for framing social movement actions. Identity constructions are pressing in as much as they capture and accentuate diversity within a social category stemming from partly different, partly overlapping experiences of injustices and hierarchies. Romani women form a diverse social group differentiated by age, language, family background, marital status, education, place of residence, sexuality and other sources of groupness. At the same time however, they share common experiences of racialized ethnicity and gender. This complexity makes the label 'Romani women' relevant and legitimate for a critical analysis of intersectionality. Mieke Verloo's ongoing research and reflections on intersectional politics, in both policymaking and social movements, serve as a source of inspiration for my inquiries into Romani women's struggles for voice, recognition and justice. She addresses interferences between inequalities that are mirrored in how social movements and policy debates create and relate intersectionally positioned people and groups. In social movements, she identifies four types of approach that offer different opportunities to escape from constraining categorical definitions, and to open up to cross-movement coalitions (Verloo 2013: 908–10). To avoid the naive suggestion that intersectional politics easily leads to reconciliation, solidarity and alliance-building, Verloo also asserts that social movements addressing intersectional hoarding connect and separate groups of rather similar positions in relation to centres of power.

Romani Women's Claims in the Context of Political Intersectionality

A growing body of literature offers comprehensive accounts of how Romani women – much like other women belonging to marginalized or minority communities – are especially vulnerable to intersecting forms of domination and oppression (Kóczé 2009, 2011; Lamoreux 2011; Jovanović, Kóczé and Balogh 2015). These power practices, resulting in social phenomena ranging from ignorance to exploitation, are generated by both mainstream society and Romani communities, as well as the enduring inequalities between them. In addition to the multiple disadvantages Romani women suffer in the labour market, and in education, health and housing, several sensitive and controversial issues have recently gained more prominence in the debates, particularly regarding violence against women, including domestic violence, human trafficking and forced marriage (Jovanović 2015). Romani women have continuously been exposed to coerced sterilization in mainstream medical institutions, and have also been subjected to extremist, nationalist and racist attacks owing to their alleged role as reproducers of 'undesirable' social groups. Feminist scholars (see, for instance, Vincze 2014) have also explored how Romani women's sexuality is disciplined: while Romani women are often perceived by their own community as obliged to biologically reproduce their own ethnic group, they have simultaneously also become the targets of racist fertility control and dehumanizing discourses, according to which they give birth to 'inferior' children.

An expanding group of feminist thinkers proposes that the negligible attention paid to intersectional issues in current European political and policy actions stems from the limited opportunities of the Romani women's movement to influence political and policy debates (Izsák 2008; Kóczé 2011; Jovanović, Kóczé and Balogh 2015; Kóczé et al. 2019). As a matter of fact, Romani women have claimed a place in some key human rights developments and, over the last twenty-five years, have become visible time and again at influential international events. During some of these events, Romani women's voices have not only been heard, but have also impacted on the discursive frames of key political statements. For instance, during the 2001 Durban conference on antiracism, the issue of forced sterilization of Romani women in socialist and postsocialist states was powerfully addressed (Kóczé 2011). Moreover, in 2003, during the international conference in Budapest that inaugurated the Decade of Roma Inclusion 2005–2015, the presence and voice of several prominent Romani women's movement leaders resulted in the inclusion of their agenda in the larger European policy frame of Roma inclusion (Open Society Institute 2003). Although such progress took place in a fragmented way, the intersectional understanding of the situation of Romani women has appeared in the key documents of the Decade of Roma Inclusion, as well as in various domestic strategic plans for Roma inclusion, developed in the second half of the 2000s. Besides the UN human rights mechanisms and the transnational policy alliance of the Decade of Roma Inclusion, Romani women activists have had to nudge and challenge various European social movement arenas in which the politics of gender equality and equal citizenship for the Roma are negotiated.

The two key categories of gender and Roma are endorsed by European political, legal and policy structures, which orient collective actions and group formations in social movement arenas (Jacquot and Vitale 2014). These transnational forms of mobilization, entangled with both domestic gender equality struggles and Romani empowerment efforts, tend to solidify collective identity constructions in accordance with firm social categories or axes of inequalities. As a consequence, Romani women's creative and effective intersectional politics have to specify domination practices and political subject positions from the perspective of their own experiences, but also with reference to social categories promoted by powerful transnational political and policy actors.

Groundbreaking Acts in the Romani Women's Movement through Articulations of Sensitive Issues

Of the many inequality problems addressed by Romani women activists, some are quintessential for revealing the overlapping practices of domination and oppression that tend to consistently render minority women at the bottom of power hierarchies. At critical academic fora, the most outspoken Romani feminist thinkers have also proposed that patriarchal norms in Romani communities are not simply the result of self-defence mechanisms, but also a means of perpetuating asymmetrical power relations based on gender (Izsák 2008; Kóczé 2011). Parallel to the landmark and frequently criticized European Framework for Roma Integration introduced in 2011, Romani women activists have elaborated critical statements on sensitive intersectional issues. Two leading Romani civil society groups, one from Romania and one from Bulgaria, have published English-language reports that have become indispensable sources for international policy discussions and Romani women's activism.

In the first report, Romanian feminist activist scholars Nicoleta Bițu and Crina Morteanu (2010) investigate early marriage practices in Romani communities, and the social and political reactions that accompany them. They argue that early marriages, imagined as a form of profound traditionalism for the preservation of the community's moral and physical health, have generated criticism in various Romani and non-Romani civic groups in Romania. In their view, early marriages violate children's (both boys' and girls') rights, and hamper the emancipation of the entire community. The authors also refer to some traditional leaders who argue that arranged marriages help to preserve the healthy moral traditions and spirit of the community, and guard against the 'ills of modern society'. The authors believe that early marriages violate the individual rights of Romani children and youth in the name of the collective rights of the community. At the same time, they understand early marriage from a historical perspective: these traditional practices should not be seen as the ethnic or cultural 'property' of Romani communities. Bițu and Morteanu also reveal how racism against Romani communities and wider gender relations significantly impact Romani women and girls. The importance of taking this intersectional dimension into account is also emphasized in the introduction to the report, in which Vincze, a non-Romani feminist ally, proposes:

[B]y treating the phenomenon of early marriages in the context of interethnic relations, the 'Roma woman' gets to be perceived by and subjected to gendered norms both in her own community and by the majority population, becoming the instrument through which the two communities interrelate and contest each other. (Quoted verbatim from Vincze 2010: 8)

The second report was composed by the Amalipe Center for Interethnic Dialogue and Tolerance in Bulgaria. Amalipe is a leading Romani civil society organization, founded and led by Deyan Kolev and Teodora Krumova, who are internationally well-known Romani activists promoting feminist values. In 2009, in collaboration with Liga Pro Europa from Romania and the Association for Social Support of Europe from Greece, Amalipe initiated the 'Preventing Early/Forced Marriages' project, which was funded through the European Commission's Daphne Programme. The initiative's main report, released in 2011, concludes that early marriages are not specific to

Romani communities, and that their elimination will not endanger Romani identity. The report reveals that early marriages were also widespread among ethnic Bulgarians, Romanians and Greeks only two or three generations ago. This reasoning on the causes and perceptions of early marriage practices resonates with that of the Romanian report, although it refers more explicitly to 'social modernization'[1] among the Roma. The report also offers refined observations on differences between various Romani groups in terms of legitimating the disputed tradition, the rigidity of the practice and the willingness of communities to transform it. The report also explores instances of structural intersectionality that shape the family practices in question. A large majority of teachers and social workers think that early marriage is an internal Roma problem that cannot be solved. If child protection authorities respond at all, their measures are often mostly administrative and formal, relying primarily on sanctions. The latter approach fuels resistance in the Romani community towards any external intervention.

Both reports assert the commonality of wider historical transformations in family and marriage patterns valued by various ethnic groups across Europe, and deconstruct the idea that early marriage is a distinctive Romani 'cultural' practice. Both documents unveil the oppressive power nexus between mainstream institutions and Romani families when analysing the reactions of the relevant social services to the subject of early marriage. I consider these reports as important *social movement acts* that have articulated unambiguous and strong political messages on behalf of Romani women activists. Although non-Romani researchers, human rights groups and even major Romani movement organizations backed the research behind the reports, Romani women activists served as their key authors and advocates. The intersectional message is relentless and vocal: young Roma, in particular girls, shall be protected from early marriages and this principle shall not be seen to endanger Romani empowerment or identity.

Interferences between the Romani and the Mainstream Women's Movements: Awakening and Cooperation

Outspoken leaders of the Romani women's movement, such as Magda Matache (2009), Carmen Gheorghe (Gheorghe and h.arta Group 2010) and Angéla Kóczé (2011), have argued that it is not only the male-dominated leadership of the Romani movement that challenges the legitimacy of the Romani women's voice. For many years in the post-Cold War struggles for women's equality, the international feminist and gender equality movement – better referred to as movements in the plural – had largely been ignorant or silent on both Romani women's intersectional position in society and the need to articulate a Romani women's agenda. Post-Cold War women's movements in Central and Eastern Europe (CEE) have gone through a gradual learning process on multiple oppressions and cross-categorical politics, facilitated since the mid-1990s by various encounters between Romani and non-Romani women activists and actions. Much remains to be learned about scholarly and activist discussions through which various ideas on multiple inequalities emerged in the period between the Beijing Conference on Women in 1995 and the first round of EU enlargement in 2004. What is already documented is that from the mid-2000s onwards, the process of UN CEDAW (Convention on the Elimination of All Forms of Discrimination against Women) shadow reporting offered important opportunities for Romani women to address multiple inequalities, not only for the wider public, but also for mainstream women's movement actors to acknowledge these proposals (Krizsán and Zentai 2012). Transnational advocacy networks supported the first engagements with the CEDAW mechanisms. The European Roma Rights Centre (ERRC), a transnational NGO dedicated to the protection of human rights and fighting racism and discrimination against the Roma, participated in the drafting of parallel CEDAW shadow reports in several CEE countries from 2006 onwards. In Romania, Romani CRISS, a major Romani NGO, and ERRC jointly wrote a Romani women's report, alongside the civil shadow report in 2006. In 2007, ERRC assisted in the composition of a second CEDAW shadow report specifically addressing Romani women to supplement the 'main' shadow report on Hungary (ERRC 2007). These reports discussed detailed intersectional agendas, and created space and recognition for various Romani women's activists and NGOs. These exercises invited and pushed mainstream women's groups to address the Romani women's cause as part of wider gender equality issues. Subsequently, the Romani women's agenda has become an integral part of the main CEDAW shadow reports regarding most countries in the region. Nonetheless, the story of the CEDAW reports does not imply that intersectional learning is a linear and smooth process in the broader women's movement.

The Roma Women's Initiative (1999–2005), supported by the Network Women's Program of the Open Society Institute, tangibly enlarged the European and wider transnational space for Romani women's activism in CEE (see also Schultz, this volume). This initiative helped to build important institutional links between Romani and non-Romani women's activisms. But forging sisterhood between minority and majority women's equality struggles appeared to be a challenging undertaking in Europe. Fiona Williams (2003) has revealed that the European Women's Lobby (EWL) – the leading advocacy alliance for a transformative gender equality agenda in Europe – had its own uneasy trajectory of recognizing migrant women's cause and voice, and working on the necessary organizational transformations. She explains how black, ethnic minority and migrant women had to fight to make their voices heard in EU political structures, as well as in European civil society groups. They articulated their claims within the EWL, whose representatives in the 1990s framed their actions within the universal category of 'women', before moving to a greater recognition of different women's experiences, and actively supporting migrant and minority women's claim for equality.

Several years later, the major European comparative project, EUROSPHERE,[2] investigated intersectional politics regarding gender equality and ethnonational diversity within European political structures following the economic crisis of 2008 (Mokre and Siim 2013). It examined the interrelations between norms and discourses concerning the equality axes of gender and ethnicity among major political and policy actors. One strand of the analysis compared two key European transnational advocacy organizations, the European Women's Lobby (EWL) and the European Network against Racism (ENAR) in 2009–10. The results showed that EWL members remained solely concerned with gender equality and women's rights, whereas the respondents from ENAR were interested in both antidiscrimination policies and gender equality (ibid.: 11–12). These findings also reveal the slow and reluctant engagement with multiple inequality agendas by the key European advocacy network of women's rights groups.

Although the EWL has included a Romani women's movement representative since 2004, it took several years for the organization to engage earnestly with Romani women's issues. EWL made a highly visible move by organizing an international conference on Romani women in Budapest in 2011, shortly after the initiation of the European Framework for Roma Integration. The following year, EWL published a position paper on the experiences of Romani and Traveller women who had been exposed to multiple and intersectional discrimination on grounds of gender and ethnic origin. The paper's main argument is that discrimination against Romani women has occurred within Romani communities amidst growing anti-Roma racism in mainstream society (EWL 2012). The position paper discusses two major intersectional issues. It argues that Romani women run a higher risk than non-Romani women of being exposed to all forms of violence against women – notably domestic violence, trafficking and exploitation – while facing additional obstacles in accessing protection. Most importantly, limited protection from the authorities often discourages women from seeking legal help. Romani women fear further victimization by the police, as well as loss of support from their communities. These arguments fully resonate with those spelled out in the two reports on early marriage among the Roma – and which are quoted as direct reference sources for EWL.

The position paper also discusses the problem of trafficking and prostitution by arguing that Roma are highly vulnerable to trafficking because of structural forms of discrimination, poverty and exclusion. The document concludes that policies dedicated to combating trafficking and prostitution are ineffective, owing to the dramatic failure of protection systems. The EWL's articulation of the trafficking problem seems to rely on a tactical presentation of data, by boldly pitching the highest estimates as evidence of unusually high margins for any statistical data (30 to 40 per cent). These dramatic figures promulgating Romani women's vulnerability run the risk of endorsing a stigmatizing understanding of the Roma as 'natural' victims of criminal acts (Jovanović 2015). In sum, however, the EWL document presents an advanced account on various aspects of multiple discrimination against Romani women. The authors of the document received fundamental intellectual support from gender equality thinkers and leading Romani women activists from CEE. The EWL report is a symbolically and politically salient opening and response to Romani women activists' understanding of intersectional equality problems.

In this chapter, I will not examine how EWL has followed up this landmark engagement with the rights and claims of Romani women.[3] Yet I think we can conclude that the wider European political and social environment for various inequality struggles has fundamentally changed since 2011. Broadly speaking, gender equality mechanisms and the political attention paid to them have been significantly weakened, despite their groundbreaking inclusion at the Istanbul Convention, whereas the European Framework for Roma Integration has helped to keep the Roma's claims for equality relatively high on the European political and policy agenda. Both equality grounds, however, started to suffer from backlashes against the wider European human rights and equality norms and struggles following the 2008 financial and economic crisis.

Recent Reactions to Women's Claims in the Romani Movement

It is noteworthy that two internationally recognized Romani women activists-experts from CEE have articulated the major puzzle in intersectional politics for Romani women with saliently different emphases. On the one hand, Alexandra Oprea (2004) has argued that it has become more difficult to speak about the specificities of oppression that minority women face when increased racism affects the group as a whole. At the same time, Rita Izsák (2008) has proposed that one cannot tackle racism unless gender discrimination is addressed in the first place. In Romani women's internal discussions and public manifestos, these priority statements are not exclusive; they are viewed and referred to as impactful complementary or combined perspectives. Relating gender and racial marginalization in social justice discussions shows less flexibility, however, in the leading international fora of the Romani movement.[4]

In a recent, widely disseminated public statement, several internationally recognized political actors within the Romani movement have offered insights into the master frames of Romani participation in European and wider public spaces. Since its publication, the volume edited by András Bíró, Nicolae Gheorghe, Martin Kovats and Will Guy (Bíró et al. 2013) has served as an important reference point for academic and activist debates. The volume presents position papers and debates from a 2011 workshop, at which two generations of Romani leaders from Central and South Eastern Europe and several invited non-Romani allies took part. The discussions offer self-reflections and new visions concerning Romani politics and participation that also dwell on gender equality puzzles. The relevant chapter of the volume mirrors fault lines among workshop participants across gender and generational lines. An outspoken young woman from Romania, and a doctoral candidate at the time, Ioana Vrăbiescu, kicks off the discussion with the radical claim that any understanding of gender relations is absent from discussions on Romani identity (ibid.: 160). Without singling out any individual voice, it is fair to propose that representatives of the older generation of Romani activists argued that articulating gender equality perspectives within the wider Romani movement was irrelevant, or brought with it risky consequences. In contrast, younger Romani movement leaders (all of whom were male at this workshop), suggested that Romani women and men could relate on more equal terms if men and non-Roma – the two major power groups – were willing to manage public affairs in a power-sharing manner.

The director of the Roma Initiatives Office of OSF, Željko Jovanović, called for changing the status quo between the Roma and the mainstream. To this end, he made an unambiguous proposal for a generational shift and a new path for self-determination by reconstructing the category of Roma and redefining politics (Bíró et al. 2013: 202). An agenda of intergenerational shift avoids fissures with any other possible cross-categorical proposal within the movement, including gender equality, and articulates citizenship claims within both the dominant relations of the mainstream and the Romani minority. It is important to notice that the visionary conversations in this volume did not include the voices of leading activists from the Romani women's movement. Many years after the start of various forms of Romani women's activism, a programmatic statement for the wider politics of Roma inclusion and citizenship presented itself through an exclusively male editorial group.

In principle, through the launch of the National Roma Integration Strategies (NRIS), a new space has been created for intersectional debates for the larger Romani movement and Romani women's activists in the contemporary European policy environment. In 2012–13, various Romani organizations and actors embarked on crafting 'shadow reports' on the implementation of the NRISs and, in the non-EU states, of the Decade of Roma Inclusion Action Plans. The Secretariat of the Decade of Roma Inclusion, in cooperation with the Open Society Foundations (OSF), supported this initiative. The underlying rationale was that civil society organizations and actors produce genuine empirical knowledge that would help critical reflection on the policy performances of governments. In two consecutive rounds, six national 'shadow reports' were prepared and updated on the first group of countries.[5] Most of the civil society coalitions involved incorporated pro-Roma and Romani NGOs and, occasionally, independent experts on social inclusion policies. Although we cannot argue that these reports are authoritative statements by representatives of the Romani movements in the countries involved, they nevertheless mirror the recognition of Romani women's voice, and the acknowledgement of intersectional inequality agendas at crucial moments of European Romani politics. Any considerable attention paid to gender equality issues in the civil monitoring reports of 2012–13 could be seen primarily as the result of internal discussions or struggles that occurred within coalitions of civil society actors during the writing of these reports. This can be aptly demonstrated by a brief look at two civil society reports.

The Civil Society Monitoring Report Romania (2012) acknowledges that the country's national strategy cherishes the pivotal role of Romani women in their families and communities, and defines inclusion measures to address women's education and qualifications. Thus, the main policy objective is to assist women in enhancing their families' welfare, family cohesion and the development of future generations. The civil society coalition underscores the caring role of Romani women in so far as it results in social empowerment. The report also offers a detailed and well-informed account on trafficking issues. It refers to structural causes of the overrepresentation of Romani women and minors among the victims of trafficking, including the perpetual discrimination against Romani women in employment and education (ibid.: 122). The main conclusion of the civil society statement is that there is a need for the constant and systematic promotion of the idea of Romani women's equal participation, both in public and in private life. In terms of intersectional politics, the authors of the report rely on a well-established Romani NGO and its experiences working with and for Romani women. There were, however, no Romani women's organizations or Romani feminist thinkers directly involved in the coalition that wrote the report. The authors of the report only refer to conversations with Nicoleta Bițu, a central figure of the Romanian Romani women's movement, to endorse their key conclusions.

It is intriguing to acknowledge that the Civil Society Monitoring Report on Bulgaria of 2012 remains relatively circumspect regarding gender equality matters. The stated rationale for this is that the NRIS displays little sensitivity towards the specific challenges of Romani women's equality. The coordinating role played by the Amalipe Center in the group that developed the report implied that they were not short on expertise in gender equality. The limited attention paid in the report to gender equality issues might have been a tactical decision, or a compromise within the civil society coalition regarding the wider perspective politics of Roma inclusion in the country.

Despite the availability of sophisticated knowledge and political courage among Romani women activists in both Romania and Bulgaria – which the reports on early marriages discussed above clearly demonstrate – civil monitoring reports in these two polities offered only a modest space to elevate gender equality into the main agenda of Roma inclusion. Interestingly, the Slovak civil society report of 2012 is significantly more advanced in its gender equality awareness when compared to the other two countries discussed. This is far from being self-explanatory considering that, in both Romania and Bulgaria, Romani women's activism has developed much more prominently than in Slovakia. The invitation to engage with gender equality issues implicated in the European Framework of Roma Integration has not become a major source of inspiration for intersectional thinking within the wider Romani movement. Notwithstanding this, the mechanism of civil society monitoring in 2012–13 has generated a more accommodating space for intersectional attention than the close circle of the most powerful voices within the Romani civil movement in the flagship publication discussed above.

Compared to the examples of Romani politics within international and domestic spaces reviewed above, it appears that the inclusion of internationally well-known and leading Romani feminist activist-scholars on the governing boards and in leadership positions of new institutions represents a major leap forward, the most important case in point being the European Roma Institute for Art and Culture (ERIAC), established in 2017. With the appointment of Tímea Junghaus as its executive director, Nicoletta Bițu as chair of the board, and Ethel Brooks as a board member, these renowned Romani feminist thinkers have been granted not only visibility for the Romani women's movement, but also decision-making and discursive power (see also Magazzini, this volume). This development calls for critical attention to the ways in which these individuals can use their authority and position to redirect gender politics within and across the Romani movement and Romani politics in Europe more generally.

With vast human rights and Romani women's activist experiences, Soraya Post has conducted vocal and widely recognized political advocacy work in the European Parliament in the current cycle (2014–2019). Being elected as a member of an antiracist feminist party, in her public statements and policy work she has identified herself with intersectional feminist approaches. Further, she has become a leading and highly respected voice in the recently emerged and powerfully promoted political advocacy framework centring on the fight against antigypsyism. The intersections of race and gender in this new mobilizing framework, and the role of Romani women's activists in shaping the discursive opportunities around the framework, deserve further scholarly attention.

Romani Women's Agenda Setting Initiatives: New Tables and New Frames

In the following, I will explore discussions, claims and strategic framing moves from within the Romani women's movement that have most recently taken shape, both in domestic and international contexts. Without embarking on a wider and complex contextual mapping, it is important to signal two recent junctures in the formation of political and movement spaces for Romani women's activism. First, the 2008 economic crisis brought about massive populist reactions to social and political challenges, in which gender equality has become a prime target and scapegoat of the despised liberal order. For feminist groups, it has become even more difficult to respond adequately to the increasing attacks on 'gender ideology' from conservative factions in politics. Moreover, the mechanisms of gender equality in Europe, previously believed to be firm and well anchored, have started to weaken. This has impacted the CEE countries – where democratic equality policies are far more recent – with particular (although not exclusive) intensity. In parallel to this, new forms of precarity and social cleavages have emerged and become more socially and politically pronounced – something that has complicated or overshadowed ethnic and gender hierarchies. These trends have repositioned Romani women's voices in wider equality struggles and the social movement landscape.

In Romania, where the Romani women's movement has become the most vocal and impactful in CEE – in addition to the post-Yugoslav states – political intersectionality struggles have embarked upon novel paths in recent years. Two of the three visible and active Romani women's organizations in Romania – the E-Romnja Association and the Association of Roma Women for Our Children – have played an outstanding role in this development. Although not without precedent, new collaborative actions, statements and fora emerged between the wider women's and the Romani women's movement in the 2010s. It is enough to refer to the inspirational and creative trilingual journal *Nevi Sara Kali*, a genuine feminist product, initiated and edited in Romani and non-Romani feminist collaboration. The journal 'only' produced three volume-length issues, but it has remained an unparalleled manifestation of efforts to overcome the representational and political forms of intersectional tensions between Romani and non-Romani women.

Three Romanian feminists have recently reflected in an exceptionally innovative way on their experiences of interconnected social movement activities. Two of them are Romani – Letitia Mark and Carmen Gheorghe – and the third, Enikő Vincze, is non-Romani. Their encounter took place in 2017 as part of a joint writing process; the text of their conversation is reproduced in a recent edited volume (Kóczé et al. 2019). The two Romani women from different generations are public intellectuals and activists, and leaders of the E-Romnja Association and the Association of Roma Women for Our Children. The non-Romani feminist is an academic and housing activist in Romania. The three women pursue their activities in the Romanian cities of Cluj-Napoca, Timișoara and Bucharest. Their conceptual proposals for locating Romani women's activism converge on the notion of being 'in between', which laces together experiences of disadvantages and potentials to generate enabling liaisons of solidarity. Mark, the senior of the two Romani activists, expresses her full endorsement of a joint declaration made by Romani and non-Romani activists, artists and researchers from a number of European countries in Timișoara in 2011. A few months after the announcement of the European Framework for Roma, the Timișoara gathering voiced a powerful message:

> Disadvantaged Romani women are not only victims of multiple and intersectional discrimination, but also *agents of social change* towards promoting equal opportunities, ensuring social justice and human dignity, eliminating prejudices and unequal treatment, increasing self-esteem, and affirming economic independence, cultural recognition and civic and political representation. (Mark and Vincze 2011, emphasis added)

The emphasis on the potentialities of Romani women as capable actors, in spite of the harsh disadvantages they face, makes Mark's political vision powerfully forward looking. The common experiences of injustices are the springboard for collective action, but group affiliations and identity categories for those who want to mobilize are left largely open. It is fair to argue that the drive for this sort of transformative movement politics has been nurtured among several Romani and non-Romani feminists, even though these opportunities arrived only towards the end of the present decade.

Carmen Gheorghe, a mid-career Romani activist involved in transformative intersectional feminist thinking, explicitly argues that '[t]he theory of intersectionality does not satisfy me completely in saying that yes, I have several identities, and I come with all of them into a feminist space and find myself complete' (Gheorghe, Mark and Vincze 2019: 116). She argues that categorical identity constructions are locked in and often reproduce particular hierarchies of inequalities. Vincze advocates for intersectional feminism rooted in political solidarity among women, by targeting not only patriarchy, but also class inequalities and racialization. Through a systemic critique of capitalism, this feminism unveils the intertwined structures of domination, and advocates for gender equality embodied in a broader regime of social justice. Vincze argues that due to the experiences of socioeconomic and territorial marginalization, Romani feminists are able to centre attention on class inequalities and, in doing so, to enrich a wider radical feminist agenda, rather than a liberal one. In sum, all three activists reject the competitive intersectionality thinking along the lines of ethnicity and gender, either by decomposing category-based mobilization, proposing the addition of other inequality categories, or by replacing identity categories with elevated values of humanity to eradicate injustices.

All three feminists have developed a rich history of working with challenges of political intersectionality, in particular at the nexus of the wider Romani and the women's movement. They describe international women's and feminist meetings where Romani women's agendas were either ignored or sidelined. They also observe the limited interest of Romani women activists in supporting the wider feminist movement. Gheorghe recalls that in 2012–13, when engaging in feminist coalition building, she found only a few organizations that spoke about violence against Romani women or power relations between Romani and non-Romani women. Against this backdrop, she highlights a recent groundbreaking turn in the liaison between Romani and non-Romani women's groups. She invited feminist organizations to work together on evictions; at first they declined the invitation, but then changed their position. Some of these organizations have recently organized joint actions on housing in Bucharest and Cluj-Napoca. These collaborations, which include both Romani and non-Romani women' organizations, embody new types of alliances and have generated new spaces for actions regarding social justice. Gheorghe stresses that these collective housing actions are particularly valuable in view of the fact that some important gender equality agendas seem to have created new dividing lines within women's rights groups.[6] Gheorghe also refers to a new alliance against labour exploitation emerging within the Romanian social movement, in which non-Roma and Romani women also collaborate.[7]

Regarding organization-based movement activisms, the strategic actions of E-Romnja – an association established by Romani women activists in 2012 – seem key to highlighting the changes in intersectional politics that Romani feminists have initiated. The organization works to achieve equality and dignity for Romani women through ensuring that public representations are congruent with their diversity and 'real life' experiences. Their social diagnosis stresses Romani women's marginalized and inferior position within their communities and families, and their suffering from broader patriarchal systems, which keep them illiterate, economically dependent and subjugated to cultural traditions. The organization's mission statement highlights the invisibility of Romani women as the main barrier to improving their situation and cementing their role in the community and society more generally. E-Romnja has a saliently political agenda. In order to create an enabling framework of action, the organization's activists engage extensively with the grassroots communities that they consider not only as the location of genuine gender politics, but also as sources of political knowledge for domestic and international actions. All this serves to generate alterity to the former configurations of movement politics between the wider women's and Romani movement in both Romanian and transnational settings.

E-Romnja is also engaged in high-level and impactful advocacy work, thanks to its capacities in political communication, knowledge of the policy process and agendas, and a rich repertoire of social movement mobilization. This advocacy activity also diverges from the duality of gender and ethnicity axes utilized in Romani women's earlier intersectional political activism. E-Romnja activists pay increasing attention to the precarity of various poorly educated, often rural groups of people, but also to suburban groups who face difficult labour market conditions or are excluded from work, and often live in housing poverty or quasi-homelessness. This focus on social injustice connects E-Romnja activists with social movement actors who have identified new lines of solidarity in terms of class, but also with those who have focused on structural conditions of vulnerability through fluid identity constructions. Despite the unsettled boundaries of such new lines of solidarity, the master frame of activist engagement is unambiguous: it is 'groupness' in the making, concomitant to the domestic responses (or lack of them) to neoliberal capitalism and the 2008 economic and financial crisis, and to post-crisis policies in particular. In this emerging activist agenda, the overlap between housing poverty and exclusion patterns affecting the Roma are obvious, but the connection between gender inequalities and housing poverty remains less pronounced. This is where E-Romnja has found an important domain it can enter, and where it can articulate its social justice agenda from within the diverse perspectives of Romani women. This substantive repositioning of Romani women's struggles is taking place while the wider gender equality mechanisms in CEE are tangibly weakening, and the political support for Roma inclusion is becoming increasingly fragile.

The other high-level advocacy track along which Romani women are becoming not only partners at the table of equality politics but also civil society opinion-makers, is gender-based violence. This is a field in which women's groups often tend to overcome their differences and disagreements. More closely, domestic violence and sexual harassment are problems on which women's groups often cooperate, especially given the current conditions of backsliding in various equality policy domains in Europe and a conspicuous political resistance to furthering the Istanbul Convention. I briefly portray three written statements that discuss violence against women, composed with the involvement of Romani women's groups: a transnational public statement by Romani feminists, a joint civil society shadow report by Romanian human and women's rights groups, and a research report backed by women's rights groups.

On the occasion of a 2015 event in the European Parliament, ten Romani women activists with an international profile addressed the issue of violence against Romani women and girls by referring to the main related international conventions.[8] In their statement, these activists announced their participation in the major transnational '16 Days of Activism against Gender-Based Violence Campaign' in search of justice for Romani women, and girls as well. They revealed that different forms of violence against Romani women are deeply rooted in patriarchal relations and antigypsyism. Highlighting the distinctive forms of violence against Romani women ranging from silent ignorance to forced sterilizations, they also referred to the differential impact of violence on Romani women according to age, sexuality, social status, class and religion. The document also stresses that femicide, forced marriage and teenage pregnancies – still prevalent in some communities – should never be justified by culture and/or religion. Its broadest political claim is that living without violence should be a basic human right. In their statement, activists understand violence through structural intersectionality is interwoven with a transformative and non-competitive political intersectionality, in which social justice is pursued through pedagogical claims to power holders, both in social movements and in wider political and policy arenas. This strategic act resonates with what Mary Bernstein calls 'identity for education' (1997). Cooperation across groupness is made possible by endorsing a particular hierarchy of values – and freedom from violence is a right that cannot be compromised in any circumstances. To this end, educators must be visible through high-level statements (such as this one), and via European political opinion-making and discourse-setting bodies.

In 2017, three civil society organizations prepared a shadow report to the Romanian government's regular CEDAW report. The shadow report was jointly initiated by the E-Romnja Association, the Coalition for Gender Equality, and the Network for Preventing and Combating Violence against Women. It discusses topics covered by the CEDAW articles from the period 2009–16. It not only offers a separate chapter dedicated to Romani women's equality matters, but pays attention to the Romani women's perspective in other sections too. One of the report's main conclusions is that women's rights are ignored in all subgroups of society. Romani women are absent both from the national strategy for gender equality and the national strategy for Roma inclusion. The latter does not include specific measures to achieve gender equality, whereas the national strategy for gender equality is silent about ethnic groups and disabled or LGBTQI+ citizens. A large part of the section devoted to Romani women deals with partnership and domestic violence, and victim protection – that is, essential issues of gender-based violence in any social settings. The report unambiguously makes the problem of early marriage secondary to domestic violence, considering it a form of patriarchal injustice common to all women in society. The production of this report is a significant act of collaborative intersectionality based on shared beliefs in, and positions on, gender equality-related agendas. Whereas a decade ago, alternative or separate shadow reporting was the most visible method to draw attention to Romani women's agendas, joint reporting by groups of Romani and non-Romani women now represents a new and transformative kind of cooperation in the larger social movements within which they operate. In the context of the current chapter, I cannot provide a detailed explanation for this move, but the rapidly coalescing anti-gender equality voices and attacks in Europe and beyond (Kuhar and Paternotte 2017) can certainly be seen as a major political condition for novel intersectional political dynamics. The disempowerment of the mainstream women's movement could be another plausible assumption, although there are few signs that Romanian mainstream feminist groups are significantly weakening.

The third recent and powerful statement is included in a research report entitled 'Phenja/ Sisterhood: Violence Against Women Has No Color' (Vrăbiescu 2015). The research was conducted with the active participation of a human rights and women's group coalition, including E-Romnja. The report uncovers perceptions of the causes and consequences of gender-based violence among women in Romania, and the experiences of public authorities assigned to handle the problem and support the victims. Based on investigations in Romania, and comparing Romani and non-Romani women's accounts, the findings refute some commonly held 'facts'. For example, Romani women are more vocal than non-Romani women about their experiences of violence, both with the researchers and in their social interactions. A less surprising finding is that non-Romani women believe that violence is more common in Romani than in non-Romani families, overstating the problem as ethnically defined and distancing it from their own environment. Most importantly, the report reveals that the dominant relations of dependency are generally shared across society, and that these lead both Romani and non-Romani women to not report their suffering, and only to ask for external help as a last resort. The report can be seen as the result of a powerful alliance within the women's movement, and speaks for the shared experiences of violence, driven and perpetuated by patriarchal power relations. The overarching political message evokes practices of 'sisterhood' enacted by revealing both difference and similarities in the possibilities for escaping and avoiding violence in the lives of Romani and non-Romani women.

Conclusions

In this chapter, I have shown that fundamental transformations have occurred in the position, operation and recognition of Romani women's activism throughout the 2010s. Reports from Romani women addressing early marriage practices in Romani families have challenged both the silence regarding Romani women in the mainstream women's movement and the frequent resistance to gender equality politics within the broader Romani movement. In the European political arenas, the wider women's movements have made decisive, although not yet fully transformative steps to opening up towards intersectional politics and more inclusive agenda-setting for gender equality. Leading voices in the transnational fora of the Romani movement showed first reluctance, and then accommodation regarding the claims of Romani women. Most importantly, in recent years, Romani women activists have participated and also initiated transformative cross-categorical politics. The grounds on which they have built alliances range from the notion of multiple dispossessions to various manifestations and forms of gender-based violence. The approach of multiple dispossession widens the scope of cross-categorical politics by lacing together the fights against racism, sexism, ageism, class-based exclusion and their intersections in conditions of precarity. Addressing gender-based violence sharpens an equality agenda that – though dwelling on the specific power regime of gender – challenges violence-inducing patriarchy in its various manifestations. In these actions, the distinctive experiences of Romani women are reconsidered in relational terms, and inspire the construction of novel platforms for social movements.

All this suggests that Romani women who act in accordance with relational identity configurations and social justice agendas have addressed and advocated for strategies of *transformative anti-essentialism*, which are increasingly replacing the intersectional reasoning and punctuated strategic essentialism that inspired them in the recent past. The new movement and activist alliances have been forged not despite, but precisely because of and thanks to earlier efforts to reveal and demonstrate the intersectional distinctiveness of Romani women's experience. Oprea's earlier observation that feminist and antiracist politics in Europe are two separate struggles might still be legitimate, but Romani feminists do not seem to 'wind up in a separate, isolated sphere fighting on their own' (Oprea 2012: 18). One cannot yet know whether this will be an enduring configuration, but the social movement landscape in CEE looks quite different from what it was ten years ago. It endorses Verloo's comparative observation that social movement struggles for equality enjoy better chances for advancement when alliances across causes and communities enact a composite domain and entertain fluid identities.

Finally, the new alliances established by Romani women are not the only change in the wider context of Romani politics. Peter Vermeersch (2017: 10) and Huub van Baar and Peter Vermeersch together (2017: 133–34) reveal how young Romani activists provide living evidence of the fluidity of group boundaries that challenges entrenched associations between Romani identity and certain social problems. Anna Mirga-Kruszelnicka (2018) portrays the drives and practices of cross-categorical politics and alliance-building in the contemporary bottom-up Roma youth movement. This chapter resonates with a growing body of literature on various groups and multiple identity formations among Romani activists who seek sustained relations of solidarity by not giving up Romani empowerment goals. They revisit earlier identity claims and social justice concepts, and Romani women are playing pivotal and brave roles in this transformation.

Violetta Zentai is Research Fellow and Co-director of the Center for Policy Studies, and faculty member of the School of Public Policy and the Department of Sociology and Social Anthropology at the Central European University in Budapest, Hungary. Her research focuses on ethnic and gender inequalities, post-socialist capitalist transformations, political and policy debates on social inclusion and pro-equality civil society formations. She has also worked as expert with the Open Society Foundations for two decades on initiatives related to democratic local governance, equality mainstreaming and rights-based development. She is a co-editor of *The Romani Women's Movement: Struggles and Debates in Central and Eastern Europe* (Routledge, 2019, with Angéla Kóczé, Jelena Jovanović and Enikő Vincze) and of *Faces and Causes of Roma Marginalization in Local Contexts*

(Center for Policy Studies, Central European University, 2014, with Júlia Szalai).

Notes

The author is grateful to the editors of the volume for their thorough editing and sensitive support in crafting this chapter.

1. The notion of modernization has been part of the policy and political vocabulary of Amalipe. They consistently and vocally address the marginalization that some Romani communities face, not only due to oppression or negligence of the mainstream, but also due to their traditional values and practices.
2. An EC 6th framework-supported project, which identifies itself as follows: 'The main objective of EUROSPHERE is to create innovative perspectives on the European public spheres and to identify the conditions that enable or undermine the articulation of inclusive democratic European Public Spheres'. Retrieved 10 October 2018 from https://eurosphere.w.uib.no/.
3. Sophie Jacquot and Tommaso Vitale (2014) offer a persuasive account of two European umbrella organizations representing two major equality groups: the European Women's Lobby (EWL) and the European Roma and Travellers Forum (ERTF). In their comparative approach, EWL pursues advocacy framing based on the idea that women constitute an 'exceptional', in the literal sense 'incomparable', quality and grouping in society. This position makes EWL reluctant to embrace intersectionality politics. The inquiry makes other important proposals regarding the diverging strategic paths that the two organizations follow in European equality politics.
4. I use the term 'Romani movement' in the singular in cognizance of that it denotes a rich and dynamically changing plurality of multi-scalar collective activities.
5. As the Decade Secretariat's website has been terminated with no information on archiving efforts, the electronic version of the 2012–13 civil society reports have been uploaded to the Civil Monitor Project, coordinated by the Center for Policy Studies at the Central European University, see: https://cps.ceu.edu/roma-civil-monitor-civil-society-monitoring-reports (retrieved 2 November 2018).
6. For example, woman's rights groups are debating among themselves if the problem of human trafficking should be seen though the primacy of gender equality among the many oppressive mechanisms. Even more explosive is the debate on prostitution, more particularly on understanding the significance of coercion versus choice, and on policy visions promoting the prohibition or regulation of prostitution.
7. In Cluj, Vincze is one of the key activists coordinating the actions of citizens and civil society against evictions and housing poverty. Through the Social Housing NOW, the Women's March and other actions, activists have connected different forms of violence, hierarchy of citizenship and differential social policy in a variety of political actions with diverse social movement means. Romani and non-Romani feminists,

housing activists and Romani civil society actors team up with artists and scholars in addressing both local and domestic policymakers by issuing regular appeals to local citizens. The alliance laces together antiracist, anti-poverty and anti-patriarchy social justice framing for action. See their Facebook page: https://www.facebook.com/CasiSocialeACUM/ (retrieved 2 November 2018).

8. The event 'Forwarding the Positions of Roma Women in Politics – Romnia Feminism in the Making' was held at the European Parliament in Brussels on 18–19 November 2015, and gathered eleven Romani women feminists supported by the Feminist Initiative and the S&D Group of the European Parliament. See: http://e-romnja.ro/e-romnja/publicstatement%20.html (retrieved 2 November 2018).

References

Amalipe Center for Interethnic Dialogue and Tolerance. 2011. *Preventing Early Marriages*. Veliko Tarnovo.

Balogh, L., and A. Kóczé. 2011. 'Roma Women in Europe, Current Issues in Europe Regarding the Social and Political Inclusion of Romani Women'. Policy paper issued for the 'Roma Women in Focus' conference, Budapest, 7 April 2011, organized by Női Érdek, European Women's Lobby, Nemzeti Civil Alapprogram.

Beck, S., and A. Ivasiuc (eds). 2018. *Roma Activism: Reimagining Power and Knowledge*. New York: Berghahn Books.

Bernstein, M. 1997. 'Celebration and Suppression: The Strategic Uses of Identity by the Lesbian and Gay Movement', *American Journal of Sociology* 103: 531–65.

Bíró, A., et al. (eds). 2013. *From Victimhood to Citizenship: A Debate*. Budapest: Pakiv European Roma Fund.

Bițu, N. 1999. *The Situation of Roma/Gypsy Women in Europe*. Strasbourg: Council of Europe.

Bițu, N., and C. Morteanu. 2010. 'The Case of Early Marriages within Roma Communities in Romania: Are the Rights of the Child Negotiable?' Bucharest: Romani CRISS.

Civil Society Monitoring Reports. 2012–2013. Budapest. Retrieved 10 October 2018 from https://cps.ceu.edu/roma-civil-monitor-civil-society-monitoring-reports.

Crenshaw, K. 1991. 'Mapping the Margins: Intersectionality, Identity Politics and Violence Against Women of Colour', *Stanford Law Review* 43(6): 1241–99.

European Roma Rights Centre (ERRC). 2007. 'Written Comments of the European Roma Rights Centre Concerning Hungary for Consideration by the United Nations Committee on the Elimination of Discrimination against Women at its 39th Session'. Budapest.

European Women's Lobby (EWL). 2012. 'Tackling Multiple Discrimination of Romani and Traveller Women: A Crucial Factor for the Successful Implementation of the National Roma Integration Strategies'. Position Paper. Retrieved 10 October 2018 from https://www.womenlobby.org/Position-Paper-Tackling-multiple-discrimination-of-Romani-and-Traveller-Women-a?lang=en.

Gheorghe, C., and h.arta Group. 2010. *Privește-mă așa cum sunt: Cuvinte și imagini ale femeilor rome* [See Me As I Am: Words and Images of Roma Women]. Bucharest: American Cultural Center.

Gheorghe, C. 2016. 'Editorial: Envisioning Roma Feminism', *Analize: Journal of Gender and Feminist Studies* 7: 15–18.

Gheorghe, C., L. Mark and E. Vincze. 2019. 'Towards an Anti-Racist Feminism for Social Justice in Romania', in A. Kóczé et al. (eds), *The Romani Women's Movement: Struggles and Debates in Central and Eastern Europe*. London: Routledge, pp. 111–34.

Izsák, R. 2008. *The European Romani Women's Movement: International Roma Women's Network*. Toronto: AWID.

Jacquot, S., and T. Vitale. 2014. 'Law as a Weapon of the Weak? A Comparative Analysis of Legal Mobilization by Roma and Women's Groups at the European Level', *Journal of European Public Policy* 21(4): 587–604.

Jovanović, J. 2015. 'Challenges to Preliminary Identification of "Victims" of Forced Marriage and Forced Begging in Serbia: Recommendations to Anti-Trafficking Policy Actors'. Policy Brief. Budapest: Central European University. Retrieved 10 October 2018 from https://cps.ceu.edu/publications/policy-briefs/romani-victims-of-trafficking.

Jovanović, J., A. Kóczé and L. Balogh. 2015. 'Intersections of Gender, Ethnicity and Class: History and Future of the Romani Women's Movement'. Working Paper. Budapest: Friedrich-Ebert-Stiftung. Retrieved 10 October 2018 from: https://cps.ceu.edu/sites/cps.ceu.edu/files/fes-cps-working-paper-roma-women-gender-politics-2015.pdf.

Kóczé, A. 2009. 'The Limits of Rights-based Discourse in Romani Women's Activism: The Gender Dimension in Romani Politics', in N. Sigona and N. Trehan (eds), *Romani Politics in Contemporary Europe*. New York: Palgrave Macmillan, pp. 135–52.

———. 2011. 'Gender, Ethnicity and Class: Exposing Contemporary Romani Women's Issues and Political Activism'. PhD dissertation. Budapest: Central European University.

Kóczé, A., et al. (eds). 2019. *The Romani Women's Movement: Struggles and Debates in Central and Eastern Europe*. London: Routledge.

Krizsán, A., and V. Zentai. 2012. 'Intersectionality: Whose Concern? Institutional Responses to Intersectionality in Central and Eastern European Members States of the EU', in J. Squires, A. Krizsán and H. Skeje (eds), *Institutionalizing Intersectionality*. New York: Palgrave Macmillan, pp. 179–208.

Kuhar, R., and D. Paternotte (eds). 2017. *Anti-Gender Campaigns in Europe Mobilizing against Equality*. Lanham, MD: Rowman & Littlefield.

Lamoreux, N. 2011. 'Bridging the Gap: Romani Women, Transnational Advocacy Networks and Dismantling Roma Discrimination in Europe'. MA thesis. New York: New York University.

Mark, L., and E. Vincze. 2011. 'Conclusions of the International Conference "Romani Women for Equal Opportunities"'. Timişoara, 20 June – 2 July. Retrieved 20 October 2018 from http://www.desire-ro.eu/wp-content/uploads/conclusions-conference-romani-women-for-equal-opportunities-2011.pdf.

Matache, M. 2009. 'Gender Equality, Sense of Belonging, Both?' *Nevi Sara Kali* 1(1): 45–59.

McGarry, A. 2010. *Who Speaks for Roma? Political Representation of a Transnational Minority Community*. London: Continuum.

McGarry, A., and J. Jasper (eds). 2015. *The Identity Dilemma: Social Movements and Collective Identity*. Philadelphia, PA: Temple University Press.

Mirga-Kruszelnicka, A. 2018. '"Be Young, Be Roma": Modern Roma Youth Activism in the Current Panorama of Romani Affairs', in S. Beck and A. Ivasiuc (eds), *Roma Activism: Reimagining Power and Knowledge*. New York: Berhghan Books, pp. 197–215.

Mokre, M., and B. Siim. 2013. 'Negotiating Equality and Diversity across Europe: Multiculturalism/Migration, Citizenship and Social Justice'. RECODE Online Working Paper No. 31. Retrieved 10 October 2018 from http://www.recode.info/wp-content/uploads/2014/01/Final-RECODE-31-Mokre-and-Siim_Final_fin.pdf.

Open Society Institute. 2003. 'A Place at the Policy Table: Report on the Roma Women's Forum Budapest, Hungary, 2003'. Network Women's Program. Retrieved 29 September 2018 from https://www.opensocietyfoundations.org/sites/default/files/roma_womens_finalreport.pdf.

Oprea, A. 2004. 'Re-envisioning Social Justice from the Ground Up: Including the Experiences of Romani Women', *Essex Human Rights Review* 1(1): 29–39.

———. 2012. 'Romani Feminism in Reactionary Times', *Signs: Journal of Women in Culture and Society* 31(1): 11–21.

Polletta, F., and J. Jasper. 2001. 'Collective Identity and Social Movements', *Annual Review of Sociology* 27: 283–305.

Popa, R. 2009. 'Meanings and Uses of Intersectionality', *Nevi Sara Kali* 1: 70–80.

Schultz, D. 2005. 'An Intersectional Feminism of Their Own: Creating European Romani Women's Activism', *Journal for Politics, Gender and Culture* 4(8/9): 243–77.

Sigona, N., and N. Trehan (eds). 2009. *Romani Politics in Contemporary Europe: Poverty, Ethnic Mobilization and the Neoliberal Order*. New York: Palgrave Macmillan.

van Baar, H. 2012. 'Toward a Politics of Representation beyond Hegemonic Neoliberalism: The European Romani Movement Revisited', *Citizenship Studies* 16(2): 285–94.

van Baar, H., and P. Vermeersch. 2017. 'The Limits of Operational Representations: "Ways of Seeing Roma" beyond the Recognition–Redistribution Paradigm', *Intersections* 3(4): 120–39.

Verloo, M. 2013. 'Intersectional and Cross-movement Politics and Policies: Reflections on Current Practices and Debates', *Signs: Journal of Women in Culture and Society* 38(4): 893–915.

Vermeersch, P. 2006. *The Romani Movement: Minority Politics and Ethnic Mobilization in Contemporary Central Europe*. Oxford: Berghahn Books.

———. 2017. 'Romani Mobilization and Participation: Obstacles and Opportunities', in J. Bhabha, A. Mirga and M. Matache (eds), *Realizing Roma Rights*. Philadelphia: University of Pennsylvania Press, pp. 200–13.

Vincze, E. 2010. 'Culture, Rights and Moral Entitlements', *Nevi Sara Kali* 2: 9–28.

———. 2014. 'The Racialisation of Roma in the "New" Europe and the Political Potential of Romani Women', *European Journal of Women's Studies* 21(4): 435–42.

Vrăbiescu, I. 2015. 'Phenja/Sisterhood: Violence Against Women Has No Color'. Retrieved 10 October 2018 from http://centrulfilia.ro/new/wp-content/uploads/2015/03/Raport-Phenja-I.pdf.

Williams, F. 2003. 'Contesting "Race" and Gender in the European Union: A Multi-layered Recognition Struggle for Voice and Visibility' in B. Hobson (ed.) *Recognition Struggles and Social Movement*. Cambridge: Cambridge University Press, pp. 121–44.

Young, I.M. 1989. 'Polity and Group Difference: A Critique of the Ideal of Universal Citizenship', *Ethics* 99(2): 250–74.

PART V

❀ ❀ ❀

ART AND CULTURE

CHAPTER 9

❋ ❋ ❋

Ethnicity Unbound
Conundrums of Culture in Representations of Roma

Carol Silverman

On the ground, Roma seem to be a myriad collection of subgroups that differ in language, custom and regional history. Yet all Roma have faced and continue to face discrimination. This truism provides the legitimate backbone of the Roma human rights struggle. How does culture relate to how Roma are represented by those who seek to demonize, defend or document them? This chapter interrogates current debates about ethnicity regarding the representation of Roma in order to explore the 'conundrums of Romani culture'. Several recent publications have addressed how the label/category 'Roma' may be used – on the one hand, to essentialize a diverse group of people, but on the other, to serve as an umbrella term for political mobilization (Stewart 2011, 2012, 2013; Vermeersch 2012, 2016; Tremlett and McGarry 2013; Tremlett, McGarry and Agarin 2014; Surdu 2016; McGarry 2017). The 'difference' or 'essentialism' conundrum unmasks the tension between the danger of reifying Roma culture and the need to define it for both non-Roma and Roma.

Variously positioned actors have used culture to justify difference in the service of divergent goals. A group of 'traits' are often listed to define Roma: for example, language, nomadism, kinship, taboos, early marriage, fortune-telling, begging and music. These traits may be employed to either criticize or valorize Roma. For example, xenophobes argue for the exclusion or even deportation of Roma due to their alien, primitive and foreign culture; right-wing populists argue for surveillance of Roma, owing to their alleged criminality, begging and early marriage. Conversely, positive trait lists, such as those that require speaking the Romani language, or performing Romani arts such as music, can also be very dangerous; they are often prescriptive – individuals and groups are measured against them in terms of authenticity and legitimacy, and those who lack these may be excluded from the category of Roma. On the other hand, a certain amount of essentializing is necessary for pride, politics, advocacy, publicity and policy. In short, for identity politics, funding, music marketing and legal battles, Roma sometimes need to be perceived as a bounded, distinct group. Postcolonial critic Gayatri Spivak (1987) termed this tension 'strategic essentialism', although she later repudiated how the term was misused to support a reductionist kind of essentialism.

Advocates, researchers and Roma themselves may essentialize for various reasons. Scholars, activists, lawyers and policymakers – both Roma and non-Roma – situationally use cultural arguments for various political and emancipatory goals. Advocates for political emancipation must strategically define Roma as a disenfranchised group; ethnographers by profession emphasize difference; world music marketers capitalize on exoticism; and Roma themselves may emphasize difference, either because it is a discourse of pride and alliance or because they have internally adopted how outside experts define them (Surdu 2016). Thus, ironically, both pro- and anti-human rights discourses may sometimes appear similar (Leggio 2017). Thus, it is important to investigate who is defining Roma culture and for what purpose. As Peter Vermeersch has suggested: 'A serious analysis should not simply focus on specific forms of lifestyle, traditions, descent, language use and so forth; it should ask why and in what social and political circumstances such phenomenon have been generally accepted as markers of Romani identity' (Vermeersch 2006: 3). I illustrate the thorny role of culture by delving into the social theory literature about culture and ethnicity, and via three contrasting empirical examples. First, I examine the cultural demonization of Romanian Roma migrants to the United States via a July 2017 media frenzy; second, I reflexively examine my legal advocacy role in an Oregon court case, in which my defence of Kalderash Roma required the demonstration of cultural difference; and third, I examine an Italian case where begging was claimed as a Romani cultural practice. I suggest that culture and tradition are not static givens, but rather tools in representational projects. Like postcolonial critics Arif Dirlik, Stuart Hall and Paul Gilroy, I do not dismiss Romani claims to identity and culture as mere essentialisms, but prefer to analyse them as performative works in progress, in a hierarchical political playing field.

Debating Culture

How can we situate Roma in the social theory literature on ethnicity, essentialism and cultural representation, so that they can no longer be seen as isolated, exotic or 'unique'? Nodding towards uniqueness, Michael Stewart points out that the phenomenon of 'Gypsy Persistence' for over seven hundred years is a 'fascinating sociological puzzle'. He explains:

> Gypsies live dispersed among majority populations who, at least in the modern era ... tend to despise them; they are always more or less familiar, indeed intimate, with the cultural world around them and yet they reproduce their communities with apparent ease; and they do so without shared religion, without any form of ritual or political leadership, and without overarching or underpinning political organization. (Stewart 2013: 418)

Even if one disagrees with Stewart's list of absent cultural features, we can agree that the persistence of 'Romani-ness' for centuries is notable. However, is Romani-ness about culture or identity? If Roma still feel Romani in some core way – even without community – this might flag identity; their lived experience may have little to do with culture. Furthermore, they may inhabit their Romani identity position either in spite of or because of marginalization. In addition, identities as well as cultures are multiple and are continually changing.

To explain 'Gypsy Persistence', Stewart outlines 'three types of explanation' that scholars have offered:

> [H]istorical explanations, which focus on the distinct origins of Gypsy populations and treat them in effect as an unassimilated foreign ethnic group with a distinct ethos; structural explanations, which locate the persistence of Gypsy populations in the way they have occupied particular niches within the changing European division of labour ... and finally, culturalist explanations, which consider the internal coherence of Gypsy or Romany value systems in a self-declared holistic approach. (Stewart 2013: 418)

Taking a historical step back, I note that culture as the cornerstone of social anthropology was defined by Edward Tylor in 1871 as a 'complex whole which includes knowledge, belief, arts, morals, law, customs, and any other capabilities and habits acquired by man as a member of society' (Tylor 1871: 1). In Tylor's definition, culture, although labelled a 'whole', is actually treated as a list of elements that chart the supposed 'natural' progress of humankind from barbarism to civilization. Civilization meant 'Western civilization', the apex of evolution. In contrast, anthropology today rejects this cultural evolutionary scheme in favour of a Boasian cultural relativism.

Kwame Appiah has cogently dismantled the term 'Western civilization', plucking it from its lofty height:

> It imagines western culture as the expression of an essence – a something – which has been passed from hand to hand on its historic journey. The pitfalls of this sort of essentialism are evident in a wide range of cases. Whether you are discussing religion, nationality, race or culture, people have supposed that an identity that survives through time and space must be propelled by some potent common essence. But that is simply a mistake. (Appiah 2017)

Appiah points out that all cultures have changed; there is no 'golden nugget' of Western culture. However, remnants of the 'civilization' concept pervade racist discourses about Roma. In fact, Roma are damned from several angles. Sometimes, they are accused of not having culture, meaning they are not 'civilized'. But simultaneously their culture is labelled 'backward' and then recruited as a cause of their marginality (blaming the victim). Either they have no culture, or they have flawed culture. Their culture is neither seen in its broad multiplicity, not historicized, nor appreciated as an integral part of European history. Mihai Surdu thus criticizes anthropological approaches that are 'plagued by cultural determinism' (2016: 92), and which replaced biological determinism rooted in Indian origins.

Roma are either overdetermined by culture – for instance, Romophobes blame Romani culture for their marginalization – or underdetermined by culture – that is, they do not have any common characteristics, and their identity is a result of marginalization. Stewart's 'structural explanations' are allied with marginalization because they attribute the persistence of Roma to their particular economic niches. Jean-Pierre Liégeois and Nicolae Gheorghe have expressed this dilemma of lack of culture:

> Roma/Gypsies are thought to have no linguistic, cultural or ethnic roots. They are instead a 'social problem' requiring 'rehabilitation' and 'reintegration', who can – and must – be brought back into the fold of 'society' . . . It is this vision [that] lies behind the assumed duty . . . of active intervention, and gives rise to measures of 'assistance' opening up the way for full-scale drives aimed at 'reintegration' and 'rehabilitation'. These flawed analyses encourage a focus on the consequences of a given situation (such as health problems, poverty, illiteracy, etc.), rather than on their root causes (rejection, inappropriate provision, etc.). (Liégeois and Gheorghe 1995: 13)

We must remember that it is too easy to explain all differences through culture when, in fact, there are economic and political reasons for different life situations. Writing about Muslims, Mahmood Mamdani labels this '"culture talk", the predilection to define cultures according to their presumed "essential" characteristics, especially as regards politics' (Mamdani 2002: 766). This leads to the idea that there is something inherent in a group's culture that explains away inequalities. Roma are seen to be 'trapped' by their culture. In Mamdani's terms, they do not 'make' culture, but rather 'conform' to it: 'Their culture seems to have no history, no politics, and no debates. It seems just to have petrified into a lifeless custom. Even more, these people seem incapable of transforming their culture' (ibid.: 767). Vermeersch similarly writes: '[F]rom there it is a small step to see such marginality and exclusion simply as a symptom of Romani culture and identity, and not as a problem of inequality and socioeconomic polarization. From deprived co-citizens the Roma are turned into cultural deviants' (Vermeersch 2012: 1208). This serves to codify 'a narrative that highlights the distance between Roma and other groups of citizens, and portrays both Roma and non-Roma as homogenous bounded camps' (ibid.: 1205). Surdu points out that the 'standardization of Romani identity' through classification has a looping effect, so that 'Roma internalize these scientifically constructed stereotypes' (Surdu 2016: 6).

For many years, anthropologists have used culture as the key to defining that which was shared; this led to the assumption that groups were bounded into distinct units, known as 'cultures'. One reason for this parcelization is that culture (and ethnicity) became a proxy for race, as race became a discredited concept. Yet we should note that race did not disappear: biological racism often morphed into cultural racism. Another reason is that the concept of bounded units is derived from European nationalism, where the nation/state supposedly encloses a unified culture. This is not true, of course, but the tie between nation and culture runs deep, all the way from Herder's eighteenth-century 'romantic nationalism' to today's populist parties.

As Stewart writes: 'Our notions of "culture", of "ethnic group" or "people" are so utterly rooted in the schemas derived from ... nation states (which are, or at least strive to be, homogenous, neatly bounded states) that Romany communities appear as anomalies' (Stewart 2011: 2). Thus, essentialist categories contrast one cultural group with another; and difference becomes paradigmatic. Much of the older work on Roma by amateur non-Romani 'folkorists', such as George Borrow, Walter Starkie and Dora Yates, emphasized difference. These works were plagued by a cultural determinism that chronicled the minutiae of subgroup customs, language, trades and costume, leading to objectification and exoticism.

As Lila Abu-Lughod points out:

> Culture is the essential tool for making other ... Anthropological discourse gives cultural difference ... the air of the self-evident. In this regard, the concept of culture operates much like its predecessor – race ... The most important of culture's advantages, however, is that it removes difference from the realm of the

natural and the innate. Whether conceived of as a set of behaviours, customs, traditions, rules, plans, recipes, instructions, or programs . . . culture is learned and can change. Despite its anti-essentialist intent, however, the culture concept retains some of the tendencies to freeze difference possessed by concepts like race. (Abu-Lughod 1991: 143–44)

Thus, current anthropological definitions of culture have moved away from reified lists towards complexity, such as in this definition: 'The system of shared beliefs, values, customs, behaviours, and artefacts that the members of society use to cope with their world and with one another, and that are transmitted from generation to generation through learning'.[1] This definition, used in some North American universities, emphasizes systems, symbols and sociality, rather than differences and boundaries.

Debating Ethnicity

Since the 1970s, ethnicity rather than culture has become a more hotly debated term among social theorists. The reasons for this are multiple: the rise of ethnic 'identity politics' in this decade; the presumption that many conflicts can primarily be explained by 'ethnic difference' (Brubaker 2004); and the need to replace the discredited concept of race. However, I do not want to lose sight of the power of culture: how can it be recruited for useful analysis of ethnicity, without reproducing stereotypes about Roma?

Many scholars have underlined the divide between primordial and constructivist concepts of Roma ethnicity (Stewart 2013; Surdu 2016; McGarry 2017). Primordial approaches to ethnicity (sometimes termed 'essentialist') assume there is a clearly bounded ethnic group with shared characteristics, often listed as history, language and culture; territory is omitted for Roma. Conversely, constructivist approaches emphasize the dynamic, shifting nature of ethnicity; ethnic groups are not self-evident but are produced by many variables, often economic and/or political. This approach resonates with the structural explanations of 'Gypsy persistence' that Stewart outlined and attributed to Judith Okely, Wim Willems and Leo Lucassen (Stewart 2013: 418).

Fredrik Barth (1969), the father of constructivism in ethnicity, treated it as an ascription that changes depending on context and history. He emphasized the boundary-making mechanisms between groups via symbols and traditions, not the cultural inventories they enclose. This conceptualization has enabled scholars to concentrate upon the situational nature of ethnicity.

Rogers Brubaker (2004) argues against ethnicity from a different angle, and claims that the idea of a unified group is a 'political fiction'. He rejects the use of identity-based groups as 'categories for social analysis', because of 'groupism', which he describes as follows:

> [This is] the tendency to take discrete, bounded groups as basic constituents of social life, chief protagonists of social conflicts, and fundamental units of social analysis. I mean the tendency to treat ethnic groups, nations, and races as substantial entities to which interests and agency can be attributed ... I mean the tendency to represent the social and cultural world as a multichrome mosaic of monochrome ethnic, racial, or cultural blocks. (Brubaker 2004: 8)

For Brubaker, 'ethnopolitical entrepreneurs ... may live "off" as well as "for" ethnicity ... By *invoking* groups, they seek to *evoke* them, summon them, call them into being. Their categories are *for doing* – designed to stir, summon, justify, mobilize, kindle, and energize' (ibid.: 10, italics in original). He claims that ethnic groups are better regarded as 'projects', often fashioned from the inside by political elites. Applied to Roma, Aidan McGarry also claims that 'political elites have proclaimed Roma nationhood as a distinct transnational nation sharing a common culture' (McGarry 2017: 104).

Surdu criticizes the essentialized depiction of Roma as a bounded ethnic group that is produced in policy by schemes of classification and measurement. He contrasts social theory scholarship, which tends to be constructivist, to policy about Roma, which is based on 'considering ethnicity as an objective and measurable fact' and thus quantifiable (Surdu 2016: 8–9). Vermeersch further explains that activists '[c]onstruct a particular sectional marginal identity that not only fails to give full expression to individual identity, but is usually also "stigmatized" in the sense that it is popularly associated with standard stereotypical images and negative characteristics' (Vermeersch 2005: 451).

Although Surdu does not claim Roma are a fiction, Andzrej Mirga criticized him by stating: '[A]s a Romani person, I object to being seen simply as an ethnic subject who is constructed by those in power' (Mirga 2018: 124). Surdu writes: 'I do not affirm that Roma do not exist but I assert that the Roma population exists as negative and oppositional [to non-Roma] construction made by dominant groups and self-internalized by those labelled as Roma' (Surdu 2016: 39). Yet for Mirga, Surdu has mistakenly exposed an empty centre, the dissolution of identity, the absence of shared sociality and culture. Surdu employs ample cultural phenomena to discuss definitions of and stigmatization of Roma (ibid.: 180–84), but he does not explicitly tackle the question of culture. He dissects not only racist media accounts discrediting Roma, but also World Bank reports seeking to ameliorate their conditions by showing that 'three frames' predominate: 'poverty as an overall Roma attribute, precarious living, and traditionalism' (ibid.: 4).

In critiquing essentialism, Surdu leaves us wondering what is left – what about Roma culture? Mirga faulted Surdu's book because the lived experiences (including language) of Roma themselves seem to be absent; it seemed to him that Surdu dissolved Romani identity (Mirga 2018: 124). Similarly, Stewart quotes Mirga as saying: '[Y]ou may not know who we are, but we do' (Stewart 2011: 2). Stewart expounds that, despite constructivism, ethnicity remains bounded:

> For academic scholars, 'ethnicity' tends to be used to mean 'linguistic and cultural group' – a group sharing a historically formed traditional culture; but in that sense, of course, there is no 'Roma ethnic group' . . . rather perhaps a community of communities – as activists like Mirga understand. (Ibid.: 4–5)

Indeed, Roma are sometimes defined as a rich mosaic of groups that distinguish among themselves culturally. The diversity of Romani groups is in part due to their diaspora; some Roma became sedentary while some are nomadic to varying degrees; some assimilated more than others linguistically and culturally; and all adopted the religious beliefs of their neighbours to some extent. In 2010, the European Commission defined 'Roma' as an 'umbrella term that includes groups of people who share similar cultural characteristics and a history of segregation in European societies' (quoted in Stewart 2011: 2). Gheorghe and Acton recognize this diversity:

> While East European administrators tend to look for the 'uniqueness' and unity of a people's culture as a prerequisite for promoting distinct cultural entities . . . the Romani people is presenting itself as a huge diaspora embracing five continents, sharing the citizenship of a multitude of states, while lacking a territory of its own. The Gypsy 'archipelago' is formed by a mosaic of various groups speaking both different dialects of Romani as an oral language and a variety of languages of the surrounding societies. The Romani communities share a number of religions . . . they maintain cultural boundaries not only between themselves and the surrounding environment, but also between various Romani groups themselves. (Gheorghe and Acton 2001: 55–56)

Similarly, Will Guy states that 'in view of the diversity of Romani experience, it would be more accurate to talk of a constellation of Romani cultures and . . . a cluster of varying and related identities rather than a homogeneous identity' (Guy 2001: 28).

In a Council of Europe document, Elena Marushiakova and Vesselin Popov emphasize that

> [East European Romani cultures have] developed through a long and complex process of continuous active interaction with the culture of their surrounding population. Due to the internal heterogeneity of the Romani communities and

the fact that they live scattered among the surrounding population in different countries and in different cultural and historic regions, the result is the presence of many diverse sub-variants. (Marushiakova and Popov n.d.: 1)

The authors conclude with a Barthian structural claim that boundaries define difference, which then determines groups:

> What has been argued above should by no means be considered as a bold statement that an ethnically specific Romani culture does not exist. [Rather,] the different cultural elements by themselves are not ethnically loaded but *become ethnically specific only when perceived as such by the respective communities* who consider them as markers distinguishing them from 'other' communities. (Ibid.: 8, emphasis added)

Their claim rejects both narrow constructivist as well as essentialist views, while trying to keep the boundary of cultural difference as a valid, although shifting, reference point.

To further recruit culture back into ethnicity, it is useful to consider how Craig Calhoun takes issue with Brubaker's critique of 'groupism', because it dismisses the social and the cultural: 'In his generally salutary critique of "groupism" . . . he both underestimates the importance of particular collectivities and . . . obscures the . . . importance of the social' (Calhoun 2003b: 558). Calhoun goes on to explain why culture matters in social relations:

> I think too much gets tossed out along with the genuinely specious notion that ethnicities, nations, or other social groups are internally homogeneous, sharply bounded, and self-subsistent. Specifically, I think Brubaker underestimates the constitutive role of culture and the ways in which the general phenomenon of human embeddedness in social relations . . . takes the specific form of embeddedness in particular collectivities. Culture plays a necessary role in making persons – that is, enabling biological humans to be psychological and sociological humans. (Ibid.: 559)

Here Calhoun underlines the constitutive nature of common culture in making experience understandable and, thus, meaningful, while pointing out that these very cultures as well as the processes that produce them are contingent and changing. He also underlines the collective symbolic power of common culture while realizing that the specifics, namely 'language, norms, beliefs, and tacit assumptions, should be unpacked' (ibid.: 559). Calhoun goes on to recruit Pierre Bourdieu's practice theory to stress how culture is constantly created but appears as 'natural and necessary' (ibid.: 559). He calls attention to both the social relational power of groups as well as their contingency: 'Ethnicity . . . is not merely an attribute of individuals, nor is it any specific attribute shared by all members of one set of people and no others. It is a commonality of understanding, access to the world, and mode of action that facilitates the construction of social relationships'. He stresses that 'people participate to varying degrees in ethnicity, rather than being simply in or out of a group'. Ethnicity is 'a relational phenomenon' that is 'reproduced in ways that bind people into certain relationships'. Moreover, just because it is not a 'substance ... does not mean it is not productive of groupness' (ibid.: 560). Calhoun further expounds on the operational power of ethnicity to accomplish practical action: '[W]hy ethnicity may feel binding may be not only an effect of social relations but itself part of the organization of practical action, and may predispose people to form and value groups – even if these are not perfectly bounded, internally homogenous' (ibid.: 567). He concludes that cultural solidarities do matter to communities: 'I argue also that an approach that starts with individuals and treats culture as contingent cannot do justice to the legitimate claims made on behalf of "communities", and the reasons why "thick attachments" to particular solidarities still matter – whether in the forms of nations, ethnicities, local communities, or religions' (Calhoun 2003a: 532).

For the Romani case, we can clearly see that 'there are a variety of stakes in ethnicity' (Calhoun 2003b: 567). On the one hand, the liability of being 'Gypsy' leads people either to conceal their Romani identity and pass as higher status ethnic groups, or to emphasize other aspects of their identity. On the other hand, people may highlight their Romani ethnicity when it is an asset, such in social welfare, legal cases, or as part of exoticism in the arts. Jean and John Comaroff analyse the construction of the exoticized other: '[I]n the case of ethnic groups, [empowerment] is frankly associated with finding something essentially their own and theirs alone, something of their essence, to sell. In other words, a brand' (Comaroff and Comaroff 2009: 15). They state that 'identity is increasingly claimed as *property* by its living heirs, who proceed to manage it by palpably corporate means: to brand it and sell it, even to anthropologists, in self-consciously consumable forms' (ibid.: 29, italics in original). As Calhoun also observes, 'culture' does important identity work: 'Identities and solidarities, thus, are neither simply fixed nor simply fluid, but may be more fixed or more fluid under different circumstances ... They provide networks of mutual support, capacities for communication, frameworks of meaning' (Calhoun 2003a: 537).

Essentialist Dilemmas

Thus far I have explained how scholars have exposed the pitfalls of reifying the boundedness of ethnic groups and culture; indeed, these tactics can have disastrous consequences. Both media and policy representations often essentialize Roma via tropes of culture. Romani cultural 'difference' is regularly used to legitimize anti-Gypsy hostility (Tremlett 2009, 2014; Stewart 2012; McGarry 2017). On the other hand, I have shown that cultural symbols and practices accomplish important work in communities and are constantly adapting to changing economic, social and political contexts. For many Roma, language, rituals, work, religion, arts, costume and other cultural ways of being are the main reference points of sociality in their communities.

Now, I want to illuminate how essentializing becomes strategic. To redress current and historical abuses of Roma, we need a sense of what 'Romani' is. As Michael Herzfeld points out, 'states AND citizens both depend on the semiotic illusion – that identity is consistent; they both create or constitute homogeneity and produce iconicities' (Herzfeld 1997: 31). Although Spivak later disavowed the term 'strategic essentialism', she did not disavow the concept: 'As to whether I have given up on it as a project, that is really a different idea ... I'm much more interested in seeing the differences among these so-called essences in various cultural inscriptions' (Spivak quoted in Danius, Jonsson and Spivak 1993: 35–36).

In responding to Spivak's call for attention to how essences are employed in cultural inscriptions, I claim that identity politics and recognition frameworks require strategic essentialism. African American scholars have bravely dealt with this issue. Feminist scholar bell hooks welcomes a critique of essentialism, but warns about its 'abuses':

> [T]his critique should not become a means to dismiss differences or an excuse for the ignoring of experience. It is often evoked in a manner which suggests that all the ways black people think of ourselves as 'different' from whites are really essentialist, and therefore without concrete grounding. This way of thinking threatens the very foundation that makes resistance to domination possible. (hooks 1990: 130)

hooks remind us of the irony that intellectuals have the luxury to repudiate essentialized identities, but that oppressed people on the ground are relegated to those exact essential categories and labels. Essentialism has been so demonized in social theory that we may be afraid to fruitfully employ it. In fact, perhaps, the concept of hybridity has become so fashionable because it seems like the perfect antidote to essentialism.[2] As postcolonial scholar Dirlik writes: 'It seems that any admission of identity, including the identity that may be necessary to any articulated form of collective political action, is open to charges of essentialism' (Dirlik 2000: 188; see also 1997).

Tremlett (2009, 2014) provides a cogent analysis of how notions of Roma homogeneity still creep into pro-Roma scholarship about heterogeneity. Taking her cue from British Cultural Studies, she quotes scholars such as Hall and Gilroy who point out that antiracist activists may be just as essentialist as anti-Roma xenophobes. Tremlett (2009) recommends using terms such as 'unfinished ethnicities', 'new ethnicities' and 'ethnicity at the margins' to open up debate on the idea of boundedness. I underline that grounded activists do not have the luxury to dispense with groups. Both hooks and Dirlik remind us of the irony that elite intellectuals have the luxury to repudiate essentialized identities. These intellectuals construct 'identities and histories almost at will in those "in-between" places that are immune to the burden of the past', whereas those who suffer 'the sentence of history' are supposedly too caught up in the past and are thus misguided in their collective claims (Dirlik 1997: 221). Those fighting inequality on the ground do not have the luxury of being abstract and debating hybridity.

Thus, we should analyse claims to collective identity as dynamic representational projects. Along these lines, Nicolae Gheorghe and Thomas Acton realize that the 'multiculturality' of Roma can be a drawback to political mobilization: '[I]t is still difficult to imagine how multiculturality and multiterritoriality could become the basis for the cultural affirmation and development of a people ... [who] strive to identify themselves ... in terms of unity and specificity' (Gheorghe and Acton 2001: 56). While Mirga and Gheorghe (1997) have suggested adopting the term 'transnational minority', other activists have used, for instance, the terminology 'ethnogenesis' (Guy 2001: 19) and 'nation' (International Romani Union 2001).

An example of strategic essentialism that has emanated from the Romani rights movement is the emergence of its national symbols. I use the world symbol here not to contest truth claims, but rather to indicate a constellation that is elevated for the larger group and to public meaning. These include a unifying label (Roma), a singular narrative of Indian origin often tied to Romani language, the Holocaust as a symbol of oppression, a flag and an anthem. Each is a trope that inscribes the legitimate historical place of Roma in the world; each corresponds to the dominant European tropes of defining the heritage of a singular nation. Thus, at the same time that Roma on the ground live according to diverse, nuanced and changing identity formations, activists have engaged in classic European essentialist nationalist symbol making (Silverman 2012: 47–51).

To illustrate the 'conundrums of culture' in conflict situations involving non-Roma, I present two empirical examples from my own experience: one involves condemning cultural difference and the other defending it, plus a third case from the literature that intertwines both. Essentialism can be recruited for both pro-Roma and anti-Roma projects; therefore, it should never be dismissed but rather thoroughly analysed.

Culture: Negative

It has been widely noted that historical stereotypes depict 'Gypsies' as culturally uncivilized: as criminal, rootless and dangerous by nature and upbringing. Ian Hancock (1987, 2002, 2010) has tirelessly exposed stereotypical images and discourse demonizing Roma both in the United States and Europe, in literature, visual arts, opera and other arts, as well as in the media. Theresa Catalano (2014) recently chronicled North American media reports about Roma, showing that they reinforce assumptions of thievery, deception and swindling, and I documented a century of pervasive media racial profiling of Roma in Oregon (Silverman 2017).

With the recent westward migration of Roma from Eastern Europe after the fall of socialism, the media in Western Europe and North America has often produced sensational accounts, and the discourse of 'invasion' has appeared. Both scholars (Castañeda 2014) and journalists have reported the hysteria of Germans with reference to the 'human tidal wave' (Landler 2004: 4) of incoming Roma. Moreover, Stewart (2012) and McGarry (2017) chronicle how the rise of populism has amplified fear and condemnation of Roma migrants. Stefan Benedik (2010), for example, analyses how the menacing migrant beggar complex had been produced in cultural terms via media images and discourse in Graz, Austria since 1989. He shows how the media first culturally differentiated beggars from locals, as poor and from the East (thus as 'others') and then ethnicized them all as Zigeuner/Roma (ibid.: 76). Two strands thus combine to vilify Roma: one, the historical accusation as criminal aliens, and two, the new accusation as bogus refugees.

My example is drawn from the American landscape and involves sensational July 2017 media accounts of Romanian Roma migrants in the rural western Pennsylvania town of California. Tucker Carlson of right-wing Fox News previewed his report as follows: 'a small town in Pennsylvania trying to cope with streets covered – pardon us now, but it's true – with human faeces and headless chickens after immigration officials settle dozens of Roma – you may call them 'gypsies' – in their town. Is the federal government failing its own citizens, or do they need to just grow up and start appreciating diversity?' (Wemple 2017).

Carlson's report centres on cultural dysfunction, exemplified in public defecation. Here are several excerpts:

> I have heard a lot of people mention ... public defecation ... There are a lot of news stories around ... going back a long time in the UK. And here where groups of Roma settle in a new community and then defecate on playgrounds or sidewalks or on their front steps. That seems to me a hostile act ... When you do that, you are saying we reject you and your mores ... But we can agree that when you come to Pennsylvania, you can't 'go' on the sidewalk or the playground

... do you think that we are secure enough with our own mores that we can just say, 'Hey, knock it off?' (*Fox News*, 17 July 2017)

When American Kalderash activist George Eli tried to clarify that these are unproven allegations and are unrepresentative of Roma, Carlson rebounded: 'There is nothing vague about it – there are photographs of it online. It is deeply offensive'. He continued to say that town residents had said that Roma 'have little regard for the law or for public decency ... They chop the heads off chickens and leave trash everywhere' (*Fox News*, 17 July 2017).

It appears that Carlson's story exaggerated one isolated incident reported by the *Pittsburgh Post-Gazette* on 14 July 2017 (Majors, Strasburg and Behrman 2017): 'When it comes to public defecation, there has been a "single incident of that"' which involved a 10-year-old child (Wemple 2017). Vito Dentino, a real estate broker who rents apartments to most of the forty Roma migrants said: 'I think people around here are just overreacting ... I think they are adjusting fine' (ibid.). The *Post-Gazette* story was actually more nuanced than the *Fox News* story, and stated that 'there have been no instances of violence or aggression, and the immigrants involved in minor infractions have been duly cited and [have] paid their fines' (Majors, Strasburg and Behrman 2017). It also explained that the Romanian Roma were processed for asylum through US Immigration and Customs Enforcement, and were released to live wherever they wanted as part of the government's Alternative to Detention programme. The *Post-Gazette* quoted Ali George, 24, from Bucharest, who said they were drawn to California 'by the same things that might attract anyone – a friendly, inexpensive place to live ... We left our country, not because we are poor', said a friend of Mr George. 'We left because of racism and we're seeking political asylum' (ibid.).

Note, however, how Carlson's report omits any sympathy, and leads listeners directly from issues of defecation/chicken slaughtering/trash to 'hostile acts'. Thus, cultural difference, rooted in supposed lack of 'civilization', is imbued with hostility; he implies locals may be in danger. Carlson then accuses Roma of refusing cultural assimilation. He uses phrases such as 'integration is not going well' and 'the group doesn't seem interested at all in integrating', and he recruits Romani history to 'prove' his assertion: 'This is a distinct ethnic group originally from the Indian subcontinent. This has been a distinct ethnic group for a thousand years that hasn't ... assimilated into the cultures [by] which it's been hosted. So why would we think it would assimilate in Pennsylvania?' (*Fox News*, 17 July 2017). Carlson thus raises themes also pervasive in European media reports about migrants: Roma are dangerous, alien, uncivilized, and lack the desire to integrate. Culture again is problematic. Roma have bad/primitive culture that they are unwilling to give up to become civilized locals.

Several journalists insightfully criticized the Carlson report (Wemple 2017; *Pittsburgh Post-Gazette*, editorial, 20 August 2017). Yu Hsi Lee (2017) linked the local anti-Roma discourse to wider anti-immigrant sentiment in rural towns; she wrote: 'Nearly 1,200 people have signed onto a petition called "End Housing of Illegal Immigrants in California", which in part argued that the government is paying "local figures" to "house illegal immigrants"'. Moreover, the scandal spurred Eli and other activists to travel to Pennsylvania for several activities to help to foster better communication between Roma and locals (Tony 2017). I too was interviewed about the Fox story by the Romanian newspaper *Adevarul*. I provided a history of Roma migration to the United States, pointed out that defecation incidents were undocumented, that the stereotypic defamation formulas had a long history, and the actual numbers (forty Roma out of seven thousand residents) belied any danger. I noted an ironic fact about Western Pennsylvanians demonizing East European Roma: many Western Pennsylvanians are descendants of East Europeans. They were hated and labelled 'uncivilized' by Anglos when they arrived between the 1880s and 1920s to work in the steel mills. But they brought with them their prejudices against Roma and anyone else who appears different, and these fears are now amplified in Trump's rural America; the current median family income in the town is $43,000 and 23 per cent live below the poverty line. Unfortunately, the *Adevarul* article only mentioned a few of my comments (Grigorescu 2017).

Culture: Positive – but Exotic and Essentialized

My second example illustrates the 'conundrums of culture' via a court case involving American Kalderash, in which my testimony required positive but essentialized views of difference to mount a 'cultural defence'. To provide some context: Kalderash, the largest Romani subgroup in the United States, migrated there from various parts of Eastern Europe about a hundred years ago. Oregon is home to a large Kalderash population (Silverman 2017) who have faced long-term racial profiling. I have done advocacy work with local families for several decades, and have tried to explain Kalderash culture without essentializing it. My goal in my work, both scholarly and activist, has been to represent Roma as being just as 'normal' as any other ethnic group. However, one case challenged these assumptions.[3]

An elderly Romani widow was about to lose her house because her daughter had been convicted of elder fraud, and the house was in the daughter's name. The daughter had admitted to the fraud, served a jail sentence, and repaid the money in question plus penalties. But the non-Roma who were defrauded filed a civil case to obtain all the daughter's assets. The house had been signed over to the daughter many years previously, when she was fourteen years old. My task as a witness was to prove that the family did not believe or understand that the daughter/felon actually owned the house because of their culture.

According to legal scholar Alison Renteln, a 'cultural defence' promotes fairness in the legal system by allowing judges to 'consider the cultural background of litigants in the disposition of cases' (Renteln 2004: 5). It is usually, but not exclusively, used in criminal defences. The lawyer's strategy was to have me prove that culture trumped the legality of the document of house ownership. My testimony depended on portraying Roma as being as different as possible from 'mainstream majority Americans'. This type of essentialism is something I have fought against my whole life. But in the courtroom it was our legal strategy to make Roma into a bounded exotic subculture.

I needed to underline 'difference' via inheritance patterns that would explain why parents would sign over their large house to their youngest daughter when she was only fourteen years old. I explained that Romani culture was patrilocal and patrilineal, and that elders were respected; because the family only had female children, the youngest daughter was obliged to respect her parents by ensuring their care as they aged. The house would be 'hers' for the purpose of their security, so they could live in it until they died. I also emphasized that the parents were illiterate and could not read the document they had signed, so they had not realized what 'transferring ownership' meant.

I couched all of this in how 'different' Roma were from Americans, something I do not usually promote. My evidence was the significance of the extended family, retention of Romani language, lack of intermarriage with non-Roma, and vitality of the taboo system. The *marhime* (taboo) system was especially intriguing to the judge, who asked many questions about it; I explained the gender division and the bodily division into clean upper and 'polluted' lower halves, and that Roma do not eat in non-Romani homes, do not sit on tables, and bring their own pillows to hotels and hospitals. As I was explaining how Roma sort clothing into upper and lower for washing, necessitating two washing machines (if a family can afford them), the elderly defendant interrupted that she had four washing machines (for male and female, upper and lower)!

This revelation seemed to cinch the case for the judge in terms of insularity, exoticism and cultural difference. He ruled in favour of allowing the defendant to keep her house via 'an equitable remedy'. In 2016, the case was appealed and again the judge ruled in favour of the Romani family, stating: 'These relatively unsophisticated people managed their lives very differently from those in modern American culture. They lived by different codes. But their codes clearly included honour'. Thus, by my constructing of Roma as bounded, insular, exotic and traditional, in contrast to modern, I was able to win this case.

Begging as Culture? Essentialism Contested

In the last twenty years, begging has emerged as a practice by which non-Roma culturally define, criminalize and regulate Roma. Negative images and discourse about Roma (especially migrant Roma) who aggressively beg are abundant in the media. Benedik pointed out that in Graz, Austria, media images and discourse constructed Roma as problems in gendered terms, emphasizing that women with children begged; this presumed exploitation of children implied 'that Romani culture lacks "healthy" or "normal" gender relations' (Benedik 2010: 76).

Ironically, in a 2008 Italian case, begging was used as a cultural defence. 'Several Italian judges, including the members of the Supreme Court, have defined begging with children as a "Roma cultural practice". In response, the Italian Parliament enacted law no. 94/2009, which severely represses the practice' (Ruggiu 2016: 31). Ruggiu describes the lawyer's argument in the defence of a Romani mother: 'It is always difficult to find whether there is abuse of authority by parents . . . This is particularly true for some ethnic communities *where begging is a traditional way of life deeply rooted in the culture and in the mentality of the people* . . . It is important to consider the real situations in order to avoid criminalizing *behaviours that are part of a group's cultural tradition*' (ibid.: 32–33, italics in original). Despite ample evidence from many Romani activists and anthropologists that begging is not a historical cultural practice but rather an economic adaptation, the judges accepted the lawyer's cultural argument; they then went on to criminalize the behaviour based on exploitation of children (Ruggiu 2016).[4]

This was not an isolated incident. In 2013 in France, lawyers again offered a cultural defence not only of begging but of coerced criminal begging among children. 'Rather than focusing on the argument that the Roma are forced to resort to crime because of poverty and discrimination, it claimed that in some cases they were simply following age-old Roma traditions and generally operate outside the norms of society in "the style of the Middle Ages"' (Bilefsky 2013). In response, Lívia Járóka, a Hungarian Romani anthropologist and member of the European Parliament, said: 'The cultural explanation for Roma criminality is nonsense . . . It is about economics' (ibid.).

The above Italian and French cases illustrate how cultural arguments can have dangerous implications even when employed to defend Roma. The very title of Bilefsky's article, 'Are the Roma Primitive, or Just Poor?', belies how Roma are categorized as uncivilized. These examples illustrate how essentialist culture concepts are recruited both for pro- and anti-Roma agendas. Culture is thus distilled and simplified, and then conscripted into frameworks such as media and law. In all these examples, the institutional structures are controlled by non-Roma, and non-Roma are the primary actors, even in advocacy (Silverman 2019). However, earlier I pointed out that Roma activists have successfully used strategic essentialism to craft symbols of the human rights movement. Below I expand on how culture in Romani communities refuses reification and remains complex and dynamic. Culture is a vital realm of sociality, work and meaning, and is now being deployed in new Romani-led public projects.

Essentialism Unbound: Culture as a Creative Tool

The site of intersection between Romani communities and institutions (such as states, markets and museums) provides a fruitful context to examine cultural production in response to structural constraints. Some good work has been done in this realm, such as Okely's work on bricolage (1996, 2011) and a *Third Text* special issue dealing with Romani museum exhibits and other forms of public and cultural representations of Roma (Gay y Blasco and Iordanova 2008). My work shows how Balkan Romani musicians have negotiated the interface between community roles and world music markets, including non-Roman collaborators, managers and organizers; I also examine my own role as a non-Romani music producer (Silverman 2012, 2019).

In the future, we should examine two new projects that fall precisely at the intersection between identity politics and public institutions, and squarely deal with issues of cultural representation: RomArchive and the European Roma Institute for Arts and Culture (ERIAC).[5] Tina Magazzini's (2016) analysis of the debates about ERIAC shows that culture remains hotly contested and is intertwined with issues of legitimacy and power. ERIAC and RomArchive, both led by Roma, are already charting new trajectories. For example, the music section of RomArchive, where I am a co-curator, seeks not to be merely representative of Romani culture, but to offer materials that are not readily available elsewhere. For curators, this has raised questions about presenting new and innovative Romani music as well as traditional genres. Similarly, ERAIC is showcasing contemporary visual artists to illustrate the innovative artistry of Roma in the modern world in response to historical discrimination (see also Magazzini, this volume). We should also note the pioneering work in the United Kingdom that established in 2008 an annual 'Gypsy Roma and Traveller History Month' to raise awareness of these communities and their cultural contributions to society, and to offset negative stereotyping and prejudices.

An expanded notion of culture that is tied to the past but not constrained by it can help us to widen bounded notions to embrace new performative forms. Dirlik writes similarly about Native Americans: 'Contrary to critics ... who see in every affirmation of cultural identity an ahistorical cultural essentialism, indigenous voices are quite open to change; what they insist on is not cultural purity or persistence, but the preservation of a particular historical trajectory of their own' (Dirlik 1997: 223). Clifford notes that indigenous leaders are simultaneously loosening and reclaiming the notion of culture; sometimes authenticity can be 'a straightjacket, making every engagement with modernity (religions, technologies, knowledges, markets or media) a contamination, a "loss" of true selfhood' (Clifford 2004: 156).

Rejecting their emplacement in the past, native leaders are asserting their legitimate public place through global displays of media, art, literature and ritual. Similarly, Roma are establishing cultural centres, designing exhibits and educational centres, and producing archives. As Clifford writes, these are 'zones of contact' (1997), 'whereby authenticity thus becomes a process – the open-ended work of preservation and transformation. Living traditions must be selectively pure: mixing, matching, remembering, forgetting, sustaining, transforming their senses of communal continuity' (Clifford 2004: 156).

Clifford claims that 'what is at stake is the power to define tradition and authenticity, to determine the relationships through which ... identity is negotiated in a changing world' (2004: 157). The challenge is to reject both a pro- and anti-essentialist position and to embrace an 'anti-anti-essentialist' position:

> The two negatives, do not, of course, add up to a positive, and so the anti-anti-essentialist position is not simply a return to essentialism. It recognizes that a rigorously anti-essentialist attitude, with respect to things like identity, culture, tradition, [and] gender ... is not really a position one can sustain in a consistent way ... Certainly one can't sustain a social movement or a community without certain apparently stable criteria for distinguishing us from them. These may be ... articulated in connections and disconnections, but as they are expressed and become meaningful to people, they establish accepted truths. Certain key symbols come to define the we against the they; certain core elements ... come to be separated out, venerated, fetishized, defended. This is the normal process, the politics, by which groups form themselves into identities. (Clifford 2003: 62)

Hall makes the point that identity politics arise precisely around issues of representation:

> Though they seem to invoke an origin in a historical past ... actually identities are about ... using the resources of history, language and culture in the process

of becoming ... [N]ot 'who we are' or 'where we came from' so much as who we might become, how we have been represented, and how that bears on how we represent ourselves. Identities are, therefore constituted within, not without representation. (Hall 1996: 4)

Similarly, Huub van Baar (2011) has argued that manifestations of Roma self-articulation are not expressions of their own problematic essentialism but are related to interrogations of how essentialized renderings of Roma (mostly crafted by non-Roma) have affected them throughout history. With new projects, Roma continue to find new ways of articulating cultural identity that are not stuck in the past, but reference the past in relationship to the future. Hall's concept of identity rejects an unchanging traditional core; he questions a 'true self ... which a people with a shared history ... hold in common'; rather, identities are 'never unified, and ... increasingly fragmented and fractured, never singular but multiply constructed across ... intersecting and antagonistic discourses, practices and positions' (Hall 1996: 3–4). For Roma, identity has always been construed in relation to hegemonic powers such as patrons of the arts, states, markets, officials, scholars and funders.

The term tradition can then be reclaimed, for it 'is not a wholesale return to past ways, but a practical selection and critical reweaving of roots' whereby 'some essentialisms are embraced while others are rejected' (Clifford 2004: 157). Culture should not be read as 'endless reiteration but as "the changing same", not the so-called return to roots but a coming-to-terms-with our routes' (Hall 1996: 4). Here Hall is referencing Gilroy's (1993: 101) useful formulation of tradition as the 'changing same' in reference to the African American diaspora. Similarly, Romani cultural identity projects should be analysed in their historical contexts, paying special attention to inequalities and hierarchies. To examine how Roma are performatively crafting identities is to implicitly reframe the 'conundrums of culture'.

Carol Silverman is a Professor of Anthropology/Folklore at the University of Oregon in the US, and has been involved with Romani culture for over forty years as a researcher, teacher, activist and performer. Focusing on Roma in Bulgaria and Macedonia, and the American and West European Romani diasporas, her research explores the intersection of politics, music, human rights, gender and state policy, with a focus on issues of representation. Her current project examines the issues of appropriation, migration and race in relationship to the globalization of 'Gypsy' music. Her book *Romani Routes: Cultural Politics and Balkan Music in Diaspora* (Oxford University Press, 2012) won the 2013 book prize from the Society for Ethnomusicology.

She is curator of Balkan Music for the international digital RomArchive, and a board member of the American-based NGO Voice of Roma. Her recent articles have appeared in *Critical Romani Studies*, *Western Folklore*, *Ethnomusicology Forum*, *Oregon Historical Quarterly* and the edited volume *The Romani Women's Movement*.

Notes

I would like to thank the editors and peer reviewers of the volume for their insightful comments, and the many Roma who have shared their homes and perceptions with me.

1. Retrieved on 5 June 2018 from https://www.umanitoba.ca/faculties/arts/anthropology/courses/122/module1/culture.html.
2. Although I do not have the space to delve into this, I note that Tremlett (2009) has offered hybridity as a conceptual solution to the essentialist trap. In contrast, my work shows that hybridity has its own set of drawbacks and operates as a seductive multicultural discursive framework with little chance of dismantling injustice (Silverman 2012: 42–56; 2011, 2014). Tremlett (2014) has more recently introduced Vertovec's concept of super-diversity into Romani Studies, but it remains to be seen how she will utilize it practically.
3. Hughes v. Ephrem, Case No. 1200-25302E.
4. Although I do not have the space here to expand this argument, I must point out that the assumed neglect of children is increasingly being used by local governments to criminalize Roma.
5. See www.romarchive.eu and https://eriac.org/ (retrieved 23 April 2019).

References

Abu-Lughod, L. 1991. 'Writing against Culture', in R. Fox (ed.), *Recapturing Anthropology: Working in the Present*. Santa Fe, NM: School of American Research Press, pp. 137–62.

Appiah, K.A. 2017. 'There is no such thing as Western civilisation'. Retrieved 10 June 2018 from https://www.theguardian.com/world/2016/nov/09/western-civilisation-appiah-reith-lecture?CMP=share_btn_fb.

Barth, F. 1969. *Ethnic Groups and Boundaries*. Oslo: Universitetsforlaget.

Benedik, S. 2010. 'Harming "Cultural Feelings": Images and Categorisation of Temporary Romani Migrants to Graz/Austria', in M. Stewart and M. Rövid (eds), *Multi-Disciplinary Approaches to Romany Studies*. Budapest: CEU Press, pp. 71–90.

Bilefsky, D. 2013. 'Are the Roma Primitive, or Just Poor?' *New York Times*, 20 October, SR4.

Brubaker, R. 2004. *Ethnicity Without Groups*. Cambridge, MA: Harvard University Press.

Calhoun, C. 2003a. '"Belonging" in the Cosmopolitan Imaginary', *Ethnicities* 3(4): 531–53.
———. 2003b. 'The Variability of Belonging: A Reply to Rogers Brubaker', *Ethnicities* 3(4): 558–67.
Castañeda, H. 2014. 'European Mobilities or Poverty Migration? Discourses on Roma in Germany', *International Migration* 53(3): 87–99.
Catalano, T. 2014. 'The Roma and Wall Street/CEOs: Linguistic Construction of Identity in U.S. and Canadian Crime Reports', *International Journal of Comparative and Applied Criminal Justice* 38(2): 133–56.
Clifford, J. 1997. *Routes: Travel and Translation in the Late Twentieth Century*. Cambridge, MA: Harvard University Press.
———. 2003. *On the Edges of Anthropology*. Chicago, IL: Prickly Paradigm Press.
———. 2004. 'Looking Several Ways: Anthropology and Native Heritage in Alaska', *Current Anthropology* 45(1): 5–30.
Comaroff, J., and J. Comaroff. 2009. *Ethnicity, Inc.* Chicago, IL: University of Chicago Press.
Danius, S., S. Jonsson and G. Spivak. 1993. 'Interview with Gayatri Chakravorty Spivak', *boundary* 20(2): 24–50.
Dirlik, A. 1997. *The Postcolonial Aura: Third World Criticism in the Age of Global Capitalism*. Boulder, CO: Westview.
———. 2000. *Postmodernity's Histories: The Past as Legacy and Project*. Lanham, MD: Rowman & Littlefield.
Gay y Blasco, P., and D. Iordanova (eds). 2008. 'Picturing "Gypsies": Interdisciplinary Approaches to Roma Representation', *Third Text* special issue 22(3): 297–425.
Gheorghe, N., and T. Acton. 2001. 'Citizens of the World and Nowhere: Minority, Ethnic, and Human Rights for Roma', in W. Guy (ed.), *Between Past and Future: The Roma of Central and Eastern Europe*. Hatfield: University of Hertfordshire Press, pp. 54–70.
Gilroy, P. 1993. *The Black Atlantic: Modernity and Double Consciousness*. Cambridge, MA: Harvard University Press.
Grigorescu, D. 2017. 'Sute de americani au semnat o petiție împotriva țiganilor români care i-au șocat cu obiceiurile lor' [Hundreds of Americans have signed a petition against the Romanian Gypsies who have shocked them with their customs], *Adevarul*, 18 July.
Guy, W. (ed.). 2001. *Between Past and Future: The Roma of Central and Eastern Europe*. Hatfield: University of Hertfordshire Press.
Hall, S. 1996. 'Introduction: Who Needs Identity?' in S. Hall and P. DuGay (eds), *Questions of Cultural Identity*. London: Sage, pp. 1–17.
Hancock, I. 1987. *The Pariah Syndrome: An Account of Gypsy Slavery*. Ann Arbor, MI: Karoma.
———. 2002. *We Are The Romani People: Ame Sam e Rromane Džene*. Hatfield: University of Hertfordshire Press.
———. 2010. *Danger! Educated Gypsy*. Hatfield: University of Hertfordshire Press.
Herzfeld, M. 1997. *Cultural Intimacy: Social Poetics in the Nation-State*. London: Routledge.
hooks, b. 1990. *Yearning: Race, Gender, and Cultural Politics*. Boston, MA: South End.
International Romani Union. 2001. 'Declaration of a Roma Nation'. Retrieved 10 June 2018 from http://www.hartford-hwp.com/archives/60/132.html.

Landler, M. 2004. 'A Human Tidal Wave, or a Ripple of Hypsteria?' *New York Times*, 5 May, A4.

Leggio, D.V. 2017. 'Critiquing Stereotypes: Research Engagement with UK Local Authority Supporting Roma Migrants', *ANUAC Journal of the Italian Society of Cultural Anthropology* 6(1): 119–40.

Liégeois, J.-P., and N. Gheorghe. 1995. *Roma/Gypsies: A European Minority*. London: Minority Rights Group International.

Magazzini, T. 2016. 'Cultural Institutions as Combat Sport: Reflections on the European Roma Institute', *The Age of Human Rights Journal* 7: 50–76.

Majors, D., S. Strasburg and E. Behrman. 2017. 'Romanians seeking asylum are in California, PA, as part of U.S. immigration program'. *Pittsburgh Post-Gazette*. 14 July.

Mamdani, M. 2002. 'Good Muslim, Bad Muslim: A Political Perspective on Culture and Terrorism', *American Anthropologist* 104(3): 766–75.

Marushiakova, E., and V. Popov. n.d. 'Roma Culture', Council of Europe. Retrieved 10 June 2018 from http://romafacts.uni-graz.at/index.php/culture/introduction/roma-culture.

McGarry, A. 2017. *Romophobia: The Last Acceptable Form of Racism*. London: Zed Books.

Mirga, A. 2018. 'Book Review of *Those Who Count: Expert Practices of Roma Classification* by Mihai Surdu', *Critical Romani Studies* 1(1): 114–26.

Mirga, A., and N. Gheorghe. 1997. *The Roma in the Twenty-First Century: A Policy Paper*. Princeton, NJ: Project on Ethnic Relations.

Okely, J. 1996. 'Trading Stereotypes', in J. Okely, *Own or Other Culture*. London: Routledge, pp. 45–61.

———. 2011. 'Construction Culture through Shared Location, Bricolage and Exchange', in M. Stewart and M. Rovid (eds), *Multi-Disciplinary Approaches to Romany Studies*. Budapest: CEU Press, pp. 35–54.

Renteln, A.D. 2004. *The Cultural Defense*. Oxford: Oxford University Press.

Ruggiu, I. 2016. 'Is Begging a Roma Cultural Practice? Answers from the Italian Legal System and Anthropology', *Romani Studies* 26(1): 31–61.

Silverman, C. 2011. 'Gypsy Music, Hybridity and Appropriation: Balkan Dilemmas of Postmodernity', *Ethnologia Balkanica* 15: 15–32.

———. 2012. *Romani Routes: Cultural Politics and Balkan Music in Diaspora*. Oxford: Oxford University Press.

———. 2014. 'Global Balkan Gypsy Music: Issues of Migration, Appropriation, and Representation', in S. Krüger and R. Trandafoiu (eds), *The Globalization of Musics in Transit: Musical Migration and Tourism*. London: Routledge, pp. 185–208.

———. 2017. 'Oregon Roma (Gypsies): A Hidden History', *Oregon Historical Quarterly* 118(4): 518–53.

———. 2019. 'From Reflexivity to Collaboration: Changing Roles of a non-Romani Scholar/activist/performer', *Critical Romani Studies* 1(2): 43–63.

Spivak, G. 1987. *In Other Worlds: Essays in Cultural Politics*. London: Routledge.

Stewart. M. 2011. 'Introduction', in M. Stewart and M. Rovid (eds), *Multi-Disciplinary Approaches to Romany Studies*. Budapest: CEU Press, pp. 1–9.

———. (ed.) 2012. *The Gypsy 'Menace': Populism and the New Anti-Gypsy Politics*. London: Hurst & Co.

———. 2013. 'Roma and Gypsy Ethnicity as a Subject of Anthropological Inquiry', *Annual Review of Anthropology* 42: 415–32.

Surdu, M. 2016. *Those Who Count: Expert Practices of Roma Classification*. Budapest: CEU Press.
Tony, M. 2017. 'Film event set up to bridge knowledge gap about Roma in California', *Herald Standard*, 20 September.
Tremlett, A. 2009. 'Bringing Hybridity to Heterogeneity in Romani Studies', *Romani Studies* 19(2): 147–68.
———. 2014. 'Making a Difference without Creating Difference: Super-Diversity as a New Direction for Research on Roma Minorities', *Ethnicities* 14(6): 830–48.
Tremlett, A., and A. McGarry. 2013. 'Challenges Facing Researchers on Roma Minorities in Contemporary Europe: Notes towards a Research Program'. Working Paper No. 62. European Centre for Minority Issues.
Tremlett, A., A. McGarry and T. Agarin. 2014. 'The Work of Sisyphus: Squaring the Circle of Roma Recognition', *Ethnicities* 14(6): 727–36.
Tylor, E. 1871. *Primitive Culture: Research into the Development of Mythology, Philosophy, Religion, Art, and Custom*. London: John Murray.
van Baar, H. 2011. *The European Roma: Minority Representation, Memory and the Limits of Transnational Governmentality*. Amsterdam: F&N.
Vermeersch, P. 2005. 'Marginality, Advocacy and the Ambiguities of Multiculturalism', *Identities* 12(4): 451–78.
———. 2006. *The Romani Movement: Minority Politics and Ethnic Mobilization in Contemporary Central Europe*. Oxford: Berghahn Books.
———. 2012. 'Reframing the Roma: EU Initiatives and the Politics of Reinterpretation', *Journal of Ethnic and Migration Studies* 38(8): 1195–212.
———. 2016. 'The Plight of Eastern Europe's Roma', in A. Fagy and P. Kopecky (eds), *The Routledge Handbook of East European Politics*. London: Routledge, pp. 225–35.
Wemple, E. 2017. 'In his quest to demonize immigrants, Fox News's Tucker Carlson misses a good story', 20 July. Retrieved 10 June 2018 from https://www.washingtonpost.com/blogs/erik-wemple/wp/2017/07/20/in-his-quest-to-demonize-immigrants-fox-newss-tucker-carlson-misses-a-good-story/?tid=ss_fb-bottom&utm_term=.0559df054cbc.
Yu Hsi Lee, E. 2017. 'The truth about the immigrants Tucker Carlson claims are defecating in the streets of Pennsylvania', 20 July. Retrieved 10 June 2018 from https://thinkprogress.org/roma-refugees-cal-pa-3997faa966c/.

CHAPTER 10

❋ ❋ ❋

IDENTITY AS A WEAPON OF THE WEAK?

Understanding the European Roma Institute for Arts and Culture – An Interview with Tímea Junghaus and Anna Mirga-Kruszelnicka

Tina Magazzini

Interview with Tímea Junghaus, Executive Director of the European Roma Institute for Arts and Culture (ERIAC), and Anna Mirga-Kruszelnicka, its Deputy Director

In keeping with this volume's aim to go beyond the binary between constructivism and essentialism in debates about Romani identity in contemporary Europe, this interview with the directors of the European Roma Institute for Arts and Culture (ERIAC) intends to provide a first-hand account of one of the most symbolic and debated sites of Romani culture and identity recognition of recent times.

Stemming from broader reflections on the role that a minority cultural institution could play in the current European landscape (Magazzini 2016), interviews with the executive director and deputy director of ERIAC were conducted in July and September 2018, and then combined.[1] The first set of questions addresses the origins and development of ERIAC, its internal structure and principles, as well as issues of membership and ethnicity; the second set analyses the institute's positioning towards other Romani or pro-Roma organizations, touching on the politics of culture and identity; and the final set clusters questions on knowledge production, cultural production and the meaning and relevance of 'elitism'.

While the account that emerges stresses the directorship's attempt at maintaining a certain distance from both relevant political and academic fora, the institution and its members remain fundamentally involved in ongoing debates regarding the politics of culture and identity, particularly at a time when right-wing populist movements seem to be successfully appealing to identity. In this respect, ERIAC and its ongoing development can offer a starting point to discuss the relationship between cultural and social inclusion, as well as problems of democratic representation more broadly. The hope is that more situated and contextualized accounts of the expectations one could reasonably have of cultural knowledge production sites such as ERIAC can help us to overcome some of the misunderstandings between activism and academia – not by further separating them, but by constructively engaging with each other on issues regarding Romani culture and identity.

The Making of ERIAC

Tina Magazzini (TM): Can you explain what ERIAC is, how it has emerged and developed, and what exactly your job at ERIAC is?

Anna Mirga-Kruszelnicka (AMK): ERIAC, the European Roma Institute for Arts and Culture, is a first of its kind, and a unique institution. Its mission statement is to combat antigypsyism through the means of art and culture, history and commemoration, media and information, and knowledge production – which are ERIAC's key areas of competence and the thematic sections around which the ERIAC associate membership is organized. The establishment of the institute is a historic moment, in the sense that the struggle for its creation should be looked at from a longitudinal perspective. It is not the case that a few years ago, a bunch of people got together and invented ERIAC; rather, it emerged from a legacy and history of fighting for an institution that would be independent and work to safeguard and promote Romani cultural heritage and Romani artistic and cultural creations. We can trace back the attempts at creating such an institution, at both national and international levels, to the 1970s, but only recently, in 2017, did such an institution crystallize in the form of ERIAC. In 2013, the idea of ERIAC was taken up effectively by a group of Romani activists, intellectuals and artists from different countries, who got together and revived the idea of trying to create an institution for Romani arts and culture at the European level. Eventually, this group of people formed the 'Alliance for the European Roma Institute' and became the motor behind the initiative, working with the Open Society Foundations and eventually also securing the support of the Council of Europe.

Tímea Junghaus (TJ): ERIAC is the first transnational institution with a single and unique mandate focused on recognition of arts and culture of Roma – the largest European ethnic minority of about ten to twelve million people. This minority has been advocating for an institution at the European, transnational level that represents their arts and culture. This idea had already emerged in 1971 at the first Roma World Congress in London. I understand ERIAC as the embodiment of the long-time efforts of Romani intellectuals, artists, public speakers and politicians who have been involved in the Romani movement and who have lobbied for this over the past decades. Of course, there have always been non-Romani allies who support this movement but, at the same time and for years, there has been a persistent paternalizing discourse in the European public sphere that focuses on the question: 'When do the Roma finally take responsibility for their future and act for their own people?' I see ERIAC as a perfect answer to such narratives. When you walk into our institute's building, on the wall you see the logo of the Open Society Foundations next to that of the Council of Europe. Then, next to the logos of these prestigious organizations, there is a small plaque that says, 'Alliance for the European Roma Institute'. It is very important for us to remember that ERIAC was the initiative of seventeen brilliant Romani intellectuals who united their efforts in their respective countries, convinced their own governments, lobbied with ambassadors and went to the meetings of the Council of Europe to explain why we needed such an institution. Being part of this development is both a huge honour and a gigantic responsibility.

The initial informal network was the initiative of a small number of concept drafters. I believe it was Ethel Brooks who, in the beginning, wrote the conceptual draft for a transnational organization. Deciding on the name was different too; it was called 'European Roma Institute' at that time. However, even before Ethel's draft, there were so many drafts for a museum, or for a European space, an institution with doors and windows that does not exist exclusively on a website, on paper or in a framework strategy. ERIAC is not a concept, it is an actual institution, a legitimate space that you can walk into. It was Ethel who invited several experts to contribute to this development: Nicoleta Bițu, Ciprian Necula and others contributed to that original concept too. And then, since the concept changed from a general institution to the field of culture, cultural experts were invited because it was necessary to represent the cause in the Council of Europe meetings and at cultural events, and to speak up for this movement for ERIAC: Katalin Barsony from Hungary for film expertise, Dijana Pavlović from Italy for expertise on performing arts, Sead Kazanxhiu from Albania for expertise on visual arts in the Balkans, among others. All these individuals deployed their own time and resources to lobby, network and advocate for ERIAC during the four-year process that finally led to its creation.

As ERIAC's executive director, I am responsible for reporting to the board about ERIAC's activities: we have a myriad of projects here, and almost every month we have two or three international events, including exhibitions. We have major grants that we are running, and I am reporting to the donors of these grants. I also coordinate the organization financially and administratively.

TM: *What does working as ERIAC's deputy director/executive director consist of in practical terms, on a daily basis?*

AMK: We have a very small staff and this is also a very dynamic and exciting moment of birth, of creating something that has no precedent; there is no previous similar experience on which we can easily rely. All of this is new, so having a small staff and being in this process of institution-building, our day-to-day operation entails everything from drafting grant proposals to contacting our partners through the extended network made up of a number of institutions and individuals, to setting up the office. We have a beautiful art space and office here in the centre of Berlin and it has street access with large glass windows, which generates a lot of visibility. Once ERIAC was created and started its operations, quite a big deal of curiosity arose around it. We have been continuously receiving requests for collaboration from across Europe.

TJ: At the moment (September 2018), ERIAC has already started the second outreach programme, so we are done with the first. Only the coordination and physical location of ERIAC is in Berlin; we really try to focus on the European and the transnational. In September 2018, the second outreach programme started with the support of the German Federal Foreign Office. The first programme focused mainly on Central and Eastern Europe, while the second will focus more on the Balkans. We are starting to identify the country coordinators and the partners, so that we can schedule these events and we will conduct conferences, exhibitions, discussions, public forums and concerts in all the countries covered by the project [Croatia, Albania, Serbia, Macedonia, Italy, Spain and France].

TM: *At the beginning of the process of creating ERIAC, how did you decide whom to debate and engage with?*

AMK: Creating ERIAC was a kind of self-regulating practice, at least in the sense of contribution, because those who joined the process [leading to the creation of ERIAC] did so because they believed in the idea and were driven by this dream of having an institution for ourselves [the Roma].

Some of them contributed with their own resources to try to realize this idea. The Alliance for ERI is not a group of isolated individuals who are disconnected: we come from Romani communities, we live in extended networks of families, friends, collaborators, people we work with, local communities – all sorts and at different levels. To make the establishment of ERIAC possible, we brought together different inputs and ideas, each from our own background. And then we engaged with the process; the point was to reach some kind of maturity in terms of having an idea in written form, some concept, some potential framework, and this is where we began a process of consultation. There were many different venues that we engaged with, from the 'Dikh he na Bister' Roma Genocide Remembrance Initiative in Krakow that organized the Roma Holocaust Memorial days [where we organized consultations with the participants in 2014], to the yearly Khamoro Festival in Prague and the Romani Summer Schools organized at the Central European University (CEU). We identified different places, different people to discuss with, and laid out our initial idea to hear their feedback and contribution, and to identify people who were willing to help. The entire process required several different movements, amongst them political lobbying at the national level too, because, since the Council of Europe had to be convinced that this project was something they were going to support and fund, we knew that we needed supporting countries. Thus, members from Romani communities started to lobby their own governments by saying 'Look, we really think this is an important idea that you should support'. Many of the documents were also available online, like the initial concept paper, and all these documents were made available even before the institute was founded, as the result of brainstorming. We made all these things available online, as much as we could, to make the rationale behind ERIAC feasible and visible.

TM: From a practical point of view, what language of communication do you use, considering the large diversity of nationalities and backgrounds involved?

TJ: Language-wise, at ERIAC we work in about nine or ten languages. The staff is international. We have graduates from CEU who are placed here as interns; the country coordinators are all English-speaking people who also speak the local language. We have only one person in our office who speaks Romanes fluently, but frequently we receive Romanes Facebook messages. We have four pillars at ERIAC: media and information; knowledge-production and academia; arts and culture; and commemoration and history. However, the board has decided to introduce a fifth section on language. Thus, language also groups members interested in engaging with how ERIAC will endorse Romanes in the future.

TM: *Speaking of membership, what is the role of ethnic Romani identity in your criteria for membership and partnership? In one of your own articles (Mirga-Kruszelnicka 2018), you stress the importance of challenging essentialist representations of Roma and the importance of academic knowledge produced from within the Romani subjectivity to do so. Do you ask those who want to become members of ERIAC whether they self-identify as Roma, and if that is the case, how – if at all – would you deal with cases such as those of Rachel Dolezal?*[2]

TJ: Initially, the Barvalipe Academy[3] was formed within ERIAC. The board nominated ERIAC's first seven members; afterwards, members applied through our online platform. Once we had opened this platform, people and organizations had about two months to submit their applications and indicate in what section they would like to work. Our management made a review of the applications. Then, the board reviewed them and, as a result of this process, we had a final list of those accepted. There are currently around ninety Romani and non-Romani individuals and organizations that want to engage in ERIAC's activities.

AMK: I very much like the trans-racial, trans-ethnic discussions. Yes, we set a quota, but only for the Barvalipe Academy.[4] ERIAC is based on six founding principles, one of which is Romani leadership and participation. This does not imply that we want to be exclusive, but that we want to organize our institution as a space in which Roma can have influence. This also serves as a mechanism of protection. The academic field of knowledge production is the most emblematic and exemplary in this respect, because the existing networks of academic Romani studies tend to be dominated and led by non-Romani scholars. It is not that these networks exclude Roma because they are racist; it is more about the fact that academia is generally based on merit and meritocracy. For several reasons, we are now faced with the best-educated generation of Roma in history, even though the number of Romani scholars and Romani university graduates is still rather small. As a minority, we must understand what being deprived of a voice and of a certain control over identity framing does, and how this directly and indirectly influences policymaking, for example. This is why we felt it was really important to have an institution explicitly by, for and about Roma.

Of course, we do not do blood tests [laughs]... and we do not ask relatives to confirm that one really is indeed Roma. We do ask whether an applicant is Roma to understand who is applying; this is a self-declared kind of option. In the online application form, there is an optional question on ethnic background where one can declare it.

I think that the Dolezal case is an interesting sign of our times. Here, we reach the point at which there is so much relativism and diluting of identities that it really becomes hard to keep track of racial and ethnic borders. How do we describe people of flesh and blood who escape our fixed definitions, or who reveal the limitations of the concepts we use? Perhaps there are also 'Roma wannabes', but I think we have not yet arrived at the point where being Roma is so 'cool' that we have to explicitly deal with such cases.

One of the six principles on which ERIAC is founded is that of plurality and diversity of Romani identities and cultures. Our point is that there is not *one way* of being Roma, but that there are many different ways of being and performing Roma. Thus, identities can and will change and are contextual; they are involved in dynamic processes for individuals and for entire communities. Therefore, I think that ERIAC can offer a safe space in which we can bring together the experiences coming from different Romani communities throughout Europe, but certainly also those coming from non-Roma. ERIAC wants to offer a space where we can sit down and discuss, and try to come up with assertive, evidence-based and negotiated responses to the questions that academics have been asking for centuries: what does it mean to be Roma and who is 'Roma'? I think it is important that we have our own space to discuss how we can unite in the diversity we face; to discuss the fact that multiculturalism is our everyday reality and how these issues affect our solidarity, ethnic identifications across countries and groups, dialects and so on. Since we have never had such spaces before, ERIAC can really make a change. This is the first time we have a space to negotiate, reinvent and also to argue: it is not that we are going to come up with one single, 'true' answer, but it is important that this is a space to discuss these issues about identity and to provide the ground for plural responses.

TM: Could you tell us about the relationship between the Barvalipe Academy and the Pakiv Board?[5] *What roles do they play in ERIAC?*

AMK: Barvalipe and Pakiv are the two governing bodies of the institute. The Pakiv Board is the highest organ of ERIAC. It includes three founding members, one from each of the institutions involved – thus, from the Alliance for the European Roma Institute, the Open Society Foundations and the Council of Europe. There will be two additional members from Barvalipe. Barvalipe is a mid-level governing structure that is meant to connect the Pakiv Board with our members. Barvalipe is also the strategic body that shapes most of the content, ERIAC's vision and its broader lines. Barvalipe is made up of fifteen outstanding personalities in the fields of arts and culture, with incredible curriculums, and who provide input and more specific guidance to our work. The first seven members of Barvalipe are nominated by the Pakiv Board, and the remaining eight are appointed by the members themselves. The members are affiliated to the thematic sections and they self-organize within the section, so they will have their own delegates. It sounds perhaps a bit complex, but it is through this kind of dynamic that we hope to create synergies that work in both directions, creating a channel of communication between the founders and the members. So, you can develop a space for thematic work, which is more specific, but you can also have a kind of visionary body that provides guidance and direction. Finally, you have the board that oversees and controls that everything is in line with the statutes, ERIAC's mission and the founding principles.

TM: How were the six basic principles of ERIAC developed and adopted?

AMK: It was a process of intensive brainstorming [driven by the members of the Alliance]. Some of the principles were clear and unanimously agreed upon. These principles were not even the minimum that everyone could agree upon, but involved points we felt strongly about. The principle of diversity and plurality, for instance, was very clear from the very beginning, and we also really wanted ERIAC to be a space of quality and prestige. High-quality standards in what ERIAC does and how ERIAC operates, the cultural production that comes out of it; we want ERIAC to be the best arts and culture institute in our field of competence and we know the quality is there. Non-partisanship and independent leadership, two of the other principles, were also very important for ERIAC from the beginning; they are paradigmatic.

TJ: The founding principles were key issues that were fostered by the Alliance because, during the founding negotiations, it became obvious that ERIAC was included in power structures that continuously challenged our institution in the making. During this period, it was vital to focus on the founding principles. So, after a while, the Alliance and its members harmonized their activities to make sure that we were operating on one and the same level; this is also how the principles became the leading values and catalysts for the institute.

ERIAC's Positioning, Partnerships and Institutional Relations

TM: One of this six founding principles is 'Political autonomy and non-partisanship, openness for collaboration with public authorities and political institutions as partners'. How do you realize this principle in ERIAC's practices?

TJ: This principle implies that we do not engage with any political party, even if they have an interest in supporting ERIAC and developing a partnership.

This principle retains our political autonomy, and this is particularly important because we are a German-registered association. To maintain our independent status, we must stay politically autonomous. When we are creating our programmes, we always take our founding principles into account, and this also happened, for instance, when the board nominated the first members of the Barvalipe Academy.

TM: You mentioned the fact that ERIAC generated some controversy. Could you elaborate on this and on how you, as an institution, have dealt with it?

AMK: Well, in general, I think it is a very interesting moment in time. When you look at scholarship, political activism and artistic production among Roma over the last five years or so, you can see that there is a new type of militancy, a new discourse, that tries to break with previous methods and narratives [see also Tremlett and Le Bas, this volume]. In a way, this is a sign of maturity and of growth of the Romani movement. I think that this is ultimately a question of power and control, and there has been quite a lot of misunderstanding and a bit of bad will from some during this process [leading to the establishment of ERIAC]. I believe that some of the ingredients that have come into this pot have resulted in tensions. These tensions mainly emerged because the Alliance's core group, who have also become the most vocal advocates for ERIAC, had an academic background. Particularly in academia, one can observe ongoing power struggles over definitions, influence in policymaking and shaping public discourses. Thus, many of these struggles are rooted in scholarship.

Now, we have been able to notice the emergence of an increasingly critical mass, made up of scholars of Romani background who have started to speak from Romani positionality, from within it, with a Romani voice – not necessarily claiming a more legitimate voice, but a very necessary voice that has been marginalized and not been heard for long. I think that some factions of the academic 'establishment', if I may say so, have interpreted this kind of militant voice for self-recognition and self-determination as an attack on them, rather than as a way of self-emancipation. These tensions along ethnic lines have become most visible in the field of scholarship. Interestingly, though, when you look at other fields, such as those of Romani activism or arts and culture, we see an entirely different trend. There, both Roma and non-Roma have very much welcomed and supported ERIAC. Thus, the controversy mainly started in academic circles and I think it makes no sense to mention names and point fingers. There were certain processes that resulted from personal conflicts on the individual level that became public, instead of remaining an argument between some of the intellectuals and academics involved. The problem is that, at some point, the controversies surrounding

ERIAC shifted from the idea itself to the people behind the idea, and became a series of attacks that were quite personalized in nature; these were often disrespectful and really did not contribute to any kind of academic or intellectual debate. It is important to remember this genealogy, and I think that the article you wrote (Magazzini 2016) is important because it bears witness to what happened at a certain moment in time, even though I think that time will prove us right. The entire philosophy behind ERIAC is not about attacking or excluding anyone; it is about advancing, and it is a collective progress that we should make as societies – as Roma of course, but I think also in partnership with our [non-Romani] allies throughout Europe.

TM: This leads me to ask about your allies: what kinds of collaborations and linkages does ERIAC have with other artistic and cultural institutes?

AMK: ERIAC is a Romani institute, evidently, so our mandate and scope focus predominantly on Roma. There are, however, several issues here: one is that, for us, it is important to articulate the universality of the Romani struggle and, thus, to interconnect with others with similar experiences. Many of the things that we as Roma face are not unique to us but shared by many communities that are kept on the margins of our world. The history and dynamics of both the troublesome status quo as well as the struggle against it, the processes of resisting and overcoming; all can be very instructive to us as Roma and, thus, looking into the experiences of other minority struggles is very informative and inspiring. Of course, there are many linkages – historical and contemporary – between Roma and other minority struggles, both in cultural and artistic terms, and also especially those of political activism and scholarship. We look into African-American struggles, Afro-American scholarship, into the First Nations movement in Canada, and indigenous struggles in Latin America: all of these have become sources of inspiration. Not all our connections and networks necessarily turn into formalized partnerships, but there are many inspirations. I think that the emphasis on the universality of the Romani struggle is crucial, as it points at these connections and linking the Romani debate with similar discussions that are taking place elsewhere in the world.

For example, one of the first events at ERIAC's space in Berlin was organized within the framework of the International Cultural Outreach Program. For the programme's final event we invited professor Gayatri Chakravorty Spivak to our office. We also invited a group of Romani feminists from different countries to sit together and speak about visions for a new future, so it was really about building upon experiences from Roma, but also about discussing with scholars such as Spivak about the role that Roma can play as an avant-garde, in order to try to find answers, or at least inspiration and arguments, for the future. In this case, the event focused on feminism and the importance of power structures in society, but we want to continue these kinds of collaborations and want to expand working with intellectuals and artists from other minority groups that face similar struggles to ours.

TM: How do you balance the international and European dimensions of this ambitious project with local realities?

TJ: When we enter a location with a cultural programme, we try to explore the most burning issues, the most exciting discussions or most timely debates in terms of the local context. Then we try to upscale the events, so that we can embed local discussions into international ones. In the Spanish context, for instance, UNESCO has declared flamenco a Spanish Intangible Cultural Heritage of Humanity. Romani/Gitano communities in Spain, on the other hand, have an awareness and their own knowledge of how flamenco is an art form shaped by Romani/Gitano resistance.[6] We provided a platform for local flamenco artists to organize a public conference and develop a strategy on how to approach this topic in a professional and culturally acceptable manner, in a protocol that followed the event. There were gorgeous performances of the best flamenco artists of Spain of Gitano origin. We engaged in this debate to accommodate this local discussion, and have tried to scale it up to the UNESCO level and give it visibility internationally. Another example is the way in which we have addressed the issue of Romani cultural heritage in Budapest. 2018 was the European Year of Cultural Heritage and there was not even one small initiative about Roma or organized by them. Much of the heritage of Romani arts and culture is rotting in public collections – where it is not properly archived, exhibited, researched or published. The usual argument is that there is no public funding for the conservation, inventory, research and presentation of these collections. We managed to cooperate with an EU-funded project that focused on vulnerable communities and minority cultures – the REACH project[7] – and this enabled us to invite international experts on cultural heritage who advised on the possibilities for preserving these forgotten and neglected Romani collections.

TM: What role does the 'European' component play in ERIAC?

AMK: The 'Europeanness' of our institute is inevitable and it has been debated. For me, the 'Global Roma Institute' or something with similar meaning would have been the most accurate name for our institute, because I consider us a global diaspora and we have also received contributions from all around the world, not just Europe. But because of the kind and type of struggle we currently face in Europe, and also because the Council of Europe became one of the founders, the name 'ERIAC', with the 'E' for European, was chosen.

TM: Do you think that the fact that ERIAC is largely funded by the Council of Europe impacts on what you (can) do, say and organize as an institution?

AMK: There is always a trade-off. The fact that the Council of Europe contributes to the funding and support of ERIAC is of vital importance. ERIAC could also have been founded as any other NGO; it could have been registered in Brussels or Skopje or anywhere really. This could have happened, and it would have been a much easier, less painful and quicker process. But the point was that ERIAC was not envisaged to be 'yet another' NGO. We wanted an institution that has access to the most important stakeholders, because in this way we could generate change most effectively. We want ERIAC to function bi-directionally: we work both with our own communities, our creators – most notably in artistic production – and with the main stakeholders in the field – majority arts and culture spaces, mainstream public and private cultural institutions – because they allow us to generate impact. Having the Council of Europe among our main supporters is important, because it gives us access to various governmental levels. Besides, the Council of Europe is the only intergovernmental organization that has competencies in the fields of arts and culture.[8]

On the other hand, the Council of Europe is shaped by its members and these are national governments that are becoming increasingly more hostile, racist and nationalist. So, the support from the Council of Europe that we now have might decline in time, but it is still the only intergovernmental space that we can access and simultaneously try to influence somehow through the development of a new narrative of recognition and dignity towards the Roma. We try to promote the idea of cultural inclusion, which we consider as the sine qua non of social inclusion.

TM: How do you perceive the relationship between ERIAC and the European Roma and Travellers Forum (ERTF)? In this context, some have claimed that a political institution has been 'replaced' by a cultural one. How do you see such statements?

TJ: To my mind, the 'usual' story is that one Roma organization has been replaced by another, thus ERTF by ERIAC. But this is very much a kind of institutional racism, because if you look at the institutions of the EU, you realize that there is usually place for only one token partner organization and not for others. This is outrageous if you consider the fact that ten to twelve million people should be represented. It is very important to emphasize that ERIAC is an organization that wants to reflect on and respect the cultural history of the movement. ERIAC is primarily a cultural organization with a completely different mandate and organizational structure from the ERTF. The ERTF considered itself an umbrella organization, while ERIAC is a membership-based cultural organization. The dominant discourse about replacement can itself be considered as a product of cultural and institutional racism, because of the implicit suggestion that there can only be one Roma organization serving as a partner of the Council of Europe. ERIAC aims to be a constructive organization that does not compete with but supports other organizations, and scales arts initiatives up to the international level. We would never appear as something that has challenged or contested ERTF's past and legacy. This is my personal opinion; ERIAC was never requested to form an institutional statement about the ERTF.

AMK: It is important to acknowledge that ERIAC is by no means a substitution or replacement for either the ERTF or the European Academic Network of Romani Studies (EANRS). Each of these three initiatives – ERIAC, EARNS, ERTF – is completely different, even while some have tried to frame the birth of ERIAC as a replacement of the Academic Network or the ERTF. This is something that has never been the objective, and it is incorrect – especially with regards to the ERTF, because ERIAC is not a place of political representation, and our field of competencies is also not that of policymaking. In fact, we claim no representation or political mandate, although we can argue that culture and arts can be quite political. In our statute we describe our mandate; we can only provide policy input if we are requested doing so – and in the fields of arts and culture – and, thus only if our expertise as an institution of arts and culture is requested for whatever reason. We are not a space of political representation.

Personally, I think the ERTF should continue, and that those who are involved try to redirect it as a space of international political representation. At this point in time, we do not need *a* Romani voice, but Romani *voices*. It's not about *an* institution, *an* ERTF, *a* network; it is rather about having numerous actors that operate together and have the capacity to ally strategically, collaborate and understand how they can complement rather than compete with one another. The often-heard discourse about 'a Romani voice' and the question about a lack of representativeness or legitimacy have led to a badly framed discussion. Indeed, we can question the representativeness of any democratically elected government or politicians in our majoritarian societies as well. This discussion needs to be reshaped and not framed as something specifically related to Roma; the questions relate to more general problems of representation and legitimate mandates. We are here at ERIAC with a niche of arts and culture, but we do not claim to compete or to be representative of the Roma in Europe.

Knowledge (Production) Is Power: Identity Politics and the Social Responsibility of Arts and Culture

TM: You have raised an important point when you spoke about the political responsibility of arts and culture. Do you think that culture has some sort of political responsibility? How, for instance, does ERIAC position itself in cases directly related to antigypsyism? In July 2018, for example, Italy's Minister of the Interior, Matteo Salvini, declared that he wanted to collect census data particularly on Roma, and to expel all of them who were 'illegally' residing in the country. How does ERIAC relate to such events, and does it, for instance, plan on making public statements on such cases?

TJ: Culture has absolutely a dimension of social responsibility. I say this in a lot of interviews; that culture is the only transformative field in the Romani context, because in all the other dominant discourses – such as the major ones about housing, employment, health and education – Roma are primarily contextualized as a 'problem'. It is almost impossible to manoeuvre in these settings when you want to mobilize any kind of empowerment or inspiration. For the time being then, culture seems to be the only field in which the Roma are contextualized more positively. Particularly when it comes to antigypsyism, culture is actually *the* transformative field par excellence. Indeed, when Roma finally take ownership of their own image and are able to create counter-arguments, counter-images and counter-propaganda about themselves, the transformative power of arts and culture becomes obvious for everybody. I think we find ourselves at the moment just before a key political transformation – unfortunately, right in the midst of rising far-right propaganda; from my perspective, this is a dangerous moment. Against this background, it is very important that Roma are actively engaged in political processes. I leave it to my colleagues who are political theorists to discuss this in greater detail.

AMK: We are still learning about what the input of ERIAC would and could be. If we denounce manifestations of antigypsyism too often, our role as ERIAC might be mixed up with that of other actors already out there. We are neither the European Roma Rights Centre (ERRC), nor a kind of Roma Federation; we are not a political actor in that regard. On the other hand, it is very important for us to contribute to these discussions from the perspective of arts, culture and identity. Here I want to recall Nancy Fraser's important paradigm of recognition and redistribution, which implies that you really need both to achieve social justice (Fraser and Honneth 2003). ERIAC can feed into the recognition dimension. We are still learning how to do that, and what exactly ERIAC's role could or should be. I think there are very legitimate ways for us to contribute, but I do not think that it should be at a level of, strictly speaking, political activism. One of ERIAC's thematic sections deals explicitly with history and commemoration. In the case of Italy, for instance, I would like to emphasize that it is among the very few countries that has still not recognized the Roma Holocaust. In Italy, Roma are also still not recognized as a national minority, despite the fact that Italy has officially recognized twelve minorities.[9] Salvini's proposal of 2018 can be linked to Mussolini's government and its Roma census of 1940, as some other organizations have also done. But for the moment, it is important that we are not confused with other actors who are specifically dedicated to tackling such manifestations of antigypsyism.

TM: Seen from your perspective – and not necessarily one that is representative of ERIAC's position – what would be your take on affirmative action?

AMK: Eventually, we should reach a point where affirmative action is not something that we practice. We should strive for a post-ethnic world in which ethnic identity would be an asset, part of a personal history that we all have, since we all have our own backgrounds and cultures, and they all are worth being protected and promoted. Unfortunately, we are not yet there. I think that a certain level of positive discrimination through affirmative action is currently required to remedy the societal disadvantage rooted in historical and current patterns of exclusion. So, while eventually we should not have affirmative action, we need it today. Similar discussions are currently ongoing regarding gender quotas, for example, in political representation; or regarding quotas for university students in Latin America or the United States. There is always a level of backlash from within majorities, particularly from those who feel 'discriminated against' by such measures of affirmative actions – but we also see that they can really bring important results.

At this moment in time, unfortunately, we are in a situation in which we need to have some kind of remedial action, some type of preferential treatment as a way of seeking social justice and equality. The problem is that such calls are often misinterpreted and abused by the political right. Now we see Europe more and more shifting towards the right, we also see an increasing opposition from majority societies against initiatives such as the EU Framework for Roma and investments made to improve the situation of the Roma. There is no opposition when you invest in infrastructure. But when you invest in Roma, it is understood as 'giving money to the dirty

Gypsies', rather than as an investment in a future workforce that we need in our countries because European populations are aging. There is always a risk of backlash towards policies aimed at specific groups, and with European attitudes being what they are today, I fear that the Roma will increasingly be faced with hostility.

TM: *You (TJ) are both ERIAC's executive director and on the board of the Critical Romani Studies (CRS) journal. How do you balance the two, and what do you think the role of culture can be in academic knowledge production and scholarship? Are the CRS journal and ERIAC two separate and different things or two aspects of the same process?*

TJ: I think that a critical turn in Romani Studies has picked up speed only recently. Many of our cultural theorists and political theorists have started exploring how to decolonize scholarship regarding the Romani minority, and how to confront this epistemic and physical violence with our own strategies in the field of knowledge production. I think this is a field in which we are seeing exciting developments, not just because we now have our first feminist scholars with doctorates, such as Nicoleta Bițu and Angéla Kóczé, but because we have many more Roma with higher education qualifications. This is a moment in Romani history – if I may make a comparison to the Afro-American civil rights movement – similar to when bell hooks and Cornel West founded the first Afro-American Studies at Yale University in the US. Just a year ago, Angéla Kóczé and Iulius Rostas started the Romani Studies Program at CEU, and one of its first key products is the *Critical Romani Studies* journal. I hope that this will be the journal of our cultural movement and of the desired critical turn in discourse in which Roma are taking knowledge production about themselves into their own hands.

AMK: Different processes have been initiated and they respond to different struggles, even while they are parallel to each other and coincide at this moment in time. Their background and simultaneity have to do with the new militancy to which I referred earlier, and those who are involved sharing many of its leading principles. However, these different processes also relate to different institutional structures: the journal *Critical Romani Studies* is primarily tied to CEU and to the fact that, recently, a brand-new Chair of Romani Studies has been established there, occupied by Iulius Rostas. A CRS journal has long been overdue – one that provides an academic space of relevance, that provides Romani scholars a platform of the same importance and status as other sources of knowledge, and that looks critically at the legacy of Romani Studies [not necessarily of the homonymous journal, but rather as a field of academic involvement that deals with Roma]. Tímea is on the editorial board of the journal and we as ERIAC are collaborating closely, because we also would like to support a platform in which arts, culture and the performativity of identity can be discussed from academic perspectives, possibly in collaboration with Romani artists. What is also important to mention, and what may cause some confusion about the collaboration between CRS and ERIAC, is that ERIAC is a membership-based organization. We are closing the first intake of members at the moment [July 2018]. We have organized membership thematically, in four areas, and one of them is related to knowledge production and research in the fields of arts and culture. We want Romani and non-Romani individuals and organizations to join ERIAC, and then to try to discuss together what types of knowledge, debates and topics we could or should deal with. Knowledge production is of course critical for shaping self-crafted narratives on Roma and taking control over images and discourses about us, and it overlaps with aspects of the other sections as well.[10]

TM: What do you think that the role or attitude of the European Academic Network of Romani Studies (EANRS) could or should be?

AMK: Speaking from the point of view of a scholar, I think it is important to work as a network. Having spaces in which we can exchange and discuss is incredibly enriching: from these experiences we learn and, as a scholar, staying connected is very valuable. The initial idea of the European Academic Network of Romani Studies was very good and, when I was still a PhD candidate, I was among the first to join. However, it failed to be a safe space for discussion; it failed to be a space of respectful, content-based debate. At some point, the tone of discussions became quite intimidating, especially for young scholars, and even more so for those with a Romani background. Most of them [young Romani scholars, and members more broadly] stayed silent; which is a pity, because the network has about four hundred members, which in itself is a huge resource. EANRS could have been a space for discussion, but it became the main space for polarization and politicization within academia, and also cultivated a completely arbitrary and counterproductive Roma/non-Roma divide. Network members did not manage to redirect it or use its great potential.

The work of the secretary, László Fosztó, is very valuable and still provides references for publications, posts for summer schools and so on; this is important, because it works as a source of knowledge and information. But EANRS is no longer a legitimate space for academic discussion. Presently, its members will not position themselves as a network in any productive way – at least, I doubt it, because officially the network no longer exists – and if it does, the scientific committee, the steering committee, none of the structures have a mandate any longer, because they have not been re-elected. They were supposed to hold elections that were called off, which is something that I pointed out in a public forum and, in turn, I was attacked by several scholars on that forum as well. It's okay, I think it is fine. Many of the Roma who are not vocal in this network decided to stay silent, because it is not a space for legitimate discussion for us, it is not a space we recognize, nor one in which we feel safe so that we can engage in respectful discussion among adults.

TM: *Thus far, it seems that the criticism that ERIAC has received has primarily come from those who have been involved in knowledge production related to Roma or in pro-Roma activities. Have you received negative attention from right-wing governments or groups?*

AMK: The right-wing governments in Europe are simply not supportive, or ignore us. On the other hand, with Berlin as our visible headquarters, we have probably managed to develop a safe space for ourselves; I could imagine that if we were based in a different country, we would probably have had to deal with more attacks and direct forms of harassment. In Berlin, we are in a very open and tolerant, welcoming environment, in which it is good to be and work. Yet, occasionally, social media can really turn into a hostile space, where we are sometimes attacked – you know, nasty comments, articles and those kinds of responses.

TM: *You mentioned that ERIAC has made considerable efforts to consider dimensions such as gender equality, multiculturalism and representation from different countries. How do you see the emphasis on these dimensions in relation to the fact that, as you were saying, ERIAC emerged as a product of Romani intellectuals and artists? How do you respond to suggestions that ERIAC embodies the Romani elite, rather than being representative of the Romani minority in Europe more broadly?*

AMK: I do not have problems with how ERIAC emerged out of a group of Romani intellectuals and artists. I find the entire critique of the elitism that would have been involved quite silly, because if you look at social movements and how they emerge and evolve, the role of elites is always key. This involvement of elites is fundamentally a question of resources, connections and also of capacity. So, it is not surprising or exceptional at all those initiatives such as ERIAC are not born out of a Romani mahalla [neighbourhood] but emerge from collaborations between Roma who have a certain level of privilege, whether it is by birth or their own merit. What is important to recognize is that those who were involved in ERIAC's establishment developed a vision, an idea that was shared and considered essential and inspiring enough to realize, and to which time and energy should be dedicated. But the idea was never to create something perfect out of nothing: it was about creating a strong but still provisional framework that could then be developed further. ERIAC is that kind of framework; it is a space that allows content to be created. The idea was: 'Okay, let's do whatever is in our power; let's use our resources and knowledge, and our own money, to advance this idea and create an institution that can then become a communicator and a space in which everybody can interact who wants to'.

At this moment in time [summer 2018], we are in another, still somewhat peculiar phase, in which we are completing the bodies and governing institutions of ERIAC. Once all the bodies are in full operation, the strategy of ERIAC will also be defined more prominently, through and by these bodies and the members of the Barvalipe Academy. Eventually, we hope that other countries will also embrace this idea of having Roma cultural institutes; in the future, we would like to develop local branches in different countries in which the specific role played by Roma communities and cultures throughout history and in contemporary societies can be represented adequately. The content that we want to develop within and with the support of ERIAC will come from our people – from their experiences and their knowledge on the ground, where there is so much richness and so much talent. ERIAC is here to upscale.

TJ: Often, people connect ERIAC to elitism but, unfortunately, there is never enough money to do anything really elitist in the Romani context. Let me give you an example of our 'elitism': we are based in Berlin and we have €400,000 institutional support and €200,000 in project funding. Just one kilometre away from our office, there is the Haus der Kulturen der Welt [House of the World's Cultures], which is supposed to be a competitor of ours and which organizes a barbeque every summer that costs €800,000. That's not their cultural programme; that's chicken wings and hot dogs. As a tiny and vulnerable Romani organization, located in Berlin's fancy Reinhardstrasse, we are supposed to run a cultural programme in twenty-eight EU member states with exactly this amount of money and with three employees! How elitist is that? We are still struggling against unrealistically high expectations.

TM: What kind of public are you aiming at? Who would you like to attract to ERIAC? And how would you like people to approach ERIAC?

AMK: For ERIAC to be successful, it is important that we work effectively with our own people, with our communities, so that we can really become a useful tool for them. But maybe it is even more important that we establish very strong partnerships with mainstream institutions. I mean not only with governmental institutions, but also with the mainstream cultural ones, such as with mainstream film festivals, with the archives and national galleries, and so on. Through such collaborations and partnerships, we can create a space in which Roma are recognized as contributors and creators in the same capacity as everybody else. At this moment in time, no matter whether it is in the field of knowledge production, or media or visual arts, we are still faced with a considerable level of the marginalization or orientalization of Roma. Roma are often still not recognized as a people with a very valuable culture and identity. Due to this climate, it is still very difficult for our contemporary artists, for example, to exhibit in contemporary galleries and other art spaces. Instead, they and their works are often relegated to the more traditional and often orientalist ethnographic museums. One of ERIAC's main aims is, therefore, to create an open space for Roma in which organizations and individuals can embrace Romani arts and culture without these prejudices. For example, working towards the inclusion of a Romani Pavilion in the Venice Biennale is important in terms of presenting the work of Romani artists in the context of the most prestigious contemporary art event in the world.

So far, we have attracted different types of audiences. In our office space in Berlin, a lot of people come without 'invitation' and just walk in. These are people who just pass by and are generally driven by curiosity; they could be students, elderly couples or tourists. Furthermore, there is quite a lot of interest on behalf of public institutions, particularly German ones; they really wanted to have ERIAC in Berlin. However, we do not want to be seen as a German stakeholder, replacing existing structures. There is a very rich scene here in Germany and there are very many different Roma groups, because there are traditional Sinti groups, the immigrant Roma from the Balkans and so on. We have not yet organized school visits, but this is also an avenue to be explored.

TJ: This is an arts and culture organization, so we try to target an audience interested in arts and culture with the highest quality standard. We are reaching out to, supporting, and in dialogue with a network of over six hundred Romani organizations and individuals active in Europe. When we work at the country level, we first reach out to our members and engage with NGOs and individuals in each working theme. I want to stress, though, that we need more organizations. We need to avoid putting all expectations onto ERIAC; we should have many European and transnational initiatives. We also have to forget all the ideas about competition. Instead, we have to learn a completely new pedagogy of aligning our interests and allying ourselves across countries, across institutions, across sectors, with Roma and non-Roma, in order to create real transformation in Europe.

Tina Magazzini is a Research Associate at the Robert Schuman Centre for Advanced Studies of the European University Institute (EUI) in Florence, Italy, where she works on the project 'GREASE – Radicalisation, Secularism and the Governance of Religion: Bringing together European and Asian Perspectives'. Her research interests are in the fields of comparative politics, migration and integration policies, diversity management, identity and the relationship between majorities, minorities and states. Recent publications include articles for *Migration Letters, Policy & Politics* and *International Migration*, and an edited volume for the Springer IMISCOE series. Prior to joining EUI, she worked with several NGOs, the European Commission, the Council of Europe and UNESCO in the areas of social inclusion, Roma integration policies and minority rights in Portugal, the United States, Guatemala, Belgium, Hungary, Spain and Zimbabwe. She holds a BA in Political Science (University of Florence), an MA in International Relations (CCNY) and a PhD in Human Rights (University of Deusto).

Tímea Junghaus is the European Roma Institute for Arts and Culture executive director, an art historian and contemporary art curator. Previously, Junghaus was Research Fellow of the Working Group for Critical Theories (Institute for Art History, Hungarian Academy of Sciences, 2010–2017). She has researched and published extensively on the conjunctions of modern and contemporary art with critical theory, with particular reference to issues of cultural difference, colonialism and minority representation. She is completing her PhD studies in Cultural Theory at the Eötvös Lóránd University, Budapest. In recognition of her curatorial activities, Junghaus received the Kairos – European Cultural Prize in 2008. Her curatorial works include the Roma component of the Hidden Holocaust exhibition in the Budapest Kunsthalle (2004), Paradise Lost – the First Roma Pavilion at the 52nd Venice Contemporary Art Biennale (2007), the Archive and Scholarly Conference on Roma Hiphop (2010), and The Romani Elders and their Public Intervention for the Unfinished Memorial to the Sinti and Roma Murdered Under the National Socialist Regime, at the 7th Berlin Biennale (2012).

Anna Mirga-Kruszelnicka is the European Roma Institute for Arts and Culture deputy director, an anthropologist and a Roma activist. She earned her PhD in Social and Cultural Anthropology at the Universitat Autònoma de Barcelona (UAB) in 2016. She has authored policy evaluations, reports and articles, and co-edited the book *Education for Remembrance of the Roma Genocide: Scholarship, Commemoration and the Role of Youth* (Libron, 2015). From 2013–2015, she was an OSF Roma Initiatives Fellow, conducting a comparative study of the Roma associative movements across Latin America and Europe. From 2015 to 2017, she was the coordinator and curator of the Academic Section (aka Roma Civil Rights Movement Section) in the RomArchive – Digital Archive of the Roma. From 2017 to 2018, she was a Post-Doctoral Research Fellow of the Romani Studies Program at the Central European University (CEU) in Budapest.

Notes

I would like to thank Tímea Junghaus and Anna Mirga-Kruszelnicka for their time and willingness to share their experiences during the conducted interviews, as well as Angéla Kóczé and Huub van Baar for their constructive feedback and for including this contribution in their volume regarding the broader debate on Romani culture and identity.

1. An interview with Dr Anna Mirga-Kruszelnicka took place on 10 July 2018, and with ERIAC's executive director Tímea Junghaus on 4 September 2018, both via Skype. Both interviews addressed roughly the same issues, and while I alone am responsible for combining the two interviews around what I saw as the three core themes of (a) the making of ERIAC, (b) ERIAC's positioning and (c) knowledge-production and the political responsibility of arts and culture, the edited version of this chapter was sent back to the interviewees to ensure accuracy and that no misinterpretation had occurred in merging them. Regarding the selection of the material, all answers were kept in their entirety, with the exception of a few passages that the interviewees felt it was better to remove or rephrase to better convey what they meant. Minor linguistic revisions were made in the editing phase.
2. Rachel Dolezal, an American former civil rights activist who self-identifies as black, triggered a debate on ethnic identity when her 'white' parents publicly stated that she was a 'white' woman passing as 'black'. For an overview of debates regarding this case, see Brubaker 2016.
3. *Barvalipe* means richness or pride in the Romani language. The Open Society Foundations Roma Initiatives Office has organized Barvalipe schools since 2011, aimed at supporting the emergence of young Romani leaders. In ERIAC, the Barvalipe Academy is its agenda-setting and strategic body. See also https://eriac.org/barvalipe-academy/.
4. According to the statute, two-thirds of academy members must openly declare their Romani ethnicity, respecting the diversity among the Romani communities. Gender balance must also be ensured.
5. In the Romani language, *pakiv* means to obey, respect, honour or esteem. It can also be used for ceremonial celebrations to honour special guests. ERIAC's Pakiv Board oversees the work of the institute, safeguards its values and approves the financial and activity plans. See also https://eriac.org/pakiv-board/.
6. Conversi (2018) has convincingly argued that flamenco was primarily constructed as a Spanish 'national' cultural marker abroad, particularly in Paris, despite the fact

that it originated from an ethnically and geographically bounded identity that had little to do with the Spanish nation-state.
7. For information on the REACH project see https://www.reach-culture.eu/.
8. For instance, through the Council of Europe's Framework for Minority Languages and its Framework for Minority Rights and Protection. These dimensions are also relevant for impact in the field of Roma Holocaust education.
9. In 1999, the Italian government passed a law (482/1999) for the protection of those minorities identified as 'national' or 'Historic Linguistic Minorities', aimed at safeguarding 'the languages and culture of the Albanians, Catalans, Germans, Greeks, Slovenians and Croatians, as well as of those speaking French, Franco-Provençal, Friulan, Ladino, Occitan and Sardinian' (Italian Government 1999a: art. 2, Italian Government 1999b: 3). The law established a national fund for the protection of linguistic minorities to ensure the teaching of minority languages and cultural traditions, and for their use in official acts at various administrative levels, as well as in the media (Council of Europe 2016: Chapter 5.1; Italian Government 1999a: 31). The absence of Romanes as a recognized minority language in this setting is telling. According to the 'first report' on the status of minorities in Italy of 1994 (Ministero dell'Interno 1994), as well as to a previous draft of law 482, Roma and Sinti were considered a linguistic minority, but in the final stages of the law approval they were eventually excluded from the scope of the law because of the resistance of a significant section of the Parliament, who argued that Roma and Sinti failed the 'territoriality' criterion required by the state for the protection of minorities (Tavani 2012: 209–11). In other words, '[t]he impression is that not all cultural and linguistic groups are a constitutive part of the multicultural Italian nation' (ibid.: 207).
10. The other three sections are 'Arts and Culture', 'History and Commemoration', and 'Media and Information in the Fields of Arts and Culture'.

References

Brubaker, R. 2016. 'The Dolezal Affair: Race, Gender and the Micropolitics of Identity', *Ethnic and Racial Studies* 39(3): 414–48.
Conversi, D. 2018. 'The Nation in the Region: Flamenco and *canzone napoletana* as National Icons in Modern Spain and Italy (1880–1922)', *Nations and Nationalism* 24(3): 669–94.
Council of Europe. 2016. 'Cultural Policies and Trends in Europe: Italy, General Legislation'. Retrieved 4 September 2019 from https://www.culturalpolicies.net/web/profiles-news.php?pcid=1250.
Fraser, N., and A. Honneth. 2003. *Redistribution and Recognition? A Political-Philosophical Exchange*. London: Verso.
Italian Government. 1999a. Law No. 482 (1999). Norme in materia di tutela delle minoranze linguistiche storiche. Vol. 297, art. 1.1: 2–4. Retrieved 7 November 2018 from: http://www.camera.it/parlam/leggi/99482l.htm.
———. 1999b. First Report submitted by Italy on the Framework Convention for the Protection of National Minorities. Retrieved 10 October 2018 from: https://rm.coe.int/CoERMPublicCommonSearchServices/DisplayDCTMContent?documentId=090000168008af0e.

Magazzini, T. 2016. 'Cultural Institutions as a Combat Sport: Reflections on the European Roma Institute', *The Age of Human Rights Journal* 7: 50–76.
Ministero dell'Interno. 1994. Primo rapporto sullo stato delle minoranze in Italia. Ufficio centrale per i problemi delle zone di confine e delle minoranze etniche. Retrieved 10 October 2018 from: https://ebiblio.istat.it/SebinaOpac/resource/primo-rapporto-sullo-stato-delle-minoranze-in-italia-1994/IST0016757.
Mirga-Kruszelnicka, A. 2018. 'Challenging Anti-Gypsyism in Academia: The Role of Romani Scholars', *Critical Romani Studies* 1(1): 8–28.
Tavani, C. 2012. *Collective Rights and the Cultural Identity of the Roma. A Case Study of Italy*. Leiden: Martinus Nijhoff Publishers.

CHAPTER 11

❉ ❉ ❉

A *GYPSY REVOLUTION*
The Ongoing Legacy of Delaine and Damian Le Bas

Annabel Tremlett and Delaine Le Bas

> I wanna really do something for Travellers so there is a legacy for the future generations, telling our great-great-grandkids...
> —Damian Le Bas, 7 June 2012, Worthing

This chapter is based on a conversation between artists Delaine le Bas and Damian le Bas and academic Annabel Tremlett at Delaine and Damian's home in Worthing, UK, in June 2012. The conversation itself was a precursor to a paper we (Delaine and Annabel) wrote for a conference,[1] and this chapter is based on that co-written paper. At the time, we were working with a Traveller community near Southampton, and the conversations we had in and around that work – how art can afford space for interactions and mobilization – inspired this chapter. The devastating news that Damian had passed away suddenly in December 2017 led to a surge of feeling that Damian's legacy should not end with his death, but should be ongoing. By taking his and Delaine's work as examples, this chapter discusses the role of their work in the contemporary Roma art movements and in the challenges for recognition, both politically and personally.

This one recording cannot do justice to Delaine and Damian's work as artists, or Damian's devotion to his family life and his commitment to his diverse range of friends. The energy generated by the crowds gathered in the pub at Worthing directly after his funeral spoke far more about him as a person. So this is neither an obituary for Damian nor a situation of his work in the past; there are plenty of other sources that do him far more justice.[2] This chapter is rather about the ongoing 'Gypsy Revolution' that both Damian and Delaine continue to stimulate, a testament to their work that forms, in Damian's words, a continuing legacy for all of our 'great-great-grandkids'.

From Identity Politics to Emancipation

The image of the gadjo-hating Roma, Gypsy or Traveller who opposes 'mainstream' societal norms and legal rules is frequently deployed by the media. In the UK, for example, Travellers stopping in their caravans are frequently reported as 'invaders' whose purpose is 'antagonizing the settled community' (Richardson 2006: 90). In Central and East European countries such as Hungary and Slovakia, where Roma/Gypsy people are generally sedentary, the predominant media and public image is still based on their deviance and antipathy to the (supposed) 'norms' of their non-Roma neighbours (Csepeli and Simon 2004; Messing and Bernáth 2017). What the dominant public representations do not show are Roma, Gypsy or Traveller people who get on with their neighbours, who do not automatically hate non-Roma, who might also be from mixed backgrounds and who actually work towards a better society for all. This is where Delaine and Damian Le Bas step in: two artists with very different styles and Traveller backgrounds who, both as individuals and as a couple, exude creativity, curiosity and kindness in an often pernicious society. Their aim has always been to expose and interrogate such animosity through a *Gypsy Revolution* – also the title of one of their exhibitions (2012) – that aims to integrate art with community events and actions that they describe as 'militant'. But their 'militancy', whilst confrontational, is never venomous or aggressive, but embedded in a generosity of spirit, in collaborations and affiliations (see also van Baar, Chapter 1, this volume).

The term 'identity politics' can be ridiculed – a 'modern addiction' says the *New Statesman* (Lilla 2017); its meaning can become 'flimsy' or 'shallow' says *The Guardian* (Foster 2018). Yet with Delaine and Damian, 'identity politics' becomes something emancipatory, based on learning about oneself in order to understand others. Damian hones in on the importance of understanding the personal – in his case why, despite having a large family and going 'off the rails' in his childhood, he became interested in drawing:

> Well I know we do the political stuff and that a lot more now but part of it, for me anyway, was that I almost learned through searching into myself as a person. You

know, that's why with my roots or whatever, made me the way I am. Why I fell off
the rails, why I never got any exams or . . . it's only why, that's why I'm the sort of
person that I am, you know? . . . Why all of these things happen and you don't . . .
you've got such an enormous family but then you end up just sort of on your own,
doing your little doodles in your little room in Worthing (Laughter). You know?

The 'political stuff' only comes about when you understand the vivid contrasts *and* connections between the intimate and wider positioning that evolves from you sitting on your own, drawing.

This wonderful image of Damian doodling in his 'little room in Worthing' is not the image of some romantic Traveller artist; Worthing is an average, middle-class Victorian seaside town, a 'Terry and June' type of place[3] in southern England, whose ordinariness is only compounded by comparisons to its fast-paced, trendy neighbour Brighton. Damian thus sees his identity as rooted in the ordinary, highlighted not only by the setting but also in his use of the modest term 'doodle'. From humble 'little doodles' emerge fantastic art pieces, often huge in size and stature yet communicating an intimate expression of experiencing Traveller life and culture. This is true for both artists: Delaine speaks of coming back from Traveller fairs and being inspired to do figurative drawings in the early days, whereas Damian talks of hearing about racehorses from the Irish Traveller side of his family (his great-grandfather was a horse trainer and coachman), and collecting little pictures of racehorses that inspired his early artworks and later formed the basis of his portfolio for the Royal College of Art. Figurative drawings and collecting pictures of racehorses are not instances of elite culture – they are not claiming some wider, grand authenticity – but rather a close, private, individual experience that happens to link to wider notions of 'Traveller' identity – to what Homi Bhabha (1996) might call an example of 'vernacular cosmopolitanism'.

The ways in which their work as artists provides a dialogue between academia and creativity are profoundly exciting. For both artists, art becomes an expression of specific memories that they work into broader politics. Damian's propensity for drawing maps in many of his works, for example, draws on his own feelings of not belonging, which also becomes about reclaiming a place in the world for Travellers, and a way of recognizing their histories along with his own. 'I work on old maps and turn them into art,' he says, 'and it's to do with the fact that I don't feel like I belong anywhere on the map, or any particular country.' Reclaiming such spaces by inscribing – as Damian does – Romany faces and caravans on maps of Ireland, Europe and beyond, echoes Ethel Brooks's subversive reclamation of 'Roma camps' (both the camps people lived in and concentration camps of persecution) and 'encampment', a set of practices that create the camp. In her view, '[t]o embrace Roma encampment would mean a radical rejection of the power embedded in the buildings, monuments and marble halls of the dominant; the camp is another engagement with space, embodiment and permanence' (Brooks 2013: 122). Damian's maps become a means to reimagine a landscape where borders are easily crossed – in fact they do not exist quite as we remember – and we are drawn into his maps intrigued and challenged by the familiar mapping juxtaposed with faces and caravans that belong/do not belong (see also van Baar, Chapter 1, this volume).

Brooks's notion of encampment thus creates a sense of belonging, even when 'not belonging' is a prominent aspect of that experience. Delaine's exhibition *Witch Hunt* (2009 ongoing) is another example of this. A striking theme in the exhibition is small dolls with sweet faces peering out from what seems to be cloaks made from black bin liners (Figure 11.1).

As you look at the dolls, the effect is curious: it is not a straightforward repulsion of the blue-eyed dolls' faces juxtaposed with menacing darkness, because they still look very innocent. Delaine says the dolls remind her of her early days at school:

> It's that strange mixture of being attractive but a bit strange at the same time . . . a lot of it reverts back to when I was a child and I started school. I was completely unaware of how . . . maybe how much venom there is towards people who are different. It was only when I started school that I realized that . . . but also maybe because my best friend at primary school was a little girl who was being cared for by some foster parents in Worthing who were from Africa. And we were very, very close friends and I think maybe because I was the way I was, because I never really had a proper school uniform, and I had my ears pierced – which isn't uncommon now, but when I started school in 1970 there was only one set of girls who had had their ears pierced that early, and that was the Traveller girls. So my friend and I we were both different in our own ways.

In Delaine's experience, 'difference' was an experience imposed on her in an institutional setting, and the dolls appear to capture that ambivalent position of having good feelings in this setting – for instance, becoming close friends with someone at school – alongside a growing awareness of being singled out as different through certain 'markers' of identity. As a child in the 1970s, this 'marker' was her pierced ears and lack of conformity in her school uniform that gave away her Traveller (English Romany) identity. Whilst many young girls today have their ears pierced, Travellers are still marked out as 'deviant' through other means – for example, their style of talking or where they live, the vehicles they drive or the music they listen to. Moving beyond biological racism – without losing its vicious doctrines – this cultural racism is still pernicious in its shifting goals of acceptance and rejection.

Figure 11.1 'Bin Bag Dolls', Delaine Le Bas, 2005. Image taken from ROOM catalogue. Courtesy of The Le Bas Archive & Collection. Photographic credit: Tara Darby.

Moving to wider politics, such subversive pieces show a strong rejection of the ways prominent images of Travellers and Gypsies are circulated in society and take up so much space in the public's imagination of 'who' the Gypsies are. In *The Buccaneers*, we see a painting of a Carmen-like woman (see Figure 11.2), easily recognizable as the 'true Gypsy' constructed by the late nineteenth-century romantic period, and early twentieth century art and literature in which Gypsy folklore was popularized, but had more to do with the writers' desires and political and artistic climate at the time and less to do with an actual way of life for a defined group of people (Willems 1997).

Figure 11.2 'The World of Gypsy Romance?' (Carmen painting, detail), Delaine and Damian Le Bas. From the exhibition *The Buccaneers*, 2012. Courtesy of The Le Bas Archive & Collection. Photographic credit: Delaine Le Bas.

Yet the painting has been disfigured with red paint, so it appears as though the woman's mouth is bleeding – such vandalism is emblematic of the anger against stereotypical images that overtly sexualize Gypsy and Traveller women. The violence symbolized by the blood can be interpreted in many

FIGURE 11.3. 'Don't Tell Us Who We Are' and 'Gypsy Anarchy' print, Delaine and Damian Le Bas. Original artwork produced in 2011 for HIAP Residency, Finland. Courtesy of The Le Bas Archive & Collection. Photographic credit: Delaine Le Bas.

ways, but we know that the woman is no longer just a pretty, romantic image. She bleeds like any human (see also van Baar, Chapter 1, this volume).

Similarly, the work 'Head in Scarf' by Delaine Le Bas and Damian James Le Bas from *The Romany Cultural & Arts Company* exhibition in 2012 depicts a mannequin's head and face covered entirely by a colourful scarf. It makes a clear statement about the inability of the Traveller or Gypsy woman to speak out. We cannot see her face; we cannot hear her speak. The potent image of the scarf symbolizes Gypsy traditions but it is this image that covers and strangulates her – from without and within, or both? But we cannot help noticing that it is also a beautiful scarf; once again, the tensions between attraction and repulsion, the internal and external forces of integration and exclusion we saw with the dolls in *Witch Hunt* and Damian's map paintings, are interrogated.

The reclaiming of space continues in 'Don't Tell Us Who We Are' (taken from *Gypsy Revolution*, see Figure 11.3). The title of the work is graffitied over a book page showing an old black and white image of two laughing men. 'Photographing people and referring to them as "untitled" totally hides their identities and makes them into a thing that represents "Gypsies", rather than exploring their actual lives and feelings', comments Delaine. Photographers, albeit often unwittingly, contribute to this, she says, as they 'can't help but bring an agenda' because they are attracted to a certain 'aesthetic' that comes from a template of an imagined Gypsy:

> I think that photographers bring with them an idea ... it's very much an external thing and I think it is hard ... I actually think it's really, really hard, because obviously if you go to a particular place, there's something about the aesthetic of the way things are put together and you're going to be ... if you've got any sort of visual eye then you're going to be attracted to that. So, for example, the way someone's dressed because it's a bit off-kilter – you're going to want to capture that, and then that becomes all about an idea of 'the Gypsies'.

The 'external' influence is the idea of the other, exotic, the 'off-kilter' look that attracts the photographer's eye, and this then links to wider notions of 'Gypsies' and allows the photographer's 'agenda' to be fulfilled, perpetuating the cycle of circulated stereotypes.

In this theme of outsider perception, Damian speaks of how constraints often come from how others see him. One example he gives was when he was asked to do a video for the Irish Traveller movement, and how he could not make himself understood that he was from a mixed background:

> I was explaining, you know, that I'm from a mixed background, you know? I'm part Irish Traveller, but also English Traveller as well, from Derby and different places. And I saw myself as being mixed – this, that and the other – but people, they'd like to be able to put you in a perfect little box ... and Delaine and myself being together [Delaine is from an English Romany background], we're not unique, we're like from a total mixed bag.

This recognition of being from 'a total mixed bag', 'this, that and the other', what cultural studies might call the 'hybrid' nature of identities, is still a coalescing debate in academic work with Traveller, Gypsy or Romani communities (Tremlett 2014; Surdu 2016; Magazzini 2017; Kóczé and Rövid 2017; Fremlová and McGarry 2019; Silverman, this volume; van Baar with Kóczé, Introduction, this volume). Delaine also mentions struggles with positivist and fixing ideas of a 'Traveller' or 'Gypsy' identity, saying it is 'a lot to do with stereotypes and what people think you should be because of who you are in that sense. So a lot of the work is about some myth busting'. Delaine and Damian's work provides fascinating insights into their experiences of plural and mixed identities: not only is their work regularly referenced with the play on 'Gypsy' stereotypes, but also with experiences of the interface between British, English and Irish national identities, and Traveller or English Romani identities (see, for example, Figure 11.4).

FIGURE 11.4 'The Fighting Irish', Damian Le Bas, 2008. Courtesy of The Le Bas Archive & Collection. Photographic credit: Huub van Baar.

Expressing notions of hybridity and experiences of inclusion/exclusion through art has the potential to provide a more liberating visual medium than photography, which, as Delaine comments, can too easily fall into a preset agenda.

The strong need to tackle stereotypes is something that has been noted in Roma art. 'Roma artists . . . need to reverse the existing stereotypes created in the media, by making images of the Roma that oppose the ones created in the mainstream culture', says Tímea Junghaus (2006: 7). This viewpoint leads to the question of whether the continual need to combat stereotypes constrains the type of art that can be produced by such artists. Faced with this question, both artists are emphatic that their artworks come first; 'We're still just making art at the same time', says Delaine. Their art is informed by their background and from that emerged their politics. As artists their politics, their personal lives, their connections to wider identities and their art live and breathe together. Junghaus's line that 'opposition is not enough' (n.d.) is emblematic of their work, as is Gayatri Spivak's (2012) 'making the visible and staging'.

In fact, it was Spivak who said, after visiting *Safe European Home?* for the first time, that the exhibition represented a particular 'theorizing grid'. *Safe European Home?* highlights the plight of Roma migrants from Central and Eastern Europe who continue to be forcibly ejected from European cities, finding themselves in impossible situations, unable to sustain a home or work life, and often ending up without identity papers. The exhibition/installations in a high-profile location outside the parliament building in Vienna bring the focus onto other situations such minorities find themselves in. Spivak called this 'theory as theatre':

> Theorizing, as making visible and staging, is not separate from art practice. I try to show this by suggesting that Damian and Delaine Le Bas's fragile staging of Roma life and history is just that: theory as theatre. Even if our birth certificate says 'Roma', we must pray to be haunted there because 'I cannot be in the other's place', especially historically – 'in the head of this other' – even if it is supposed to be my own history, history does not belong to anyone ... Delaine and Damian Le Bas's staging of the question mark in *Safe European Home?* is to be on a grid of theorizing, rather than caught in a theory-practice or theory-material opposition. I hope this will be clear – theorizing is an activity – in what I have to say in the time that remains. In some ways then, the way we look at theory or theorizing is a sabotaging of the classical Greek European model. (Spivak 2012)

As Spivak points out, it is not only the artworks themselves that provoke questions of difference and inclusion/integration, but also the 'stagings', the spaces and activities in which these artworks are exhibited, and which the next section now goes on to explore.

Spatial Politics: Art Creating Spaces for Solidarity

The previous section explored how Delaine and Damian's art moves from personal experience to becoming embedded in wider discourses of exclusion and stereotyping of Traveller, Gypsy and Roma minorities. We saw how artworks produced by both Delaine and Damian play with stereotypical images and explore tensions or ambiguities of representations. This section now turns to examining the spaces where these artworks are exhibited as sites that become politically interactive spaces.

Delaine and Damian have both exhibited individually and together in a wide range of settings, from Appleby Horse Fair to the first Roma art pavilion, called *Paradise Lost*, at the 2007 Venice Biennale. These settings have always stimulated interactions or become catalysts for political action that produce social change. Here we look at some examples, and argue that more attention should be paid to such events, utilizing Spivak's 'grid of theorizing'. This sees activism around terms such as 'social inclusion', not just as some formulaic transition from an imagined periphery to centre, but as active social change.

Their presence at their exhibitions and their direct engagement with their audiences is instrumental to their art as activism. One such example was their involvement in the 2006 exhibition *Second Site – Avre Yakha – Avere Thana – Wavver Yoks – Wavver Tans*. Initiated by long-standing activist and then-professor of Romani Studies at the University of Greenwich, Thomas Acton, the exhibition included a variety of artists and toured various locations in the UK, including the Stephen Lawrence Gallery at Greenwich, GRATAS in Leeds, the Appleby Horse Fair and the Museum of East Anglian Life. At each location, the artists held a number of workshops for young people to become engaged with the art practices they were viewing. There were many young people from Traveller and Gypsy backgrounds at these workshops who had never engaged with art before. Both Delaine and Damian say that the young people seem especially drawn to their own personal stories of struggling through education, whilst still managing to succeed. In Delaine's words:

> We don't hide anything, do we? [gesturing to Damian] About like the fact I didn't go to school that much and Damian got thrown out of school, but we managed to get the qualifications we've got, and now we do what we do all the time. So it's also saying to them that actually, if you really want to do something, if you put your mind to it, you can do it as well.

The young people attending the workshops were then encouraged to enter a poster competition launched to celebrate the first ever Gypsy Roma Traveller History Month. The prize giving, held within the Houses of Parliament, meant the presence of people from Traveller and Gypsy backgrounds in the centre of politics. As Delaine comments, 'never have so many Gypsies been within the walls of an institution that has done so much to persecute them'. Thus, an art exhibition became instrumental in encouraging members of the communities to become engaged with art and wider politics, as well as helping to establish a project promoting awareness of the histories of these communities, and which has now become a fixed point in the curriculum of many schools in the UK. This chain of events in itself reinforced the statement that Acton had made within the *Second Site* catalogue: 'This exhibition is an act of affirmation, not one of defence' (Acton 2006: 30).

Connections formed during the touring of *Second Site* then opened up opportunities for other networking: exhibitions have led to collaborations with social work students at the universities of Northumbria and Portsmouth, for example. This connection with social work departments links to the artists' desires to connect to a wider audience. As Delaine says, 'it's also about speaking out against discrimination, for anyone who feels belittled or marginalized'. Exhibitions are thus able to produce connections that reach through the artwork to produce situations of interactions between professions to debate practices of social inclusion. This links to Brooks's notion of encampment that does not exclude: 'Through the camp, another world is possible – for everyone, not just for we Roma' (Brooks 2013: 122).

A more detailed example is the 2011 *Reconsidering Roma* exhibition in Kreuzberg, Berlin. The opening of *Reconsidering Roma* coincided with the forced eviction of many Travellers from their homes at Dale Farm in Essex, UK. This news story dominated the British press for weeks, as a stand-off between residents, activists, bailiffs and the police made for sensationalist and racist headlines (Okely and Houtman 2011). Delaine organized an impromptu reading of a dozen news stories taken from the British press, read out by people attending the exhibition. Delaine reports how the audience members were shocked at the scale and ferocity of the anti-Traveller sentiment, thus raising awareness of the potency of discrimination in different contexts.

Such collaborative projects, epitomized in Damian and Delaine's 2011 *Safe European Home?*, are, as Damian says, where he wants his legacy to be:

Damian: The legacy – I've got to quickly get this out – is what I wanted to do. So we did *Safe European Home?* and we're building these shanty towns that are like the shanty towns that they're pulling down all over the place, in Italy and so on . . . so it's looking at all the Traveller places they are pulling down here, there and everywhere.

Delaine: But also for other people as well you know, providing some kind of support.

Damian: Yes, for other people as well.

Delaine: That's the thing with *Safe European Home?* We tried to open up, particularly, you know. It just so happens that even though we did it last year, we couldn't see how bad the recession was going to get in the light of the study of what has happened in Greece and stuff, and that actually people who never ever could have imagined themselves as being homeless are now homeless.

By focusing on points of solidarity – anyone can become poor and be evicted, anyone can be persecuted – such artistic interaction builds awareness and creates a collaborative environment for political and social change.

Not only have their exhibitions reached out to produce solidarity through collaborations, but they have also stimulated the notion of 'Roma art'. Junghaus, an art curator of Roma background herself, has been a central figure in encouraging and producing networks that promote artists from such backgrounds. Junghaus visited London to see the *Second Site* exhibition, which spurred her on to work towards her own vision for *Paradise Lost*, the first Roma Pavilion at the Venice Biennale, in 2007. Junghaus and her team in Budapest started to collate as much information as possible to find Roma artists across Europe, producing the book *Meet Your Neighbours*,[4] one of the first publications to bring together art from Traveller, Gypsy and Roma communities across Europe as 'Roma art'.[5] The workshop was the first major step in bringing these artists together and consolidating a network that would stretch across the borders of Europe.

For many of the artists involved, this would be their first major exposure to the art world at an international level. Moreover, despite difficult problems and constraints, detailed in the next section, the exhibition's impact on the art world cannot be underestimated either, for this was also a truly cross-European Pavilion with sixteen artists from eight different European countries. Relationships were formed here that still exist and continue to build an extensive network across Europe that has seen 'Roma art' grow dramatically since 2007. Such collaborations connect the experiences of Traveller, Gypsy and Roma minorities from across Europe, and lead to a greater exposure of discrimination directed at such communities. Nonetheless, the Roma Pavilion was also beset by problems, showing how encounters between 'Roma' and 'public space' continue to become fraught with politics and tensions, as the final section now moves on to discuss.

'The Roma Pavilion Got Lost': Constraints and Labelling

The dynamic and interactive way 'Roma art' is developing as a space for self and collective expression of social change does not come without certain limitations. Firstly, while art may have the potential to be a freer and more inclusive medium, the 'art world' of exhibition spaces, galleries and curators all construct their own barriers. As Delaine points out:

> I think it's much more rigid than people think it is. I think people have this idea that the art world is just a crazy place with all these eccentric characters doing amazing work, and they're really supporting it, but actually it's the complete opposite. It's very rigid. It has a really strict, tight set of rules, and if you don't abide by them, and you don't behave in a certain way, you get completely ostracized for it.

For example, whilst the first Roma Pavilion *Paradise Lost* at the 2007 Venice Biennale was hailed as a great success,[6] the project was beset with set-up problems, with inadequate time and space for the number of artists involved. This led to some artists not having enough access to their building prior to opening to adequately set up their paintings. There was also a lack of sign-posting to the building, so it was difficult to find. The subsequent Roma Pavilion in 2009 did not materialize because of internal politics and funding, leading to Damian Le Bas's postcard 'Roma Pavilion Got Lost' (see Figure 11.5). Being an artist clearly requires great dependence on the work and advice of art curators, who require a high level of art-world literacy to successfully negotiate all the different institutions and funding bodies.

Secondly, there are problems with authenticity: as 'Roma art' becomes a movement, funding bodies have a sudden, but temporary, inclination to have a 'Gypsy moment', as Damian puts it, only funding certain short-term projects that base themselves on an idea of 'authentic Gypsy' without understanding the complexities of diverse identities and socioeconomic positioning. Both artists are frequently told they do not dress or talk in the 'right' way to be identified as Travellers or Gypsies, and such comments have come from people with both Traveller (or Gypsy/Roma) and non-Traveller backgrounds. 'It's something we have to deal with all the time,' says Delaine, 'because you know we're always getting told you don't look like this, you don't know that, you don't talk like this, you don't do that.' Along with just continuing their artwork and attempting to engage with lots of different people with open minds, another way they deal with these criticisms is to continually play on the way they look and the labels they use. 'Chavi' (see Figure 11.6), for instance, shows how labels and looks become a way of reacting to and challenging notions of authenticity. This reverberates academic discussions on what 'authentic' means. Their play on their own identities echoing Stuart Hall's insistence that ethnicity has 'no guarantees in Nature' (Hall 1992: 253–54).

This leads to the third limitation: the use of labels such as 'Gypsy', 'Traveller' and 'Roma'. A major obstacle in the first Roma Pavilion at the 2007 Venice Biennale was the label 'Roma'. 'People kept talking to us in Italian about art from Rome' says Damian. 'We [were] stuck with the label "Roma"; this term is coming from certain Central and Eastern European groups, and [it] doesn't mean much to those who don't think of themselves as coming from those groups'. At the same time, other labels carry their own histories and politics: 'Travellers' has a definite British feel to it, while 'Gypsy' is still strongly associated with pejorative sentiments. Nonetheless, both artists agree that 'Gypsy' is the word that most people recognize and understand, and this is why they chose to call their collaboration *Gypsy Revolution*. 'Gypsy', they say, is deliberatively provocative – a way to motivate people to be aware of the politics of

Figure 11.5 'Roma Pavilion Got Lost', Delaine and Damian Le Bas, 2009. Intervention postcard: 'Roma Europe', Damian Le Bas, 2007. Courtesy of The Le Bas Archive & Collection.

Figure 11.6 'CHAVI', Delaine and Damian Le Bas, 2007. Invitation for *Chavi Exhibition: Daniel Baker, Damian Le Bas, Delaine Le Bas*, Novas Contemporary Urban Centre London, 2007. Courtesy of The Le Bas Archive & Collection. Photographic credit: Karl Grady.

labelling and the history of that labelling. 'It's a mixture of education and art that feeds into an ongoing discussion', Delaine said; 'it's about being militant about putting our objectives on the table, to say that we exist and we have histories, and we are doing stuff now and it's exciting'.

Conclusion: A Living Legacy

'It's time to get militant. Unless we are,' says Delaine, 'nothing will change' (see also Magazzini, this volume). When asked what counts as 'militancy', Delaine talks about drawing upon Black art and politics from the 1960s onwards, confronting difficulties and engaging with people for the purpose of empowerment:

> I think it's [militancy] about talking about things that people don't want to talk about. And I think it's about bringing that to people's attention. I think it's having discussions . . . if there is argument, then there is argument as well because I think you have to have that for stuff to come out of it. And I think always being passive is

not necessarily... it doesn't necessarily get the results that are needed to happen. I don't want to feel like in thirty years' time, that a kid like I was, who wants to be an artist, who comes from my community, can't do it.

This commitment to dialogue through art echoes Hall's interest in the ways that Black British art created certain 'moments' (Hall 2006: 3). Hall said that this is where, in these art pieces, 'enormously profound ideas and indeed concepts are at work, that art is a kind of thinking also; it's a way of feeling and a way of looking, but it's also a kind of thinking' (Hall in Dibb and Jaggi 2009, cited in Jordan 2015: 14).

'Roma art' is the place where these 'kinds of thinking' can happen, but even labelling is to be discussed, resisted and reinvented. For example, Damian discusses 'Gypsy Dada' as a new means to describe some of the more surrealist influences being used in Roma art. In using the term 'Gypsy Dada', he refers particularly to the work of his friend and fellow artist Gabi Jiménez and their work at the Berlin Gallery Kai Dikhas. But as soon as he introduces the term, he also rejects it:

> ... and it is sort of Dada really and that is what it is and ... But we don't, we weren't sure about the ... I wasn't sure about the Dada ... you know like what we do is Dada or that stuff but it is not really, you know, it's a reference but it's not really what we're doing. We're doing what we do.

'Doing what we do' sums up Delaine and Damian's approach to art. As Delaine says:

> I've got to compare it to one of Damian's maps ... we happened to draw our own map, because no one has ever navigated this territory before. And we've got to navigate in the best way we can, because you know, it's no good us denying that there are racist attitudes institutionalized in certain establishments. And that perhaps is the community we come from. We have to deal with that constantly. And I wish I didn't have to say that. And I wish it wasn't true, but it is.

Their art emerges from this navigation through racist attitudes and difficult territories. Reclaiming 'Gypsy' – but equally using 'Romani Revolution' or 'Roma art' if felt appropriate – is a part of that, as well as reaching out for other stigmatized labels. One of their exhibitions ('Chavi' 2007) centres on the term 'Chav' used as a derogatory term for white working-class people in the UK (see Jones 2011), particularly from the town of Chatham in Kent, a county well known for having a high number of people from Traveller and Romany roots. The label 'chav' – sometimes said to be an acronym for 'Council Housed And Violent' – is lesser known for its connection with Traveller and Gypsy people. As Damian points out, its roots can also be said to come from the Romani word 'chavvie', meaning children, and even the working-class trend for wearing leisure wear with flash jewellery (associated with 'chavs') is evident, and probably emanated from Traveller culture. The artists' embrace of 'chav' and their visual embodiment of the term mixing Traveller/working-class imagery (see Figure 11.6) is a classic example of how 'Gypsy' blends histories, cultures and identities, drawing people together.

Furthermore, Damian and Delaine's artworks and exhibitions speak to debates in academia and policymaking, the profound 'kinds of thinking' that Stuart Hall was talking about. In this chapter, we have seen how their exposition of Roma, Gypsy and Traveller identities, in which labelling is always evaded, always reclaimed, and always reinvented, talks to notions of hybridity that, in Werbner and Modood's words, moves 'even beyond postcolonial intellectual elites' (Werbner and Modood 2015: xviii). Their reinvention of 'chav', their reclaiming and rejection of labels such as 'Roma', 'Gypsy' and 'Gypsy Dadaism', along with their own presentations of self as a 'total mixed bag' of cultures and heritage, of being 'this, that and the other', is an example of Bhabha's 'local, vernacular cosmopolitans' that 'combine a demand for democracy, equality and transparency, rearticulated with a local culture, traditions and history' (ibid.).

Their approach to art also acts as a stimulant for thinking through the ubiquitous call for the 'social inclusion' of Roma minorities from the EU and its many institutions – there was even a Europe-wide 'Decade of Roma Inclusion 2005–2015' (see also Rostas, this volume; van Baar, Chapter 5, this volume). Their art stretches EU notions of 'inclusion as integration', and views inclusion as emblematic of social change. While EU ideas of integration are focused on getting Roma into employment, education and housing, this leads to the criticism that the Roma person becomes constructed as a kind of deficit outsider, in need of extra training/civilizing in order for 'them' to be accepted into 'our' education, employment and housing (Tremlett 2009; see also Kóczé, this volume; Szalai, this volume). Instead, Delaine and Damian's work offers sites for dialogues around what counts as skills, expertise and living. These dialogues are not easy, as Huub van Baar has commented: 'Damian and Delaine Le Bas's artworks express discomfort . . . their works express indignation over the parallel erection of boundaries between "us" and "them"' (van Baar 2013: 72). They provide a deep critique of the social rhetoric of trans/national policies, and produce alternative ways of imagining the Roma as *already* a part of Europe. Inclusion is often seen in narrow, formulaic terms about the integration of a group from an (imagined) periphery who are encouraged/cajoled into an (imagined) mainstream. Delaine and Damian's artwork and exhibitions reveal that to be a fallacy, and dynamically show how inclusion should be about listening to oneself and to others, facing challenges, and pushing for social activism and social change.

Damian's legacy includes all the above, and despite his bewildering and far too early departure, this legacy lives on. In this conversation in 2012, at his home in Worthing, he spoke about wanting his legacy to be built on his idea of an alternative to the Venice Biennale – a Gypsy Biennale. This he envisaged upon an encounter with skinheads in a bar in Austria:

> What I've been now planning for the last couple of years . . . I just had this mad idea when we were in Graz in Austria, weren't we? And it was really right wing, and I'd been accosted by all these sort of skinheads in a wine bar and I was just so pissed off and I thought of the Pavilion just petering out . . . And I thought, no, you know, this is just a collateral event, and I thought why is it just a collateral event? Why isn't it now a proper Pavilion and all the rest of it . . . so I said right, Dee, in our lifetime we're gonna have a Gypsy Biennale, I said, with a guest 'Gorgie' pavilion and that could be France or anywhere you know, but it's just like turning the whole thing on its head, and we could have it in countries at the same time . . . it could be the only true transnational event where it is really genuinely what it's supposed to be, and avoid all the politics.

So, Damian was the initiator of the first Gypsy Biennale, which was finally realized as the 'Roma Biennale', in collaboration with Roma Trial, the Gorki Theatre and many other artists, after his death, in April 2018. Dedicated to Damian, the Biennale was focused on art and performance, and was held at the Maxim Gorki Theatre in the centre of Berlin. Damian's work was not only seen in a retrospective, alongside artists Gabi Jiménez and Karol Radziszewski, but he had also designed the set for the theatre play *Roma Armee*, in which a cast of Roma actors and their non-Roma accomplices explore what it means to be the only people who have never started a war. Damian's maps form the backdrop with the words 'Gypsyland Europa' – his legacy realized, his legacy with Delaine and many other collaborators living on.

Annabel Tremlett is a Senior Lecturer at the University of Portsmouth in the UK. Her research interests include investigating the life stories and everyday experiences of people from minority or marginalized groups. She is particularly interested in how to challenge misleading representations and has extensive expertise in ethnographic and photo elicitation research. She has gained external funding from the British Academy/Leverhulme Trust and publishes her work in journals such as *Identities*, *Ethnicities* and *Ethnic and Racial Studies*, as well as at exhibitions and other community events.

Delaine Le Bas studied at the St Martin's School of Art in London and is a cross-disciplinary artist creating installations, performance, photography and film. She was one of the sixteen artists exhibited at *Paradise Lost: The First Roma Pavilion* at the Venice Biennale of 2007. She worked with her late husband, the artist Damian Le Bas, on their installations *Safe European Home?*, *Gypsy Revolution* and *Gypsy DaDa*. Delaine created *Romani Embassy* in 2015. Her works have been included in the Prague Biennale (2005, 2007), Venice Biennale (2007, 2017, 2019), Gwangju Biennale (2012), Zacheta National Gallery of Art (2013), MWW Wroclaw Contemporary Art Museum (2014), The Third Edition of the Project Biennial of Contemporary Art D-0 Ark Underground Bosnia & Herzegovina (2015), Off Biennale Budapest (2015), Goteborg International Biennale for Contemporary Art Extended (2015), Critical Contemplations Tate Modern (2017), and ANTI Athens Biennale (2018). Delaine was one of the curators for *Come Out Now! The First Roma Biennale* (2018), which her late husband Damian initiated.

Notes

Our thanks to the editors and the reviewers for their comments and suggestions; we hope we have done them justice. We just wish Damian was still here.

1. The original paper this chapter is based on is called 'Reclaiming "Gypsy": Art as Activism', presented at the UACES (The academic association for contemporary European Studies) 42nd annual conference in Passau, Germany, 3–5 September 2012.
2. See, for example: 'Obituary Damian Le Bas', *The Times*, 11 January 2018, retrieved 10 August 2018 from https://www.thetimes.co.uk/article/damian-le-bas-obituary-562ckk8jf. 'What is Soul – Damian Le Bas Special' on 20 January 2017 on 1Brighton FM, retrieved 10 August 2018 from Mixcloud: https://www.mixcloud.com/steve-mcmahon2/what-is-soul-damian-lebas-special-20117-on-1brightonfm/.
3. *Terry and June* was a popular UK television sitcom of the 1980s about a middle-aged, middle-class suburban couple and their humorous trials of life (BBC1, 1979–1987). The *Guardian* called Worthing 'Terry & June country' in their article about moving to the town (Dyckhoff 2016).
4. This 2006 collection of Roma art, *Meet Your Neighbours*, takes its title from a 2005 campaign by the British tabloid paper the *Sun* against Traveller sites in the UK. The *Sun* called their campaign a 'war on Gipsy free-for-all', invited readers to 'stamp on the camps' and featured photographs of Traveller sites with piles of rubbish, faceless groups of people standing around bonfires, and huge dilapidated caravans. Such reportage is well recognized as tapping into wider Gypsy stereotypes and deep-veined anti-Gypsy sentiment, emblematic of the 'pariah syndrome' (Hancock 1987) embedded in European cultures. In contrast to such negative stereotypes, the artwork in the collection shows a rich seam of activity that reveals the depth, breadth, variety and beauty of art produced from a range of people from various Roma and Gypsy backgrounds across Europe.

5. It is important to acknowledge the previous work of Roma activists and artists that paved the way for the possibility of the publication of *Meet Your Neighbours*; see Daróczi 2013 for an overview.
6. See Junghaus and Székely 2007.

Referenced Artworks

CHAVI: Reclaiming Gypsy Representation, 2007. Exhibition of work by Daniel Baker, Damian Le Bas and Delaine Le Bas including contributions by Tara Darby, Karl Grady, Jamal Jimenez and Paul Ryan, held at the Novas Gallery, London.

Gypsy Revolution, 2012. *Gypsy Revolution* was developed during a residency at HIAP Suomenlinna, Finland, curated by Marita Muukkonen and exhibited at the Cable Gallery, 2–26 February 2012, with a parallel exhibition at Kunstahalle Kallio, both in Helsinki.

Paradise Lost: The First Roma Pavilion. La Biennale Di Venezia, 2007. Munich: Prestel Publishers.

Reconsidering Roma – Aspects of Roma and Sinti Life in Contemporary Art, 2011, included work from Daniel Baker, Delaine Le Bas, Ceija Stojka and Karl Stojka. Curated by Lith Bahlmann and Matthias Reichelt at the Kunstquartier Bethanien Gallery, Berlin.

Safe European Home? is an ongoing art project initiated in 2011 by Damian Le Bas and Delaine Le Bas, first constructed outside the parliament building in Vienna in 2011 and has subsequently been installed in various forms in Berlin, Copenhagen, Dublin, Hastings and Thessaloniki. It was also exhibited in Worthing Museum & Art Gallery under the title *Safe European Home? (Past, Present, Future)* from 12 May to 13 October 2018.

Second Site – Avre Yakha – Avere Thana – Wavver Yoks – Wavver Tans, 2006. Catalogue of an exhibition by Daniel Baker, Ferdinand Koci, Damien Le Bas and Delaine Le Bas at the Stephen Lawrence Gallery, University of Greenwich. Compiled and edited by Thomas Acton and Grace Acton.

The Buccaneers exhibition, 2012 with work by Damian Le Bas and Delaine Le Bas. State Hall, Hastings.

The Romany Cultural & Arts Company exhibition, 2012, including works by Delaine Le Bas and Damian Le Bas, part of *The Cardiff Story* at The Old Library, The Hayes, Cardiff, June–August 2012.

Witch Hunt, 2009. Exhibition of work by Delaine Le Bas commissioned by Aspex Gallery, Portsmouth.

References

Acton, T. 2006. 'Second Site', in T. Junghaus and K. Székely (eds), *Paradise Lost*. Budapest: Open Society Institute. Retrieved 10 August 2018 from https://www.opensociety-foundations.org/reports/paradise-lost-first-roma-pavilion-venice-biennale.

Bhabha, H. 1996. 'Unsatisfied: Notes on Vernacular Cosmopolitanism', in L. Garcia-Morena and P.C. Pfeifer (eds), *Text and Nation*. London: Camden House, pp. 191–207.

———. (1997) 2015. 'Foreword', in P. Werbner and T. Modood (eds), *Debating Cultural Hybridity: Multicultural Identities and the Politics of Anti-Racism*. London: Zed Books, pp. ix–xviii.

Brooks, E. 2013. 'Reclaiming: The Camp and the Avant-Garde', in D. Baker and M. Hlavajova (eds), *We Roma: A Critical Reader in Contemporary Art*. Utrecht: BAK/Valiz, pp. 114–39.

Csepeli, G., and D. Simon. 2004. 'Construction of Roma Identity in Eastern and Central Europe: Perception and Self-identification', *Journal of Ethnic and Migration Studies* 30(1): 129–50.

Daróczi, A. 2013. 'The Birth of Roma Visual Arts – Hungary, 1979', in D. Baker and M. Hlavajova (eds), *We Roma: A Critical Reader in Contemporary Art*. Utrecht: BAK/Valiz, pp. 140–51.

Dibb, M., and M. Jaggi. 2009. 'Personally Speaking: A Long Conversation with Stuart Hall', DVD. Northampton, MA: Media Education Foundation.

Dyckhoff, T. 2016. 'Let's move to . . . Worthing, West Sussex: Don't mention the B word', *Guardian*, 28 October 2016. Retrieved 10 August 2018 from https://www.theguardian.com/money/2016/oct/28/worthing-west-sussex-property-guide-lets-move-to.

Foster, K. 2018. 'Identity politics has veered away from its roots. It's time to bring it back', *The Guardian*, 5 May 2018. Retrieved 22 October 2018 from https://www.theguardian.com/commentisfree/2018/may/05/identity-politics-veered-ideals-kimberly-foster.

Fremlová, L., and A. McGarry. 2019. 'Negotiating the Identity Dilemma: Crosscurrents across the Romani, Romani Women's and Romani LGBTIQ Movements', in A. Kóczé et al. (eds), *The Romani Woman's Movement: Struggles and Debates in Central and Eastern Europe*. London: Routledge, pp. 51–68.

Hall, S. 1992. 'New Ethnicities', in J. Donald and A. Rattansi (eds), *'Race', Culture & Difference*. London: Sage, pp. 252–59.

———. 2006. 'Black Diaspora Artists in Britain: Three "Moments" in Post-war History', *History Workshop Journal* 61(1): 1–24.

Hancock, I. 1987. *The Pariah Syndrome: An Account of Gypsy Slavery and Persecution*. Ann Arbor, MI: Karoma.

Jones, O. 2011. *Chavs: The Demonization of the Working Class*. London: Verso.

Jordan, G. 2015. 'Beyond Essentialism: On Stuart Hall and Black British Arts', *International Journal of Cultural Studies* 19(1): 11–27.

Junghaus, T. 2006. 'Foreword', in T. Junghaus and K. Székely (eds), *Meet Your Neighbours: Contemporary Roma Art from Europe*. Budapest: Open Society Institute, pp. 6–11.

———. n.d. 'Opposition is not enough. The role of Roma art in the contemporary constellation'. Retrieved 10 August 2018 from: http://romologiafolyoirat.pte.hu/?page_id=1202&lang=en.

Junghaus, T., and K. Székely (eds). 2007. *Paradise Lost: The First Roma Pavilion*. Munich: Prestel.

Kóczé, A., and M. Rövid. 2017. 'Roma and the Politics of Double Discourse in Contemporary Europe', *Identities: Global Studies in Culture and Power* 24 (6): 684–700.

Lilla, M. 2017. 'How the modern addiction to identity politics has fractured the left', *The Statesman*, 18 September 2017. Retrieved 22 October 2018 from https://www.newstatesman.com/politics/uk/2017/09/how-modern-addiction-identity-politics-has-fractured-left.

Magazzini, T. 2017. 'Making the Most of Super-diversity: Notes on the Potential of a New Approach', *Policy & Politics* 45(4): 527–45.
Messing, V., and G. Bernáth. 2017. 'Disempowered by the Media: Causes and Consequences of the Lack of Media Voice of Roma Communities', *Identities: Global Studies in Culture and Power* 24(6): 650–67.
Okely, J., and G. Houtman. 2011. 'The Dale Farm Eviction', *Anthropology Today* 27(6): 24–27.
Richardson, J. 2006. *The Gypsy Debate: Can Discourse Control?* Exeter: Imprint Academic.
Spivak, G.C. 2012. *Making Visible*. Retrieved 10 August 2018 from https://www.igkultur.at/artikel/making-visible.
Surdu, M. 2016. *Those Who Count: Expert Practices of Roma Classifications*. Budapest: CEU Press.
Tremlett, A. 2014. 'Making a Difference without Creating a Difference: Super-diversity as a New Direction for Research on Roma Minorities', *Ethnicities* 14(6): 830–48.
van Baar, H. 2013. 'Homecoming at Witching Hour: The Securitization of the European Roma and the Reclaiming of Their Citizenship', in D. Baker and M. Hlavajova (eds), *We Roma: A Critical Reader in Contemporary Art*. Utrecht: BAK/Valiz, pp. 50–73.
Werbner, P., and T. Modood. (1997) 2015. 'Preface to the Critique Influence Change Edition', in P. Werbner and T. Modood (eds), *Debating Cultural Hybridity: Multicultural Identities and the Politics of Anti-Racism*. London: Zed Books, pp. ix–xviii.
Willems, W. 1997. *In Search of the True Gypsy: From Enlightenment to Final Solution*. London: Frank Cass Publishers.

EPILOGUE

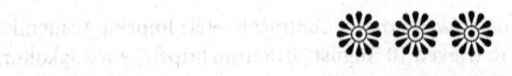

❋ ❋ ❋

THE CHALLENGE OF RECOGNITION, REDISTRIBUTION AND REPRESENTATION OF ROMA IN CONTEMPORARY EUROPE

Angéla Kóczé and Huub van Baar

The year 2019 marked thirty years since the collapse of state socialism and the beginning of the imagination of a free, unified and democratic Europe. In retrospect, and in many ways substantiated by the analyses included in this study, we know that for Roma minorities these thirty years of liberal democracy in Europe have rather led to a situation of an often-paralysing contradiction between, on the one hand, the strengthened structural violence based on the intersecting classed, racialized and gendered societal divisions implicated in neoliberal capitalism and, on the other hand, the opportunities of a new emancipatory grammar of political claim-making constituted in heterogeneous Roma movements. In the mid-1990s, Nancy Fraser discussed the political changes in Europe, and in Central and Eastern Europe in particular, as a shift towards a new 'postsocialist' imaginary in which the fundamental condition of justice was significantly reconceptualized:

> Many actors appear to be moving away from a socialist political imaginary, in which the central problem of justice is redistribution, to a 'postsocialist' political imaginary, in which the central problem of justice is recognition . . . The result is a decoupling of cultural politics from social politics, and the relative eclipse of the latter by the former. (Fraser 1997: 2)

In the context of these influential changes, the struggles for racial and gender justice were largely reconceptualized as an identity or cultural politics that tended to exclude key questions of distributive and social politics. In her contribution to this volume, Debra Schultz substantiates the false antithesis between recognition and redistribution by suggesting that the hegemonic focus on civil and political rights even in the emerging Roma women's movement occluded any discussion on social and economic rights that could expose the destructive impact of neoliberal capitalism on the socioeconomic situation of Roma, the exercise of their citizenship and their access to justice in the broadest sense of redistribution *and* recognition.

The overarching European social inclusion project dedicated to Roma and supported by the EU, other main international players and philanthropic organizations, such as the Open Society Institute, has resonated with the political shift from redistribution to recognition through the partial decoupling of the politics of recognition of Roma from the European – more specifically, the EU member states – economic and social politics of redistribution, and from any substantial and convincing development towards a social Europe more generally. Despite the fact that 'Roma ethnicity' and 'Roma equality' have become central principles in, for instance, the European Social Cohesion Fund's attempts to combat social exclusion, these endeavours were doomed to 'fail' in a context where the emphasis on welfare was diminishing and where material inequality drastically deepened in the newly developed social and economic landscapes throughout Europe. The basic premise of this edited volume has been to investigate the constitutive political and economic features of 'postsocialist' Europe in conjunction with the emergent politics of recognition and representation that have constantly shaped the Roma struggles for identity, notwithstanding the pitfalls of identity politics. Our critical approach has been to go beyond the paradigm of 'either/or' binary choices and to challenge any one-sided approach that rigorously rejects identity politics and overlooks or dismisses the opportunities of what we, in our Introduction to this volume, have called 'a critical politics of identity'.

What is more, the contributions to this volume have clarified that combining recognitive and redistributive trajectories, and securing the participation and representation of Roma in the development of such combined strategies in the contexts of public policies, politics, culture, citizenship, development, rights and social movements, are necessary but certainly not sufficient steps (see also van Baar and Vermeersch 2017). In this context, once again, Nancy Fraser's insights are a useful point of reference. To challenge what she has creatively called 'interlinked injustices of maldistribution and misrecognition', the articulation of a kind of 'meta-injustice', situated 'above and beyond those first-order injustices', is required, she suggests

(Fraser 2005: 305). To articulate this meta-injustice, she argues, we should move from the recognitive and redistributive dimensions and trajectories to the dimension of representation, where representation involves not merely the sphere of political or cultural representation, but the ability to (re)frame disputes about justice. Fraser has largely limited her discussion about representation to feminist politics and the interrelated context of gender justice, and suggested that transnational feminism is 'reconfiguring gender justice as a three-dimensional problem, in which redistribution, recognition and representation must be integrated in a balanced way' (ibid.).

More recently, Huub van Baar and Peter Vermeersch have mobilized Fraser's ideas to recontextualize the situation of Roma in Europe, Roma-related policies and politics, and the interlinked injustices of maldistribution and misrecognition affecting many Roma. In particular, they argue that, to a significant extent, these injustices are interconnected to what they call the overwhelming dominance of 'operational representations' that, particularly in policy formations and political discussions, categorize Roma one-sidedly as either 'risky' or 'at risk' (van Baar and Vermeersch 2017: 131–34; see also Introduction, this volume). As they explain, the perverse confluence of the neoliberal and participatory democratic projects have led, in a highly ambiguous fashion, to the emergence of a politics of welfare redistribution that tends to categorize 'the poor' along the lines of deservingness and to identify Roma as a racialized 'problem group', thereby implicitly but effectively materializing injustices through combined misrecognition and maldistribution. Therefore, based on Fraser's attempt to move beyond a debate in terms of mere redistribution and recognition, van Baar and Vermeersch have proposed a political and scholarly agenda that significantly invests in exploring the opportunities for a more fundamental debate about Roma-related representation.

As various contributions to this volume (see, most notably, the chapters by Kóczé, Rostas, Silverman, Szalai and van Baar) have demonstrated, in the fields of labour, housing, education, citizenship, development, culture and European and national politics and policymaking, the sustained and structural injustices of maldistribution and misrecognition affecting Roma have been largely caused by the difficulty of challenging effectively the ways in which Roma have been one-sidedly framed and problematized, at local and individual, as well as (trans)national and collective levels. However, as the chapters concentrating on practices of solidarity and political claim-making have shown in particular (see, most notably, the chapters by Magazzini, Schultz, Trehan, Tremlett and Le Bas, and Zentai; see also van Baar, Chapter 1, this volume), within the increasingly diversifying Roma movement, many debates and practices focus explicitly on the reframing and re-problematization of contemporary disputes about (in)justice and on the need for developing a sustainable politics of representation in Fraser's sense.

This book has offered various entry points into debates about the scholarly, activist and political re-problematization of disputes about present-day and historical (in)justices that have affected Roma in and beyond Europe. Some contributions have underscored the crucial importance of claiming Roma history and gaining ownership over its dominant discourses, imageries, sources and political and cultural representations (see, most notably, Trehan, Magazzini, Tremlett and Le Bas, and van Baar, Chapter 1, this volume). In Chapter 3, for instance, Nidhi Trehan has demonstrated the importance of reconsidering historical sources to challenge and thus refine often-expressed suggestions that Roma and their allies were unable to problematize the ways in which they were framed and approached in socialist public policies. In different but somewhat similar ways, Tina Magazzini (Chapter 10), Annabel Tremlett and Delaine Le Bas (Chapter 11) and Huub van Baar (Chapter 1) have all shown how Roma stakeholders have gained and regained ownership over the ways in which Roma have always been approached and represented in European cultures, memories and histories. Gaining ownership over archives and creating new ones have been among the strategies that have enabled a re-politicization of issues of historical and contemporary injustice. The development of new regimes of visuality (through strategies of mimicry or mapping, for instance), which critically target prevailing trends to hyper-visibilize Roma as representatives of deviant cultures, has contributed to the problematization of the figure of 'the Gypsy' in visual and discursive cultures, as both van Baar (Chapter 1) and Tremlett and Le Bas (Chapter 11) illuminate.

Júlia Szalai (Chapter 2), Angéla Kóczé (Chapter 4) and Huub van Baar (Chapter 5) have argued that intersectional approaches to the situation of Roma help to shed a more complex light on sustained and structural injustices of maldistribution and misrecognition that affect Roma and, thus, how intersectionality enables a scholarly re-problematization of how we should strive for more equal and just societies. While Szalai has primarily articulated the intersections of housing, labour and education, and Kóczé those of race, class and gender, van Baar has focused on the security–citizenship and security–development nexuses. Relatedly, in Chapter 9, Carol Silverman has clarified the crucial importance of understanding culture, identity and ethnicity in the context of shared commonalities. By so doing, she argues, we can reject both pro- and anti-essentialist positions towards Roma identity and ethnicity, and help to reframe the role of identity beyond the opposition between essentialism and constructivism, also in terms of debates about (in)justice. In Chapter 6, Iulius Rostas has shown how the ways in which Roma have been problematized in the design, process, implementation and evaluation of European policies have significantly, and often highly problematically, impacted on the ability of these policies to address adequately the social injustices that Roma face. By so doing, he explicitly problematizes the ways in which one-sided Roma representations have been operationalized in public policies, suggesting that substantially more attention should be paid to this key dimension of (trans)national policymaking.

Last but not least, in different but overlapping ways, Debra Schultz (Chapter 7) and Violetta Zentai (Chapter 8) show how the struggles of identity in the present-day Roma women's movement have very much developed along the more general lines of Fraser's discussion of feminist politics and the context of gender justice. At the same time, Schultz and Zentai clarify and specify how the situation of a multiple displacement – vis-à-vis the more general Roma movement, but also vis-à-vis the global women's and feminist movements – has confronted the main actors in the Roma women's movement with the difficult demand to develop strategies that could challenge dissimilar but equally problematic framings of Roma. As both contributions show in different ways, Roma women in the movement have slowly but surely managed to develop such strategies, even while their work, like that in other fields discussed in our volume, could probably best be qualified as work in progress, characterized by ongoing trial and error tactics.

The Roma and Their Struggle for Identity in Contemporary Europe emphasizes the need for a more integrative analytical perspective regarding the position of Roma in Europe, as well as for cultural, social and political changes in a Europe that has continued to present itself one-sidedly as 'in crisis' and, accordingly, permanently mobilizes crisis narratives and instruments to irregularize and securitize the identities and practices of its most vulnerable minorities and migrants. After thirty years of democratization, political integration and socioeconomic restructuration, 'Europe has reached a dangerous point', as Paul Gilroy (2019) stated in his Holberg Laureate lecture:

> As ailing capitalism emancipates itself from democratic regulation, [so] ultra-nationalism, populism, xenophobia and varieties of neo-fascism become more visible, more assertive and more corrosive of political culture. The widespread appeal of racialized group identity and racism, often conveyed obliquely with a knowing wink, has been instrumental in delivering us to a situation in which our conception of truth, law and government have been placed in jeopardy. In many places, [a] pathological hunger for national rebirth and the restoration of an earlier political time have combined with resentful, authoritarian and belligerent responses to alterity and the expectation of hospitality. (Gilroy 2019)

These racist, neo-fascist reactions quite often target racialized Roma who are living in precarious and austere conditions in Europe. However, the alienation and racialization of Roma is not a new phenomenon brought about by recent right-wing nationalisms. It is rather a constitutive mechanism that is deeply rooted in Europe's colonial, imperial and racist history, and that continuously tends to transform the manifestation of the racialization and inferiorization of Roma, based on specific social, economic and political conditions. This volume has tried to contribute to a historically informed analytical perspective that helps to formulate conceptually and theoretically articulated questions and arguments regarding the current position of Roma in Europe. However, the advocated multidimensional analytical perspective – based on the complex, intersecting dimensions of recognition, redistribution and representation – will neither change asymmetrical power relations nor address the sustained and reproduced political-epistemic violence without strong connections to forces on the ground: the social, political and cultural struggles and movements that are required to ground the multidimensional perspective and, in doing so, to enable linkages and solidarities between various racialized and marginalized groups and beyond artificial and counterproductive majority–minority binaries. Our hope is that this volume enters into a conversation about the opportunities for these linkages and solidarities, and helps its readers to better understand the position of racialized and marginalized groups in Europe such as Roma, who are struggling for identity at a time of proliferation of identity politics and the troublesome erosion of democratic and just political cultures.

Angéla Kóczé is an Assistant Professor of Romani Studies and Academic Director of the Roma Graduate Preparation Program at Central European University in Budapest, Hungary. In 2013–2017, she was a Visiting Assistant Professor in the Department of Sociology and Women's, Gender and Sexuality Studies Program at Wake Forest University in Winston Salem, NC, USA. She has published several peer-reviewed articles and book chapters with various international presses, including Palgrave Macmillan, Ashgate, Routledge and CEU Press, as well as several thematic policy papers related to social inclusion, gender equality, social justice and civil society. In 2013, the Woodrow Wilson International Center for Scholars in Washington, DC, honoured Kóczé with the Ion Ratiu Democracy Award for her interdisciplinary research approach, which combines community engagement and policymaking with in-depth participatory research on the situation of the Roma. She is a co-editor of *The Romani Women's Movement: Struggles and Debates in Central and Eastern Europe* (Routledge, 2018, with Violetta Zentai, Jelena Jovanović and Enikő Vincze).

Huub van Baar is an Assistant Professor of Political Theory at the Institute of Political Science at the Justus-Liebig University of Giessen in Germany. He is also a Senior Research Fellow at the Amsterdam Centre for Globalisation Studies (ACGS) at the Faculty of Humanities of the University of Amsterdam, and an affiliated researcher at the Amsterdam Centre for European Studies (ACES). He coordinates a research project on the formation and transformation of Romani minorities in modern European history, which is part of the research programme Dynamics of Security: Forms of Securitization in Historical Perspective (2014–2021), funded by the German Research Foundation (DFG). He has published widely on the position and political and cultural representation of Europe's Romani minorities, predominantly from the angle of how their situation has changed at the nexus of citizenship, security and development. He has published peer-reviewed articles in, for instance, *Social Identities, Antipode, Journal of Ethnic and Migration Studies, City, Third Text, Citizenship Studies, International Journal of Cultural Policy* and *Society and Space*. He is the author of *The European Roma: Minority Representation, Memory and the Limits of Transnational Governmentality* (F&N, 2011) and the main co-editor of *Museutopia: A Photographic Research Project by Ilya Rabinovich* (Alauda, 2012, with Ingrid Commandeur) and *The Securitization of the Roma in Europe* (Palgrave Macmillan, 2019, with Ana Ivasiuc and Regina Kreide). He is currently finalizing a monograph entitled *The Ambiguity of Protection: Spectacular Security and the European Roma*.

References

Fraser, N. 1997. *Justice Interruptus: Critical Reflections on the 'Postsocialist' Condition*. London: Routledge.
———. 2005. 'Mapping the Feminist Imagination: From Redistribution to Recognition to Representation', *Constellations* 12: 295–307.
Gilroy, P. 2019. 'Never Again: Refusing Race and Salvaging the Human', Holberg Laureate lecture, 4 June, University of Bergen. Retrieved 10 June 2019 from https://www.hol bergprisen.no/en/news/holberg-prize/2019-holberg-lecture-laureate-paul-gilroy.
van Baar, H., and P. Vermeersch. 2017. 'The Limits of Operational Representations: "Ways of Seeing Roma" beyond the Recognition-Distribution Paradigm', *Intersections* 3(4): 120–39.

INDEX

❋ ❋ ❋

Abdelal, Rawi, 181–82
activation, 128–29, 133, 138, 162, 164, 165
activism, xiii, 5, 6, 50, 104, 106, 115, 271
   and agenda setting, 8, 33, 156, 166, 179, 184, 208, 209–14, 216, 221, 223, 225, 230, 233, 234, 236, 242–48, 331
   and art, 35, 46–62, 215, 223–24, 281–327
   and categorization, 180, 267–68, 274
   civil rights, 6–7, 70, 118, 209, 210, 241, 296, 329
   feminist, 20, 206, 209, 214, 220, 222, 224, 225, 234, 242, 243
   and grassroots, 85, 208, 217–19, 223, 315
   and gender, 33, 101, 203–53, 298–99
   human rights, 117–18, 207–8, 221
   impact of, 5–8, 13, 32–35, 219–22
   intersectional, 13, 208, 222, 235, 235–38, 240, 243–44
   and identity politics, 22–23, 25–27, 38n7, 39n11, 194, 206, 208, 219–22, 258, 263, 294–300
   LGBTQI+, 8, 13, 19, 186, 247, 222
   networks, 8, 20, 164, 249
   and Roma rights, 205, 211, 215, 220, 221
   and scholarship, xiii, 25–27, 38n7, 39n11, 194–95, 222, 236, 239, 287–88, 289–90, 296–98, 315
   travelling, 13
   women's, 33, 101, 203–53

Acton, Thomas, 25, 39n11, 188, 199n3, 264, 268
   Second Site, 315
agency, 11, 30, 96, 117, 119n1, 153, 163, 263
   historicization of, 28–29, 174n2
Alliance for the European Roma Institute, 282, 283, 285, 287, 288, 289
Amalipe, 234, 241, 250n1
ambiguity, 11, 12, 13, 14, 22–23, 29, 84, 117, 118, 159, 164, 166, 169, 170, 172, 314
anti-essentialism, 18, 25, 34, 262, 331
   anti-, 34, 275
   transformative, 33, 230, 249
antigypsyism, 4, 15–17, 95, 102, 153, 172, 184, 186–87, 194–96, 198, 242, 246, 267, 282, 294–95
   gendered, 142
   reasonable, 17, 37n5
   See also anti-Roma racism, Romaphobia
anti-policies, 11
anti-Roma racism, xi, 99, 207, 216, 218, 223, 237, 268, 271. *See also* antigypsyism
antisemitism, 172
Appadurai, Arjun, 17, 22, 25, 141, 144
Appiah, Kwame, 260
archive, 7, 30, 37n2, 57, 94–123, 274–75, 300, 331
Arendt, Hannah, 225

artivism, 57–58
assimilation, 4, 97, 99, 101, 103, 106, 163, 187, 188, 207, 210, 259, 264, 270
Association of Roma Women for Our Children, 242, 243
Association for Women's Rights in Development (AWID), 213
asylum, 10, 14, 164, 166, 270

Barsony, Katalin, 283
Barvalipe, 286–88, 289, 299, 302n3
begging, 100, 257–58, 269
  as culture, 273–74
Benedik, Stefan, 10, 269, 273
Bhabha, Homi, 28
  hybridity, 28, 171, 267–68
  mimicry, 28, 29, 331
  vernacular cosmopolitanism, 307, 322
biopolitics, 12, 13, 132, 170
  of development, 168
Bíró, András, 239
Bițu, Nicoleta, 211, 214–15, 216, 217, 223–24, 225, 234, 241, 283
Bogdal, Michael, 28, 54, 174n1
border(s), 12, 19, 59–62, 108, 118, 165, 170, 181, 216, 287, 308, 317
  biopolitical, 12, 153–178
  as epistemological viewpoint, 170–72
  politics, 165–67
  regime of EU, 5, 11, 14, 155, 164, 165–67, 174n5
  securitization of (*see under* securitization)
  studies, 13, 14, 170
Brexit, 9, 174n4
Brooks, Ethel, 171, 225, 241, 283
  reclaiming the camp, 307–8, 316
Brubaker, Rogers, 24, 34, 262–63, 265, 302n2
The Buccaneers, 309–10
Bulgaria, 3, 4, 15, 113, 136, 193, 205, 234, 241

Calhoun, Craig, 24–25, 265–66
Carlson, Tucker, 269–71
Carmen, the figure of, 54–58, 309–10
cartography, xvii, 59–62

CEDAW, 236, 246–47
Central European University (CEU), xiv, xvi, 222, 224, 285, 296
  Romani Studies Program, 224, 296
  Romani Summer Schools, 285
Chakrabarty, Dipesh, 12, 28, 38n7, 58
Chaplin, Charlie, 60
Chavi, 318, 320, 321
citizenship, xi, 8, 11, 12, 29–31, 33, 71, 87, 90–92, 129, 142, 153, 158, 164–67, 169–70, 194, 233, 239, 264, 329, 330, 331
  EU, 31, 154, 165–67
  European, 31, 167, 172, 174n5
  irregular(ized), 129, 142, 164–67
  rights, 11, 30, 69–93
  second-class, 30, 89–91, 195
  and security (*see under* security)
  socialist, 110
  studies, 13, 14, 22
civil society, 115–16, 138, 193, 194, 205, 208, 209
  organizations, 156, 163, 192, 234, 237, 240–41, 246
class, 6, 22, 30–31, 33, 69–70, 77, 89–91, 96, 103, 114, 116, 124–28, 130–33, 136–39, 144, 153, 180, 187, 207, 210, 216, 244–46, 321–22, 328, 331
classification, 26–29, 74, 160, 162, 166, 188, 261, 263
Clifford, James, 25, 28, 34, 275–76
Coalition for Gender Equality, 247
communism, 3, 7, 95, 101, 115
  fall of, 3, 179
community, xii, 25, 35, 71–72, 76, 83–91, 103, 111, 113, 143, 153, 162, 164–65, 168, 187, 208, 214, 218–19, 220, 223, 224, 234–35, 245, 259, 264, 269, 274, 275, 306, 321
  self-protection, 79–83
constructivism, 11, 18, 22–23, 25–27, 262–64
  versus essentialism debate, 4, 25–29, 34, 174n2, 262–64, 281, 331
contestation, 6, 21, 23, 27, 31, 118, 126–27, 142, 162, 170, 172, 181, 215, 234, 273–74, 293

Costache, Nora, 217
Council of Europe, 34, 62, 112, 179, 188–90, 199n4, 282–83, 285, 287, 291–93
Crenshaw, Kimberlé, 125, 207, 231
criminalization, 5, 102, 132, 214, 258, 273, 277n4
crisis, 37n3, 126, 129, 332
  constitutional, xiv
  financial, 37n3, 126, 133, 137, 237, 238, 242, 245
  narratives, 10, 13, 14, 332
  'refugee/migration', 13–14, 37n3
critical race theory, 12, 13, 14, 22, 32, 38n7, 180, 182, 186, 197, 207
Critical Romani Studies, 22
Critical Romani Studies (journal), 296
Csalog, Zsolt, 103–04, 108, 110
culturalization, 132, 168, 172, 259
culture, xi–xii, 4, 6, 18, 25, 33–34, 47, 50–54, 75, 87, 88, 101, 103, 114, 138, 153, 163, 170, 187, 195, 207, 221, 223, 246, 257–304, 307, 313, 322
  visual, 46–64, 305–27
Czechoslovakia, 3, 96, 99
Czech Republic, 72, 128, 137–38, 193, 195, 205

Daróczi, Agnes, 7, 98, 225
Davis, Angela, 18
Decade of Roma Inclusion, 84, 116, 179, 191, 194–95, 199n1, 212, 219–20, 233, 240, 322
decoloniality, 28, 61, 296
De Genova, Nicholas, 12, 13, 14, 169
dehumanization, 5, 54, 99, 223, 232
democracy, 99, 117, 124, 183, 186, 205, 222, 231, 293, 322, 330, 332–33
  illiberal, xi, 95, 118
  liberal, xiv, 19–20, 91, 94–95, 158, 181, 328
  transition to, 117–18, 208, 219–20
depoliticization, 164
deportation, 10, 11, 12, 14, 258
deportability, 166, 169
deprivation, 71–74, 79, 81, 83, 87–89, 98, 108

deservingness, 69, 83, 126, 129, 132, 139, 186, 197, 198, 330
development, 6, 8, 11, 22, 31, 77, 84, 88, 142, 155, 158, 161, 162, 163–64, 167–69, 195–97, 329–31
developmentalism, 172
  institutional, 161
  postcolonial, 167–68
  postsocialist, 167–69
diaspora, xi–xiii, 264, 291
difference, xii, 28, 51, 52, 72, 75, 79, 81, 87, 114–15, 125, 136, 186, 188, 190, 218, 222, 235, 257–72, 308, 314
differential inclusion. *See under* inclusion
differentiation, 12, 14, 23, 24, 27, 37n5, 71, 78, 80, 81, 87, 126, 155, 167, 169–72, 186, 231, 246, 269
Dikh he na Bister Roma Genocide Remembrance Initiative, 285
Diósi, Ágnes, 104, 112
Dirlik, Arif, 28, 258, 267–68, 275
discrimination, 8, 9, 18, 20, 81, 104, 108, 139, 153, 179, 194–96, 207, 213, 236–38, 240, 243, 257, 273, 316
  multiple, 207, 212, 221, 224, 238
  positive, 210, 217, 295–96
displacement, 8, 9, 10, 32, 95, 155, 170
diversity, xiii, 28, 103, 171, 187, 231, 237, 245, 264, 287–88
Donert, Celia, 7, 30, 96, 97
donors, 33, 206, 212, 284

early/forced marriage, 207, 212, 214, 232, 234–35, 237, 241, 247, 248, 257–58
elite, 38n8, 110–11, 114, 116, 118, 184, 263, 268, 298–99, 307, 322
  elitism, 281, 298–99
Eminova, Enisa, 211, 213, 216, 218, 224, 225
emancipation, 20, 26, 100, 136, 142, 144, 219, 234, 258, 289, 306–14
employability, 74, 78, 197
employment, 73, 76–78, 80, 82, 84, 87–88, 90, 97, 101–6, 116, 125, 126, 128–30, 133–34, 137–38, 141, 192, 194–97, 212, 240, 294, 322

empowerment, 6, 131–32, 142–44, 161, 164, 165, 167, 168, 206, 211, 219, 224, 230, 233, 235, 240, 249, 266, 294, 320
encampment, 307–8, 316
Enlightenment, 26, 27, 174n2
epistemology, 30, 33, 39n11, 50–54, 94, 159–60, 170, 207, 221, 223
equality, 8, 19, 33, 36, 83, 84, 194, 207, 213, 230, 233, 235–50, 295, 298, 322, 329
E-Romnja Association, 242, 243, 245, 247, 251n8
essentialism, 18, 22–23, 33–34, 257–60, 264, 267, 272, 273–77
 anti-, 18, 33, 230, 249
 strategic, xii, 18, 33, 258, 267, 268
 versus constructivism, 5, 25–29, 34, 174n2, 281, 331
ethnicity, 6, 15, 22–25, 32–34, 70, 103, 106, 112–15, 126, 136, 153, 172, 179–202, 210, 214, 216, 231, 237, 244, 245, 257–80, 281, 302n4, 318, 329, 331
 'without groups', 24, 263, 265–66
EU Framework for Roma, 32, 84, 156, 158, 179–80, 189, 191–202, 234, 237–38, 241, 243, 295
EU Roma Policy Coalition (ERPC), 194
Eurocentrism, 31, 172
 methodological, 12, 154, 172
European history, xi–xiv, 7, 26, 52, 99, 100, 161, 260, 334
European Academic Network of Romani Studies (EANRS), 293, 297–98
European Commission, 166, 180, 183, 189–93, 195, 212, 234, 264
European Court of Human Rights, 16, 37n4, 221
European Roma Information Office (ERIO), 194, 199n6
European Roma Institute for Arts and Culture (ERIAC), 7, 34, 223, 274, 281–304
 Barvalipe Academy, 286–88, 289, 299, 302n3
 emergence of, 282–88

 founding principles of, 286, 288–89
 Pakiv Board, 287–88, 302n5
European Roma Rights Centre (ERRC), 4, 8, 15, 16, 37n4, 194, 206, 213, 224, 236, 294
European Roma and Travellers Forum (ERTF), 34, 190, 250n3, 292–93
European Union (EU), xi, 31, 69, 129, 154, 179, 194, 205
European Union Agency for Fundamental Rights (FRA), 130, 131, 133
European Women's Lobby (EWL), 221, 236–38, 250n3
Europeanization, xi–xiv, 17, 153, 155, 157
 as governmentality, 31, 154–55, 160–62, 169
 of borders, 165, 167
 of migration, 165, 167
 of Roma discourse, 154, 157, 159, 160
 of Roma identity, 31, 154, 157, 159, 160
 of 'Roma issue', 31, 154, 155–59
 of Roma minority, 127, 162
 of Roma policy, 31, 154, 157, 159, 160
 of 'Roma problem', 12, 84, 156
 of Roma representation (*see under* Europeanization of Roma representation)
 of security policies, 165
Europeanization of Roma representation, xii, 8, 12, 13, 31, 154, 159–64, 169–70
 epistemological dimension, 159–60
 genealogical dimension, 162–64
 governmental dimension, 160–62
eviction, 10, 12, 16, 37n3, 76, 81, 88, 223, 244, 316
evictability, 169
exclusion, 5, 11–15, 23, 29, 35, 58–59, 73–74, 79, 82, 87–90, 97, 99, 102, 104, 137, 155, 169, 173n1, 182, 187, 194, 195, 230, 238, 245, 248, 257, 261, 295, 311, 313,
 and education, 73, 75, 194
 residential (*see under* segregation)
 social, 71, 106, 130, 133, 138, 183, 190, 199n2, 213, 329
exoticization, 53, 214, 258, 259, 261, 266, 271–73, 312

expertise, 163–64, 171, 212, 283, 293, 322
extremism, 4, 10, 20, 158, 166, 232

fascism, 95, 98, 225
  neo-, 332
feminism, xi, 13, 18, 20, 33, 38n7, 96, 124, 130, 138, 142, 205–29, 232–35, 240–49, 296, 330, 332
  Black, 207, 209, 267
  transnational, 206, 208–14, 221–26, 290–91, 330
Ferge, Zsuzsa, 112, 128, 129, 139
FIDESZ, 112, 114, 141, 192
Fonseca, Isabel, 51
Fosztó, László, 297
Fraser, Nancy, 28, 142, 294–95, 328–332
France, 10, 11, 169, 193, 195, 273, 284, 323
Fremlová, Lucie, 8, 222
Foucault, Michel, 28, 142, 143, 160, 161
Fukuyama, Francis, 19, 22, 25, 181

Gay y Blasco, Paloma, 52
Gelbart, Petra, 225
gender, xii, 6, 8, 18, 22, 25, 28, 30–33, 50, 96, 124–49, 153, 186–88, 194, 203–53, 272, 273, 275, 295, 298, 302n4, 328–32
genealogy, 162–64, 170
genocide, 7, 37n1, 99, 100, 153, 181, 285.
  See also Holocaust
Germany, 7, 10, 14, 46, 54, 99, 163, 269, 284, 300
Gheorghe, Carmen, 235, 243–44
Gheorghe, Nicolae, 214, 217, 223, 239, 260, 264, 268
ghettoization, 75, 78, 125, 171
Gilroy, Paul, 28, 258, 267, 276, 332
Goldberg, David, 16–17
Gorki Theatre, Maxim, 46, 47, 323
governance, 100, 110, 127, 130, 154–56, 158, 162–63, 165, 172
  'ethnic minority', 14, 15, 31, 151–202
  of poverty, 31, 126, 131, 133–38
governmentality, 18, 28, 31, 100, 127, 143, 155, 160–64, 167, 169–70, 174nn3–4
groupism, 24, 263, 265
Guy, Will, 25, 157, 239, 264, 268

'Gypsies', xiii, 6, 26, 50–54, 62, 100, 163, 269, 296, 311, 312
  as backward, 51, 99, 101, 167, 260
  as 'historyless' people, 50–54, 163
  as premodern, 53, 163
  time of the, 50–54
'Gypsy'
  imageries and narratives, 50–54
  'persistence', 259–60, 262
  as a textual effect, 51
  as a trope, 50, 114, 132
Gypsy Dada, 48, 321–22
'Gypsy Question', xi, 12, 30, 53, 95, 99, 101–3, 106, 110, 112–13
Gypsy revolution, 62, 306, 321
Gypsy Revolution (artwork), 306, 311, 318
Gypsy Roma Traveller History Month, 315
'Gypsyland', 35, 48–50, 323

Hall, Stuart, 23–25, 28, 119n1, 258, 267, 275–76, 318, 321, 322
Hancock, Ian, 7, 25, 98, 100, 163, 174n2, 187, 269, 324n4
health care, 4, 8, 70, 103, 106, 112, 116, 119n4, 130, 131, 143, 161, 168, 192, 194–97, 199n1, 212, 217, 232, 294
hegemony, 100, 127, 169, 207, 276, 329
Helsinki Watch, 3–4, 8
Holocaust, xi
  Roma, 7, 37n1, 226, 268, 285, 295, 301
  See also genocide
hooks, bell, 28, 267–68, 296
hostility, 82, 86, 267, 270, 296
housing, 4, 22, 30, 69, 70, 72, 75–77, 79, 82, 88–89, 91, 97, 102, 106, 116, 119n4, 130, 180, 192, 194–96, 199n1, 212, 232, 244–45, 250n7, 294, 322, 330, 331
  market, 9, 88
Hungary, 13–14, 30, 72–73, 94–123, 126, 129, 133–36, 140–41, 143, 192, 193, 195, 205, 208, 216, 224, 225, 236, 283, 306
Kádárist, 95–96
hybridity, xiii, 28, 127, 153, 171, 267–68, 277n2, 313, 322

identification, 5, 6, 17, 50, 287
  outside, 5, 6, 9–11
identity
  'beyond', 19–25, 34, 262–63
  and citizenship, 29–30, 31, 69, 71,
    83–92, 129, 167, 172, 264, 329, 330
  claims, 7–8, 22, 33, 34, 53, 54, 57, 58,
    82, 85, 183, 191, 193–95, 206, 232–33,
    238, 239, 242, 249, 258, 266, 268, 275,
    289, 307, 311, 321–22, 330–31
  collective, 18, 23, 33, 52, 71, 74, 81,
    180–87, 206, 231, 243, 268
  construction, 22–23, 79, 214, 231, 233,
    244–45, 286
  cultural, 194–95, 219, 257–80, 281–304
  deconstruction of, 22–29, 257–80, 331
  de-ethnicize, 25–27
  denial of, 3, 4, 96
  dilemmas, 17–18, 22, 257–80
  ethnic, xii, 3, 22–29, 34, 172, 179–202,
    257–80, 295, 302n2, 307, 312, 331
  and 'Europeanness', 31–32, 155–59,
    167, 170
  formation, 9, 11, 12, 18, 25, 34, 38n9,
    96, 222, 249, 268
  hiding, 5, 9, 10, 98, 311, 315
  homogenization of, 6, 22–29, 38n7, 88,
    100, 220, 260, 264
  Hungarian, 14, 98, 110, 120nn6–7, 135
  national, 6, 7, 12, 19, 20, 22, 33, 86, 117,
    153, 158, 171, 216, 260, 268, 312,
    332
  negative, 5, 11, 26–27, 29, 83, 108, 263,
    273, 274, 275, 324n4
  objectified, 52, 100, 260, 261, 266
  personal, 18, 24, 33, 35, 71, 217, 306,
    307, 314
  in policy studies, 155–59, 160, 180–87,
    197–98
  politics (*see under* identity politics)
  predatory, 17, 20, 22, 141, 144
  racialized, 12, 13, 14–15, 17, 20, 22,
    31, 52, 99–101, 114, 117, 124–49,
    171–72, 217, 231, 244, 330, 332, 333
  struggles, 3, 5, 7, 16, 18–19, 26, 28, 95,
    172, 208, 215, 230, 249, 290–91, 312,
    329, 332–33
  transformation, 8, 9, 11, 18, 33, 35, 75,
    187, 243, 247
  as a weapon of the weak, 281–304
identity politics, 17–29, 85–86, 155–59,
  212, 219–26, 239–40, 258, 262, 267,
  274–75, 281–82, 294–300, 305–27
  and activism (*see under* activism)
  critical, 23–25, 29, 59, 329
  and emancipation, 20–22, 26, 34, 35,
    142, 144, 219–22, 258, 289, 306–14,
    328
  and gender (*see under* gender)
  and groupism (*see under* groupism)
  and homogenization, 24, 258, 267
  and intersectionality, 230–53 (*see also*
    intersectionality)
  limits of, 19–23, 38n7, 155–59, 219,
    329
  and the personal, 18, 24, 33, 35, 217,
    305–8, 314
  proliferation of, 5, 19–22, 333
  recuperative, 11, 22–23, 29, 30
  and solidarity, 18, 24–25, 30, 81, 82, 91,
    94, 224–26, 232, 243–45, 249, 266,
    314–17, 333
  and strategic essentialism (*see under*
    essentialism)
  'white', 19–22
illiberalism, xi, 95, 118
inclusion, 6, 9, 12, 35, 63n1, 73, 92, 114,
  153–55, 157, 160, 167, 190, 194,
  196, 212, 222, 241, 246–47, 313–14,
  322
  differential, 155, 169–72
  social, 36, 143, 155, 158, 161–62, 165,
    169, 190, 194, 240, 282, 292, 315–16,
    322, 329
  See also Decade of Roma Inclusion
Ingram, Helen, 185–86, 197
injustice, 81–82, 231, 243–45, 247,
  329–32. *See also* justice
insecurity, 4, 76, 89, 90, 124–49, 168
integration, xi, 96, 97, 98, 100, 102, 104,
  106, 108, 110, 113, 115–17, 120n10,
  187, 196, 208, 212, 214, 260, 270, 311,
  314, 322, 332
  European, xii, xiii, 129, 155, 165, 167

See also National Roma Integration
    Strategies
intelligentsia, xi–xiii, 26, 116
intersectionality, xii, 6, 17, 22, 30, 33,
    38n7, 71–72, 74–78, 90–91, 103, 125,
    130, 133, 138, 171, 186, 196, 205–29,
    230–53, 331
  political, 230–31, 242, 244, 246
  structural, 231, 235, 246
  theory, 125, 206–9, 230–32
invisibilization, 17, 19, 59, 84, 89, 125, 134
irregularization, 10, 23, 52, 166, 170–72,
    332
  of citizenship, 10, 166, 170–72
  of migration, 10, 166, 170–72
Islamophobia, 172
Istanbul Convention, 238, 246
Italy, 10, 61, 195, 258, 273, 283, 284,
    294–95, 303n9, 316
Izsák-Ndiaye, Rita, 215, 238

Járóka, Lívia, 192, 273
'Jewish Question', xi, 13, 100
Jews, xi–xiv, 51, 100
Jiménez, Gabi, 321, 323
Jobbik, 140–41, 145n2
Jovanović, Jelena, 221–22
Jovanović, Željko, 239
Junghaus, Tímea, 34, 224, 241, 281–304,
    313, 314, 317
justice, 8, 19, 153, 158, 194, 198, 232,
    328–32
  gender, 329, 330, 332
  social, 33, 35, 222, 239, 243–45, 249,
    295

Kai Dikhas, 47, 54, 321
Kalderash, 258, 270, 271
Kazanxhiu, Sead, 283
Kemény, István, 103, 104
kinship, 153, 187–88, 257
Kirkby Stephen and Appleby, 48
Khamoro Festival, 285
Kolev, Deyan, 234
Kossuth Klub, 110–11, 120n13
Kovats, Martin, 8, 26, 29, 109–10, 114,
    116, 120n15, 167, 239

Kóczé, Angéla, 22, 96, 103, 171, 206–7,
    210, 215–17, 219, 224, 225, 226, 232,
    233, 235, 296
Krumova, Teodora, 234
Kurtić, Vera, 8, 222

labour, 18, 22, 30, 71, 74, 76, 90, 125, 139,
    162, 169, 170, 259, 330, 331
  cheap, 76–77, 129
  child, 76, 273
  domestic, 77, 138, 139
  exploitation, 9, 90, 125, 128, 129, 237,
    244
  market, 9, 37n3, 70, 73, 76, 78, 80, 87,
    90, 117, 130, 137, 196, 232, 245
Ladányi, János, 103, 134, 135, 188
Lakatos, Menyhért, 96, 98–99
Lakatos, Szilvia, 216
Le Bas Damian James (jr.), 311
Le Bas, Damian John (sr.), x–xi, xvi–xvii,
    25, 35–36, 46–65, 305–27
Le Bas, Delaine, x–xi, xvi–xvii, 35–36, 48,
    54–58, 62, 305–27
Lucassen, Leo, 25–27, 29, 172, 262

Macedonia, 190, 215, 216, 218, 224, 284
Magazzini, Tina, 7, 274
Majtényi, Bálazs, 97, 117
Majtényi, György, 97, 117
maldistribution, 329–31
mapping, 46, 48, 58–62, 307–8, 311, 321,
    323, 331
marginalization, 5, 7, 8, 11–15, 17, 21, 26,
    29, 31, 71, 99, 101, 108, 114, 116, 118,
    124, 125, 127, 133, 135, 143, 155, 169,
    170, 208, 210, 213, 214, 216, 223, 231,
    239, 244, 245, 250n1, 259, 260, 289,
    300, 316, 333
Mark, Letitia, 208, 243
Matache, Margareta Magda, 21–22, 33,
    213, 225, 235
Matras, Yaron, 25, 27, 38n10, 39n11, 154,
    163, 174n2
  and scientism, 27, 174n2
Maya, Ostalinda, 215
McCormack, Kerieva, 224, 225
McGarry, Aidan, 22, 207, 222, 263, 269

Index

media, 5, 6, 10, 11, 13, 14, 17, 63n3, 113, 117, 128, 140, 141, 166, 184, 214, 258, 263, 266, 269, 270, 273, 274, 275, 282, 285, 300, 306, 313
  Adevarul, 271
  Fox News, 269–70
  Pittsburgh Post-Gazette, 270–71
  social, 113, 298
Meet Your Neighbours, 317, 324n4, 325n5
Memedova, Azbija, 211, 215, 216, 217–18, 224, 225
memory, 6–7, 50–53, 63n1, 153
Mezzadra, Sandro, 155, 168, 169–70, 172, 216
migration, xi, 9–11, 80, 95, 155, 162, 166, 170, 195, 224, 269, 271
  'crisis', 13–14, 37n3
  policies, 165–66, 172
  'poverty', 10
  securitization of (*see under* securitization)
  studies, 13, 14, 22, 170
militancy, 47, 84, 289, 296, 306, 320–21
mimicry. *See under* Bhabha, Homi
minority, 62, 83, 90, 91–92, 95, 110, 113, 117, 163, 168, 171, 172, 173n1, 182, 187, 190, 195, 221, 224, 232, 233, 236, 239, 268, 283, 286, 290, 333
  governance (*see under* governance)
  rights, xiv, 70, 83, 115, 155, 158, 212
Mirga, Andrzej, 263–64, 268
Mirga-Kruszelnicka, Anna, 34, 181–204, 249
misrecognition, 329–31
mobility, 70, 88, 165, 167, 168
  social, 9, 18, 30
mobilization, 7, 34, 85, 91, 143, 153, 157, 231, 233, 245, 257, 268, 305
modernity, 50, 51, 53, 87, 275
Moldava nad Bodvou, 15–16, 37n4
Morteanu, Crina, 234
movement
  African-American civil rights, 13, 19, 209, 290, 296
  feminist, 13, 206, 210, 211, 224, 244
  free, 12, 162, 165
  freedom of, 165–66, 194

indigenous, 13, 224, 290
intellectual, 53, 283, 291, 296
LGBTQI+, 8, 19, 222
religious, 37n6, 170
Romani, v, xvi, 5–8, 19, 70, 85, 117, 153, 162, 205–6, 208, 211, 217, 220, 222, 235, 239–41, 244, 249, 250n4, 268, 283, 289, 312, 328, 330
Romani art, v, xvi, 33–35, 47, 54, 305, 318
Romani women's, xii, 8, 32–33, 203–53, 329, 332
  theory, 13, 14, 222, 231–32
  women's, 213–14, 219, 220–21, 236

'National Question', 12, 13
National Roma Integration Strategies, 32, 84, 116, 156, 179, 191–97, 199n1, 240–41
nationalism, xi, xiii, 10, 13, 19, 95, 114, 157, 158, 181, 232, 261, 268, 292, 332–33
Necula, Ciprian, 283
Network for Preventing and Combating Violence against Women, 247
Network Women's Program, 209, 211, 212, 219, 236
neoliberal capitalism, 124–25, 169, 245, 328, 329
neoliberalism, 38n8, 118, 126–33, 142–43, 174n3
neoliberalization, 17, 174n3
  of development, 168
  of welfare, 126, 130, 134, 137
Nevi Sara Kali (journal), 243
NGOs, 70, 104, 106, 114, 117, 118, 131, 132, 163–64, 193–94, 212, 214, 217, 220, 236, 240, 292, 300
NGO-ization, 164, 214
nomadization, 167
normalization, 10, 60, 126, 139, 158, 160, 161–62

Okely, Judith, 25, 27, 262, 274
Open Method of Coordination, 158, 161
Open Society Foundation (OSF), 143, 239, 240, 282, 283, 287

Open Society Institute (OSI), 115, 163, 191, 199n1, 218, 233, 236, 329
Oprea, Alexandra, 210, 214, 216, 219, 223, 225, 238, 249
Orbán, Viktor, 13, 94, 114, 118, 120n6, 134, 192, 226
Organization for Security and Cooperation in Europe (OSCE), 163, 167, 168, 179, 188, 199n1
orientalism, 21, 26, 28, 38nn7-8, 100, 108, 167, 300
origins, 26-28, 62, 188, 259
  Indian, 27, 260
  linguistic, 27
  narratives of Roma, 26-28
ownership, 7, 8, 29, 88, 294, 331

Palmái, Marika, 216
participation, 5-9, 18, 31, 32, 72, 74, 80, 115, 161, 165, 182-83, 194, 231, 239, 240, 246, 247, 286, 329
  in decision-making, 192-93, 199n5, 329
  in education, 73, 115, 185, 219, 222, 224, 296
  labour market, 76-77
  political, 83-90, 92, 192-93, 199n1, 239, 329
  programs, 115, 129, 162, 179, 208, 209, 218, 219, 222, 224, 236, 296 (*see also* National Roma Integration Strategies)
  in public works, 89, 128, 129, 133, 162 (*see also* activation)
paternalism, 80, 85, 89, 126, 138, 283
Pavlović, Dijana, 283
penalization, 125, 126, 131
Pogány, István, 96, 106
police, 4, 15-16, 57, 63n3, 99, 102, 103, 166, 215, 237, 316
  violence, 4, 10, 15-16
policies, 11, 13, 19, 91, 113, 116, 127, 131, 133, 155, 237
  assimilation, 4, 97, 99, 101, 106, 163, 187
  ethnic, 27, 190
  development (*see under* development)
  European, xiii, 31, 32, 69, 154-72, 179-80, 191-98
  on Roma integration (*see under* Decade of Roma Inclusion, National Roma Integration Strategies)
  socialist, 95-111, 331
  welfare (*see under* activation, welfare)
policy
  analysis theory, 32, 180, 197
  design theory, 32, 180, 197
  formation, 156, 158, 165, 166, 187, 330
  implementation, 6, 11, 32, 106, 112, 129, 156, 158-59, 164, 179, 180, 184-86, 191, 193, 197, 213, 240, 331
  process, 180, 198, 245
  transfer, 156, 158, 199n5
policymaking, 10, 18, 21, 72, 118, 164, 179-202, 231, 286, 289, 293, 322, 332
  European, 31, 179-202, 330
politicization, 10, 18, 20, 26-27, 60-61, 70, 83, 85-86, 153, 162, 164, 168, 208, 297, 331
politics
  authoritarian, xiii, 95, 118
  cultural, 281-82, 328-29
  of declaration, 115-17
  democratic, 19, 94-95, 104, 110, 118, 183, 332, 333
  of dialogue, 115-17
  feminist (*see under* feminism)
  of identity, 23-25, 29, 59, 329 (*see also* identity politics)
  of recognition, 7, 19, 23, 26, 82, 114, 153, 161, 199n1, 209, 214, 231, 267, 295, 328-34
  of redistribution, 19, 131, 135, 139, 153, 198, 295, 328-34
  of representation, 328-34
  social, 328-29
  spatial, 314-17
  See also Roma politics
populism, xiii, 10, 13, 20, 94, 95, 134, 158, 166, 198, 242, 258, 261, 269, 282, 332
positionality, 210, 289
Post, Soraya, 242
postcolonial theory, xi, xii, xiii, 12, 21, 22, 28, 38n7, 210-11, 258, 267

poststructuralism, 18, 28
poverty, xii, 8, 10, 11, 19, 30–31, 70–71, 77, 79, 81, 83–84, 89–91, 103–4, 108, 112–14, 117, 124–49, 153, 168, 180, 190, 194–97, 207–8, 213, 216–17, 238, 245, 260, 263, 271, 273
   governance (*see under* governance)
precarity, 9, 125, 127, 130, 132, 153, 166, 167, 172, 242, 245, 248, 263, 332
prejudice, xi, 21, 30, 75–76, 94–95, 98–99, 101, 187, 207, 216, 218, 243, 271, 274, 300
privatization, 125, 128, 143
privilege, 16, 17, 21, 61, 131, 186, 187, 223, 298
   white, 21–22, 139
problematization, 59, 131, 159–60, 165–69, 174n4
   of Roma, 12, 14, 16, 28, 31, 32, 118, 141, 145, 160, 163, 166–67, 184, 191, 330–32
public order, 16, 166
public works. *See under* activation

race, 6, 15, 17, 22, 30, 31, 94, 125, 126, 127, 133, 207, 209, 210, 216, 242, 260, 261–62, 276, 331
racial reversal, 9, 16–17, 37n5
racial violence. *See under* violence
racialization, 12–17, 20, 22, 37n3, 52, 99, 114, 117, 168, 171, 172, 244, 328, 330, 332–33
   of ethnic minority governance, 14–15
   gendered, 30–31, 124–49, 231
   of social security, 133–42, 144, 190, 217
racism, 8, 11, 16–18, 20–22, 26, 37n5, 94, 99, 100, 101, 104, 113–14, 120n12, 132, 134, 138, 139, 141, 153, 180, 182–83, 186–87, 199n1, 206–11, 213, 218, 221, 223, 226, 232, 234, 236–38, 248, 260, 261, 263, 270, 286, 292–93, 308, 316, 321, 332
Radziszewski, Karol, 323
reasonable accommodation, xi–xiii
redistribution. *See under* politics
recognition. *See under* politics
Reconsidering Roma, 316, 325

religion, xi, 6, 37n6, 79, 80–81, 168, 170, 172, 181, 188, 214, 246, 259, 260, 264, 266, 267, 275
repoliticization, 18, 162, 164
representation, 6, 82, 84, 85, 91, 97, 181, 183, 214, 240, 243, 245, 282, 293–95, 314, 328–34
   artistic, 46–65
   canonical, 60, 140
   cultural, 33, 194, 257–80
   operational, 10–11
   media, 113, 306
   minority, 6, 193
   Roma, 8, 10–11, 12, 31, 33, 35, 46–65, 84, 108, 154, 159–65, 169–70, 173n1, 187, 189, 195, 257–80 (*see also* Europeanization of Roma representation)
   self-, 5, 6, 9, 54, 154, 163
   stereotypical, 53, 56, 62, 139–40, 286
   terrorizing, 47, 58
   See also politics
resistance, xiv, 15, 57, 80, 96, 132, 207, 219, 225, 226, 231, 235, 246, 248, 267, 291
responsibilization, 18, 143
rights, 26, 71, 72, 73, 82, 87, 91, 98, 154, 158, 234, 329
   activism (*see under* activism, movement)
   children's, 73, 194, 224, 234
   citizenship (*see under* citizenship)
   civil, 118, 207, 209, 210, 296, 329
   cultural, 118, 190, 207
   economic, 21, 118, 329
   human, 3, 15–16, 70, 96, 103, 114, 117–18, 153, 155, 158, 166, 179, 193–94, 207–8, 212, 213, 221, 223, 232–33, 235–36, 238, 242, 247, 257, 274
   minority (*see under* minority)
   political, 30, 86, 118, 195, 207, 329
   social, 21, 30, 31, 87, 88, 89, 91, 118, 124, 133, 207
violation, 4, 37n5, 88, 153, 166
women's, 206–7, 210, 211, 213, 216, 219, 221, 230, 237–38, 244, 246–47

risk, 10, 75, 80, 81, 90, 130–31, 137, 158, 160, 171, 190, 195, 199n2, 237, 238, 330
Roma
 -centrism, 171–72
 language, 4, 26, 27, 38n10, 96, 117, 163, 187, 188, 190, 199n3, 258, 264, 267, 268, 272
 politics, xi, 22–23, 26–27, 35, 59, 84–86, 116, 205, 207–8, 210, 212, 214, 218–20, 222, 225, 230–31, 233, 238–41, 243, 245–46, 248–49, 281–82, 306–7, 314–17, 323, 328–34
 securitization towards (see under securitization)
 voice, 5, 6, 8, 33, 53, 97, 108, 110, 117, 210, 215, 232, 233, 235, 237, 239, 240, 241, 248, 286, 289, 293
Roma Armee, v, xvii, 35, 36, 46–48, 323
Roma Biennale (Berlin), xvii, 35, 323
Roma Holocaust
 Memorial days, 285
 Remembrance Initiative, 285
 See also Holocaust
Roma Women's Forum, 212–13
Roma Women's Initiative (RWI), 33, 205, 208–14, 218, 224, 225, 236
'Roma Question', xi, 13. See also 'Gypsy Question'
Romani CRISS, 213, 217, 236
Romani Embassy, 56–58
RomArchive, 7, 37n2, 274
Romani movement. See under movement
Romani Studies, xii, xiii, xvi, 22, 27, 28, 38n7, 39n11, 96, 171, 221–24, 286, 293, 296–97, 315
Romania, 3–4, 10, 11, 15, 72, 193, 195, 205, 208, 214, 215–17, 234–35, 236, 239, 240–47, 258, 269, 270, 271
Romaphobia, 153, 172. See also antigypsyism; anti-Roma racism
Romaversitas Program, 219, 224
Rostas, Iulius, 222, 296

Safe European Home? (artwork), xvii, 58, 59, 60, 314, 316, 325
Said, Edward, 21, 28, 38n9

Schneider, Anne, 185, 186, 197
scholarship, 28, 31, 125, 126, 142, 263, 290
 disciplinarization of, 171
 ghettoization of, 171
 on Roma, 13, 14, 20, 21–22, 25, 26, 28, 38n7, 96, 97, 124, 153, 154, 155, 171, 231, 267, 289, 296
scientism, 27, 174n2
Second World War, xi, xii, 7, 51, 95, 98, 225
securitization, 153–78, 332
 of migration, 165, 167–68
 of borders, 165, 167–68
 towards Roma, 10, 11, 16, 17, 167–68
security, 10, 16, 76, 155, 158, 161, 164, 169, 170, 272
 human, 8, 162, 168
 national, 16, 168
 social, 88–89, 124–49 (see also activation; welfare)
security-citizenship nexus, 11, 22, 31, 165–67, 331
security-development nexus, 11, 22, 31, 167–69, 331
segregation, xii, 4, 8, 11, 12, 15, 18, 29–30, 69–93, 135, 196, 264
 in education, 4, 75–76, 78, 80, 85, 87, 102, 180, 195
 regarding labour, 73, 89–90, 135 (see also activation)
 multifaceted, 72–78, 89–92
 residential, 4, 15, 69–70, 75, 78, 88, 102, 125, 126, 130, 137–38, 195
Selimović, Sandra, 36, 47
Selimović, Simonida, 36, 47
Serbia, 47, 72, 216, 222, 284
sexism, 20, 207, 208, 248
Shuto Orizari, 218
Silverman, Carol, 28, 171
Sirovátka, Tomáš, 128–29
Slovakia, 15–16, 37n4, 72, 110, 128, 136, 137, 195, 205, 221, 241, 306
socialism, 4, 12, 30, 94–123, 207, 219, 233, 269, 328, 331
solidarity, 18, 24, 25, 30, 81, 82, 91, 94, 97, 108, 118, 132, 134, 218, 219, 224, 232, 243–45, 249, 266, 287, 314–17, 330, 333

Solt, Ottilia, 103, 112
Soros, George, 115, 211
   Foundations, 115, 209, 211, 213, 218, 224
spectacle, 10, 11–12, 16, 17, 19
Spain, 10, 52, 209, 215, 223, 284, 291
Spivak, Gayatri, 28, 38n7, 210, 267, 290, 315
   on Roma art, 314–15
   strategic essentialism, 258, 267
   subalternity, 211
   theory as theatre, 35, 57, 314
sterilization, 4, 99, 212, 221, 232, 233
Stewart, Michael, 12, 25, 38n7, 52, 101, 112, 259, 260, 261, 262, 264, 269
stigmatization, 5, 17, 25–29, 95, 108, 129, 131–32, 135, 138, 140, 142, 144, 172, 174n2, 190, 238, 263, 321
stratification, 126, 133, 135, 181, 187–88
superdiversity, 171
Surdu, Mihai, 26–27, 29, 258, 260–64
Szelényi, Iván, 135–36, 188
Szilvási, Marek, 196, 222

temporality, 50–54, 58
territorialization, 60, 61, 62, 168
timelessness, 50–53
trafficking, 11, 132, 166, 212, 232, 237–38, 240, 250n6
transition, 30, 50, 103, 106, 110, 112, 114, 117–18, 124, 127, 129, 137, 174n3, 207–8, 217, 223
Traveller(s), 188–89, 213, 237, 305–27
   Irish, 307, 312
   life and culture, 307, 322
   movement, 312
Tremlett, Annabel, 171, 267–68, 277n2
tribalism, 22, 38nn7–8
Trump, Donald, 19, 20, 226, 271
Trumpener, Katie, 50–54, 57, 63n1

unemployment. *See under* employment

Vajda, Violeta, 20–22, 33
Vámosi, Gyula, 216

van Baar, Huub, xii, 10, 27–29, 249, 276, 322, 330
   Europeanization of Roma representation, 8, 12, 31, 154, 159–64
   reasonable antigypsyism, 17, 37n5
   travelling activism, 13
Venice Biennale, xvi–xvii, 35, 194, 300, 315, 317–18, 323
   Paradise Lost, 315, 317–18, 325
Verloo, Mieke, 231–32, 249
Vermeersch, Peter, 10, 153, 157–58, 249, 258, 261, 263, 330
   on identity politics, 22–23, 261, 263
Vidra, Zsuzsanna, 134–35, 174n3
Vincze, Enikő, 234, 243, 244, 250n7
violence, 46, 58, 100, 195, 270, 296, 310
   domestic, 8, 212, 232, 237, 246–48
   epistemic, 100, 296, 333
   racially motivated, 4–5, 8, 15–17, 195
   sexual, 208, 212, 232, 237, 246–48
   structural, 125, 135, 139, 144, 328
visibilization, 8, 59, 84, 241, 284, 291
   hyper-, 10, 11, 13, 214, 331
visuality, 11, 49, 331

Wacquant, Loïc, 125
welfare, 30–31, 73–74, 76, 77, 88–89, 124–49, 161, 163, 169, 174n3, 222, 240, 266, 329, 330
whiteness, 20–22, 33
Willems, Wim, 21, 25–29, 38n7, 38nn9–10, 163, 171, 174n2, 262
Witch Hunt, 308, 311
women's activism. *See under* activism
workfare, 124, 126–34, 140–41, 144. *See also* activation
World Bank, 112, 163, 167, 168, 179, 191, 199n1, 211, 212, 220, 263
The World of Gypsy Romance? (artwork), 54, 55, 310

Yugoslavia, 96, 166, 205, 218